REFERENCE GUIDE TO MILTON

REFERENCE GUIDE
TO
MILTON

FROM 1800 TO THE PRESENT DAY

DAVID HARRISON STEVENS

The University of Chicago

NEW YORK / RUSSELL & RUSSELL

REISSUED, 1967, BY RUSSELL & RUSSELL
A DIVISION OF ATHENEUM HOUSE, INC.
BY ARRANGEMENT WITH DAVID H. STEVENS
L. C. CATALOG CARD NO: 66–24764

PRINTED IN THE UNITED STATES OF AMERICA

TO RUTH

PREFACE

The titles in this volume have been arranged to supply, under various headings, a chronological record of the interest in John Milton and his works from the year 1800 to 1928, inclusive. Originally, the end in view was to survey only literary and critical documents of that period, but it soon appeared that in the editions of Milton was lodged much of the most valuable material. Even the simpler school editions of *Paradise Lost* and brief articles showing slight originality have been included as evidences of the condition of public taste. Many of these trivial items have a value for students of historical and literary tradition; for such persons rather than for the true bibliographer the work should have a definite usefulness. It is intended to serve such ends of scholarly research as are met in other fields by Carpenter's *Reference Guide to Edmund Spenser* and Northup's *Bibliography of Thomas Gray*, forming a bridge of reference material between the encyclopedic footnotes of eighteenth-century editions and the classed bibliographies now issued annually by institutions and societies.

Financial assistance has been forthcoming from the General Education Board, the University of Chicago, and the American Council of Learned Societies. The invaluable aid from these sources is gratefully acknowledged. Many individuals have turned in stray items, and officers of various libraries have been most helpful. In the final operations of preparing the materials for printing, Mr. George A. White, of the Graduate School of the University of Chicago, has given faithful and able service.

The abbreviations of references to those periodicals used most frequently are as follows:

Acad.	*Academy*
AHR	*American Historical Review*
Archiv	*Archiv für das Studium der neueren Sprachen und Literaturen*
Athen.	*Athenaeum*
Beiblatt	*Beiblatt zur Anglia*
EHR	*English Historical Review*
EJ	*English Journal*
ER	*English Review*
ES	*Englische Studien*
GM	*Gentleman's Magazine*
GRM	*Germanisch-romanische Monatsschrift*

JEGP	*Journal of English and Germanic Philology*
LM	*London Mercury*
LQR	*London Quarterly Review*
LR	*London Review*
MLN	*Modern Language Notes*
MLR	*Modern Language Review*
MP	*Modern Philology*
N & Q	*Notes and Queries*
PQ	*Philological Quarterly*
PMLA	*Publications of the Modern Language Association of America*
QR	*Quarterly Review* (London)
RES	*Review of English Studies*
RAA	*Revue anglo-américaine*
RCC	*Revue des cours et conférences*
RC	*Revue critique*
RELV	*Revue de l'enseignement des langues vivantes*
RHL	*Revue d'histoire littéraire de la France*
RH	*Revue historique*
RLC	*Revue de littérature comparée*
RSH	*Revue de synthèse historique*
SR	*Saturday Review* (London)
SRL	*Saturday Review of Literature* (New York)
SNPL	*Studies and Notes in Philology and Literature*
SP	*Studies in Philology*
TLS	*Times Literary Supplement* (London)

D. H. S.

University of Chicago
December 20, 1928

CONTENTS[1]

[1] The first ten divisions contain references to editions and to critical writings on the works in question. The Index supplies a further analysis of the section containing general criticism.

I. BIBLIOGRAPHICAL AND REFERENCE WORKS

Older works in this section have in their footnotes and appendixes much bibliographical data. This material is supplemented by the variorum footnotes in the editions of Milton's poetry prepared by Todd, Warton, and even earlier scholars. For summaries of publications in the critical journals after 1928, reference is given to such digests as appear in the annual bibliographies of the Modern Language Association (American), the Modern Humanities Research Association (English and American), the *Philological Quarterly* (American), *Studies in Philology* (American), as well as to the many monthly or quarterly lists in English, American, and European journals devoted to literary studies.

1 Henry J. Todd. Some Account of the Life and Writings of John Milton. London, 1809. Pp. 217.

Volume I of the 1809 edition. A number printed with separate title-page. List of editions, pp. 189–217. Volume VI of this, the second, edition of Todd, has a verbal index to the poems that is full but faulty in reference. Abundant bibliographical matter in footnotes.

2 A Catalogue of the Very Valuable and Highly Interesting United Libraries of Thomas Hollis, Esq., and Thomas Brand Hollis, Esq., including Likewise the Theological and Political Library of . . . . John Disney . . . . Sold at Auction by Mr. Sotheby, Tues. April 22, 1817, and Seven Following Days. . . . . London, [1817].

Miltoniana, pp. 25–41.

3 Retrospective Review, XIV (1826), 282–305.

Valuable data on first editions of the prose works. Based on Pickering preface. Published also in the *Museum*, XI (1827), 114–23.

4 Athenaeum, September 3, 1842, pp. 783–84.

Review of Vericour's *Milton et la poésie épique* has a list of translations of *Paradise Lost.*

5 Henry J. Todd. The Poetical Works of John Milton. 4 vols. London, 1842.

See IV, 525–44, for lists of editions, translations, and alterations of the poetic texts and for various pieces of criticism.

6 Auguste Geoffroy. Étude sur les pamphlets politiques et religieux de Milton. Paris, 1848. Pp. 295.

Bibliography, *passim*. Appendix has a good record of editions.

7 O. W. Wheeler. Verbal Index to the Greek [Latin and Italian] Poems of Milton. [1857.]

Manuscript of sixty-nine folios (Boston Public Library).

8 G. L. Prendergast. A Complete Concordance to the Poetical Works of Milton. [In 4 parts.] Madras: Pharoah & Co., 1857–59. Pp. 416.

Review in *Athen.*, October 10, 1857, p. 1267.

9 Samuel Leigh Sotheby. Ramblings in the Elucidation of the Autograph of Milton. London, 1861. Pp. xxviii+263.

Reproductions of manuscript matter, descriptions of the 1667 issues of *Paradise Lost*, data on early editions, association copies, and early sale prices.

10 H. Dircks. A Biographical Memoir of Samuel Hartlib, Milton's Familiar Friend; with Bibliographical Notices of Works Published by Him, and a Reprint of His Pamphlet Entitled *An Invention of Engines of Motion*. London: J. R. Smith, 1865. Pp. x+124.

11 Charles Dexter Cleveland. A Complete Concordance to the Poetical Works of John Milton. London: Sampson, Low & Marston, 1867.

An advertisement in the *Athen.*, No. 2128, August 8, 1868, shows that a second printing had been made by that date.

12 Edward Arber. Addison's Criticism on Milton's *Paradise Lost.* "English Reprints." London: Murray & Son, 1868.

Bibliography, *passim.*

13 Samuel Austin Allibone. A Critical Dictionary of English Literature and British and American Authors. Philadelphia: Lippincott & Co., 1870.

See II, 1296–1324.

14 "Paradise Lost." *Leisure Hour*, XXVI (1877), 269–70.

Account of the issues of the first edition; condensed from Masson.

15 Contributions to a Catalogue of the Lenox Library, No. 6. New York: Printed for the Trustees, 1881.

Contains Allibone's materials for his biographical article on Milton: bibliography, sale prices, tributes, some collations.

16 "The First Edition of the *Paradise Lost.*" *Booklore*, III (1886), 72–75.

Description of the nine title-pages of the first edition, and possible reasons given for the changes.

17 Mary E. Plummer. A Reference List for the Study of Milton. [St. Louis], 1889. Pp. 3.

No. 10 of the St. Louis Public Library reference lists for readers and students. Elementary.

18 [Agreement with Samuel Simmons regarding *Paradise Lost.*] London: British Museum, 1890. One-sheet folio.

Reproduced by lithography.

19 Richard Garnett. Life of John Milton. London: W. Scott, 1890. Pp. 205.

Bibliography of J. P. Anderson, pp. i–xxxix, as Appendix.

20 Gustav Jenny. Milton's Verlorenes Paradies in der deutschen Literatur des 18 Jahrhunderts. St. Gallen, 1890.

21 R. Sinker. "The Milton Manuscripts." *Churchman* (London), N.S., VI (1891–92), 12–18.

22 British Museum. Department of Printed Books. . . . . Catalogue of Printed Books. Milton. London: Printed by W. Clowes & Sons, 1892. 56 cols.

23 G. Körting. Grundriss der Geschichte der englischen Litteratur von ihren Anfängen bis zur Gegenwart. Münster, 1893.

Milton items, pp. 255–71.

24 John Bradshaw. A Concordance to the Poetical Works of John Milton. London: Sonnenschein, 1894. 8vo. Pp. 412.

Published also by Macmillan (New York). Omits the Psalms and works in other languages. His strictures on Prendergast blame Indian typesetters, but for Cleveland's shortcomings no excuse is given. A work of merit, invaluable to students of Milton.

Reviews in *Beiblatt*, VI (1895), 65–70; *Nation*, LX (1895), 59; *JEGP*, I (1897), 498–502.

25 Edward Almack. A Bibliography of the King's Book or Eikon Basilike. London: Blades, East & Blades, 1896. Pp. 143.

Titles of works, with bibliographical descriptions of the editions and of replies to the work by contemporaries.

26 Milton's *Paradise Lost.* Books I and II. Edited with Notes and an Introduction by Edward Everett Hale, Jr. New York: Longmans, Green & Co., 1896. Pp. 112.

Bibliography, pp. lix–lxii.

27 The Poetical Works of John Milton. With Introductory Memoir, Notes, Bibliography . . . . [and Preface, by L. Valentine]. London: F. Warne & Co., 1896.

Scant bibliography.

28 I. T. Myers. A Study of Epic Development. "Yale Studies in English," Vol. XI. New York: Holt, 1901. Pp. 160.

Bibliography, pp. 149–56.

29 J. F. Payne. "A Lost Tract of Milton's." *Athen.*, December 28, 1901, p. 877.

Copy of second edition of *Ready and Easy Way* described; usually regarded as a lost book.

30 W. Thomas. De epico apud Joannem Miltonium versu. Paris: Hachette, 1901. Pp. xii+89.

Bibliography, pp. vii–x.

31 Comus. Facsimile Edition with an Introduction by L. S. Livingston. New York: Dodd, Mead & Co., 1903. Pp. vii+35.

First issued in the *Bibliographer* (New York), Vol. I (1902).

32 "The Manuscript of *Paradise Lost.*" *TLS*, II (1903), 365.

Describes the manuscript of Book I and indicates its textual value. *See* Item 36.

33 "Milton's Manuscript." *Independent*, LV (1903), 3138–40.

Notes sale of the manuscript of Book I of *Paradise Lost* and comments on corrections.

34 Transactions of the Bibliographical Society, VI (1903), 152.

Wynne Baxter on the printing and binding of the several issues of the first edition of *Paradise Lost.*

35 John Downing. Testimonies and Criticisms Relating to the Life and Works of John Milton. 1903.

Bibliography, *passim.*

36 The Original Manuscript of the First Book of *Paradise Lost.* London: Sotheby, Wilkinson & Hodge, 1904. Pp. 7.

Careful description of the manuscript, which has been shown by Hanford to have been used by the printer. The manuscript was offered for sale on January 25, 1904. It now is in the Morgan Library and is to be edited with exhaustive notes. See *MP*, XXV (1928), 313–17.

37 John Martin Telleen. Milton dans la littérature française. Paris: Hachette, 1904. Pp. 148.

A review in *TLS*, III (1904), 268, gives added references. A valuable record.

38 Grolier Club, New York. A Catalogue of Original and Early Editions of Some of the Poetical and Prose Works of English Writers from Wither to Prior. 3 vols. New York, 1905.

39 Ettore Allodoli. Giovanni Milton e l'Italia. Prato: C. & G. Spighi, 1907.

Bibliography, *passim.*

40 Laura E. Lockwood. Lexicon to the English Poetical Works of John Milton. New York, 1907.

Review in *Athen.*, I (1908), 255.

41 Marianna Woodhull. The Epic of *Paradise Lost:* Twelve Essays. New York: Putnams, 1907. Pp. xi+375.

Bibliography, pp. 351–68.

42 Charles F. Adams. "Knowledge of Milton in Early New England." *Nation*, LXXXVII (1908), 599–600.

Milton's poems unknown in New England until 1750. No edition of *Paradise Lost* in America until 1750. First Massachusetts edition, 1794.

43 Cambridge University. Christ's College. Milton Tercentenary. The Portraits, Prints and Writings of John Milton. Exhibited at Christ's College, Cambridge, 1908. [Cambridge: J. Clay, 1908.]

44 Grolier Club, New York. Catalogue of an Exhibition Commemorative of the Tercentenary of the Birth of John Milton, 1608–1908; including Original Editions of His Poetical and Prose Works, together with Three Hundred and Twenty-seven Engraved Portraits . . . . held at the Grolier Club Dec. 3, 1908 to Jan. 9, 1909. New York: DeVinne, [1908]. Pp. vi+116.

The Lycophron listed here is in the possession of Mr. A. T. White, Brooklyn, New York.

45 John Rylands Library, Manchester. Catalogue of an Exhibition of Original Editions of the Principal Works of John Milton, Arranged in Celebration of the Tercentenary of His Birth. [Manchester.] Printed by order of the governors, 1908.

Reproduces title-pages of early editions.

46 Stoke Newington Public Library. Milton Tercentenary Celebration. Programme of Entertainment and Catalogue of Exhibits. [Privately printed], December 9, 1908. Pp. 55.

Contains data on the title-pages of *Paradise Lost.*

47 *Nation*, LXXXVII (October 1, 1908), 311.

Critic asserts that Henry G. Bohn was wrong in distinguishing eight separate title-pages of the first edition of *Paradise Lost*, and limits the number to six.

48 Milton's *Paradise Lost*. First Edition. [London, 1908.]

A pamphlet of sixteen pages showing six title-pages and variants in the text. See the Sandys collation in the Pickering facsimile edition.

49 "Early Editions of Milton's Works in the Library of Wynne E. Baxter." *Bibliophile*, III (May, 1909), 119.

50 Worthington C. Ford. "Paradise Lost." *Athen.*, May 22, 1909, p. 617.

Tells of recently discovered variant of the first edition of *Paradise Lost*. Unusual feature is date of 1667 and name of Simmons as publisher.

51 Fernand Henry. Les petits poèmes de John Milton (Sonnets—"L'Allegro"—"Il Penseroso"—"Lycidas"). Paris, 1909.

Various French translations mentioned.

52 Massachusetts Historical Society. Pp. 4.

Reproduces a title-page of *Paradise Lost*, dated 1667 and bearing the name of S. Simmons.

This same title-page is described in Christ's College Tercentenary as "eighth binding of the first edition," with the very important exception of the date, which is two years earlier.

53 Alfred W. Pollard. "The Bibliography of Milton." *The Library*, N.S., X (1909), 1–33.

Textual data and comments on the first editions of Milton's works and of a few dated after 1700; locations of various copies and some manuscripts are noted.

54 *The Tenure of Kings and Magistrates*, by John Milton; edited . . . . by W. T. Allison. New York: Holt, 1911. Pp. liii+185.

Bibliography, pp. 173–81.

55 The Cambridge History of English Literature. New York: Putnam's Sons, 1911. Vol. VII.

Pages 469–79 contain a Milton bibliography by G. A. Brown, to which is added a note on the basic manuscript sources. Pages 158–61 offer a conspectus of the prose works, with notes on the first editions and a sketch of the sources of the texts of the poems.

56 S. J. S. and Others. "Milton's Bibles." *N & Q*, Ser. XI, No. III (1911), pp. 1, 70, 109.

57 John S. Smart. "Milton's Copy of Dante's *Convivio*." *Ibid.*, Ser. XI, No. VIII (1913), p. 49.

58 Enrico Pizzo. Milton's Verlorenes Paradies im deutschen Urteile des 18. Jahrhunderts. Berlin: Felber, 1914. Pp. 144.

59 Charles Scribner's Sons. Superb Collected Sets of the First Editions of Eliot, Milton, Coleridge, Swinburne, Wordsworth. New York, [1923]. Pp. 88.

60 W. P. Courtney and D. N. Smith. A Bibliography of Samuel Johnson. Oxford, 1915.

Has data on the editions of Samuel Johnson's essay.

61 T. de Vries. Holland's Influence on English Language and Literature. Chicago: C. Grentzebach, 1916. Pp. 398.

Bibliography on the Milton-Vondel question, pp. 297–98.

62 William Jaggard. "Treasure Trove: Milton's Latin Bible." *Athen.*, May, 1916, p. 251.

On the discovery in Devonshire of a Latin Bible having Milton's signature on the title-page.

63 Elbert N. S. Thompson. John Milton. A Topical Bibliography. New Haven: Yale University Press, 1916. Pp. xi+104.

Review by Clark S. Northup, *JEGP*, XVI, 482–84.

64 Allan H. Gilbert. A Geographical Dictionary of Milton. "Cornell Studies in English," Vol. IV. New Haven, Connecticut: Yale University Press, 1919. Pp. viii+322.

A useful reference work. Reviews in *MP*, XVII (January, 1920), 551–52; *ES*, LIII, 444–45; *MLR*, XVII (1922), 205.

65 H. Glicksman. "The Editions of Milton's *History of Britain*." *PMLA*, XXXV (1920), 116–22.

Asserts that Toland in 1698 possessed Milton's own copy of the *History*, containing his emendations. Conjectural.

66 A Catalogue of the Milton Collection Formed by Wynne E. Baxter .... Which Will Be Sold by Auction July 12, 1921. London, 1921. Pp. 51.

67 Sydney William Grose. Early Editions of Milton's Works in Christ's College Library. Cambridge: Cambridge University Press, [1921]. Pp. 8.

Reprinted from *Christ's College Magazine*, Vol. XXXIII (1921). Contains items not in Dr. Williamson's Appendix to the Milton tercentenary catalogue.

68 E. Lehmann. Tendenz und Entstehungsgeschichte von Milton's *History of Britain*. Diss. Berlin, 1921. Pp. 40.

Discussion of sources, with summaries.

69 John Milton . . . . List of Books . . . . [on sale by] J. Tregaskis. London, 1921. Pp. 20.

Full lists of works, chiefly modern editions, portraits, and critical works.

70 Denis Saurat. "La Cabale et la philosophie de Milton." *Revue des études juives*, LXXIII (1921), 1–13.

Bibliography of source materials.

71 "Early Editions of Milton's Works in Christ's College Library." *Christ's College Magazine*, XXXIII (1922), 102–10.

72 Thornton S. Graves. "Recent Literature of the English Renaissance."

Annual compilations of references to Milton literature in *SP*, XIX (1922), 278–80; XX (1923), 277–80; XXI (1924), 449–51; XXII (1925), 319–22; Hardin Craig, XXIII (1926), 276–81; XXIV (1927), 350–53.

73 Raymond D. Havens. The Influence of Milton on English Poetry. Cambridge, Massachusetts: Harvard University Press, 1922. Pp. xii+722.

Bibliography, *passim*.

74 Lane Cooper. A Concordance of the Latin, Greek, and Italian Poems of John Milton. Halle (Saale): M. Niemeyer, 1923.

A valuable and necessary addition to Bradshaw and Lockwood. Based on Beeching's text.

Reviews in *Beiblatt*, XXXIV (1923), 310–11; *Archiv*, CXLVII (1924), 155; *Neophilologus*, XII (1927), 145–46.

75 James Holly Hanford. "The Rosenbach Milton Documents." *PMLA*, XXXVIII (1923), 290–96.

Documents described as throwing light on Milton's financial condition in 1665.

76 F. F. Madan. "Milton, Salmasius, and Dugard." *Library*, 4th Ser., IV (1923), 119–45.

Bibliography of editions.

77 Denis Saurat. "La conception nouvelle de Milton." *Revue germ.*, XIV (1923), 113–41.

Bibliography of Milton scholarship, 1917–21, pp. 133–41.

78 S. de Ricci. A Catalogue of Early English Books in the Library of John L. Clawson.

Has a tentative list of existent copies of the 1637 *Comus.*

79 W. P. Courtney and D. N. Smith. A Bibliography of Samuel Johnson. Oxford, 1925.

The 1915 edition, with some additions.

80 John Keats. "Notes on Milton." *The Book Collector's Quarterly* (New York), No. 3 (1925), p. 20.

Printed from notes in the 1807 *Paradise Lost* preserved in the Dilke collection.

81 F. P. Magoun, Jr. Miltoniana. *Harvard Library Notes*, No. 15 (1925), pp. 49–56.

Lists acquisitions of the Harvard Library.

82 Denis Saurat. Milton; Man and Thinker. New York: Dial Press, 1925. Pp. xvii+363.

References to significant articles on Milton since 1917, pp. 342–52.

83 E. H. Sugden. A Topographical Dictionary to the Works of Shakespeare and His Fellow Dramatists. Manchester: University Press; and London: Longmans, Green & Co., 1925.

Has data on "Arcades" and *Comus*.

84 [Manuscript listed by Ellis, Catalogue 205, 1926. Item 234.]

The Digression in *The History of Britain*, Book III, in a seventeenth-century autograph, on six small quarto leaves. Listed at £63. The deleted passage "was never published in its entirety, all later printed editions following the separate issue of the passage in 1681 by Lord Anglesey; this begins imperfectly in the middle of a sentence. The two opening pages of this MS have not been printed and it shows other variants."

85 John Drinkwater. "Notes of S. T. Coleridge in 'Milton's Poems,' by Thomas Warton." *LM*, XIV (1926), 491–505.

Coleridge received volume (1791 edition) as a gift, probably from member of Gillman family. Reproduces Coleridge's annotations on Warton's comments.

Reprinted in *A Book for Bookmen*, 1926.

86 James Holly Hanford. A Milton Handbook. New York: Crofts, 1926. Pp. x+304.

Bibliography, pp. 287–96.

87 C. Ainsworth Mitchell. "New Light on a Milton Mystery." *Discovery*, VII (1926), 79–83.

Shows by expert evidence that the poem written on a blank leaf of a copy of 1645 edition is not Milton's, as Morley asserted. Initials of author are indisputably "P. M." and handwriting is not Milton's.

88 David H. Stevens. "The Bridgewater Manuscript of *Comus*." *MP*, XXIV (1926–27), 315–20.

Description of the manuscript. Not in hand of Henry Lawes. Represents a shortened version of the Trinity College manuscript. Milton's revision of stage directions due to the judgment of Lawes.

89 W. N. C. Carlton. "The First Edition of Milton's *Comus*, 1637." *American Collector* (New York), V (1927), 107–13.

Notes the 1926 sale of a *Comus* at $21,500; lists other copies known; erroneously locates the Bridgewater MS of *Comus* in the Huntington Library, whereas it is still at Bridgewater House, London.

90 C. J. Sawyer and F. J. H. Darton. English Books, 1475–1900: a Signpost for Collectors. London: Sawyer, 1927. 2 vols.

91 Annual Bibliography of English Language and Literature, Edited for the Modern Humanities Research Association, Vol. VIII, for 1927. Cambridge: Bowes & Bowes, 1928. Pp. viii+200.

Preceding volumes equally valuable for references to current publications. The continuance of such bibliographical annuals will provide proper supplements to such special works as the present volume.

92 James Holly Hanford. "The Manuscript of *Paradise Lost*." *MP*, XXV (1927–28), 313–17.

Asserts that the manuscript of *Paradise Lost* now in the Morgan Library, and described by Sotheby, 1861, as an independent transcript made for the licenser, "is indeed part of the copy prepared by amanuenses at Milton's direction for the press and .... was actually used in setting Book I of the 1667 text."

93 Thomas O. Mabbott. "On Milton's Letters." *TLS*, February 16, 1928, p. 112.

Notice of the discovery of letters to Oldenburg. Full details to be given in the Columbia University edition of Milton.

94 Justin Winsor. Miltoniana.

A manuscript in the Harvard Library.

Bibliographical notes on the works of Milton, with letters and clippings from sales catalogues.

95 English Literary Autographs, 1550–1650. Selected for Reproduction and Edited by W. W. Greg, in Collaboration with J. P. Gilson, Hilary Jenkinson, R. T. McKerrow, A. W. Pollard. Oxford: Oxford University Press, 1929. 2 vols.

Volume II has a specimen of the *Comus* manuscript and evidence on Milton's change of form for his letter *e*.

II. COLLECTED WORKS: PROSE AND POETRY

Though a few issues of both the prose and poetical works have appeared in uniform format, these collections do not contain all the known Milton material. Interest in the full body of Milton's prose has never been such as to warrant commercial ventures more extensive than that of the "Bohn Library" Milton, which has an incomplete and uncritical text. Now, however, the Columbia University Press is ready to produce in full both the prose and poetry. The purpose of the American scholars working under Professor Frank A. Patterson as general editor is to present faithful representations of the seventeenth-century texts and also all variants from editions issued during the lifetime of Milton. No notes on allusions or background will be given. A few letters hitherto unpublished are to be included, but the greatest significance of the Columbia University Milton will lie in its presentation of all the known documents with their original spelling and punctuation. Students of seventeenth-century language will possess a new tool for examination and explanation of English word-forms. Later editors of Milton may profit as well through having this material during the preliminary stages of work on their critical texts. It is expected that the first volumes will appear before the present comment is printed.

96 The Prose Works of John Milton; with an Introductory Review by R. Fletcher. London: Westley & Davis, 1833. Pp. xliii+963.

Issued as a companion volume to the *Poetical Works*.
Frequently reprinted in stereotype (1834, 1835, etc.).
Index added in an issue published by William Ball in 1838.

97 Milton. I, Prose Works. II, Poetical Works. Paris: A. and W. Galignani & Cie, [*ca.* 1836].

Two volumes in one; the text from the London edition of Westley and Davis.

98 The Prose Works of John Milton . . . . with a Preface, Preliminary Remarks, and Notes, by J. A. St. John. "Bohn's Standard Library." London: Bell, [1848]–1881. 5 vols.

Original issues, only Volume V by G. Bell & Son.
Volume IV has a revised edition of Sumner's translation of *De doctrina.* Review in *Athen.*, October 7, 1748. Frequently reprinted. The 1843 edition of the poetry (2

vols.; Tilt and Bogue) gave a complete set of Milton in seven volumes that has been perpetuated in reprints, with additions, in the "Bohn Library." This set, however, lacks minor items and is not a critical production from the standpoint of texts or its few footnotes.

99 The Works of John Milton in Verse and Prose, Printed from the Original Editions with a Life of the Author by the Rev. John Mitford. London: Pickering, 1841. 8 vols.

Lacks *De doctrina* and some minor items. Facsimile issued 1863 by Bickers and Busch, London; in 1873 the *Poetical Works* (Vols. I and II) were reissued by the same house. Contains new material in the life, illustrations, a reproduction of the Simmons agreement, etc.

III. POETICAL WORKS

100 The Poetical Works of John Milton. New York: Leavitt & Allen, [*ca.* 1800]. Pp. 368.

Sheldon & Co., New York, same text (n. d.).
Montgomery's memoir; plates.

101 The Poetical Works of John Milton. New York: Charles Wells, [*ca.* 1800]. 2 vols.

102 The Poetical Works of John Milton. With the Principal Notes of Various Commentators. To Which Are Added Illustrations with Some Account of the Life of Milton. By H. J. Todd. London: J. Johnson, etc., 1801. 6 vols.

Other editions 1809, 1826, 1842. The compendium of Milton scholarship in the eighteenth century. Contains Addison's criticism on *Paradise Lost*, Johnson's remarks on versification, and Burney's observations on the Greek verses. Later editions have various additions.

103 The Poetical Works of John Milton, to Which Is Prefix'd the Life of the Author. Edinburgh: Cupar Fife, 1804. 2 vols.

104 The Poetical Works of John Milton in Three Volumes. With a Preface, Biographical and Critical, by John Aikin. London: Heath & Kearsley, 1805.

Volumes XII–XIV in "The Works of the English Poets" by Samuel Johnson. New issue in 1806.

105 The Poetical Works of John Milton. Collated with the Best Editions: by Thomas Park. . . . . "The Works of the British Poets." London: printed . . . . for John Sharpe. 1805. 2 vols. Illus.

106 The Poetical Works of John Milton Complete in Two Volumes. London: W. Suttaby, B. Crosby & Co., and C. Corrall, 1806. 2 vols.

107 The Poetical Works of John Milton. Collated with the Best Editions: by Thomas Park. London, 1808. 3 vols.

The 1805 edition, with an added volume containing Addison's criticism and Johnson on versification; reprinted, 1815.

108 The Poetical Works of John Milton, with Notes of Various Authors. To Which Are Added Illustrations, and Some Account of the Life and Writings of Milton, by . . . . H. J. Todd. Second edition, with considerable additions and with a Verbal Index to the whole of Milton's poetry. London: J. Johnson, etc., 1809. 7 vols.

Harvard has an undated edition which may represent another issue of either the first or second printing of the first six volumes.

109 The Poetical Works of John Milton. With the Life of the Author, by Samuel Johnson. London, 1809. 3 vols.

110 The Poetical Works of John Milton. From the Text of Doctor Newton. With the Life of the Author. New York: printed for Richard Scott, by D. & G. Bruce, 1809.

111 The Poetical Works of John Milton. With the Life of the Author, by Samuel Johnson. "Select British Poets." . . . . London: printed for the Proprietors by G. Hazard, 1810.

112 Milton's Life and Poetical Works with Notes by William Cowper. Edited with a Life of Milton by W. Hayley. With Adam, a Sacred Drama [translated from the Italian by W. Cowper and W. Hayley]. Chichester, 1810. 4 vols.

Has translations of the Latin and Italian poems in Volume III.
The British Museum set has John Mitford's autograph notes.

113 The Poetical Works of John Milton. Edited by Samuel Johnson . . . . with Remarks by John Aikin. London, 1810.

114 The Poems of John Milton. London, 1810.

In Chalmers' "The Works of the English Poets," VII, 269–540. Includes Todd's "An Inquiry into the Origin of *Paradise Lost*."

115 The Poetical Works of John Milton. Consisting of *Paradise Lost* and *Regained*, and *Poems on Several Occasions*, from the Text of Dr. Newton. With the Life of the Author. Brookfield: published by Isaiah Thomas, jun.; E. Merriam & Co., printers, 1810.

116 The Poetical Works of John Milton. Albany: Packard, 1811. Pp. xxvi+484.

Newton's text and Aikin's essay.

117 *Paradise Lost*, *Paradise Regained*, *Samson Agonistes*, and Other Poems. Edited by David McNicoll. Liverpool, 1812.

118 The Poetical Works of John Milton. Baltimore: Lucas and Cushing, 1813. 2 vols.

119 The Poetical Works of John Milton. With the Life of the Author. New York: J. Forbes & Co., 1815. 3 vols.

120 *Paradise Lost* by John Milton. . . . . To Which Is Added a Complete Collection of His Miscellaneous Poems, Both English and Latin. London: F. C. and J. Rivington, 1817. 2 vols.

Introductory pages have Fenton's life and Johnson's essay. Portrait and engraved title-pages.

121 Milton. Poetical Works in English. Illustrated by Engravings from the Designs of R. Westall. London: J. Sharpe, 1817. 4 vols.

Volumes I and II, *Paradise Lost;* Vols. III and IV, *Paradise Regained, Samson Agonistes, Comus,* "Arcades," and *Poems on Several Occasions.*

122 The Poetical Works of John Milton, to Which Is Prefixed the Life of the Author. "Walker's British Classics." London: J. Walker, 1818. Pp. vii+549.

123 The Poetical Works of John Milton. With a Life of the Author by Ezekiel Sanford. "The Works of the British Poets," Vols. VII and VIII. London, 1819. 2 vols.

Published also in Philadelphia, 1819–23.

124 The Poetical Works of John Milton. Philadelphia: J. Stevenson, 1821. 2 vols.

The English poems and Fenton's life.

125 The Poetical Works of John Milton. New York: Bartow, 1822. 3 vols.

126 The Poems of John Milton. "The British Poets . . . . ," Vols. XVI–XVIII. London, [1822].

127 The Poetical Works of John Milton. New York: Paul, 1824. 2 vols.

Fenton's life. Published also as two volumes in one.

128 The Poetical Works of John Milton, with Notes of Various Authors, Principally from the Editions of T. Newton, C. Dunster, and T. Warton, to Which Is Prefixed Newton's Life of Milton. By E. Hawkins. Oxford: printed by W. Baxter for J. Parker and C. B. Whittaker, London, 1824. 4 vols.

129 The Poetical Works of John Milton. With a Life of the Author, by Elijah Fenton, and a Critique by Samuel Johnson. Glasgow: R. Malcolm, 1825. 2 vols.

130 The Poetical Works of John Milton in Three Volumes. London: W. Pickering, 1826.

Life by Edward Phillips and text of Hawkey's (1757) Dublin edition.

131 The Poetical Works of John Milton. With Notes of Various Authors. Third Edition, with Other Illustrations; and with Some Account of the

Life and Writings of Milton, Derived Principally from Documents in His Majesty's State-Paper Office, Now First Published. By . . . . H. J. Todd. London: C. and J. Rivington, 1826. 6 vols.

The *Life* (pp. vi+370+lxvii) was issued separately as well in 1826.
Review in *QR*, XXXVI (1827), 29–61.

132 The Poetical Works of John Milton, Printed from the Text of Todd, Hawkins, and Others; to Which Is Prefixed the Poet's Life by Edward Philips. Leipsic: printed for Ernest Fleischer, 1827. Pp. xxviii+392.

Greek and Latin poems included; no notes. Reprinted, 1834.

133 The Poetical Works of John Milton. "The Aldine Edition of the British Poets." London: Pickering, 1832. 3 vols.

Edited by Mitford.
Reviews in *Athen.*, December 17, 1831, pp. 814–15; *GM*, CI (1831), 615–16; *Athen.*, June 2, 1832, p. 353; *New Monthly Magazine*, XXXIV (1832), 581–82.

134 The Poetical Works of John Milton. New York: J. H. Turney, 1832. 2 vols.

Same plates used in 1857 by Phillips, Sampson & Co.; reprinted 1859. Fenton's life.

135 The Poetical Works of John Milton, to Which Is Prefixed the Life of the Author. London: Longmans, Green & Co., 1832. Pp. xi+551.

Fenton's life.

136 The Works of John Milton (Verse and Prose) with Introduction by R. Fletcher. London: Westby & Davis, 1833.

Lowndes: "A stereotype edition frequently reprinted."

137 The Poetical Works of John Milton, with a Life by John Mitford "Aldine Poets," Vols. XVII and XIX. London: Pickering, 1834. 3 vols.

Reprinted in Boston by Hilliard, Gray & Co., 1834, 1836, 1838, 1839, 1841.

138 The Poetical Works of John Milton. Edited by Sir Edgerton Brydges, with Imaginative Illustrations by J. M. W. Turner. London, 1835. 6 vols.

Other editions, 1842, 1848, 1853 in 8vo; 1862.
Volume I, reviewed in *Athen.*, June 13, 1835; Vol. VI reviewed in *Athen.*, December 5, 1835, pp. 902–3.

139 The Poetical Works of John Milton. . . . . With a Memoir and Six Embellishments. London, 1836. Pp. 527.

140 The Poetical Works of John Milton. With Notes, and a Life of the Author. A New Edition. Boston: Hilliard, Gray & Co., 1836.

Mitford's edition; two volumes in one.

141 The Poetical Works of John Milton. London and Berlin: A. Asher, 1837. Pp. 479.

The English poems only.

142 The Complete Poetical Works of John Milton, with Explanatory Notes and a Life of the Author by the Rev. H. Stebbing. To Which Is Prefixed Dr. Channing's "Essay on the Poetical Genius of Milton." London: Scott, Webster & Geary, 1839.

Other editions in 1841 and 1846.

143 The Poetical Works of Milton, Thomson and Young. Edited by the Rev. H. F. Cary with a Biographical Notice of Each Author. London: W. Smith, 1841.

144 The Poetical Works of John Milton. . . . . Edited by H. J. Todd. London: Rivington, 1842. 4 vols.

The fourth and last edition of Todd. Has copious notes, critical comment of Boyd on tragedy and on Lauder's interpolations, and an Appendix on Baron's *Cyprian Academy*.

145 The Poetical Works of John Milton. With a Memoir and Critical Remarks on His Genius and Writings by James Montgomery . . . . with One Hundred and Twenty Engravings from Drawings by William Harvey. London: Tilt & Bogue, 1843. 2 vols.

Reprinted by Leavitt & Allen (New York) in 2 vols., 1843, and by Harper & Bros. (New York) in 2 vols. [1847].

The basis of the Bohn edition.

146 Milton's Poetical Works, Consisting of *Paradise Lost, Paradise Regained*, the Mask of *Comus, Samson Agonistes*, and *Poems on Several Occasions;* Together with the Life of the Author. New York: E. Kearny, 1843. 2 vols.

Omits the Latin poems.

147 The Complete Poetical Works of John Milton with Explanatory Notes and a Life of the Author, by the Rev. H. Stebbing. To Which Is Prefix'd Dr. Channing's Essay on the Poetical Genius of Milton. New York: Appleton, 1843. Pp. xvi+552.

Reprinted 1850, 1852, 1853; in 16mo, 1851, 1855, 1856.

148 The Poetical Works of John Milton with a Memoir and Seven Embellishments by Fuseli, Westall, and Martin. London, 1844. Pp. 527.

No notes.

149 The Poetical Works of John Milton. London: William Pickering, 1845. 3 vols.

150 The Poetical Works of John Milton. With Notes and a Life of the Author. A New Edition. Boston: C. C. Little & J. Brown, 1845. 2 vols.

151 The Poetical Works of John Milton; to Which Is Prefixed the Life of the Author. London, 1845. Pp. 576.

152 Milton: I, Prose Works; II, Poetical Works. Introductory Review by Robert Fletcher. London: Bohn, 1847.

Two volumes in one.

153 The Poetical Works of John Milton. A New Edition with Notes and a Life of the Author. Lowell: Bixby, 1848. 2 vols.

Mitford's edition.

154 The Poetical Works of John Milton. Hartford: S. Andrus & Son. 1848. 2 vols.

James Montgomery's edition. Reprinted, 1856.

155 The Poetical Works of John Milton: with Life and Notes. Edinburgh: Oliver & Boyd, [1848]. Pp. 539.

156 The Poetical Works of John Milton. New York: Clark, Austin & Co., 1849. Pp. 232.

These plates and illustrations, from the Appleton edition of 1843, were used by Edward Kearney in an undated New York edition.

157 The Complete Poetical Works of John Milton. New York: Appleton & Co., 1850. Pp. 552.

The Stebbing edition. *See* Items 142 and 147.

158 The Poetical Works of John Milton. Boston: Phillips, Sampson & Co., 1850. 2 vols.

The Mitford edition. *See* Item 133. The same plates used by W. P. Hazard, Philadelphia, 1864. Reissued, 1853.

159 The Poetical Works of John Milton. *Paradise Lost* and *Paradise Regained*. Leipzig, 1850. Pp. vi+358.

Tauchnitz collection of British authors, Vol. CXCIV.

160 The Poetical Works of John Milton. "Cabinet Edition of the British Poets." London: Bohn, 1851. 4 vols.

161 The Works of John Milton in Verse and Prose, Printed from the Original Editions, with a Life of the Author. Edited by John Mitford. London and Boston: Pickering, 1851. 6 vols.

Lacks *Christian Doctrine* and some minor items. Reissued by Bickers and Bush (London, 1863), and in 1873 the poetical works (Vols. I and II) were reissued by the same house.

Review in *North British Review*, XVI, 295–335; *Literary World*, IX, 86–87.

162 The Poetical Works of John Milton, Printed from the Original Editions, with a Life of the Author by the Rev. John Mitford. London: William Pickering, 1851. 2 vols.

Review in *GM*, XXXVI (1851), 160–61.

163 The Poetical Works of John Milton: with Explanatory Notes and a Life of the Author by the Rev. H. Stebbing, D.D. To Which Is Prefixed Dr. Channing's "Essay on the Poetical Genius of Milton." London: Bohn, 1851.

164 The Poetical Works of John Milton; with a Memoir; Embellished with Engravings after Designs by Fuseli, Westall, and Martin. London: Bohn, 1852. Pp. vii+527.

Reprint of the edition of 1841.

165 The Poetical Works of John Milton, Printed from the Original Editions, with a Life . . . . by the Rev. John Mitford. Boston: Phillips Sampson, 1852. 2 vols. Pp. cxxix+371+478.

Issued in one volume, 1853.

166 The Complete Poetical Works of John Milton with Explanatory Notes and a Life of the Author by the Rev. H. Stebbing. To Which Is Prefix'd Dr. Channing's "Essay on the Poetical Genius of Milton." New York: Appleton, 1852.

See Items 142 and 147.

167 The Poetical Works of John Milton . . . . with a Life by the Rev. John Mitford. Boston: Little, Brown & Co., 1853. 3 vols.

168 The Poetical Works of John Milton, with a Life of the Author; Preliminary Dissertations on Each Poem; Notes Critical and Explanatory; an Index to the Subjects of *Paradise Lost;* and a Verbal Index to All the Poems. Edited by Charles Dexter Cleveland. Philadelphia: Lippincott, Grambo & Co., 1853. Pp. 688.

The English poems only included.

Asserted in Preface that Todd's verbal index contains 3,362 mistakes in contrast to the accuracy of this new index. Brydges' text used, but corrected and compared with others. It is evident that Cleveland had no seventeenth-century texts. Allibone calls the 1854 reprint a second edition. Issued in 8vo by Leypoldt (Philadelphia), 1865.

169 The Poetical Works of John Milton. Halifax: Milner & Sowerby, 1853. Pp. 431.

The Channing essay is included, as well as translations of the shorter poems in foreign languages. Reprinted, 1862.

170 The Poetical Works of John Milton. Complete Edition. London: Nelson & Sons, 1853. Pp. xxx+523.

Lacks the Latin poems.

171 The Poetical Works of John Milton. "The Universal Library," I, 389-551. London: Ingram, Cooke & Co., 1853.

172 The Poetical Works of John Milton. Edited by George Gilfillan. "The Library Edition of the British Poets." Edinburgh, 1853. 2 vols.

173 The Poetical Works of John Milton . . . . Edited by J. R. Boyd. New York: A. S. Barnes & Co., 1854. Pp. 552.

174 The Poetical Works of John Milton. Boston: Little, Brown & Co., 1854. 3 vols.

Reprinted, 1859.

175 The Poetical Works of John Milton. Boston: Phillips, Sampson & Co., 1854. Pp. 858.

The Bridges edition (1835). Reprinted, 1855, 1857.

176 The Complete Poetical Works of John Milton. Edinburgh: Gall & Inglis, [1855]. Pp. xx+491.

177 The Poetical Works of John Milton. With a Life by the Rev. John Mitford. Boston: Little, Brown & Co., 1856. 3 vols.

178 The Poetical Works of John Milton. New York: D. Appleton & Co., 1857. Pp. 569.

Introduction by "I. P.," dated 1826, pp. 1–21; Biography by Phillips, pp. 22–42. Asserted that the text is new.

179 The Poems of John Milton, with Notes by T. Keightley. London: Chapman & Hall, 1859. 2 vols.

Important for its original notes.

Review in *Athen.*, September 17, 1859, pp. 360–61; *North American Review*, LXXXII, 388–404.

180 The Poetical Works of John Milton. To Which Is Prefixed a Biography of the Author by His Nephew, Edward Phillips. New York: D. Appleton & Co., 1859. Pp. 574.

181 The Poetical Works of John Milton, with a Memoir and Critical Remains of His Genius and Writings, by James Montgomery, and One Hundred and Twenty Engravings by John Thompson, S. and T. Williams, O. Smith, J. Linton, from drawings by William Harvey. London: W. Kent, 1859. 2 vols.

182 The Poetical Works of John Milton. A New Edition with Notes, and a Life of the Author by John Mitford. Boston: Crosby, Nichols, Lee & Co., 1860. 2 vols.

183 The Poetical Works of John Milton, with a Memoir and Critical Remarks on His Genius and Writings by James Montgomery, and One Hundred and Twenty Engravings. . . . . New Edition. With an Index to *Paradise Lost;* Todd's Verbal Index to All the Poems; and a Variorum Selection of Explanatory Notes by H. G. Bohn. London, 1861. 2 vols.

Based on the 1843 edition. First issue of Todd's Index after 1809. Reprinted (1884–87) in "Bohn's Standard Library."

184 The Poetical Works of John Milton. London: H. G. Bohn, 1862.

Includes all the poems; has H. Stebbing's life and Channing's essay. Stebbing's text.

185 The Complete Poetical Works of John Milton. Boston: Crosby & Nichols, 1863. 2 vols.

Fenton's life and the English poems.

186 The Works of John Milton, in Verse and Prose, Printed from the Original Editions, With a Life of the Author by the Rev. John Mitford. London: Bickers and Bush, 1863. 8 vols.

The 1851 edition.

187 The Poetical Works of John Milton. A New Edition with Notes and a Life of the Author by John Mitford. Philadelphia: Hazard, 1864. 2 vols.

188 The Poetical Works of John Milton. With Illustrations by E. H. Corbould and J. Gilbert. London: T. Nelson & Sons, 1864.

Photographs of Milton's tomb in St. Giles and of Ludlow Castle; ten zinc etchings. Only the English poems.

189 The Poetical Works of John Milton: with a Life of the Author; Preliminary Dissertations on Each Poem; Notes Critical and Explanatory; an Index to the Subjects of *Paradise Lost;* and a Verbal Index to All the Poems. By Charles Dexter Cleveland. New York and Chicago: A. S. Barnes & Co., [*ca.* 1865]. Pp. 688.

190 English Poems by John Milton. Edited with Life, Introduction, and Selected Notes by R. C. Browne. Oxford: Clarendon Press, 1866. 2 vols.

Life, Introduction, and notes that merited the many reprintings of this edition. The text is not important. *See* Item 239.

191 The Poetical Works of John Milton. "The Aldine Edition of the British Poets." London: Bell & Daldy, 1866. 3 vols.

Mitford's life.

192 Milton's Poems. Boston: Ticknor & Fields, 1866. 2 vols.

The text of Keightley's library edition.

193 The Poetical Works of John Milton. With Life, Critical Dissertation, and Explanatory Notes. . . . . The Text Edited by Charles Cowden Clarke. Nichols' "Library Edition of British Poets." Edinburgh: J. Nichols, etc. 1866.

194 The Poetical Works of John Milton. Edited by Sir Egerton Brydges. . . . . Illustrated with Engravings, Designed by John Martin and J. W. M. Turner. New York: W. I. Pooley, 1867.

195 The Poetical Works of Milton and Young. London: Griffin & Co., [*ca.* 1868].

Illustrated. Milton's poems, pp. 1–171.

196 The Poetical Works of John Milton. Reprinted from the "Chandos Poets." With Memoir, Explanatory Notes, etc. London: F. Warne & Co., 1868.

A few footnotes from Newton and others. Reprinted without date at least once (1872).

197 The Poetical Works of John Milton. With a Memoir. Boston: J. R. Osgood & Co., 1868–74. 3 vols.

198 The Poetical Works of John Milton. With Life, Critical Dissertation, and Explanatory Notes. The Text Edited by Charles Cowden Clarke. Edinburgh: W. P. Nimmo, 1869. 2 vols.

199 The Poetical Works of John Milton. Illustrated by F. Gilbert. London: J. Dicks, 1870.

Cheaply printed; no notes.

200 Poems by John Milton. Edited with Life and Notes, Critical and Philological, by John Merry Ross. London: Nelson & Sons, 1871.

School edition; life, notes, and glossary.

201 The Poetical Works of John Milton. Edited, with a Critical Memoir, by William Michael Rossetti. Illustrated by Thomas Seccombe. London: F. Moxon, Son & Co., [1871].

Reprinted, 1880 and 1881.

202 The Complete Poetical Works of Milton and Young. New Edition. Illustrated. London: Blackwood, [1872].

In Blackwood's "Universal Library of Standard Authors."

Printed from the plates used by Griffin in 1868. Illustrated with zinc etchings, one being of "the house in which Milton was born."

203 The Poetical Works of John Milton. With Life of the Author, and an Appendix Containing Addison's "Critique upon the Paradise Lost and Dr. Channing's "Essay on the Poetical Genius of Milton." London: Blackwood, [1872].

With illustrations.

204 The Poetical Works of John Milton, Printed from the Original Editions, with a Life of the Author by A. Chalmers. London: Bickers & Son, [1873].

205 The Poetical Works of John Milton. With Life, Critical Dissertation and Explanatory Notes [by Gilfillan]. The Text Edited by C. C. Clarke. London: Cassell, [1874]. 2 vols.

No notes.

206 The Poetical Works of John Milton. Edited, with Introductions, Notes, and an Essay on Milton's English by David Masson. London: Macmillan & Co., 1874. 3 vols.

Still a standard edition because of the introductory essays. Known as the "Cambridge edition." Issued 1882 in 12mo and in 1890 in 8vo. Re-edited in 1890; text corrected, poems put in chronological order, and a memoir added at that time.

207 The Poetical Works of John Milton. With Introductions and Notes by David Masson. "The Golden Treasury Series." London: Macmillan & Co., 1874. 2 vols.

This edition appeared at the same time as the larger one of the same year, but with abridged notes.

208 The Poetical Works of John Milton. Edited by Sir Egerton Brydges. Illustrated with Engravings from Drawings by J. M. W. Turner. A New Edition. London: W. Tegg, [1876].

From the six-volume edition of 1835.

209 The Poetical Works of John Milton. With Introductions by David Masson. London: Macmillan & Co., 1877.

The Globe edition. Has the introductory matter of the Golden Treasury edition, with revisions. The text is not significant. Frequently reprinted.

210 The Poetical Works of John Milton. London, [1878].

211 The Poetical Works of John Milton. Edited with Notes, Explanatory and Philological, by John Bradshaw. London: Allen, 1878. 3 vols.

A good text with an index to the notes.

Reviews in *Athen.*, August 3, 1878, pp. 134–35; *SR*, XLVI (1878), 723–25.

212 The Poetical Works of Milton and Marvell, with a Memoir of Each. "Riverside Edition of the British Poets." Boston: Houghton, Osgood & Co., 1878. 2 vols.

Published also by "Houghton and Company" with this date. Reprinted in the eighties.

The Milton memoir is Masson's. The notes are from Mitford.

213 The Poetical Works of John Milton. London: Ward, Lock & Co., [1878].

No notes; popular edition.

214 The Poetical Works of John Milton. Reprinted from the Best Editions, with Biographical Notice, etc. New York: Crowell, [*ca.* 1880].

215 The Poetical Works of John Milton. With a Sketch of His Life. New York: American Book Exchange, 1880.

216 The Poetical Works by John Milton. A New Edition, ... Revised from the Text of T. Newton [by T. A. W. Buckley]. "Excelsior Series." London: Routledge & Sons, [1880].

217 The Poetical Works of John Milton. London: W. Kent & Co., 1880. 2 vols.

218 The Poetical Works of John Milton, Printed from the Original Editions. With a Life of the Author by A. Chalmers. . . . . With Twelve Illustrations by R. Westall. London: Bickers & Son, 1881.

219 The Poetical Works of John Milton. With Life. Engravings on steel. "The Landscape Series of Poets," Edinburgh, [1881].

220 The Poetical Works of John Milton. Edited with a Critical Memoir by William Michael Rossetti. Illustrated by Thomas Seccombe. London: Ward Locke & Co., [1881]. 8vo.

A stereotype reprint on larger paper appeared in the same year.

221 The Poetical Works of John Milton. Edited, with Memoir, Introductions, Notes, and an Essay on Milton's English and Versification, by David Masson. London: Macmillan & Co., 1882. 3 vols.

Issued to supply a format between the Globe and Cambridge editions, the Golden Treasury edition being out of print. Chronological order of poems attempted, and more editorial matter as well as changes in the introductory essays. Reprinted, 1890.

222 The Poetical Works of John Milton. With a Biographical Notice. New York: W. E. Russell, [1884]. Pp. 562.

223 The Poetical Works of John Milton. Edited with Notes, Explanatory and Philological, by John Bradshaw. 2d ed. London: W. H. Allen & Co., 1885. 8vo. 2 vols.

A student's edition, with notes used by the editor in the University of Madras.

224 The Poetical Works of John Milton. London, [1886], 2 vols.

225 The Poetical Works of John Milton . . . . by David Masson. Chicago and New York: Belford, Clark & Co., 1886. Pp. li+627.

A cheap reprint of Masson.

226 The Poetical Works of John Milton. "Miniature Library of Poets." London: Cassell & Co., [1886]. 2 vols.

227 The Poetical Works of John Milton. "The Aldine Edition of the British Poets." London, 1886–88. 3 vols. in 2.

228 The Poetical Works of John Milton. "The Parchment Library." London: Kegan, Paul & Co., 1887. 2 vols.

No notes. Fifty copies on large paper.

229 The Poetical Works of John Milton, with Biographical Notice by John Bradshaw. "The Canterbury Poets." London: Walter Scott (Newcastle-on-Tyne), 1887–88. 2 vols.

The life and *Paradise Lost* are in the first volume (1887).

230 The Poetical Works of John Milton, with a Memoir. . . . . Fully Illustrated with New Wood-Engravings. With a Border by George Wharton Edwards. New York: Stokes, 1888.

231 The Poetical Works of John Milton. Edited by A. Waugh. London and Glasgow: Collins Clear Type Press, [*ca.* 1890].

Illustrated. Biographical sketch.

232 The Complete Poetical Works of John Milton, with a Life of the Poet and Notes on His Works by T. Newton. Illustrated with Fifty

Photogravures from Designs by Great Artists. Philadelphia: Gibbs & Co., 1890. Folio.

233 The Poetical Works of John Milton, with Memoir, Introductions, Notes, and an Essay on Milton's English Versification. Edited by David Masson. London: Macmillan & Co., 1890. 3 vols.

Another printing in 1894.

234 The English Poems of John Milton. Oxford: Clarendon Press, 1890–91. 2 vols.

235 The Cambridge Milton for Schools. Edited by A. W. Verity. 10 vols. "The Pitt Press Series." Cambridge: Cambridge University Press, 1891–96. 8vo.

Each volume offers the same biographical sketch, glossaries, notes, and appendixes on Milton's cosmology, blank verse, etc.

Volume I reviewed in *Athen.*, January 23, 1892, p. 113; *QR* (by L. Stephen), CXCIV, 102–25.

236 The Poetical Works of John Milton. . . . . Edited, with a Bibliographical Introduction, Life of Milton and an Analysis of Addison's Criticism on *Paradise Lost*, by John Bradshaw. London, 1892. 2 vols.

Replaces Mitford in the Aldine edition. Few notes; seven pages of bibliography. Comment on the Milton window in St. Margaret's, Westminster, on the portraits of Milton, etc.

Review in *N & Q*, Ser. VIII, No. I, pp. 179–80.

237 The Poetical Works of John Milton; with Introductions by David Masson. . . . . Biographical Sketch by Nathan Haskell Dole. New York and Boston: T. Y. Crowell & Co., [1892]. Pp. xiii+618.

238 The Poetical Works of John Milton. "Sir John Lubbock's Hundred Books." London: Routledge & Sons, 1893.

T. A. Buckley nominal editor, but the brief footnotes are not critical.

239 English Poems by John Milton Edited with Life, Introduction, and Notes by R. C. Browne. New Edition, with the Etymological Notes Revised by Henry Bradley. Oxford: Clarendon Press, 1894. 2 vols.

Reprinted frequently.

240 The Poetical Works of John Milton. Edited with Memoir, Introductions, Notes, and an Essay on Milton's English and Versification, by David Masson. New York and London: Macmillan & Co., 1894. 3 vols.

Another printing in 1896.

241 The Poetical Works of John Milton. With Introductory Memoir, Notes, Bibliography . . . . [and Preface by L. Valentine]. London: F. Warne & Co., 1896. 8vo.

Scant bibliography; few footnotes.

242 The Poetical Works of John Milton. "The Apollo Poets." London: Bliss Sands & Co., [1897].

Portrait; brief biographical sketch.

243 The Complete Poetical Works of John Milton. Edited by William Vaughan Moody. Cambridge edition. Boston: Houghton Mifflin Co., [1899].

Notes and critical prefaces to individual poems and translations of the Latin poems. The criticism shows discriminating judgment of literary values but is occasionally wrong in its premises. Issued under various dates; reprinted 1924 in the Students' Cambridge edition.

Review in *Poet-lore,* XI (1899), 438–39.

244 The Poems of John Milton. Philadelphia: H. Altemus, [*ca.* 1899]. Pp. 192.

245 The Poetical Works of John Milton. Edited after the Original Texts by H. C. Beeching. Oxford: The Clarendon Press, 1900. Pp. xiii+554.

Issued the same year on India paper with less leading of lines. No notes, but two collotypes of Milton's handwriting and nine facsimile title-pages are given.

246 The Complete Poetical Works of Milton, from the Edition of H. C. Beeching. "The Oxford Miniature Edition." London: Henry Frowde, 1900. 16mo.

Reprinted, 1922.

Reviews in *Athen.*, March 31, 1900, p. 398; *QR* (by Leslie Stephen), CXCIV, 102–25.

247 The Poems of John Milton. London: Newnes, 1901. Pp. viii+526.

248 The Poems of John Milton with a Critical and Biographical Introduction by Brander Matthews. New York, 1902. Pp. 514.

249 The Poetical Works of John Milton. Edited with Critical Notes by William Aldis Wright. Cambridge: The University Press, 1903. Pp. xxiv+607.

A critical text; notes on variants, pp. 547–607. The Preface has typographical descriptions of title-pages and comments on various editions. The texts are based on manuscripts and the earliest editions, with some indebtedness to Capell's unpublished material now preserved at Trinity Library. Many anonymous conjectures are included. Issued in heavy and thin paper editions. Reviews in *Athen.*, July 4, 1903, p. 60; *TLS*, August 7, 1903, pp. 237–38; *ES*, XXXIV (1904), 394–95; *Beiblatt*, XIX (1908), 378.

250 The Poetical Works of John Milton, Edited after the Original Texts by . . . . H. C. Beeching. London: Henry Frowde, 1904. Pp. xiii+554.

Preface of 1899. Reprint of the 1900 edition. "Reproduces for the first time the scarce small octavo of 1645," whereas Mitford followed that of 1673.

See J. Caro, *Beiblatt*, XXV (1914), 211–12.

251 The Poetical Works of John Milton. Etchings, Mezzo-tints and Copper Engravings by William Hyde. London: Astolat Press, 1904. Large 4to. Pp. 194.

Beeching's text with excellent plates.

252 The Poetical Works of John Milton. "Library of English Classics." London: Macmillan & Co., 1904. 2 vols.

Bibliographical note (I, i–xv) by A. W. Pollard. Masson's text, with some changes of capitalization and italic type.

253 The Complete Poems of John Milton, Written in English; with Introductions, Notes and Illustrations. "The Harvard Classics." New York: P. F. Collier & Son, [1909].

254 The Poetical Works of John Milton. "Everyman's Library." London: J. M. Dent & Co.; New York: E. P. Dutton & Co., [*ca.* 1909].

255 The Cambridge Milton for Schools. Edited by A. W. Verity. "The Pitt Press Series." Cambridge: Cambridge University Press, 1891–1910.

The revised Verity edition of *Paradise Lost* (1910) is the most learned in annotation of all modern editions. This was added to the 1891–96 series.

256 The Poetical Works of John Milton. With Introduction by Edmund Gosse. London: Ward Locke & Co., [1911]. Pp. xix+423.

Refers to the 1637 *Comus* as "unauthorized," and charges Milton's blindness to glaucoma.

257 The English Poems of John Milton. Edited from Beeching's text. "World's Classics." Oxford: University Press; London: H. Milford, 1913. Pp. 488.

Modernizes use of capitals and punctuation.

Reviews in *MLR*, XI (1916), 117; *Beiblatt* (by J. Caro), XXV (1914), 211–12.

258 The Poetical Works of John Milton. Edited after the Original Texts by H. C. Beeching. Oxford, 1922. Small 8vo.

259 The Complete Poetical Works of John Milton. Edited by William Vaughan Moody. "Students' Cambridge Edition." Boston, New York: Houghton Mifflin Co., [*ca.* 1924]. Pp. xxxiv+419.

The translations of the 1899 edition revised by E. K. Rand.

260 John Milton [poetical works]. With an Introduction by Henry Newbolt. London and Edinburgh: Nelson & Sons, [1924]. Pp. xiv+530.

Scant biographical and political accounts. The lines are not numbered. Of the Latin poems, only Elegies 6 and 7 are included. No use is made of the new facts in Smart's edition of the sonnets.

261 The Poems of John Milton: English, Latin, Greek, and Italian, Arranged in Chronological Order with a Preface by H. J. C. Grierson. London: Chatto & Windus, 1925. 2 vols.

Volume II, *Paradise Lost.*

The attempts to save only such archaic spellings as signify the older pronunciation and to punctuate logically are notable additions to the values of this edition arising from the editor's search for evidence on dates of composition. The prefatory matter is more marked by studious care for recent scholarship than appears in any other modern edition. Apart from a failure to utilize some of Smart's evidence on the sonnets, the text is most ably prepared.

Reviews in *RAA*, III, 346–47; *LM*, XII, 432; *TLS*, May 21, 1925 (see corr., *ibid.*, June 4, 1925); *Bookman*, LXVIII (1925), 233–37; *Nation-Athenaeum*, XXXVII (1925), 297; *TLS*, November 19, 1925; *Spectator*, November 14, 1925.

262 Poems in English by John Milton, with Illustrations by William Blake. London: The Nonesuch Press, 1926. 2 vols. Pp. 352; 283.

Review in *TLS*, August 19, 1926.

IV. THE *MINOR POEMS* AND SELECTED MINOR POEMS

263 Robert Deverell. Discoveries in Hieroglyphics and Other Antiquities. London, 1813. 6 vols.

Volumes IV and VI contain texts of "L'Allegro," "Il Penseroso," and *Comus* "put in a light now entirely new." Commentary and wood engravings.

264 Poems on Several Occasions. . . . . The Author, John Milton. London: [J. Sharpe], 1817. Pp. 188.

Added title-page engraved with vignette reads, "*The Minor Poems of John Milton* . . . . 1816." Bound with his *Paradise Regained*, 1817.

265 Poems on Several Occasions. London, 1817. 2 vols.

Fenton's life and Johnson's criticism.

266 Poems on Several Occasions. London, 1827.

Westall's plates.

267 Milton's Poem of *Comus* . . . . with Notes by Francis Henry Egerton, now Earl of Bridgewater, and Others. Paris: Galignani, 1829. Pp. 72.

Includes "L'Allegro," "Il Penseroso," and "Lycidas."

268 Milton's *Comus*, "L'Allegro," and "Il Penseroso." With Numerous Illustrative Notes Adapted for Use in Training Colleges and Schools. By John Hunter. London: Green, Longmans, Roberts & Green, 1864. Pp. xix+78.

269 Milton's *Comus*, "Lycidas," "L'Allegro," "Il Penseroso," and Selected Sonnets. With Notes by H. R. Huckin. London: Seeley & Co., 1871.

270 Milton's *Comus*, "L'Allegro," and "Il Penseroso." With . . . . Notes . . . . by John Hunter. . . . . Revised Edition, with a New Appendix. London: Longmans & Co., [1874]. Pp. xix+95.

271 "L'Allegro," "Il Penseroso" and "Lycidas." With Life of Milton, Introduction and Notes by F. Storr. "English School Classics." London, 1874. Pp. 61.

Reprinted 1878, 1884.

272 The "Lycidas" and "Epitaphium Damonis." . . . . Edited with Notes and Introduction (including a Reprint of the Rare Latin Version of the

Lycidas by William Hog, 1694), by C. S. Jerram. London: Longmans & Co., 1874. Pp. xi+141.

Extensive notes, etymologies, translations of the Latin poem by Symmons and Masson. Second edition, 1881.

273 "L'Allegro," "Il Penseroso," and Other Poems. . . . . Illustrated. Boston: Osgood & Co., [1877]. Pp. 96.

274 Milton's "L'Allegro," "Il Penseroso" and "Lycidas": Edited, with an Introduction, Paraphrase and Vocabularies, by . . . . F. S. Aldhouse. London, 1879. Pp. 48.

275 Milton's "Arcades" and Sonnets, with . . . . Notes . . . . by . . . . John Hunter. London: Longmans & Co., 1880. Pp. 48.

276 "Lycidas" and "Epitaphium Damonis." London, 1881.

Edited by C. S. Jerram. Second edition, revised. *See* Item 272.

277 "L'Allegro," "Il Penseroso," and the "Hymn on the Nativity." Illustrated. London: Cassell & Co., 1885. Pp. 57.

278 Miscellaneous Poems, Sonnets, and Psalms . . . . edited by G. T. Bettany. "Popular Library of Literary Treasures." London: Ward, Lock & Co., 1886. Pp. 126.

279 Milton's Earlier Poems, including the Translations by W. Cowper of Those Written in Latin and Italian. "Cassell's National Library." London: Cassell, 1886. Pp. 192.

280 The *Minor Poems* of John Milton. Edited with Notes, by William J. Rolfe. New York: Harper & Bros., 1887. Pp. viii+229.

281 The Shorter Poems of John Milton. With . . . . Illustrations by Samuel Palmer. London: Seeley & Co., 1889. Fol.

Preface by H. Palmer.

282 Milton's "L'Allegro," "Il Penseroso," "Arcades," "Lycidas," Sonnets . . . . ; with Introduction and Notes by W. Bell. London: Macmillan & Co., 1889. Pp. xv+183. 8vo.

283 Milton's "Lycidas," Sonnets. . . . . Edited by W. Bell, with Introduction and Notes. London: Macmillan & Co., 1889. Pp. 183.

Fourteen reprints by 1919.

284 Milton. "L'Allegro," "Il Penseroso," "Lycidas," "On the Morning of Christ's Nativity." "Royal English Classics." London: Nelson & Sons, 1890. Pp. vi+48.

285 Milton's "Ode on the Morning of Christ's Nativity," "L'Allegro," "Il Penseroso," and "Lycidas." With Introduction, Notes, and Indexes by A. W. Verity. "Pitt Press Series." Cambridge, 1891. Pp. li+172.

Full notes and verbal index as in all of Verity's editions. Reprinted nine times by 1924.

286 Milton's *Comus*, "Arcades," and Sonnets. Edited by Oliver Elton. Oxford, 1893.

287 Milton's Lyrics. Boston, 1892. Pp. 102.

"L'Allegro," "Il Penseroso," and *Comus*.

288 "L'Allegro," "Il Penseroso," *Comus*, and "Lycidas." Edited by Louise Manning Hodgkins. "Students Series of English Classics." Boston: Leach, Shewell & Sanborn, [1893]. Pp. xii+102.

289 "L'Allegro," "Il Penseroso," *Comus*, and "Lycidas" . . . . with Biographical Introduction and Notes. New York: American Book Co., 1894. Pp. 74.

290 Milton's "L'Allegro," "Il Penseroso," and "Lycidas." With Explanatory Notes . . . . by F. Gorse. London: Relfe Brothers, [1894]. Pp. iv+48.

Footnotes and guides for paraphrasing by young students.

291 "L'Allegro," and Other Poems, by John Milton; with a Biographical Sketch, Introductions, and Notes. "The Riverside Literature Series." Boston: Houghton Mifflin Co., [1895]. Pp. 96.

292 Select Minor Poems of John Milton. "Hymn on the Nativity." "L'Allegro," "Il Penseroso," *Comus*, "Lycidas." With Biography, Introductions, Notes, Edited by James E. Thomas. "Studies in English Classics." Boston and New York: Silver, Burdette & Co., 1895.

293 John Milton's "L'Allegro," "Il Penseroso," *Comus*, and "Lycidas," Edited with Notes and Introductions by William P. Trent. "Longmans' English Classics." New York and London: Longmans, Green & Co., 1895. Pp. xviii+181.

294 Three Poems of John Milton. Ashendene, County of Hereford: privately printed, 1896. Pp. iv+42.

"L'Allegro," "Il Penseroso," "Hymn." Printed by St. John Hornby "from types cast from matrices given to the University of Oxford by Bishop Fell in or about the year 1670." Designs by C. Barclay. Fifty copies only.

295 The Early Poems of John Milton. Seen through the Press by Charles Sturt. The Decorations Are Designed and Cut on Wood by Charles Ricketts. London: Hacon & Ricketts, [1896]. Pp. ciii.

Three hundred and ten copies; printed by the Ballantyne Press.

296 Select Minor Poems of John Milton. Edited by J. E. Thomas. With Biographical Introduction and Notes. Boston: Silver Burdette & Co., 1896.

297 Milton's Poems. "L'Allegro," "Il Penseroso," *Comus*, and "Lycidas." With Introduction and Notes by A. Cameron. Halifax, Nova Scotia: Allen & Co., 1898. Pp. v+53.

298 The Shorter Poems of John Milton, including the Two Latin Elegies and Italian Sonnet to Diodati and the "Epitaphium Damonis," Arranged in Chronological Order. With Preface, Introduction, and Notes by Andrew J. George. New York: Macmillan Co., 1898. Pp. xxv+299.

Translations of the Latin and Italian pieces.

299 The Minor Poems of John Milton. Illustrated and Decorated by A. Garth Jones. London: Bell & Sons, 1898. Pp. xiv+206.

One hundred copies on Japanese vellum.

300 "Lycidas," "L'Allegro," "Il Penseroso" by John Milton. Edited with Life, Introduction, Notes Arranged and Classified, Paraphrasing .... by Thomas Page. London: Moffatt & Paige, 1898.

301 *Comus* and "Lycidas." Edited with Introduction, Notes .... by A. W. Verity. "Cambridge Series for Schools." Cambridge: Cambridge University Press, 1898. Pp. lv+208.

302 Milton's Shorter Poems and Sonnets. Arranged in Chronological Order, and Edited with Introduction and Notes, by Frederick Day Nichols. "Twentieth Century Text-Books." New York: D. Appleton & Co., 1899.

303 Milton's *Comus*, "Lycidas," and Other Poems, and Matthew Arnold's "Address on Milton." Edited with Introduction and Notes by Andrew J. George. .... "Pocket English Classics." New York and London: Macmillan, 1899. Pp. xxxviii+178.

304 Facsimile of the Manuscript of Milton's Minor Poems Preserved in the Library of Trinity College, Cambridge. University Press: Cambridge, 1899.

Edited, with an Introduction, by W. Aldis Wright.
Reviews in *Athen.*, February 10, 1900, pp. 174–75; *QR*, July, 1901, pp. 101–25.

305 "L'Allegro," "Il Penseroso," *Comus*, and "Lycidas." Edited by E. E. Hale, Jr. New York, [1900]. Pp. 140.

306 "L'Allegro," "Il Penseroso," *Comus*, and "Lycidas." Edited with Introduction and Notes by T. F. Huntington. Boston: Ginn & Co., 1900. Pp. 130.

307 Milton's Minor Poems; "L'Allegro," "Il Penseroso," *Comus*, and "Lycidas." Edited for School Use, by W. A. Neilson. "Lake English Classics." Chicago: Scott, Foresman & Co., 1900. Pp. 165.

308 Select Minor Poems of John Milton. . . . . Edited, with Introduction, Notes, etc., by A. P. Walker. Boston: D. C. Heath & Co., 1900. Pp. x+186.

309 "L'Allegro," "Il Penseroso," *Comus*, and "Lycidas." Edited for School Use by E. E. Hale, Jr. New York and Chicago: Globe School Book Co., [1900].

310 Milton's "L'Allegro," "Il Penseroso," *Comus*, and "Lycidas." Edited with Introduction and Notes by T. F. Huntington. . . . . "Standard English Classics." Boston: Ginn & Co., 1900. Pp. 130.

311 "L'Allegro," "Il Penseroso," *Comus*, "Lycidas." Edited with Introduction and Notes by E. S. Parsons. "Cambridge Literature Series." Boston: B. H. Sanborn & Co., [1900]. Pp. xxxviii+138.

312 Milton's Shorter Poems and Sonnets. Edited . . . . by F. D. Nichols. New York: Appleton & Co., 1901. Pp. 153.

313 The Lyric and Dramatic Poems of John Milton. Edited with Introduction and Notes by Martin W. Sampson. London: Bell; New York: Holt, 1901. Pp. 345.

Long introduction, notes, metrical apparatus.
Review in *Athen.*, January 18, 1902, p. 78.

314 Milton's Minor Poems . . . . with Introduction and Notes by S. Thurber. "Academy Series of English Classics." Boston and Chicago: Allyn & Bacon, [1901]. Pp. xxiv+129.

315 Lycidas and Other Odes by John Milton. With Illustrations by R. Anning Bell. London: Bell & Sons, 1903. Pp. 54.

316 Milton's Minor Poems. Edited by Mary A. Jordan. New York: American Book Co., 1904. Pp. 179.

A good edition of "L'Allegro," "Il Penseroso," "Arcades," *Comus*, and "Lycidas."

317 Milton's Shorter Poems and Sonnets. Arranged in Chronological Order, and Edited with Introduction and Notes, by Frederick Day Nichols. New York: D. Appleton & Co., 1904. Pp. x+153.

318 Ode on Time. Illumination on Vellum by Edith Horwood, with Writing by Graily Hewitt. *International Studio*, XXV (1905), 61.

319 Milton's Minor Poems: "L'Allegro," "Il Penseroso," *Comus*, and "Lycidas"; a Plan for Study, with a Biographical Sketch, Suggestions to Teachers and Notes for Students, by Mary Devereux. Chicago: A. Flanagan Co., [1905]. Pp. v+181.

320 Poems by John Milton. Introduction by Sir Walter Raleigh. London: Blackie & Son, 1905. Pp. x+231.

The usual briefer poems in English, the Psalms and classical translations in paraphrase.

321 *Comus*, and Other Poems. Cambridge: Cambridge University Press, 1906. Pp. 85.

Has eighteen of the sonnets and the other minor poems in English. Only 250 copies printed. *Comus* is taken from the 1645 and 1673 editions and the manuscript autograph, but with no description of the procedure used.

322 "Lycidas," *Comus*, "L'Allegro," "Il Penseroso" and Other Poems. Edited by J. W. Abernethy. New York: Maynard, Merrill & Co., [1906]. Pp. 198.

323 "Lycidas," *Comus*, "L'Allegro," "Il Penseroso," and Other Poems, by John Milton. Edited by Julian W. Abernethy. "Maynard's English Classic Series." New York: Maynard, Merrill & Co., [1906]. 2 vols.

324 Milton: Early Poems, *Comus*, and "Lycidas." Edited by S. E. Goggin and A. F. Watt. London: University Tutorial Press, 1906. Pp. 184.

325 "Il Penseroso," "L'Allegro," and "Arcades." London: De la Mare Press, 1907. Pp. 30.

326 Minor Poems by John Milton. With Biographical Introduction by H. Bennett. London: Long, 1907. Pp. xvi+138.

No notes.

327 Selected Poems of John Milton: "L'Allegro," "Il Penseroso," *Comus*, "Lycidas." Edited . . . . by Clara H. Whitmore. New York: University Publishing Co., [1907].

328 The Shorter Poems of John Milton. Introduction by T. Cartwright. London: Heinemann, 1908. Pp. xiv+79.

No notes.

329 Minor Poems . . . . Chosen by A. T. Quiller-Couch. "Select English Classics." Oxford: Oxford University Press, [1908].

330 Milton's *Comus*, "Lycidas," and Other Poems, and Matthew Arnold's "Address on Milton." Edited . . . . by A. J. George. New York: Macmillan Co., 1909. Pp. xxxviii+178.

331 [Minor Poems] edited by Oliver Elton. Oxford: Oxford University Press, 1897–[1910].

Dates given on title-pages are: "L'Allegro," 1893; "Il Penseroso," 1897; *Comus*, 1898; "Lycidas," 1900. "Arcades" and the sonnets are not dated; British Museum has 1910. Review in *RELV*, XXVIII (1911), 35.

332 *Comus*, "L'Allegro," "Il Penseroso," and "Lycidas," with Other of Milton's Shorter Poems. Edited with Introduction and Notes by Clarence Griffin Child. New York: C. Scribner's Sons, 1910. Pp. xxx+163.

333 Milton's Shorter Poems. Edited by G. B. Sellon. London: Blackie & Son, 1910. Pp. x+135.

334 "Song on May Morning." *Chautauquan*, LXII (May, 1911), 407.

335 Minor Poems, by John Milton; with Notes for Careful Study, by Henry W. Boynton, and Suggestive Questions and Comments by Charles Swain Thomas. Boston: Houghton Mifflin Co., [1911].

336 "L'Allegro," "Il Penseroso," *Comus*, and "Lycidas." Edited by Philo M. Buck, Jr. New York: American Book Co., [1911]. Pp. 84.

337 The Shorter Poems of John Milton. London: St. Catherine's Press, [1912].

Texts of "Lycidas," "L'Allegro," "Il Penseroso," and the "Hymns."

338 Milton's "L'Allegro," "Il Penseroso," *Comus*, and "Lycidas." Edited by Martin W. Sampson. New York: Holt, 1912. Pp. xxxii+96.

339 Milton's *Comus*, "Lycidas," and Other Poems, and Matthew Arnold's "Address on Milton"; Edited with Introduction and Notes, by Samuel Edward Allen. New York: Macmillan Co., 1912. Pp. lxxvi+164.

340 The Minor Poems . . . . edited by Edmund Dale. London, [1913].

341 [Milton's] Shorter Poems. Edited by Fred Le Roy Homer. Chautauqua, New York: Union Book Co., [1913].

342 Milton's Minor Poems. Edited by R. T. Kerlin. Richmond, Virginia: Johnson Publishing Co., [1913]. Pp. 171.

343 John Milton's Rendition into Verse of the Eighth Psalm, August 14, 1653. San Francisco: Taylor, Nash & Taylor, [1914].

Only 350 copies printed.

344 Minor Poems, by John Milton; with Notes for Careful Study, by Claude M. Fuess . . . . and Suggestive Questions and Comments, by Charles Swain Thomas. Boston, New York, etc.: Houghton Mifflin Co., [1914].

345 Milton's Minor Poems: "L'Allegro," "Il Penseroso," *Comus*, and "Lycidas." Edited for School Use by William Allan Neilson. Chicago: Scott, Foresman & Co., [1919].

346 The Minor English Poems. With an Introduction and Notes by H. C. Beeching. London: Methuen, 1923. Pp. xxxvii+116.

The materials were first published in the "Little Library," 1903.

347 John Milton: Minor Poems. London: Noel Douglas, 1924. Pp. ix+120.

The 1645 text in a photographic facsimile of less interest than the type facsimile of the same year.

348 Milton's Poems 1645: Type-facsimile. Oxford: Clarendon Press, 1924.

"Set up from rotographs of the Bodleian copy, and the proofs were compared with the three copies in the British Museum." One thousand copies printed on linen-rag paper.

Reviews in *QR*, CXLIII (1925), 277; *LM*, XI (1925), 306; *Library*, V (1925), 383.

349 The Minor Poems of John Milton. New York: Payson, [1927]. Pp. 120.

Portrait; original title-pages reproduced from the 1645 edition; no Latin poems.

CRITICISM

350 E. H. Barker. "Error in Milton's Latinity Noticed. . . ." *Classical Journal*, VII (1813), 393–98.

351 C. Symmons. "Observations on Milton's Latin Poetry." *Ibid.*, IX (1814), 338–44.

352 "Milton's Minor Poems." *Dublin University Magazine*, LXIII (June, 1864), 619–25.

Appreciation of "Lycidas," *Comus*, "L'Allegro," and "Il Penseroso."

353 A. de Morgan. "The Milton Difficulty." *Athen.*, January 8, 1870, p. 72

On points of style in the paraphrases of the Psalms unlike those in the other early poems.

354 C. Wordsworth. "On Some Faults in Milton's Latin Poetry." *Classical Review*, I (1887), 46–48.

355 E. Walford. "Milton's Pronunciation of Latin." *N & Q*, Ser. VIII, No. VI, pp. 146, 253, 489; No. VII, p. 436.

356 G. Serrell. "Milton as Seen in His Latin Poems." *Temple Bar*, CXV, (1898), 547–63.

357 A. H. Mabley. "Milton's Latin Poems." *Western Reserve University Bulletin*, II (1899), 49–72.

358 Charles G. Osgood, Jr. "Milton's 'Elm Star-proof.'" *JEGP*, IV (1902), 370–78.

Phrase illustrates how Milton expressed his own observations of nature in language reminiscent of his reading. Comments on the possibility of Milton's acquaintance with Countess Dowager of Derby in 1633.

359 Mark Pattison. "Milton in His Latin Poems." *GM*, CCC (1906), 497–512.

Milton's Latin poems distinguished by being a vehicle of genuine emotion.

360 Ernest H. Coleridge. "A Note on Milton's Shorter Poems." *Milton Memorial Lectures* (Oxford, 1909), pp. 23–38.

361 Laura E. Lockwood. "Milton's Corrections to the *Minor Poems*." *MLN*, XXV (1910), 201–5.

Valuable inferences made as to Milton's method of writing; based on a study of the facsimile of the Trinity College manuscript.

362 Frederico Olivero. "Keats and the *Minor Poems* of Milton." *ES*, XLIII (1910), 242–51.

The aesthetic development of Milton and Keats compared. Keats first influenced by the *Minor Poems*, then by the two epics and *Samson Agonistes*.

363 Sir Edwin Durning-Lawrence. Milton's Epitaph to Shakespeare. London: Truslowe & Bray, [1912]. Pp. 7.

Through comparison of the page in the New York Public Library copy of the Second Folio bearing the Epitaph with six other copies, it is shown that this one reading "Starre-ypointed" is unique. Presumption is taken that the word is equivalent to "beacon," then pronounced "bacon."

364 Allan H. Gilbert. "The Tower of Fame in Milton." *MLN*, XXVIII (1913), 30.

Speculates on location of the tower described in "In quintum Novembris," ll. 170–73.

365 Alden Sampson. Studies in Milton. New York, 1913. Pp. 310.

Among the most pleasing critical interpretations of the shorter poems.
Review in *Nation*, XCVIII, 266–67.

366 Samuel A. Tannenbaum. "Milton's Starre-ypointing Pyramid." *Dial*, LV (1913), 401.

Refutes Lawrence's arguments.

367 Edward Chauncey Baldwin. "Milton and the Psalms." *MP*, XVII (1919), 457–63.

Scholarly and suggestive discussion of Milton's translations.

368 George W. Sherburn. "The Early Popularity of Milton's *Minor Poems*." *MP*, XVII (1919–20), 259–78, 515–40.

An important collection of evidence showing the popularity of the *Minor Poems* from 1637 to 1740. Refutation, by means of imitative passages and quotations, of Warton's assertion in 1757 that Milton had been neglected until that year.

369 John A. Himes. "Some Interpretations of Milton." *MLN*, XXXV (1920), 441–42.

Notes on "Lycidas," ll. 17, 30, 31, 110; *Comus*, ll. 93–94; "On the Death of a Fair Infant," l. 53.

370 ———. "Further Interpretations of Milton." *MLN*, XXXVI (1921), 414–19.

Comments on *Comus*, l. 93; "Death of a Fair Infant," ll. 53, 76–77; "Lycidas," ll. 50 ff.; "L'Allegro," ll. 136 ff.

371 ———. Miltonic Enigmas. Gettysburg, Pennsylvania: privately printed [1921]. Pp. 23.

Empirical interpretations of lines from some of the *Minor Poems*.

372 E. K. Rand. "J. and I. in Milton's Latin Script." *MP*, XIX (1922), 315–19.

Evidence to show that the letters *J* and *I* in Milton's Italian handwriting are identical.

373 J. A. Nairn. "Milton's Latin Poetry." *Fortnightly Review*, CXXIII (1925), 501–13.

Brief exposition of passages from the Latin poems, which show Milton a poet of first rank, combining strong originality with an intimate knowledge of Latin literature. Has the unusual assertion that Milton used "Elegiarum Liber" to refer to his theme rather than to his meter.

374 Marian H. Studley. "Milton and His Paraphrases of the Psalms." *PQ*, IV (1925), 364–72.

Milton's interest in the Psalms, and his use of all available texts in making paraphrases held unusual, as well as his self-expression in the paraphrases.

375 Harris F. Fletcher. "Milton and Thomas Young." *TLS*, January 21, 1926.

Reviews the traditional date for the Fourth Latin Elegy (i.e., 1627), and from ll. 33–38 deduces that it was written before March 26, 1625. See Grierson's comment in the issue for February 11, 1926.

376 H. W. Garrod. Milton's Lines on Shakespeare.

In *Essays and Studies by Members of the English Association*, XII (1926), 1–23, the author repeats Baxter's 1913 statement that Milton revised the poem twice. Errs in asserting that the poem was omitted from the Fourth Folio; also, is not convincing in use of parallels from contemporaries as a means of discrediting the 1630 date.

Review in *TLS*, December 23, 1926, p. 947.

377 John Drinkwater. A Book for Bookmen. New York: Doran, 1927.

"Coleridge, Milton, and Warton," pp. 61–91, deals with the copy of the 1791 Warton given to Coleridge. Reproduces in full Coleridge's strictures on Warton's notes. See also *LM*, XIV (1926), 491–505.

378 George Reuben Potter. "Milton's Early Poems, the School of Donne, and the Elizabethan Sonneteers." *PQ*, VI (1927), 396–400.

In his use of conceits, Milton followed the sonneteers rather than Donne.

379 Robert M. Smith. The Variant Issues of Shakespeare's Second Folio and Milton's First Published Poem: a Bibliographical Problem. Bethlehem, Pennsylvania: Lehigh University, 1928. Pp. 62.

Using evidence from the title-pages of 124 copies of the Second Folio, Mr. Smith proves that Milton wrote "starre-ypointing" in the *Epitaph*. His method is in admirable contrast to that of Sir Edward Durning-Lawrence. There are many other useful additions to our knowledge of the typography of the folios.

V. INDIVIDUAL WORKS FROM THE *MINOR POEMS*

1. "ODE ON THE MORNING OF CHRIST'S NATIVITY"

380 Milton's "Ode on the Morning of Christ's Nativity." Illustrated by Eminent Artists. London, 1868. Pp. 44.

Forty-two drawings in black and white. Republished in London (*ca.* 1870) and in New York (Scribners, Welford & Armstrong).

381 The Nativity. Words from Milton. Composed for Chorus, Solo Voices, and Orchestra by J. K. Paine, [1883].

382 The Nativity of Christ: Milton. With Illustrations in Colour from the Works of the Old Masters. London: Marcus Ward & Co., [1892]. Pp. 15.

383 Milton. "Ode on the Morning of Christ's Nativity." Oxford: Daniel, 1894. Pp. 21.

Only 200 copies printed.

384 On the Morning of Christ's Nativity. John Milton. . . . . With Christmas Greetings of All Souls' Church, Chicago. [Chicago]: R. R. Donnelley & Sons Co., 1896.

Finely illuminated edition of the text.

385 Milton's "Hymn on the Morning of Christ's Nativity." With Illustrations by Emily J. Harding and I. H. Robinson. London: G. Allen, 1897.

386 " 'Ode on the Nativity.' With Colored Illustrations." *Century*, N.S., LXI (December, 1900), 161–77.

387 Milton's "Ode on the Morning of Christ's Nativity," Prefaced by an Appreciation Taken in Part from the Works of Henry Hallam. Chicago: R. F. Seymour, 1901.

Illustrated; ornaments by the publisher; on handmade paper.

388 "On the Morning of Christ's Nativity. . . . ." *Critic*, XXXIX (1901), 483–502.

Illustrated.

389 Milton's "Ode on the Morning of Christ's Nativity." Edited by Mary Olivia Kennedy. London: Blackie & Son, 1902.

390 Milton's "Ode on the Morning of Christ's Nativity." With an Introduction by G. L. Swiggett. Sewanee, Tennessee: University Press, [1906]. Pp. 32.

391 "Ode on the Morning of Christ's Nativity," by John Milton; with an Introduction by Walter Taylor Field. "The Abbey Classics." San Francisco and New York: P. Elder & Co., [1907].

392 On the Morning of Christ's Nativity. John Milton. Illustrated by R. T. Rose. London: T. E. and E. C. Jack, [1908].

393 "Ode on the Morning of Christ's Nativity," by John Milton. Portland, Maine: Mosher, 1909. Pp. 26.

394 "Ode on the Morning of Christ's Nativity" by John Milton and "A Hymn of the Nativity" by Richard Crashaw. London: St. Catherine Press, [1912]. Pp. 28.

395 On the Morning of Christ's Nativity. Milton's Hymn with Illustrations by William Blake and a Note by Geoffrey Keynes. Cambridge: Cambridge University Press, 1923. Pp. 32.

Presents new Blake drawings preserved in Whitworth Institute, Manchester. Reproduces the 1645 text.
Review in *TLS*, XXII (1923), 907.

396 "Milton. 'On the Morning of Christ's Nativity.' " *Primary Education*, XXXIII (1925), 657.

CRITICISM

397 "Milton's 'Hymn on the Morning of Christ's Nativity.' " *N & Q*, Ser. IX, No. XI (1903), pp. 88, 193, 475; No. XII, p. 56.

Comments on the punctuation.

398 Albert S. Cook. "Two Notes on Milton." *MLR*, II (1907), 121–28.

"Namancos" ("Lycidas," l. 162) equals "Nemancos"; parallel passages from the "Ode" and Mantuan.

399 Albert S. Cook. Notes on Milton's "Ode on the Morning of Christ's Nativity." [Reprinted from the] *Transactions of the Connecticut Academy of Arts and Sciences*, XV (1909), 307–68.

An important document covering source materials and points of structure.
Review by Theo. Mühe, *Beiblatt*, XXIII (1912), 143.

400 John Monaghan. "Two Poets Went over to Bethlehem." *Catholic World*, CXVIII (1923), 381–83.

Contrasting the poems of Crashaw and Milton on the Nativity, the author stresses the humility of the courtier and the arrogance of the "Puritan."

2. *COMUS* AND ADAPTATIONS

401 Comus. A Mask Presented at Ludlow Castle, 1634, before the Earl of Bridgewater . . . . by John Milton. Ludlow: Printed and sold by W. Felton, 1803. Pp. 38.

402 Comus. A Mask by John Milton. . . . . Printed from the Text of . . . . Henry John Todd, with Selected and Original Anecdotes and Annotations, Biographical, Explanatory, Critical and Dramatic, with Splendid Embellishments. London: Mathews & Leigh, 1808.

In *The Cabinet*, Vol. V.

The 1798 edition, published at Canterbury, with additional notes from Warton and others. Both works contain unique material on the background and circumstances of the first production, but the text variants are incomplete.

403 *Comus:* a Masque, in Two Acts. As Performed at the Theatre Royal, Drury Lane. Altered from Milton by George Colman. London, 1809.

In Inchbald's *Collection of Farces*, VII, 295–315.

Reprinted, 1815.

404 *Comus*, a Mask: Now Adapted to the Stage, as Altered from Milton's Mask. London, 1811.

In *The Modern British Drama*, II, 571–85.

Dalton's three-act version. See Colman's version of two acts in this five-volume collection of plays; V, 1–7. Reprinted, 1824.

405 Milton's *Mask of Comus.*

In *Discoveries in Hieroglyphics and Other Antiquities, in Progress, to Which Many Favorite Compositions Are Put in a Light Now Entirely New, and Such As Rendered Them Infinitely More Amusing As Well As More Instructive to Readers of Earlier Times*, by Robert Deverell. London, 1813.

Long footnotes; the whole work a freak of scholarship.

406 Comus. A Mask. Altered from Milton. Correctly Given, from Copies Used in the Theatres, by Thomas Dibdin. London: printed at the Chiswick Press for Whittingham and Arliss, 1815. Pp. 24.

In *Dibdin's London Theatre*, Vol. II.

407 Milton's *Comus:* a Masque, in Two Acts. . . . . The Original Music by Handel and Arne, with Some Additions by Bishop and Kelly; the Overture by Cherubini, the Dances by M. Ware. London: J. Miller, 1815.

408 Milton's *Comus:* a Masque, in Two Acts, as Revived at Covent-Garden, April, 28, 1815. London: J. Miller, 1815. Pp. 29.

409 The *Masque of Comus* by John Milton. Adapted for Theatrical Representation .... with the Life of the Author by Dr. Johnson and a Critique by R. Cumberland. London: C. Cooke, [1817]. Pp. xlviii+37.
In *The British Drama*, Vol. II.

410 *Comus*, a Mask: Now Adapted to the Stage, as Alter'd from Milton's Mask. London, 1824.
In *The British Drama*, II, 1380–93.
Dalton's three-act version.

411 Comus. A Mask. London, 1824.
In *The London Stage*, Vol. II. Altered from the adaptations of Dalton and Colman. In verse; two acts.

412 *Comus*, a Masque, in Two Acts, by John Milton; Printed from the Acting Copy. London: J. Cumberland, [1829].
In *Cumberland's British Theatre*, XXXII, 1–22.
A Cruikshank frontispiece.

413 Comus. Philadelphia: Isaac Bird, 1833.
In *The British Drama*, Vol. II.

414 Songs, Duets, Choruses, Etc., in Milton's *Comus:* a Masque in Two Acts, with Additions, from the Author's Poem, "L'Allegro," and from Dryden's Opera of *King Arthur*. The Music Principally Selected from the Works of Handel, Purcell, and Arne, Adapted and Arranged by Mr. J. H. Tully. As Revived at the Theatre Royal, Covent Garden, on Wednesday, March 22, 1842. London, [1842].
Printed without the music.

415 *Comus:* a Masque, in Two Acts. Altered from Milton. London: Sherwood & Bowyer, 1845. Pp. 29.

416 *Comus:* a Masque, in Three Acts. By John Milton. An Adaptation. Philadelphia, 1850.
In *The British Drama*, II, 1380–93.
A reprint of the 1824 edition.

417 *Comus;* a Mask. .... Printed from the Text of .... H. J. Todd, with Selected and Original Anecdotes and Annotations. .... London, 1854.
In *The Book of Celebrated Poems*.

418 Comus. A Mask by John Milton, with Thirty Illustrations by Pickersgill, Birket Foster, Harrison Weir. London: Routledge, 1858. Pp. 91.
Text and notes.

419 Milton's *Comus*. London: Christian Knowledge Society, [1860]. Pp. 35.

Published again (1861) with introductory matter.

420 Milton's *Masque of Comus*. Theatre Royal, Drury Lane, Easter Monday, April 17, 1865. London: E. Harrison, 1865. Pp. 19.

421 Milton's *Comus*. With Notes by W. Wallace. London, 1871.

422 Comus. A Mask. London, 1872.

In *The British Drama*, Vol. III. Illustrated. Two acts. Altered from the adaptations of Dalton and Colman.

423 *Comus* . . . . with Introduction and Notes. "Collins School Classics." Glasgow: W. Collins, 1873.

424 The Mask of Comus. . . . . Edited with Copious Explanatory Notes and with Exercises in Synonyms for the Use of Classes in Reading, Analysis, and Parsing, by Homer B. Sprague. New York: Schermerhorn & Co., 1876.

In *Masterpieces in English Literature*, pp. 251–82.

425 Milton's *Comus*, Annotated with a Glossary and Notes Grammatical and Explanatory for the Use of Students, with Three Introductory Essays upon the Masque Proper and upon the Origin and History of the Poem. Edited by B. M. and F. D. Rankin. London: West, 1878. Pp. vi+76.

426 *Comus*, ... Condensed for the Use of Schools, by A. F. Westmacott. Oxford: James Russell, 1884. Pp. 23.

Slight changes. No added stage directions.

427 Milton's *Comus*, with Introduction and Notes. "Chambers Reprints of English Classics." London, 1884. Pp. 48.

428 [Music for *Comus*.]

Trinity College Library, Cambridge, has the autograph full score of Sir C. H. H. Parry's setting of Milton's "Blest Pair of Sirens." Author's note: "Finished Jan. 7, 1887."

429 Milton's *Comus*. Edited, with Introduction and Notes, by A. M. Williams. London: Longmans & Co., 1888. Pp. 91.

Review in *Athen.*, II (1888), 382.

430 Illustrations to Milton's *Comus*, by William Blake. London, 1890.

Reproductions of eight drawings.

431 Milton's *Comus*. With Introduction and Notes by W. Bell. London: Macmillan & Co., 1890. Pp. 117.

432 Milton's "Arcades" and *Comus*. With Introduction, Notes, and Indexes by A. W. Verity. "Pitt Press Series." Cambridge: Cambridge University Press, 1891. Pp. lxxvi+208.

"Arcades" was issued separately as well in 1905, 1906, and 1908.
Review in *Athen.*, April 1, 1891, p. 157.

433 Comus. Edited with Notes by Oliver Elton. "Clarendon Press Series." Oxford: Clarendon Press, 1893. Pp. 101.

434 *Comus* by John Milton. Edited with Life, Introduction, Notes Arranged and Classified, Paraphrasing . . . . by Thomas Page. London: Moffatt & Paige, 1897. Pp. 150.

Good introduction and full notes. Third edition, revised, published in 1904.

435 John Milton: *Comus* and "Lycidas." Cambridge: Cambridge University Press. 1898. Pp. lv+208.

The texts of the "Pitt Press Series," with textual variants of "Lycidas" and a glossary. Reprinted six times before 1925.

436 Milton's *Comus*. Edited by H. R. Huckin. New York: Maynard Merrill & Co., 1898. Pp. 47.

437 Milton's *Comus*. A Complete Paraphrase. By E. E. Denney and P. L. Roberts. London: Normal College Press, [1899]. Pp. 28.

438 *Comus*, a Mask. Printed under the Care of C. R. Ashbee, at the Essex House Press, with a Wood Block Frontispiece by Reginald Savage. London: E. Arnold; and New York: S. Buckley & Co., 1901.

One hundred fifty copies, on vellum.

439 *Comus*, a Maske, by John Milton. New Rochelle, New York: Elston Press, 1902. Pp. 29.

From the 1637 edition. One hundred and sixty copies printed.

440 Comus. London, 1902.

A facsimile reprint issued in supplements to the *Bibliographer*, Vol. I (1902).

441 Comus. Facsimile Edition with an Introduction by L. S. Livingston. New York: Dodd, Mead, & Co., 1903. Pp. vii+35.

442 Milton's *Comus*. Edited by G. M. Handley. London: Normal Press, [1904].

443 Milton's *Comus*. Edited by E. A. Phillips. London: Blackie & Son, 1904. Pp. xlix+68.

Review in *Athen.*, October 22, 1904, p. 549.

444 Comus. A Masque by John Milton. With Illustrations by Jessie M. King. London: Routledge & Sons, 1906. Pp. 82.

445 A Maske [*Comus*] Presented at Ludlow Castle, 1634. Cambridge: Cambridge University Press, 1906.

A type reproduction of the first edition.

446 Sir Frederick Bridge. The *Masque of Comus*—the Original Music by Henry Lawes and Other Contemporary Composers. London: Novello, 1908.

447 A Maske [*Comus*]. Edited by A. W. Verity. Cambridge: Cambridge University Press, 1909. Pp. xlvi+143.

Biographical introduction, notes, glossary, and a comment on the English masque.

448 Milton's *Comus*, being the Bridgewater Manuscript, with Notes and a Short Family Memoir, by the Lady Alix Egerton. London: Dent, 1910. Pp. viii+99.

Unusual material from the family papers and contemporary portraits; notes; some facts regarding variants.

Review in *Athen.*, July 2, 1910, p. 12.

449 Comus . . . . Abridged and Arranged for School Performance by Lucy Chater. London: Allen & Co., 1911. Pp. 32.

Illustrations for costuming; music.

450 Comus. . . . . Edited by S. E. Goggin and A. F. Watt. London: University Tutorial Press, 1912. Pp. 86.

451 Comus. . . . . Abridged and Arranged for School Performance, by Lucy Chater. Boston: Baker, [1913]. Pp. 32.

Copyrighted 1889. Music given.

452 *Comus*, by John Milton. Illustrated by Arthur Rackham. London: W. Heineman; New York: Doubleday, Page & Co., [1921]. Pp. xviii+76.

Review in *SR*, CXXXII, 718.

453 Comus. Edited by A. W. Verity. Cambridge: Cambridge University Press, 1921. Pp. xlvi+143.

"Partly a recast of the earlier editions of this poem in the Pitt Press Series." First ed., 1909; reprinted, 1921.

454 Comus, a Mask. . . . . With Eight Illustrations by William Blake. Edited from the Edition of 1645 and the Autograph Manuscript, with a Preface . . . . by D. Figgis. London: Benn, 1926. Pp. xxiv+35.

Uncritical text.

Review in *TLS*, April 1, 1926.

CRITICISM

455 The Gentleman's Magazine, LXXXV (May, 1815), 405.

Reprint of a notice from the *Times* referring to stage revivals of *Comus* at Covent Garden.

456 William Hazlitt. [Criticism of *Comus* as acted at Covent Garden Theatre.] *Examiner*, June, 1815.

Quoted in *Christ's College Magazine*, XXIII, 63.
Hazlitt saw the distorted 1738 version and was affected unfavorably.

457 "Milton's *Comus*." *Colburn's New Monthly Magazine*, VII (1823), 222–29.

The masque is treated as "a specimen of our best poetry" that is out of favor because we love not pure "moral virtue."

458 [*Comus*, l. 45.] *Edinburgh Review*, L (January, 1830), 372–96.

In a review of F. Inghirami's *Monumenti Etruschi* the critic indicates Milton's error in giving an Italian locality for the scene of the abduction of Bacchus.

459 J. P. "Milton's *Comus*." *GM*, C (December, 1830), 505–7.

Suggests that Milton took the part of Comus at the first performance. No evidence.

460 "A Visit to the Scene of *Comus*." *Every Saturday*, I (February 17, 1866), 188–92.

Description of Ludlow Castle and the surrounding country.

461 T. F. A. Croker. "On Milton's *Masque of Comus*." *Journal of the British Archaeological Association*, XXIV (1868), 44–51.

462 W. E. A. Axon. Milton's *Comus* and Fletcher's *Faithful Shepherdess* Compared. Manchester, 1882.

A reprint from the *Manchester Quarterly* for July, 1882. It is noted that the first performance of Fletcher's work was a failure, but that the title-page of the third edition reported it as acted "divers times with great applause at the private house in Black Friars." Poor as pastoral and marred by the characterization of Cloe. Milton considered superior to Fletcher in style and in reasoning. Only the Attendant Spirit clearly drawn from material in the earlier work.

463 John W. Hales. "An Unexplained Passage in *Comus*." *Athen.*, April 20, 1889, pp. 507–8.

Comment on lines 230–35.
See *Folia literaria* (1893), pp. 231–45.

464 William Blake's Illustrations of Milton's *Comus*. Reproduced by William Griggs. London, 1890.

465 Jonathan Boucher. "Wordsworth's 'Ode on Intimations of Immortality.'" *N & Q*, Ser. VII, No. X (1890), p. 110.

Wordsworth's indebtedness to Milton's *Comus* shown.

466 Joseph Jacobs. "Childe Rowland." *Folklore*, II (1891), 182–97.

On Milton's use of that story in *Comus*.

467 F. C. B. Terry. "Milton's *Comus*." *N & Q*, Ser. VIII, No. VII, p. 354.

Refers to query in Ser. VIII, No. VI, p. 187, and points to a verbal parallel in Shakespere for line 297. Page 472 of the same volume has another trifle of the same sort.

468 P. M. Buck, Jr. "Note on Milton's *Comus*." *MLN*, XXI (1906), 17–18.

Parallel to *Comus* in Spenser's account of adventures of Amoret in palace of Busyrane, *Fairie Queene*, Book III, Cantos xi–xii.

469 Paul Shorey. "A Greek Source of Milton." *Ibid.*, p. 192.

Indicates parallels to passages of *Comus* in Porphyrio's *De Abstinentia*, I, 16–17; and in *Dio Chrysostomus*, Or. 30 (I, 340, Teubner).

470 "The Music in *Comus*." *Christ's College Magazine*, XXIII (1908), 64–80.

Lawes altered text of Milton to provide a song both at beginning and end for himself. Lawes had no music for entrance of Sabrina; no music known for various dances in *Comus*. Music given "for strings in a pianoforte score."

471 Marian Mead. "Milton's *Comus* in Western Woods." *Dial*, XLV (1908), 108.

Account of performance of *Comus* at Ravinia Park, Chicago. An excellent presentation. See another account of same performance in *University of Chicago Magazine*, I (1909), 96–97.

472 Charles Sayle. "Comus." *Christ's College Magazine*, XXIII (1908), 57–62.

On family of the Earl and incidents of first performance. Lord Brackley, then twelve, was acting rôle of Elder Brother before his father. But two older sons were already buried in St. Giles', Cripplegate.

473 Herman Spencer. "A Greek Source for *Comus*, 30." *MLN*, XXIII (1908), 30.

Suggests Aeschylus, *Supp.*, ll. 254–55.

474 Bertha Badt. "Milton's *Comus* und Peele's *Old Wives Tale*." *Archiv*, CXXIII (1909), 305–9.

Peele's work analyzed as one source of Milton's story.

475 Albert S. Cook. "Milton, *Comus*, 598." *MLN*, XXIV (1909), 55.

Source in Job 26:11.

476 Maud Elma Kingsley. "Examination Questions [on *Comus* and 'Lycidas']." *Education*, XXXIII (1912), 50–51, 113–14.

477 F. B. Snyder. "Literary Parallels." *MLN*, XXVII (1912), 63.

Between *Comus*, ll. 36 f., and *Pamela*, letter 32; Collins' "Ode to Evening" and "Lycidas."

478 J. F. Bense. "The Conduct of the Attendant Spirit in *Comus*." *ES*, XLVI (1913), 333–35.

Points out some hitherto unnoticed defects in the plot of *Comus*.

479 Edward Bensly. "*Comus* and Gray's *Elegy*." *N & Q*, Ser. XI, No. VII (1913), pp. 206, 277.

Parallel noted by P. A. McElwain between *Comus*, ll. 22–23, and *Elegy*, ll. 53–54. Other parallels noted between *Comus* and Hall's *Contemplations*, and Young's *Ocean*.

480 P. A. McElwaine. [*Comus* and Gray's *Elegy*.] *Ibid.*, p. 206.

Compares *Comus*, ll. 22–23, to *Elegy*, ll. 53–54.

481 Henry Newbolt. "John Milton." *ER*, XIV (1913), 517–34. Also in *Living Age*, CCLXXIX, 73–85.

Relation of Milton's early life to early poems; change in Milton between years of "Lycidas" and *Paradise Lost; Paradise Lost* filled with intellectual absurdities, and inferior to *Samson Agonistes*.

482 Henry Newbolt. "The Poets and Their Friends." *Ibid.*, XVII (1914), 11–29.

Urges that *Comus* should be studied for its own sake, not because of its literary relations with earlier works.

483 W. H. Vann. "A Note on *Comus*." *MLN*, XXX (1915), 198–99.

Thinks "the deep" (l. 733) refers to depths of the earth, not sea; and that "they below" (l. 734) refers to men.

484 J. F. Bense. " 'Meliboeus old' in Milton's *Comus*." *Neophilologus*, I (1916), 62–64.

Milton was referring to Spenser, not to Geoffrey of Monmouth, as Masson thought. Milton's debt to Spenser in *Comus* discussed.

485 C. B. Cooper. "*Comus* [ll. 706–55]." *MLN*, XXXII (1917), 436.

Source in Randolph's *The Muse's Looking-Glass*, II, iii.

486 John A. Himes. "Some Interpretations of Milton." *Ibid.*, XXXV (1920), 441–42.

On *Comus*, ll. 93–94.

487 Alwin Thaler. "Milton in the Theatre." *SP*, XVII (1920), 269–308.

Exhaustive record of stagings of *Comus*.

488 Oliver F. Emerson. "Milton's *Comus*, 93–94." *MLN*, XXXVII (1922), 118.

Rejects Himes's interpretation of lines, because of his taking "star" to mean "constellation."

489 Frederick Houk Law. "The Volstead Act and Milton's *Comus*." *Independent*, CVIII (1922), 291–93.

Milton did not sympathize with stern puritan laws of prohibition. We, like him, should look more to education, less to law.

490 E. A. Hall. *Comus*, *Old Wives Tale*, and Drury's *Alvredus*.

In *Manly Anniversary Studies in Language and Literature* (Chicago: University of Chicago Press, 1923), pp. 140–44.

A general account of recognized source values, with new conclusions.

491 Johnson's Prologue to *Comus*, 1750. Reproduced in Type-facsimile. Oxford University Press, 1925. Pp. 16.

Noted in *TLS*, August 6, 1925; *N & Q*, CXLIX, 306.

492 F. Brie. "Das Märchen von Childe Rowland und sein Nachleben." *Palaestra*, CXLVIII (1925), 118–43.

On use in *Comus* and in two analogues.

493 H. J. Ayliffe. "Milton's Grammar in *Comus*, 238–39." *N & Q*, October 9, 1926.

See also issue of October 23, 1926.

494 R. W. Chapman. "Misprints in *Comus*." *TLS*, April 8, 1926. Pp. 264.

3. "L'ALLEGRO" AND "IL PENSEROSO"

495 G. F. Handel. *The Requiem*, or *Grand Funeral Anthem*, Composed by W. A. Mozart . . . . and "L'Allegro," "Il Pensieroso" Written by Milton, and Composed by G. F. Handel. As Performed under the Direction of Mr. Ashley at the Theatre Royal, Covent Garden, during Lent, 1801. London, [1801].

Names of performers and singers are given.

Parts II and III are arranged as dialogue in recitative with a chorus.

496 "L'Allegro" and "Il Penseroso." London, 1838.

Thirty woodcuts, done for the Art Union of London.

497 "Haste Thee, Nymph," Air and Chorus, from the Cantata of "L'Allegro." The Poetry by Milton. Composed by Handel, 1740. Arranged

from the Original Score by Henry R. Bishop, D. Almaine, 1839. Folio, music, and words.

498 Il Penseroso. With Designs by J. E. G.; Etched by J. E. G. and H. P. G. on India paper. London, 1844. Folio.

499 "L'Allegro" and "Il Penseroso" by John Milton. With Thirty Illustrations Designed Expressly for the Art-Union of London [by G. Scharf, H. O'Neil, and Others]. London, [1848]. Pp. 30.

500 L'Allegro. By John Milton. Illustrated by the Etching Club. London: J. Cundall [for the Etching Club], 1849. Pp. 20.

Plates destroyed after 300 imprints. Announces "Il Penseroso" for the year 1850.

501 Milton's "L'Allegro" and "Il Penseroso." Illustrated with Etchings on Steel by Birket Foster. London: David Bogue, 1855.

Autographs and photographs of George Cruikshank in British Museum copy.

502 "L'Allegro" and "Il Penseroso." Illustrated with Etchings on Steel, by Birket Foster. London: W. Kent & Co., 1858.

Leaves printed on one side only.

503 "L'Allegro" by John Milton. With Illustrations Engraved on Wood by W. J. Linton. London: Sampson Low, Son & Co., 1859.

Same woodcuts as in 1849 edition. Some copies have the Foster etchings inserted.

504 "L'Allegro," "Il Pensieroso," ed "Il Moderato" (composed in the year 1740), Including the Additional Songs Composed in the Year 1741; with an Accompaniment for the Organ or Pianoforte by W. H. Monk. [London], 1860.

505 "L'Allegro" and "Il Penseroso." Illustrated with Etchings on Steel, after Designs by Birket Foster. London, 1860.

506 Milton. Il Penseroso. Oxford: Clarendon Press, 1874.

507 Milton's "Il Penseroso," and Gray's "The Progress of Poesy," and "The Bard"; with Notes . . . . for the Use of Students, by William Powning, B.A. Melbourne: S. Mullen, 1874.

508 L'Allegro. "The Choice Series." London: Sampson Low & Co., [1875].

509 Milton: "Il Penseroso." With Notes. "Allman's English Classics." London, [1875].

510 Milton. Il Penseroso. Oxford: Clarendon Press, [1875]. Pp. 16.

Notes from Browne's edition.

511 *L'Allegro* by John Milton. London, 1876. Pp. 28.

511a *Il Penseroso* by John Milton. London, 1876. Pp. 28.

In "Annotated Poems of English Authors" by E. T. Stevens and D. Morris.

512 Milton's "L'Allegro" and "Il Penseroso." With . . . . Notes. "Laurie's Class-Books of Literature." London, [1877]. Pp. 44.

513 Milton's "L'Allegro." Edited, with Interpretation, Notes, and Derivations . . . . by F. Main. 2d ed. London: Stanford, 1877. Pp. 37.

514 Oxford Local Examination, 1878. Milton's "L'Allegro." With Notes. . . . . Edited by L. Evans. "Gill's School Series." London, 1878.

515 "L'Allegro" and "Il Penseroso" by John Milton, with Prefatory and Explanatory Notes. "Blackie's School Classics." London, 1879. Pp. 31.

516 Milton's "L'Allegro" and "Il Penseroso." With a Life of the Poet, Notes Grammatical, Explanatory, and Critical . . . . by J. Aikin. Poona: Orphanage Press, [1881]. Pp. 31.

517 "L'Allegro" and "Il Penseroso." With Prefatory and Explanatory Notes. New York: Clark & Maynard, 1888. Pp. 31.

518 Milton. Il Penseroso. Edited, with Notes, by Oliver Elton. Oxford: Clarendon Press, 1890. Pp. 16.

519 Milton's "L'Allegro" and "Il Penseroso." With Introduction, Notes, and Appendices. By J. H. Boardman. London: Normal Press, [1892]. Pp. 68.

520 L'Allegro. Edited with Notes by Oliver Elton. Oxford: Clarendon Press, 1893. Pp. 16.

521 "L'Allegro" and "Il Penseroso" of John Milton. With Drawings by William Hyde. [Edited by T. G. Foster.] London: Dent & Co., [1895]. Pp. 53.

Excellent illustrations; introduction.

522 "L'Allegro" and "Il Penseroso." The Junior School Milton. Edited by C. E. Brownrigg. "Blackie's English Classics." London, [1896]. Pp. 32.

523 "L'Allegro" and "Il Penseroso." . . . . With Notes . . . . by the Rev. H. Evans. London, 1896. Pp. 48.

524 L'Allegro. With Pictures by Maxfield Parrish. *Century*, LXIII (December, 1901), 163–69.

525 The "L'Allegro" and "Il Penseroso" of John Milton. Edited with Notes and Other Matter by A. J. Grieve. Madras, 1902. Pp. iv+64.

Reproduces spelling and capitalization of the 1645 edition.

526 "L'Allegro" and "Il Penseroso." John Milton. Chicago: The Blue Sky Press, [1902].

527 "L'Allegro" and "Il Penseroso." New Rochelle, New York: Elston Press, 1903. Pp. 28.

One hundred sixty copies printed.

528 "L'Allegro" and "Il Penseroso" by John Milton. London: Routledge, 1906. Pp. 42.

Illustrated.

529 Milton's "L'Allegro" and "Il Penseroso." Edited by R. P. Cowl. London: Dent & Co., [1903].

530 Milton's "L'Allegro" and "Il Penseroso." Parsed and Analysed, by E. E. Denney and P. Lyddon-Roberts. London: Normal Press, [1905]. Pp. 54.

Text not given; every word parsed.

531 Milton's "L'Allegro" and "Il Penseroso." A Complete Paraphrase. By N. Stockwell. London: Normal Press, [1905]. Pp. 9.

Trivial; for review purposes.

532 Milton's "L'Allegro" and "Il Penseroso." Edited by H. M. Percival. Oxford: Clarendon Press, 1912. Pp. 48.

533 Milton's "L'Allegro" and "Il Penseroso." Edited by J. C. Banerjea with Introduction and Notes. Calcutta, [1917]. Pp. xi+96.

534 J. Milton. "L'Allegro" and "Il Penseroso." Illustrated by Peggy Norgate. London: John Lane, 1927. Pp. 55.

CRITICISM

535 Edward Coplestone. "Advice to a Young Reviewer; with a Specimen of the Art." [1807.] *An English Garner: Critical Essays* (Westminster, 1903), VIII, 159–66.

A clever satire on supercilious journalists that evidently gained much from a high contemporary regard for Milton.

536 [Review of W. C. Harvey's *Poems, etc.*] *GM*, LXXXIX (1819), 236.

Shows that Harvey imitated "L'Allegro" and "Il Penseroso." Comment on subject matter of Milton's poems.

537 T. I. Bennett and Others. ["L'Allegro," l. 67.] *N & Q*, Ser. V, No. XI (1874), pp. 94, 153, 378.

Comments on "tells his tale."

538 E. Koelbing. "L'Allegro." *ES*, V (1881), 153–56.

39 W. H. David. "Penseroso." *N & Q*, Ser. VII, No. VIII (1889), p. 326.

Justifies Milton's spelling by referring to French-Italian dictionary, published by Chouet at Geneva, 1644.

40 J. Schipper. "English Metres." *MLN*, VI (1891), 121–23.

Comment on the meter of "L'Allegro" and "Il Penseroso."

41 "Who Is Prince Memnon's Sister?" *N & Q*, Ser. VIII, No. I (1892), pp. 87–88, 149–50.

Notes on meaning of "Il Penseroso," l. 18, by J. Bouchier, E. Marshall, and E. Venables.

42 J. D. C., F. C. Birbeck Terry, and Others. "Milton and Randolph." *Athen.*, II, (1894), 194, 225, 254, 289.

Suggestions as to source of "L'Allegro," ll. 23–24.

43 Albert S. Cook. "'L'Allegro,' 25." *MLN*, XV (1900), 160.

Suggests Horace *Odes* i. 30, ll. 5–8, as source.

44 George L. Kittredge. "The Friar's Lantern and Friar Rush." *PMLA*, XV (1900), 415–41.

Shows that "L'Allegro," l. 104, does not refer to Friar Rush. Probable that in Milton's time the *ignis fatuus* was called "friar's lantern" and thought of as a light borne by spirit of a friar.

45 Fanny Byse. Milton on the Continent; a Key to "L'Allegro" and "Il Penseroso," with Several Illustrations, a Historical Chart, and an Original Portrait of Galileo. London: E. Stock, 1903.

Poor method: fanciful argument starting with feeling that court references in "L'Allegro" must be due to real experience.

"L'Allegro": "store of ladies" = group around Catherine de Vivonne.

"Il Penseroso": girl = daughter of Galileo, who died in 1634.

Argues from descriptions in poems that they could not have been written before Italian journey.

Printed for private circulation earlier, but no copy of that issue seen.

Review in *Athen.*, October 31, 1903, pp. 575–76.

46 Frederick M. Padelford. "An Unnoted Source of 'L'Allegro.' " *MLN*, XXII (1907), 200.

Parallel to Milton's lines in *Tottel's Miscellany*.

The word "tale" (l. 67) probably means love story.

47 Harriet R. Pease. "Milton's Moods." *Journal of Education*, LXVIII (1908), 509.

Methods of presenting "L'Allegro" and "Il Penseroso" to high-school students.

548 Raymond D. Havens. "Literature of Melancholy." *MLN*, XXIV (1909), 226–27.

Literature of melancholy in the eighteenth-century owes nothing to "Il Penseroso," but belongs to the romantic and sentimental tendencies of the times. It is foreign to the mood of "Il Penseroso."

549 John Livingston Lowes. " 'L'Allegro' and the *Passionate Shepherd*." *MLR*, VI (1911), 206–9.

Relation of "L'Allegro" to Nicholas Breton's *Passionate Shepherd* (1604).

550 G. Norlin. "The Conventions of Pastoral Elegy." *American Journal of Philology*, XXXII (1911), 294–312.

Influence of Sannazaro on Milton; use of classical convention of showing blessedness of the dead in terms of mixed pagan and Christian imagery.

551 J. M. Hart. "Tells His Tale." *Nation*, XCIV (1912), 32, 158–59.

Believes *The Oxford English Dictionary* wrong in explaining phrase as meaning "tells his story." Refutes Kenyon's statements on subject.

552 John S. Kenyon. "Tells His Tale." *Ibid.*, pp. 83–84.

Disagrees with Hart, Item 551.

553 J. W. Rankin. "Tells His Tale." *MLN*, XXVII (1912), 230.

Upholds interpretation by *The Oxford English Dictionary* of "tale" as "story." Cites parallel in "Ode on the Morning of Christ's Nativity."

554 J. M. Hart. "Milton's 'Nativity.' " *Ibid.*, XXVIII (1913), 159–60.

Rejects Rankin's argument that "tale" ("L'Allegro," l. 67) means story. Shows that the parallel from "Ode on the Morning of Christ's Nativity" is wrongly drawn.

555 Alden Hewitt. " 'L'Allegro' and 'Il Penseroso'; the Study of Two Moods." *Journal of Education*, LXXX (1914), 667.

Exercises in study of the poems for young students.

556 F. M. Darnall. "Milton's 'L'Allegro' and 'Il Penseroso.' " *MLN*, XXXI (1916), 56–58.

Suggests that Diodati was the character suggested in "L'Allegro," and Milton in "Il Penseroso."

557 Alwin Thaler. "Milton's 'L'Allegro' and 'Il Penseroso.' " *Ibid.*, pp. 437–38.

Rejects Darnall's suggestion of Diodati as model for "L'Allegro," and shows others equally available to Milton.

558 F. M. Darnall. "Milton and Diodati." *Ibid.*, XXXII (1917), 377–79.

Replies to Thaler's objections to suggestion that Diodati was model for "L'Allegro." Not convincing.

;59 Mabel Day. "Milton's 'Il Penseroso,' ll. 17, 18." *MLR*, XII (1917), 496–97.

Possible source of the idea of Hemera, Memnon's sister.

;60 Edward Chauncey Baldwin. "Note on 'Il Penseroso.'" *MLN*, XXXIII (1918), 184–85.

Lines 85–90 contain reference to Plato and to Hermetic philosophy; a mixture of Neo-Platonism and oriental mysticism.

;61 Normalcy. "'L'Allegro' and 'Il Penseroso.'" *Independent*, CVIII (1922), 357–58.

Milton's poems an antidote for modern pleasure-seeking.

;62 S. B. Hustvedt. "'L'Allegro,' 45–48." *MLN*, XXXVIII (1923), 87.

Note that the one who comes to the window and bids good morrow is Dawn. Compare the opinions of Masson, Verity, Moody, and others.

;63 Heinrich Mutschmann. "Milton's Selbstdarstellung in 'L'Allegro' und 'Il Penseroso.'" *Beiblatt*, XXXIV (1923), 338–42.

;64 D. V. Smith. "Lesson on Milton's 'L'Allegro.'" *EJ*, XIV (1925), 36–46.

Teaching of Milton in secondary schools surveyed.

;65 J. Le Gay Brereton. "'*L'Allegro*,' 45–48." *MLN*, XLI (1926), 533.

Attempts to correct standard interpretation of lines.

;66 S. F. Damon. "Milton and Marston." *PMLA*, XLII (1927), 873–75.

Suggests opening lines of Marston's *Scourge of Villanie* as source for opening lines of "L'Allegro."

4. "LYCIDAS"

;67 Justa Edowardo King, naufrago, ab amicis moerentibus, amoris et μνεία σχάριν. . . . . Cantabrigiae, apud T. Buck, et R. Daniel, celeberrimae Academiae typographos, 1638. Re-impressum Dublinii, Apud R. Graisberry, Academiae typographum, 1835. Pp. xv+140.

;68 "Lycidas" by John Milton. Reprinted from the First Edition of 1638 and Collated with the Autograph Copy in the Library of Trinity College, Cambridge, with a Version in Latin Hexameters by F. A. Paley. London: Bell & Sons, 1874. Pp. vi+23.

Gives the manuscript variants. Discusses Milton's spelling and the corrections in autograph in the Cambridge proof sheet and copy of text. Refers to Calverley's translation of "Lycidas" in his *Verses and Translations* (1862) and to Todd's errors in discussing the poem.

569 Milton's "Lycidas." With Notes. . . . . "Allman's English Classics." London, [1876]. Pp. 32.

570 Milton's "Lycidas." With Introduction and Notes . . . . by T. D. Hall. Manchester: J. Galt & Co., [1876].

571 "Lycidas": with . . . . Notes . . . . and . . . . Analysis of the Text, together with a . . . . Course of Examination Exercises. Prepared . . . . by J. S. Laurie. [In] Laurie's "Specimens of English Literature." London, 1876. Pp. 44.

572 Milton's "Lycidas." Edited by Francis Main. London: Stanford, 1876. Pp. 25.

Second edition, 1876.

573 Lycidas. Edited by E. T. Stevens and B. A. Morris. "Annotated Poems of English Authors." London, 1877.

574 Milton's "Lycidas." Edited with Notes, by Homer B. Sprague. Boston: Ginn & Heath, 1878. Pp. xiii+38.

Issued with his edition of *Paradise Lost*, Books I and II, 1879; separately in later issues.

575 "Lycidas"; with Introduction and Notes . . . . by T. D. Hall. 2d ed. Manchester: J. Galt & Co., [1880].

576 Lycidas. Edited with Notes by Oliver Elton. Cambridge: Clarendon Press, 1893. Pp. 24.

577 Lycidas. . . . . With Notes by the Rev. H. Evans. London, 1896. Pp. 36.

578 "Lycidas" by John Milton. Edited by John Phelps Truit. Boston: Ginn, 1897. Pp. xvi+29.

579 Milton's "Lycidas." A Complete Paraphrase by E. E. Denney and P. Lyddon-Roberts. London: Normal College Press, [1899].

580 Milton's "Lycidas," edited by H. B. Cotterill. London: Blackie & Son, 1902. Pp. 112.

581 "Lycidas" by John Milton. Illustrations by Gertrude Brodie. London: Lane, 1903. Pp. 41.

582 Helps to the Study of Milton's *Paradise Lost*, Book VI, and Milton's "Lycidas." By A. L. Cann. London: Holland & Co., 1904.

Interleaved. Full notes, index to notes, specimen examinations. Published also separately.

583 "Lycidas" and the Sonnets. Edited by N. L. Frazer.

Noted in *TLS*, May 10, 1905, p. 155.

584 Lycidas. Edited with Notes, by Oliver Elton. Oxford: Clarendon Press, 1910. Pp. 24.

585 Milton: "Lycidas." Edited by S. E. Goggin. London: University Tutorial Press, [1910]. Pp. 40.

86 Lycidas. A Monograph by W. Tuckwell. London: Murray, 1911. Pp. 65.

An attempt to reproduce the Trinity text by typography. Analysis and commentary.

Review in *Athen.*, November 25, 1911, 659.

CRITICISM

87 William Hazlitt. On Milton's "Lycidas."

In *The Round Table.* London, 1817.

88 N. Ogle. "On the Origin of Milton's 'Lycidas.'" *Classical Journal*, XXIX (1824), 356–61.

89 A. C. Brackett. "Notes on Milton's 'Lycidas.'" *Journal of Speculative Philosophy*, I (1867), 87–90.

90 [Meaning of "Muse" in "Lycidas," l. 19.] *N & Q*, Ser. V, No. XI (1874), pp. 89, 155, 316.

Milton uses word "muse" to mean poet.

91 H. Nettleship. "'Lycidas' in Latin." *Acad.*, V (April 18, 1874), 425–26.

Relation of Milton to Vergil discussed in a review of Paley's "Lycidas."

92 ["Lycidas," "Adonais," and "In Memoriam."] *QR*, CLVIII (1884), 162–83.

Comparison of subjects, treatment, and style of the three poems.

93 ["Lycidas," ll. 130–31.] *N & Q*, Ser. VI, No. XI (1885), pp. 428, 516; XII, p. 351.

Notes on meaning of "two-handed engine," by C. A. Ward, F. C. Birbeck Terry, and others.

94 John W. Hales. "Milton's 'Lycidas.'" *Athen.*, August 1, 1891, pp. 159–60.

Points out use of name "Lycidas" by Theocritus, Sannazaro, and Giovanni Baptista Amaltei. Milton may have derived name from these writers as well as from Vergil.

Also in *Folia literaria*, 1893, pp. 231–45.

95 C. Alphonso Smith. "A Note on the Punctuation of 'Lycidas.'" *MLN*, XI (1896), 28.

Proposes a change in punctuation of lines 57–58.

596 Albert S. Cook. " 'Lycidas,' 40 ff." *Ibid.*, XV (1900), 255.

Suggests Vergil's *Eclogues* as source.

597 H. L. "The Two-handed Engine in 'Lycidas.' " *Athen.*, June 30, 1900, p. 815.

Calls attention to mention of such a sword in Sylvester's *Du Bartas* (1621), p. 18.

598 Albert S. Cook. " 'Lycidas,' 113 ff." *MLN*, XVI (1901), 92.

Parallel in Bale's characterization of John Capgrave (*Script. Illus.*, p. 582).

599 "That Two-handed Engine at the Door."

The critics offer their views through the columns of the *Athenaeum:* W. H. Ward, April 14, 1906, pp. 451–52, refers the idea to a source in Ezek. 9:1–2; M. D, April 28, p. 515, proposes "engine" = scythe; G. H. Powell, May 5, p. 547, makes the word = axe.

600 Albert S. Cook. "Two Notes on Milton." *MLR*, II (1907), 121–28.

"Namancos" ("Lycidas," l. 162) = Nemancos; parallel passages from "The Ode on the Nativity" and Mantuan.

601 Thomas K. Sidey. "The *Uncouth Swain* in Milton's 'Lycidas.' " *MLN*, XXIII (1908), 92.

Probably from Vergil's *Eclogues* iii. 26.

602 [Milton and Petronius.] S. Gaselee. "The bibliography of Petronius." *Transactions of the Bibliographical Society*, X (1909), 157.

Mere reference to the Petronius line on the title-page of the *Justa*.

603 H. F. Hamilton. "The Sources of Milton's 'Lycidas.' " *Sewanee Review*, XVII (1909), 235–40.

"Lycidas" has no prototype, and is free from trammels of classical and medieval tradition. Milton blended elegiac elements with those of the ode—made a "pastoral-elegiac ode." "Lycidas" was model for Cowley's absurd Pindaric odes.

604 Charles Read Baskervill. "Two Parallels to 'Lycidas.' " *Nation*, XCI (1910), 546–47.

Similarity to "Lycidas" in "symbolism and seriousness" of Greene's *A Maiden's Dream*. Two parallel passages in Skelton's *Colin Clout*, ll. 75–81, 125–31.

605 Archibald Brown. [Rhymeless lines in "Lycidas."] *Athen.*, May 21, 1910, p. 611.

606 James Holly Hanford. "The Pastoral Elegy and Milton's 'Lycidas.' " *PMLA*, XXV (1910), 403–47.

Reviews history of pastoral poetry. Concludes that Milton found his material in all great pastorals; that he was more indebted to Vergil than to Theocritus; and that his debt to Spenser is great. A thorough study.

07 W. Tuckwell. "Lycidas"; a Monograph. London: J. Murray, 1911. Pp. 65.

On the Trinity College manuscript, with original notes on stanzas of the text.

08 Louis Sigmund Friedland. "Milton's 'Lycidas' and Spenser's 'Ruines of Time.'" *MLN*, XXVII (1912), 246–50.

Parallel passages and similarities in mood and matter noted.

09 Franklin B. Snyder. "Literary Parallels." *Ibid.*, p. 63.

Collins' "Ode to Evening" and "Lycidas" related.

10 W. H. Pinchbeck. "Milton's 'Lycidas.'" *N & Q*, Ser. XI, No. VII (1913), p. 17.

See also *N & Q*, Ser. XI, No. VI (1912), pp. 328, 395, 476.
Compares nuptial song in Revelation with passage in "Lycidas."

11 Sir John Erwin Sandys. The Literary Sources of Milton's "Lycidas." London, [1914]. Pp. 32.

A chronological record of sources, with minute study of classical allusions. Reprinted from the *Transactions of the Royal Society of Literature*, Vol. XXXII.

12 Edward Chauncey Baldwin. "Milton and Ezekiel." *MLN*, XXXIII (1918), 211–15.

Parallel between "Lycidas," ll. 113–31, and Ezekiel, 34:2–10.

13 Albert S. Cook. "Lycidas." *Ibid.*, p. 379.

Shows that his note on "Lycidas," l. 162, antedates Georgiana Goddard King's note in *MLN*, XXXIII, 310–11.

14 Albert S. Cook. "Four Notes." *SP*, XVI (1919), 177–86.

Note III (pp. 184–85), on source of "Lycidas," l. 86.

15 John A. Himes. "Some Interpretations of Milton." *MLN*, XXXV (1920), 441–42.

Notes on "Lycidas," ll. 17, 30, 31, 110.

16 Robert F. Arnold. "Milton's 'Lycidas' deutsch." *Z. f. franz. u. engl. Unterricht*, XXI (1922), 241–53.

Comments on German translations of "Lycidas." New translation given.

17 L. Wann. "Milton's 'Lycidas' and the Play of Barnavelt." *MLN*, XXXVII (1922), 470–73.

Milton apparently borrowed from the play of Massinger and Fletcher.

18 Samuel C. Chew. "'Lycidas' and the Play of Barnavelt." *Ibid.*, XXXVIII (1923), 122.

Discredits Wann, XXXVII, 470, showing likelihood that "Lycidas," l. 71, crept into Bullen's edition of the play through a marginal note on a proof sheet.

619 R. S. Crane. "Gray's 'Elegy' and 'Lycidas.'" *Ibid.*, p. 183.

Gives quotation from John Hill's essay on Gray's Elegy, published in *London Daily Advertiser*, March, 1751, furnishing documentary evidence for suggestion offered by R. D. Havens in *The Influence of Milton on English Poetry* (1922), that there is a close affinity between the new lyricism of 1740–50 and the *Minor Poems* of Milton.

620 E. M. W. Tillyard. "Paragraphing in 'Lycidas,' Lines 23–24." *TLS*, November 13, 1924, p. 731.

621 Charles G. Osgood. "'Lycidas,' ll. 130–131." *RES*, I (1925), 339–40.

Suggests that "two-handed engine" is the iron flail of Talus, mentioned in *Faerie Queene*, Book V, Canto i, l. 12.

622 G. M. Harper. "Milton's 'Two-handed Engine.'" *TLS*, June 16, 1927, p. 424.

Proposes Spain and France as the "double threat" of Catholicism against England.

623 N. W. Hill. "Milton's 'Two-handed Engine.'" *Ibid.*, July 28, 1927, p. 520.

Discredits idea of French-Spanish alliance against England to restore Catholicism. Proposes the doors of Janus, "handed" as more poetical than "headed" being used.

624 K. N. Colvile. "That Two-handed Engine at the Door." *Ibid.*, November 22, 1928. Pp. 909–10.

To make the line of "Lycidas" a further item in the list of evils under prelacy, not a sign of punishment to the wrongdoers, the author must make the "but" adversative only to the negative in the latter part of the preceding line (i.e., "and nothing said"). Thus he puts forward the ecclesiastical and temporal powers of the Court of High Commission as "two-handed." Not a credible analysis of the crux.

625 Nowell Smith. "That Two-handed Engine at the Door." *Ibid.*, December 6, 1928, p. 965.

Disposes pretty effectually of idea that Milton aimed at Calderwood's *duplici gladio* of the Court of High Commission (*TLS*, November 22, 1928); then strays after the fancy that "the homely slighted Shepherd's trade" (l. 65) refers to King's purpose to become a college don, not to the verse-making practice of pastoralism.

5. SONNETS

626 The Sonnets of Shakespeare and Milton. London: E. Moxon, 1830. Pp. iv+186.

Review in *Athen.*, November 20, 1830, p. 727.

627 Milton's "Arcades" and Sonnets, Adapted for Use in Training Colleges and Schools. Edited by John Hunter. London: Longmans, Green & Co., 1880. Pp. xi+48.

English sonnets only.

628 The Sonnets of John Milton. Edited by Mark Pattison. "The Parchment Library." London: Kegan Paul, Trench, & Co., 1883. Pp. 227.

Issued in a fine paper edition as well. Attempts a chronological arrangement. Analysis of the form and translations of Langhorne and Cowper included. Published in New York by D. Appleton & Co.

Reviews in *Athen.*, September 1, pp. 263–65; *Acad.*, July 28, pp. 57–58; *SR*, August 25, pp. 252–53; *Spectator*, August 18, pp. 1062–63; *Nation*, November 20, p. 515.

629 Milton's Sonnets. Edited by Alden Sampson. New York: De Vinne, 1886. Pp. 72.

630 Milton's Sonnets, with Introduction, Notes, Glossary and Indexes, by A. W. Verity. "Pitt Press Series." Cambridge: Cambridge University Press, 1895. Pp. xxxii+78.

Four printings to 1908.
Reviews in *Athen.*, December 28, 1885, p. 899; *RC*, XL (1895), 231–32.

631 Milton's Sonnets. Parsed and Analysed by E. E. Denney and Lytton Roberts. "Normal Tutorial Series." London, [1905].

632 Milton's Sonnets. Edited with Notes by Walter Worrall. Oxford: Clarendon Press, 1910.

Only the English sonnets.

633 Milton's Sonnets and Coleridge's *Rime of the Ancient Mariner*. . . . . Introduction and Notes by Egerton Smith. "Longman's English Classics for India." London, 1914.

634 The Sonnets of Milton, with Introduction and Notes by John S. Smart. Glasgow: Maclehose, Jackson & Co., 1921. Pp. x+195.

Among the most valuable of recent works on Milton. Significant for its introductory study of the sonnet forms affecting Milton and for new biographical data that illuminate obscure points in the texts.

Reviews in *Edinburgh Review*, CCXLII, 165–78; *MLN*, XXXIX (1924), 45; *MLR*, XVII, 205; *Beiblatt*, XXXIV (1923), 84–86; *ES*, LVII (1924), 432–34; *MP*, XX (1922–23), 219–20.

635 Milton. The Sonnets. Edited by A. R. Weekes. London: University Tutorial Press, [1922]. Pp. 42.

Third edition. No notice of the new evidence in Smart's edition.

636 J. Milton. The English Sonnets of John Milton. Wood Engravings by Rachel Russell. Limited edition. Chelsea: Swan Press, 1927.

CRITICISM

637 "On the Sonnets of Milton, with a Translation of One of His Italian Sonnets." *Censura literaria*, VI (1908), 414–17.

Appreciative. Translation of the 4th sonnet, "Diodati, io te'l diro. . . . ."

638 St. Ives. [*History of the Ancient Family of Lawrence.*] *GM*, LXXXV (July, 1815), 12–16.

Concerned with the son of Lord Lawrence to whom Milton addressed his sonnet.

639 William Hazlitt. "On Milton's Sonnets." *Table Talk.* London, 1821.

640 [Review of Leigh Hunt's *The Book of the Sonnet.*] *Nation*, IV (1867), 26–27.

Comment on Leigh Hunt's criticism of Milton's sonnets.

641 [Milton's Sonnets.] *Ibid.*, XXXII (April 14, 1881), 262–63.

Milton compared with Shakespeare and Wordsworth as a writer of sonnets, in a review of books on the sonnet by Main and Waddington.

642 K. A. Leutzner. Über das Sonett und seine Gestaltung in der englischen Dichtung bis Milton. Halle: Niemeyer, 1886. Pp. iv+81.

Good study, but has no new theories, and accepts dogmatic ideas of peculiarities of form.

643 William Davies. "Milton's Sonnets." *Athen.*, September 29, 1888, pp. 418–19.

Points out similarities in thought and expression between Milton's sonnets and Italian work. "Rime di M. Domenico Mantova, Gentil'Huomo Bresciano," published as an appendix to *Rime di Diversi Eccellenti Autori Bresciani, Nuovamente Raccolte et Mandate in Luce da Girolamo Ruscelli* (Venice, 1654).

644 W. T. Lendrum and R. Y. Tyrrell. "Milton and Pindar." *Classical Review*, IX (1895), 10–12.

645 G. Serrell. "Milton as Seen in His Sonnets." *Temple Bar*, CXXI (1900), 27–42.

646 T. S. Bateman. Milton's Sonnets: a Complete Paraphrase. London, [1904]. Pp. 10.

647 J. Willcock. "Milton and Fairfax." *N & Q*, Ser. XI, No. IX (1914), p. 147.

Line 2 of sonnet "On the Late Massacre" taken from Fairfax's *Tasso*.

648 W. F. Smith. "Milton's Sonnet on Tetrachordon." *Ibid.*, Ser. XII, No. II (1916), p. 7.

Note on the use of word "like" (l. 10).

649 David H. Stevens. "The Order of Milton's Sonnets." *MP*, XVII (1919), 25–33.

Masson's order questioned; internal evidence examined, as well as Milton's directions in the Trinity College manuscript concerning arrangement of certain poems.

650 James Holly Hanford. "The Arrangement and Order of Milton's Sonnets." *Ibid.*, XVIII (1921), 475–83.

Adds new evidence to that adduced by Stevens. Considers the problem of the arrangement in 1673 edition.

651 The Sonnets of Milton. With Introduction and Notes, by John S. Smart. Glasgow: Maclehose, Jackson & Co., 1921. Pp. x+195.

Throughout are the most valuable comments thus far made on particular points in the sonnets, and the study of Milton's origins is from an entirely original point of attack.

652 Walter Thomas. "Les sonnets de Milton et sa vie intime." *RELV*, XLI (1924), 252–58, 289–96.

Relates composition of sonnets to periods in Milton's life. Translates the most widely known sonnets.

653 H. J. C. Grierson. "The Text of Milton." *TLS*, January 15, 1925, p. 40.

Suggests an emendation in line of sonnet "On the Religious Memory of Mrs. Catherine Thomason."

VI. *PARADISE LOST*

654 Milton's *Paradise Lost*, Illustrated by Gustave Doré; Edited by Henry C. Walsh. Philadelphia, [18—]. Pp. 319.

655 Milton's *Paradise Lost*, with Explanatory Notes by Rev. J. R. Boyd. School and Academic Edition. New York, [*ca.* 1800]. Pp. 548.

656 *Paradise Lost* . . . . with a Biographical and Critical Account of the Author and His Writings. Washington and Philadelphia: M. Carey, 1801. Pp. xvi+289.

Fenton's life.

657 Milton's *Paradise Lost*. A New Edition. Adorned with Plates Engraved Chiefly by F. Bartolozzi from Designs by W. Hamilton and H. Fuseli. London: Du Roveray, 1802. 2 vols.

There were two forms issued, one on large paper. The frontispiece portrait of Milton is not from an authenticated original.

658 Milton's *Paradise Lost* with the Life of the Author [Fenton's] to Which Is Prefixed the Celebrated Critique by S. Johnson. A New Edition. London: J. Johnson, 1802. Pp. xliii+420.

Illustrated.

659 Paradise Lost. A Poem in Twelve Books, the Author John Milton. With His Life, and Historical, Philosophical, and Explanatory Notes. Translated from the French of the Learned Raymond de St. Maur, and Various Critical Remarks from Mr. Addison, Dr. Warburton, Dr. Newton, Dr. Pearce, Dr. Bentley, Mr. Richardson, and Mr. Hume. A New Edition, Adorned with Three Elegant Frontispieces. Vienna: printed for R. Sammer, 1803. 3 vols.

660 *Paradise Lost*, a Poem in Twelve Books. A New Edition. London: H. Richardson, 1803. Pp. 294.

Fenton's life.

661 Milton's *Paradise Lost*, Illustrated with Texts of Scripture, by J. Gillies. Third Edition, with Additions. London: J. Johnson, 1804. Pp. xxxi+378.

Fenton's life. Index.

662 Paradise Lost. London, 1804. 2 vols.

With part of Newton's notes and a life by John Evans. In two forms, 12mo and 8vo. Plates.

Reprinted in 1808, 8vo.

663 Paradise Lost. . . . . Printed from the Text of Tonson's Correct Edition of 1711. London: J. Johnson, 1804. Pp. xxxv+345.

Unauthenticated portrait "from an impression of a seal of T. Simon, in the possession of the late Mr. Yeo."

664 *Paradise Lost*. . . . . With Notes Selected from Newton and Others. A New Edition, Corrected. Nottingham: C. Sutton, 1805. Pp. 336.

665 Milton's *Paradise Lost*. Edinburgh: Turnbull, 1806. Pp. xvi+288.

Fenton's life.

666 Paradise Lost. London, 1806. Pp. viii+305.

667 Paradise Lost. . . . . A New Edition, Adorned with Beautiful Plates. Edinburgh: Deas, 1807. 2 vols.

Fenton's life.

668 Paradise Lost. Philadelphia: Johnson & Warner, 1808. Pp. 318.

669 Paradise Lost. "Cabinet of Poetry." London, 1808. Vol. I.

Contains also *Comus*, "L'Allegro," "Il Penseroso," "Lycidas," and *Samson Agonistes*.

670 Paradise Lost. . . . . Printed from the Text of Tonson's Correct Edition of 1711. A New Edition, with Plates. London, 1808. Pp. xlii+372.

Fenton's life and Johnson's essay.

671 *Paradise Lost*, a Poem, with the Life of Milton. London, 1812.

Fenton's life.

672 Paradise Lost. London: W. Suttaby and B. Crosby & Co., 1812. Pp. viii+305.

A reissue of the 1806 edition by the same publishers. *See* Item 666.

673 Paradise Lost. . . . . To Which Is Prefixed the Life of the Author [by Fenton]. London: T. Tegg, 1813. Pp. vii+304.

Good illustrations.

674 Paradise Lost. . . . . A New Edition. Romsey: W. Sharp, 1816. Pp. xxxii+305.

Fenton's life and Addison's criticism.

675 *Paradise Lost* by John Milton. London: F. C. and J. Rivington, 1817. Pp. 331.

Portrait. Same publishers issued a two-volume edition of complete works in 1817. I have notes on another edition of *Paradise Lost* from the same publisher in 1817 (xlviii+384), but have not been able to verify my jottings in an English bookshop.

676 *Paradise Lost* by John Milton. Lyons, 1818. Pp. 355.

Fenton's life.

677 Paradise Lost. Baltimore: Fielding Lucas, 1818. Pp. xii+36.

678 Paradise Lost. Philadelphia: Warner, 1818. Pp. 356.

Illustrated. Reprinted, 1819; issued in 1820 with new title-page.

679 Paradise Lost . . . . To Which Is Prefixed the Life of the Author [by Fenton, and Marvell's poem]. London: Tegg, 1818. Pp. viii+304.

Fenton's life and Marvell's poem. Reissued in 1820 with a new title-page. The British Museum copy of 1820 is filled with notes.

680 Paradise Lost. Boston: T. Bedlington, 1820. Pp. viii+305.

Fenton's life. Index.

681 Paradise Lost. London: Suttaby, Evans & Fox, 1821. Pp. 305 and Index.

Illustrated. Fenton's life.

682 *Paradise Lost* by John Milton. To Which Are Prefixed, the Life of the Author by Elijah Fenton: and a Criticism of the Poem by Dr. Johnson. London: J. Bumpus. 1821. Pp. xlviii+384.

Frontispiece portrait engraved by Freeman from a portrait in the collection of the late C. Lamb, Esq., South Sea House.

683 Paradise Lost. . . . . A New Edition, with Notes Critical and Explanatory by J. B. Williams. London: G. and W. B. Whitaker, 1824. 2 vols.

Volume II has *Paradise Regained*, *Samson Agonistes* and the *Minor Poems*. The British Museum copy has autograph notes by the editor. Among others is one praising the Cleveland edition of *Paradise Lost*.

684 Paradise Lost. A Poem, in Twelve Books. By John Milton. Boston: T. Bedlington, 1825. Pp. 294.

Same in London, 1825.

685 Paradise Lost. London: Jones & Co., 1825. Pp. xii+268.

686 Paradise Lost. A Poem in Twelve Books. The Author, John Milton. London: J. Sharpe, 1825. 2 vols.

Each title-page is dated 1822. Engravings from the designs of R. Westall.

87 John Martin. [Twenty-four copper engravings representing scenes from *Paradise Lost.*] [1826.] Folio.

A separate issue of plates used in the next item.

88 *Paradise Lost,* with Illustrations Designed and Engraved by John Martin. London: S. Prowett, 1827. 2 vols. Folio.

Twenty-four plates. Issued also in 4to (1827). Other editions, 1847, 1850, 1853, 1858.

89 Paradise Lost. London: W. S. Orr & Co., [1830]. Pp. x+268.

Fenton's life. Index of names.

90 Paradise Lost. "Diamond Classic" edition. London: Pickering, 1830. 48mo.

Reprinted, 1835, 1838.

91 Paradise Lost. Edited by Forbes. New York, 1830.

92 *Paradise Lost:* a Poem in Twelve Books; with the Life of the Author. Philadelphia, 1830. Pp. 306.

93 Paradise Lost. New York: J. H. Turney, 1832. Pp. 321.

Fenton's life.
Issued also in 24mo, 283 pages, with portrait.

94 *Paradise Lost* by John Milton. With a Memoir of the Author. New Edition. London: J. G. and F. Rivington, 1833. Pp. xvi+306.

95 Paradise Lost. London, 1835.

No details of editing. Plain text.

96 Paradise Lost. Philadelphia: Kay, 1836. Pp. xii+268.

Stebbing's edition. Same published by Appleton (New York) in 1843 and 1848.

97 Paradise Lost. Philadelphia: Kay & Bros., 1839. Pp. x+312.

98 Milton's *Paradise Lost:* with Copious Notes Explanatory and Critical. Partly Selected from the Various Commentators and Partly Original: also a Memoir of His Life. By James Prendeville. London: S. Holdsworth, 1840. Pp. lxiii+452.

Good in critical comment, notes, and review of earlier criticism. Index. Review in *Blackwood's Magazine*, XLVII (1840), 691–716.

99 *Paradise Lost* and Other Poetical Works. London: Churton, 1841.

Engravings by Martin, Westall, Fuseli.
New edition, Bohn, 1848.

00 Paradise Lost. Boston: Littlefield, 1841. Pp. 294.

A new edition.

701 Paradise Lost. New York: C. Wells, 1841. Pp. 283.
Fenton's life. Index.

702 *Paradise Lost.* . . . . With Explanatory Notes by Henry Stebbing. New York: Appleton & Co., 1848. Pp. 296.

703 The *Paradise Lost* of Milton. Translated into Fifty-four Designs by J. J. Flatters. [Without letterpress], 1843. Fol.
The most elaborate illustrations of scenes in *Paradise Lost* thus far.

704 Paradise Lost. New York: E. Kearny, 1844. Pp. 283.
Fenton's life. Index.

705 Paradise Lost. . . . . A New Edition, with an Abridgment of the Copious and Learned Notes Collected by Bishop Newton, together with Additions and a Sketch of the Life and Writings of the Author. For the Use of Schools. Calcutta: Ostell & Lepage, 1844. Pp. xx+354.
Many footnotes.

706 Paradise Lost. Boston: Phillips & Sampson, 1845. Pp. 294.
Reissued in 1846.

707 *Paradise Lost*, a Poem in Twelve Bucs. By Jon Miltun. Lundun: J. Pitman. 1846. Pp. x+320.
Printed in phonetic spelling; edited by A. J. Ellis. The table of characters has twelve vowels, four diphthongs, two coalescents (*y*, *w*), one breathing, fifteen consonants, two liquids, and three nasals.

708 Paradise Lost. With Illustrations by John Martin. London: Wittingham, 1846.
Same plates used in the editions of 1849 and 1853. *See* Item 688.

709 *Paradise Lost* . . . . with "Night Thoughts" . . . . and "The Force of Religion" by Edward Young. A New Edition. Boston: Phillips & Sampson, 1847. Pp. 288.

710 *Paradise Lost* . . . . with Explanatory Notes by Henry Stebbing. New York: Appleton & Co., 1848. Pp. 296.

711 Paradise Lost. New York: Leavitt & Co., 1849. Pp. 220.

712 Paradise Lost. New York: Clarke Austin & Co., 1850. Pp. 274.
Fenton's life; index.

713 *Paradise Lost*, by John Milton. With Notes, Explanatory and Critical. Edited by Rev. James Robert Boyd. New York: Baker & Scribner, 1850.
Issued with new title-page, 1851, and reprinted in 1852. Explains need of an American edition on ground of remoteness of Milton's language. Many footnotes from earlier editors.

714 Paradise Lost. In Twelve Parts. By John Milton. Night Thoughts on Life, Death and Immortality to Which Is Added *The Force of Religion* by Edward Young, D.D. A New Edition. Boston: Phillips, Sampson & Co., 1850.

715 Paradise Lost. By John Milton. With Notes by Sir Egerton Brydges. . . . . Elegantly Illustrated with Designs by Martin. Philadelphia: G. S. Appleton; New York: D. Appleton & Co., 1851. Pp. cxiii+415.

716 Paradise Lost. A Poem in Twelve Books. By John Milton. New York: Clark, Austin & Co., 1851.

717 Milton's *Paradise Lost* with Notes . . . . by the Rev. J. R. Major. London: B. Fellowes, 1853. Pp. vii+584.

Notes chiefly from Newton. Index of references to classical authors.

718 *Paradise Lost* . . . . with a Memoir of the Author. Hartford (Connecticut): Andrus, 1853. Pp. xiv+400.

719 Milton's *Paradise Lost* and *Paradise Regained.* With Explanatory Notes . . . . by J. Edmondston. London: Nelson, 1854. Pp. 468.

Issued also with an 1855 title-page.

720 Paradise Lost. . . . . The Life of John Milton. London: Nelson & Sons, 1855. 32mo. Pp. xii+268.

Fenton's life and Marvell's poem.

721 Paradise Lost. London: W. Tegg, 1856. Pp. 223.

Illustrated by K. Meadows.

722 Milton's *Paradise Lost.* Philadelphia: Hayes & Lelly, 1857. Pp. x+311.

An electrotype of Stebbing's edition.

723 The *Paradise Lost* of Milton. With Illustrations by John Martin. London: H. Washbourne & Co., 1858. Pp. 373.

724 Paradise Lost. London, 1860.

Memoir by James Montgomery; variorum notes; woodcuts.

725 Milton's *Paradise Lost,* in Twelve Books. London: Bell & Daldy, 1861.

Volume II has *Paradise Regained* and shorter poems.

726 Paradise Lost. . . . . To Which Is Prefixed, a Life of the Author, and Dr. Channing's "Essay on the Poetical Genius of Milton." London: W. Tegg, 1862. Pp. ix+325.

727 The *Paradise Lost*, by John Milton. With Notes, Explanatory and Critical. Edited by Rev. James Boyd. "The National School Series." New York: A. S. Barnes & Burr, 1864. Pp. 552.

Original work in the notes. Another edition, 1869.

728 Milton's *Paradise Lost*. New York: Appleton & Co., 1865. Pp. 301.

Illustrated.

729 Milton's *Paradise Lost*. Illustrated by Gustave Doré. Edited, with Notes and a Life of Milton, by R. Vaughan. London: Cassell & Co., [1866]. Fol. Pp. lxii+329.

Appeared with a New York imprint in 1866 and was reprinted in 1871–72, 1882, 1888–90, 1898–99, 1904 in folio; in 1894, in octavo.

730 Paradise Lost. New York: Barnes & Co., 1867. Pp. 552.

731 *Paradise Lost*. . . . . A New Edition with Explanatory Notes. New York: Hurd & Houghton, 1869. Pp. xiv+409.

Reprinted, 1870.

732 Paradise Lost. A Poem in Twelve Books. By John Milton. Lithographed in Phonography. London: Pitman, 1871. Pp. 280.

Double columns of shorthand characters. No notes.

733 Milton's *Paradise Lost*. . . . . New Edition with Notes. New York: Hurd & Houghton, 1872. Pp. xiv+409.

Brief life, notes, and Index.

734 *Paradise Lost* in Ten Books. The Text Exactly Reproduced from the First Edition of 1667, with an Appendix Containing the Additions Made in Later Issues and a Monograph [by R. H. Shepherd] on the Original Publication of the Poem. London: Pickering (1873). Pp. 375.

No pagination. The arguments are given in the Appendix. The monograph gives data on the contract and on word variants.

735 *Paradise Lost* as Originally Published by John Milton, Being a Facsimile Reproduction of the First Edition. With an Introduction by David Masson. London: Stock, 1877.

Not so valuable as the 1873 edition of Pickering.

Reviews in *Athen.*, March 31, 1877, p. 416; *Acad.*, July 28, 1877, p. 82.

736 *Paradise Lost* by John Milton. Illustrated by Thirty-eight Designs in Outline. Thirty-four of the Plates Engraved by the Artist and Four by F. Joubert. London: Hardwicke & Bogue, 1879.

Fragments of the text. The figures are classical; the features modern, as if from life models.

737 Paradise Lost. Boston: Perkins Institution and Massachusetts School for the Blind, 1879. 2 vols.

Raised type for the blind. Second edition.

738 Paradise Lost. Boston: Nichols & Hall, [1881]. Pp. 294.

739 Milton's *Paradise Lost.* Illustrated by Gustav Doré. Edited with Notes and a Life of Milton, by R. Vaughan. London: Cassell & Co., 1882. Pp. lxii+329.

A reissue of the 1866 edition; another issue, 1888.

740 *Paradise Lost,* by John Milton. "Lovell's Library." New York: J. W. Lovell Co., [1884]. Pp. 291.

741 Paradise Lost. "The Canterbury Poets" London and New York: W. Scott, [1887]. Pp. xxviii+339.

742 Paradise Lost. "Pocket Library." London: Routledge & Sons, 1887. Pp. 381.

743 Paradise Lost. New York: Worthington Co., 1888. Pp. 366.

744 Milton's *Paradise Lost.* Illustrated by Gustave Doré. Edited, with Notes and a Life of Milton, by . . . . R. Vaughan. London: Cassell, [1888]. Pp. lxii+329.

Issued first in 1866; another issue of this form, 1898. A popular edition was out in 1894.

745 Paradise Lost. "Cassell's National Library." London: Cassell, 1889. 2 vols.

Issued with a 1904 title-page and doubtless under other dates. Introduction by Henry Morley.

746 David Masson. Paradise Lost. [In] *The Poetical Works of John Milton.* London: Macmillan and Co., 1890. 3 vols.

Distinguished by its excellent notes: Vol. III, pp. 375–558.

747 Paradise Lost. Boston: Houghton Mifflin & Co., 1894. Pp. 331.

The Salem edition.

748 Milton's *Paradise Lost.* Illustrated by Gustave Doré. Edited . . . . by R. Vaughan. . . . . Popular Edition. London: Cassell, 1894. Pp. lxviii+388.

749 Paradise Lost. . . . . Edited by W. H. D. Rouse. "Temple Classics." London, 1897. Pp. xi+372.

750 Paradise Lost. . . . . Edited by J. A. Himes. New Edition. New York, 1898.

Many original notes, some being without much authority. The work of an enthusiastic and industrious student whose knowledge was miscellaneous rather than historical.

751 *Paradise Lost*, a Poem in Twelve Books. The Author, John Milton. Hammersmith: Dove Press, 1902. Pp. 387.

A reprint of the forms of the first edition, with seven "literal faults" corrected and with the text in twelve books instead of ten. The arguments, not in the first edition, are added, and the errata as noted are observed.

752 Paradise Lost. . . . . With Twelve Photogravures after Designs by William Strang. London: Routledge & Sons, 1905. Pp. 242.

Brief footnotes. The etchings of Strang, out in 1896, were also sold separately.

753 *Paradise Lost* by John Milton. Illustrations by William Blake. Liverpool: Lyceum Press, 1906. Pp. ix+397.

Masson's text. Preface by Sydney Hyle.

754 Paradise Lost. London: Harrap & Co., [1909]. Pp. 323.

No notes. Text edited by F. E. Bumby. Pp. 323.

755 Milton: *Paradise Lost*. . . . . Edited by A. W. Verity. Cambridge: Cambridge University Press, 1910. Pp. lxxii+750.

Masson's "Globe" text with simplified punctuation. Notes, pp. 365–658. Appendix, Glossary, Index. The most complete and valuable exposition of *Paradise Lost* in print, being a revision of the materials in the earlier parts.

Reviews in *Spectator*, CIV (1910), 625–26; *Beiblatt*, XXI (1910), 336–37; *Revue germ.*, VI (1910), 477–78; *RELV*, XXVII (1911), 34–35.

756 Paradise Lost. . . . . Edited by G. H. Cowling and H. F. Hallett. London: Methuen & Co., 1926. Pp. xxix+286.

Illustrated. Notes and glossary.

CRITICISM

The comments of the earlier editors on separate points in *Paradise Lost* will be found massed in such works as the Todd, Masson, and Verity editions. In the biographies of Milton appear analyses of the meaning of various passages that are equally valuable for interpretation.

757 Henry J. Todd. An Inquiry into the Origin of *Paradise Lost.*

In *The Poetical Works of John Milton.* London, 1801. 6 vols.

758 Charles Delalot. "Review of a New Edition of *Paradise Lost.*" *Mercure de France*, XVI (1804), 57–66; 105–15; 293–300; 581–89.

759 Addison's Criticism of *Paradise Lost* and Johnson's Remarks on Milton's Versification. London: Sharpe, 1805.

760 Charles Delalot. "Review of De Lille's Translation of *Paradise Lost.*" *Mercure de France*, XIX (1805), 201–14; 295–306; 391–403.

761 Probe eines neuen Commentars über Milton's *Verlornes Paradies*. 1. Abth. als Einladungsschrift zur würdigen Feyer des Weihnachtsfestes. Hrsg. von J. F. Pries. Rostock: Gedruckt bey Alders Erben, 1809.

762 [Review of D. Stewart's *Philosophical Essays.*] *Edinburgh Review*, XVII (1810), 167–211.

Quotes Waller's unfavorable comment on *Paradise Lost* (p. 209).

763 [Quotation from one of Waller's letters regarding *Paradise Lost.*] *GM*, LXXXI (August, 1811), 155.

In review of poetical works of Anna Seward.

764 "Annotations on *Paradise Lost.*" *General Repository*, II (1812), 66–84.

Good notes on sources in Vergil, Juvenal, and medieval literature. Puts classical sources forward, not repeating what was in earlier editions.

765 T. G. C. [Milton's third marriage and documents concerning *Paradise Lost.*] *GM*, LXXXV (1815), 292.

766 "On the Original of Milton's Satan." *Blackwood's Magazine*, I (1817), 140–41.

767 Digamma. "On the Original of Milton's Satan, with Extracts from Crashaw's 'Suspicion of Herod.' " *Ibid.*, May, 1817, pp. 140–42.

Milton borrowed his Satan from Marino's "The Slaughter of the Innocents," translated from Italian by Crashaw.

768 J. A. [Passage from *Paradise Lost* Compared with One from Sir David Lindsay.] *GM*, LXXXVII (1817), 606.

769 F. Scolari. Saggio di critica sul *Paradiso perduto*, poema di Giovanni Milton, e sulli annotazioni a quello di Giuseppe Addisson aggiuntovi *L'Adamo*, sacra rappresentazione di Gio. Battista Andreini. Venice: Rizzi, 1818.

Pages 3–4, Dedication; pp. 5–25, life of Milton; pp. 26–134, criticism; pp. 137–69, annotations; pp. 174–216, "Le descrizione del Paradiso terrestre dall 'originale di Milton tradotta in varie lingue' "; pp. 217–356., *L'Adamo* of Andreini, with notes and Index.

770 "Review of P. Bagley's 'Idwal,' and Other Portions of a Poem." *GM*, LXXXIX (March, 1819), 299.

Use made of Milton's Satan.

771 "Patrick Hume's and Mr. Callender of Craigforth's Notes on Milton." *Blackwood's Magazine*, IV (1819), 658–62.

Callender (1750) plagiarized notes signed by P. H. (Patrick Hume) in Tonson's 1695 edition of *Paradise Lost.* Hume was "the first annotator of *Paradise Lost.*"

772 J. B. Yates. "An Account of an Unprinted English Poem, Written in the Early Part of the Fourteenth Century, by Richard de Hampole, and Entitled 'Stimulus Conscientiae,' or 'The Prick of Conscience.' " *Archaeologia* or *Miscellaneous Tracts Relating to Antiquity*, XIX (1821), 327–38.

Milton's supposed use in *Paradise Lost:* Book I, ll. 61 ff; Book II, ll. 596 ff.

773 "Moral Estimate of *Paradise Lost.*" *Christian Observer*, XXII (1822), 211–18, 278–84.

Paradise Lost is asserted to have serious faults, but its general character is that of "evangelical excellence."

774 "Milton's *Paradise Lost.*" *GM*, XCII (July, 1822), 13–14.

Shows a facsimile of Milton's first receipt, for £5.

775 Philo-Milton. A Vindication of the *Paradise Lost* from the Charge of Exculpating *Cain*, a Mystery. London: F. C. and J. Rivington, 1822. Pp. 60.

Answers letter to Sir Walter Scott in which censured passages of *Cain* are paralleled by some from *Paradise Lost* in order to defend Byron's piece.

776 [Milton and Caedmon.]

See Sharon Turner's *History of the Anglo-Saxon* (1815), for the suggestion of a similarity between *Paradise Lost* and the *Paraphrase.* See the fourth edition (1823), IV, 308. W. D. Conybeare carried further this suggestion to query a possible use of the Junius manuscript by Milton, in the *Illustrations of Anglo-Saxon Poetry* by Joseph Conybeare (London, 1826), pp. 186 f.

777 Angelo Fruglio. Angeleida di Erasmo da Valvasone. Udine, 1825.

On Milton's imitation of Valvasone.

778 Proposal for Printing. . . . . *Paradisi amissi* a Cl. Miltono conscripti liber primus Graeca versione donatus una cum annotationibus a R. Dawes. [With a specimen. In] Ricardi Dawesii Miscellanea critica. . . . . Editio secunda. 1827.

Proposal on pp. 623–27 is identical with that in the first edition.

779 Christian Cann. A Scriptural and Allegorical Glossary to Milton's *Paradise Lost.* London: C. and J. Rivington, [1828]. Pp. xii+282.

Notes grouped according to books of *Paradise Lost*, with some parallels.
Review in *Athen.*, December 10, 1828, p. 937.

780 Description of an Attempt To Illustrate Milton's Pandemonium Now Exhibiting in the Panorama, Leicester Square. Painted by the Proprietor, Robert Burford, from the Designs of H. C. Slons. London, 1829. Pp. 12.

Chart showing forty figures in a panorama planned to show Satan's group, then Pandemonium, and then the pagan gods and other phases of *Paradise Lost* scenes. Characters of persons based on quotations from *Paradise Lost*. A guide for use of spectators.

781 "Mr. Burford's Panorama of Milton's Pandemonium." *GM*, XCIX (1829), 448–49.

Comment on the artist's conception.

782 [Review of Robert Montgomery's "Satan: a Poem."] *Athen.*, January 1, 1830, pp. 1–2.

Comparison with Milton's Satan, much to the disparagement of Montgomery. Milton's Satan "the noblest mythological personage ever created in poetry, not excepting the *Prometheus*, of Aeschylus."

783 Eliza W. Bradburn. The Story of *Paradise Lost*, for Children. Portland, [Maine]: Shirley & Hyde, 1830. Pp. 143.

In set conversational form, with some quotation from *Paradise Lost*, the author attempts to prove the closeness of the poem and the biblical narrative of the Creation.

784 W. P. [Comment on Todd's *Milton*.] *GM*, C (July, 1830), 16–17.

Milton took description of Death from Sackville, not from Spenser, as Todd thought.

785 "Guizot and Milton." *Blackwood's Magazine*, XLIII (1838), 303–12.

Elaborates Guizot's suggestion that Milton was indebted to Bishop Avitus for ideas in *Paradise Lost*.

786 "Milton." *Ibid.*, XLVI (1839), 775–80.

Paradise Lost unique in its sublimity.
Defends Milton for use of pagan material in *Paradise Lost*.

787 The *Adamus Exul* of Grotius, or the Prototype of *Paradise Lost*. Now First Translated from the Latin, by Francis Barham. London: Sherwood, Gilbert & Piper, 1839. Pp. 51.

Dedicated to John A. Herand, editor of the *Monthly Magazine*, in a manner that shows the current interest in a national literary tradition. Translator proposed to publish the original Latin text. He also offered in his Introduction a history of literary source studies up to that day.

788 Philippe Cordova. Congrès scientifique de France. Sixième session, Sept. 1858. Paris et Clermont: Ferrand, 1839. Pp. 609–17.

Question proposed: "Quelle est la plus convenable interprétation du vers premier du *Paradis perdu*? A-t-on, jusqu'à présent, bien traduit ce vers-la?"

789 [*Paradise Lost*—French translation.] Pongerville's Text and *Addison's Essays*. Paris, 1841.

Notes on Milton, his period, and his works, by M. de Pongerville. Philological notes by M. O'Sullivan.

790 Athenaeum. September 3, 1842, pp. 783–84.

A review of Vericour's *Milton et la poésie épique* surveys Milton's influence abroad.

791 Ch. Louandre. "Le diable." *Revue des deux mondes*, XXXI (1842), 568–95.

Comment on Milton's Satan, p. 593.

792 E. di Valvasone. L'Angeleida, poema . . . . per servire d'appendice al *Paradiso perduto* di Milton trad. da Polidori. London, 1842. Pp. xxx+95.

793 David Masson. "The Three Devils: Luther's, Milton's, and Goethe's." *Fraser's Magazine*, XXX (1844), 648–66.

794 Zicari da Paola. Sulla scoverta dell'originale italiano da cui Milton trasse il suo poema del *Paradiso perduto*. Lettera di Francesco Zicari da Paola al Signor Francesco Ruffa. Napoli, 1844. Pp. 36.

L'Adamo, comico italiano.
Refers to scenes of Sin and Death, Creation, Eve and Serpent.

795 Iota. "The Two Devils: or the Satan of Milton and Lucifer of Byron Compared." *Knickerbocker Magazine*, XXX (1847), 150–55.

Byron's Lucifer the more correct. Milton's Satan excites in us pity and admiration. Byron avoided Milton's faults.

796 J. M. Gentleman's Magazine. N.S., XXVII (February, 1847), 159–60.

A review of a paraphrase of *Paradise Lost* done by a Mr. Greene of Oxford in an effort to "harmonise the versification."

797 F. A. Cox. "An Essay on the *Paradise Lost*, Considered with Reference to Its Theological Sentiments and Moral Influence." *Journal of Sacred Literature*, 1848, pp. 236–57.

798 [Milton and *Adamo Caduto* of Salandra.] *GM*, XXXV (January, 1851), 51–57.

Defends Milton against charges of plagiarism.

799 Thomas Goodwin. The Student's Practical Grammar of the English Language Together with a Commentary on the First Book of Milton's *Paradise Lost*, Containing a Practical Analysis Thereof, Critical and Grammatical, with an "Ordo Verborum" of the Difficult Passages, In-

tended for Use in Schools, and Adapted To Meet the Wants of Self-instructing Students. London: C. F. Hodgson, 1855. Pp. vi+309.

Milton study, pp. 258–309.

800 W. A. Delmotte. Drawings to Milton's *Paradise Lost.* 1856.

Four hundred and seventy-four folio plates; original drawings, dated, some few being copies of engravings.

801 [On *Paradise Lost,* Book I, l. 1.]

On the meanings given the line in translation.

In Philippe Cordova's *Congrès scientifique de France. Sixième session, septembre, 1858* (Paris, 1839), pp. 609–17.

802 William H. F. Bosanquet. *The Fall of Man,* or *Paradise Lost,* of Caedmon. Translated in Verse from the Anglo-Saxon. London, 1860. Pp. xxxviii+63.

The abrupt opening of Satan's speech in *Paradise Lost* (Book I, l. 84) traced to a specific passage. Much of the substance and expression credited to the same source.

803 L. E. Dubois. "An Inglorious Milton." *North American Review,* XCI (October, 1860), 539–55.

Thomas Peyton's *Glasse of Time* (1620) suggested as source of *Paradise Lost* plan.

804 W. H. Hilliard. Milton's Eve. An Address Delivered before the Female College, Columbia, South Carolina, June 26, 1860. Montgomery, 1860. Pp. 24.

805 Percy Bysshe Shelley. On the Devil, and Devils.

In *Works of . . . .* edited by H. B. Forman. London, 1862. 8 vols.

See Volume VI.

806 J. W. Stearns. "The Miltonic Deity." *Christian Review,* XXVIII (October, 1863), 629–45.

Milton's task an impossible one, but he awes and dazzles us.

807 L. Wiese. Miltons *Verlorenes Paradies.* Berlin, 1863. Pp. 56.

Vorwort, pp. iii–iv; Test, pp. 5–54; literarische Anmerkungen, pp. 55–56.

A brief but excellent study relating *Paradise Lost* to Greek philosophy and biblical story.

808 A. de Lamartine. Héloïse et Abélard. Paris, 1864.

Criticism of *Paradise Lost,* pp. 113–215.

809 Ferdinandus Joseph Mörs. De fontibus *Paradisi amissi* Miltoniani. Dissertatio philologica, etc. Bonn, [1865]. Pp. 30.

810 "Masson's First Lecture at Edinburgh." *Nation,* II (February 8, 1866), 181.

On a theory of composition of *Paradise Lost.*

811 Criticism on Milton's *Paradise Lost* [from the *Spectator*]. London: A. Murray & Son, 1868. Pp. 152.

In "English Reprints," edited by Edward Arber.

812 Eugenio Camerini. Profili Letterari. Firenze: Barbera, 1870. Pp. x +525.

In an essay on "Milton e l'Italia," pp. 264–74, the author discredits Rolli's Milton criticism; shows points of likeness in *Paradise Lost* and Andreini's *Adamo;* and lists Italian translations of Milton.

813 [Punctuation of *Paradise Lost,* Book I, ll. 567–71.] *Nation,* XV (November 21, 1872), 335–36.

On Johnson's error in punctuating the passage.

814 "The Daughters of Eve and the Poet of *Paradise Lost.*" *Every Saturday,* XV (1873), 543–48.

Asserts Milton's idea of woman is that of the Bible. Commends him for his ideal.

815 Jabez, C. A. Ward, and Others. [On *Paradise Lost,* Book I, ll. 258–60.] *N & Q,* Ser. V, No. XI (1874), pp. 7, 132, 217, 356.

Dealing with Milton's use of "built" as a substantive.

816 W. Münch. Die Entstehung des *Verlorenen Paradieses.* Program. Cleve, 1874.

Reviews in *Archiv,* LV (1876), 229–30; *ES,* I (1877), 366.

817 A. Baumgarten. John Milton und das *Verlorene Paradies.* Coburg, [1875]. Pp. 58.

Largely criticism, but offers German translations and English passages on opposed pages, and also Milton's letter for Cromwell to the King of France (1658).

Review in *Archiv,* LVI (1876), 457.

818 "Milton's Satan." *Dublin University Magazine,* LXXXVIII (1876), 707–14.

819 E. H. Bickersteth. Companions for the Devout Life: the St. James Lectures, Second Series. London: Murray, 1876. Pp. 161.

Lecture on *Paradise Lost,* pp. 91–110, is a heavy moralizing document. Reissued in a New York edition, 1877.

820 Buddensieg. Der Fall der Engel bei John Milton und bei Vondel. [In] *Grenzboten,* No. 33 (1877), p. 241.

821 John A. Himes. Study of Milton's *Paradise Lost.* 1878.

822 J. V. von König. [Letter to Bodmer dated May 15, 1725. In] A. Brandl, *B. H. Brockes* (Innsbruck, 1878), p. 142.

Adverse comment on E. G. Berge's (MS) translation of *Paradise Lost.*

823 E. S. Nadal. "The Cosmogony of *Paradise Lost.*" *Harper's Magazine*, LVI (1878), 137–40.

824 W. T. Dobson. The Classic Poets; Their Lives and Their Times, with the Epics Epitomized. London: Smith, Elder & Co., 1879. Pp. ix+452.

Both epics are treated in formal style.

825 Edmund Gosse. Studies in the Literature of Northern Europe. London: Kegan Paul & Co., 1879. Pp. xii+375.

Credits self with discovering Milton's fall of the rebel angels to be from *Lucifer*. Asserts Roger Williams taught Milton Dutch, and that Milton used copy of Vondel's *Lucifer* soon after it was printed.

826 "Milton and Vondel." *N & Q*, Ser. VII, No. VIII (1889), pp. 288, 377.

Influence of Vondel on Milton.

See also Ser. VII, No. I (1886), p. 246.

827 J. Th. de Visser. Daemonologie van het oude Testament. Utrecht, 1880.

828 M. H. Bailly. "Origines et caractère du Satan de Milton." [Extrait du] *Bulletin de la Société académique de Brest.* Brest, 1881.

829 S. H. Hodgson. Outcast Essays. 1881. Pp. 411.

Pages 99–180, on the "Supernatural in English Poetry." Takes exception to Milton for his free handling of Christian tradition in *Paradise Lost,* making the dubious premise that poetry is identical in aims with religion.

830 John C. H. Flood. "Masenius, Lauder, and Milton." *Antiquarian Magazine and Bibliographer*, III (1883), 221–26, 300–305.

Discussion of Lauder's charge that Milton stole his plot and many passages of *Paradise Lost* from Masenius' *Sarcotis,* and from Grotius' *Adamus Exul.*

831 K. Max Gottschalk. Über den Gebrauch des Artikels in Miltons *Paradise Lost.* Inaugural dissertation, Halle, 1883. Pp. 55.

Page 54: "Aus den angeführten Beispielen ergiebt sich, dass Milton den Artikel bei Titeln in der Apposition nicht gebraucht, also darin ganz mit dem heutigen Sprachgebrauche übereinstimmt, sich aber bei allen übrigen Fällen der Apposition eine gewisse Freiheit in der Verwendung des Artikels gestattet."

832 John A. Himes. "The Plan of *Paradise Lost.*" *New Englander*, XLII (1883), 196–211.

Attempts to prove that Milton took plan from Apocalypse of St. John.

833 William H. Stifler. "Some Phases of Theology in the *Paradise Lost.*" *Baptist Quarterly Review*, V (1883), 135–42.

Asserts that Milton's theology is inexact but inspiring. Satan drawn from classical mythology. Failure to describe the Father and Son thoroughly leaves him open to the charge of Arianism.

834 John A. Himes. "Milton's Angels." *New Englander*, XLIII (1884), 527–43.

835 Maria Mitchell. "The Astronomical Science of Milton as Shown in His *Paradise Lost.*" *Poet-lore*, VI (1884), 313–23.

Milton's work reflects the state of astronomical learning of his time.

836 M. Mull. "Mr. Mull's Edition of *Paradise Lost.*"

Letter by Mull in the *Saturday Review*, November 1, 1884. A four-page retort to a review of Mull's absurd book "restoring" *Paradise Lost* after Bentley's manner.

837 "*Paradise Lost* in Prose." *N & Q*, Ser. VI, No. XI (1885), pp. 267, 318, 492.

Query and replies concerning St. Maur's work as translation into English; here assumed wrongly to be a version of *Paradise Lost.*

See also William Freelove, *N & Q*, Ser. VI, No. XII, p. 296; and J. J. Fahie, *ibid.*, Ser. VII, No. I, p. 14.

838 George Edmundson. Milton and Vondel. London: Trübner, 1885. Pp. 223.

Among the best source-studies in Milton scholarship.

Reviews in *Nation*, XLII (1886), 264–65; *Athen.*, II (1885), 599–600.

839 ———. "Milton and Vondel." *Acad.*, XXVIII (October 31, 1885), 293–94; XXVIII (November 21, 1885), 342.

Refutes Gosse's charges in *Acad.*, XXVIII (October 24, 1885), 265–66.

840 J. R. MacIhraith. "Milton and Vondel." *Ibid.*, XXVIII (November 7, 1885), 308–9.

Comment on Gosse and Edmundson, and on Milton's probable use of Vondel.

841 J. J. Fahie. "*Paradise Lost* in Prose." *N & Q*, Ser. VII, No. I (1886), 14.

Quotes D'Israeli (*Curiosities of Literature*, I (1867), 305) on folly of translating *Paradise Lost* in prose.

842 W. T. Lynn. [*Paradise Lost*, Book II, ll. 706–11.] *Ibid.*, Ser. VII, No. XI (1886), p. 66.

Lynn thinks passage refers to a comet that appeared in 1664.

843 C. B. Mount. "Cherubim in the Celestial Hierarchy, Milton, and Shakspeare." *Ibid.*, pp. 323–24, 517–18.

Milton's meaning of "cherubim" taken from the fourth-century book of Dionysius the Areopagite, or from English books on hierarchies. Shakespeare's use of the word similar to Milton's.

844 Priggles. [Italian Translations of *Paradise Lost.*] *N & Q* (American). (Manchester, New Hampshire), III (1886), 50.

List of Italian translations, 1735–1832.

845 A. R. Shilleto. "Milton and Eyford." *Ibid.*, Ser. VII, No. XI (1886), pp. 245–46.

Tries to disprove tradition that Milton wrote part of *Paradise Lost* at Eyford.

846 Johann Baudisch. Schulcommentar zu Miltons *Paradise Lost.* Leipzig: Piehler, 1887. Pp. 146.

Review by M. Krummacher in *ES*, XI, 309–10.

847 [The spirits in *Paradise Lost.*] *N & Q* (American), VI (1889), 235, 299.

Query and answer on distance spirits fell in nine days.

848 Melville B. Anderson. [Review of Matthew Arnold's *Essays in Criticism* (2d Ser.).] *MLN*, IV (1889), 297.

Justice not done by modern critics to "the architectonies of *Paradise Lost.*"

849 L'abbé Looten (Camille Évariste Lucien). Étude sur le poète néerlandais Vondel. Lille, 1889. Pp. iii+332.

Chapter vii discusses relationship of Milton to Vondel.

850 H. Rawlings. "The Transfigured Theology of *Paradise Lost.*" *Westminster Review*, CLIII (1889), 32–41.

Milton has shown the absurdity of the Genesis fable, since even he has failed to make it seem possible. *Paradise Lost* will be more widely appreciated when its theology is regarded in the way we regard that of Homer or Vergil.

851 J. O. Westwood. "Milton and Caedmon." *Acad.*, XXXV (1889), 10.

Book IV of *Paradise Lost* intended as beginning of a tragedy. Books I–III perhaps added under influence of the Paraphrase.

852 "Precursor of Milton." *Atlantic Monthly*, LXV (1890), 33–43.

Points out parallels between Avitus' *De Initio Mundi* and *Paradise Lost;* not aware that this had been suggested by Guizot, and done later in *Blackwood's*, XLIII (1838), 303–12.

853 George Edmundson. "Milton and Vondel." *Acad.*, XXXVIII (1890), 613–14.

Further defense of his thesis that Milton was indebted to Vondel.

854 Gustav Jenny. Miltons *Verlorenes Paradies* in der deutschen Literatur des 18. Jahrhunderts. St. Gallen, 1890.

Important for reference work.

855 Franz Schwalbach. Kommentar zum ersten Buche von Miltons *Paradise Lost.* Harburg, 1890. Pp. 36.

Annotations from Anglo-Saxon, the Bible, and commentators. Nothing strikingly new.

Review by O. Glöde, *ES*, XVII (1892), 162–64.

856 Edward H. Marshall. "*Paradise Lost*, I, 587." *N & Q*, Ser. VII, No. XII (1891), pp. 456–57.

Milton's accuracy in geographical allusions illustrated.

857 August Müller. Über Miltons Abhängigkeit von Vondel. Berlin, 1891. Pp. 61.

Parallel passages used. Refers to articles by Edmundson and Beddoes.

858 Mary A. Woods. "Studies in *Paradise Lost.*" *Expository Times* (Edinburgh), III (1891–92), 295–98, 391–94, 486–90; IV (1892–93), 199–203.

859 J. W. Brouwers. Vondel en de Catalaansche dicktkunst. Redevoering uitgesproken op de plechtige jaarlijksche vergadering der Koninkijke Vlaamsche Academie, van 23 Juni, 1892. Ghent, 1892. Pp. 53.

On Milton's obligations to Vondel.

860 A. S. Cook (ed.). Criticisms on *Paradise Lost.* Boston: Ginn & Co., 1892. Pp. xxiv+200.

Compilation of articles and reviews.

Review by W. H. Hudson, *Beiblatt*, IV (1893), 138.

861 John Pickford. "Paradise Lost." *N & Q*, Ser. VIII, No. I (1892), p. 158.

Variant of legend in *Paradise Lost* indicated in Scott's *Rob Roy.*

862 Woldemar Rost. Die Orthographie der ersten Quartoausgabe von Miltons *Paradise Lost.* Dissertation, Leipzig, 1892. Pp. 76.

Used Masson's 1877 reproduction of the first edition as a basis. Finds twelve title-pages. Discusses word forms.

863 F. Blumenthal. "Lord Byron's Mystery *Cain* and Its Relation to Milton's *Paradise Lost* and Gessner's *Death of Abel.*" *Beiblatt*, III (1892), 90.

Shows a similarity between Milton's Satan and Byron's Lucifer; also between his Adam and Byron's Cain.

864 Mary A. Woods. "Milton's Primeval Man." *Expository Times* [Edinburgh], IV (1892–93), 8–9.

865 Edward E. Hale, Jr. "Certain Miltonic Conceptions." *MLN*, VIII (1893), 25–27.

Comment on Milton's conception of heaven and hell.

866 D. G. Millison. How It Happened. The Story of Milton's *Paradise Lost.* . . . . Illustrated with Zincs from Doré's Pictures. Wichita, Kansas: Beacon Publishing Co., 1893. Pp. 81.

Paraphrase in prose.

867 R. Sprenger. "Anklänge an Milton in Goethe's *Faust.*" *ES*, XVIII (1893), 304–6.

Goethe's indebtedness to Milton shown through parallel passages of *Paradise Lost* and *Faust.*

868 F. Hübler. Milton und Klopstock mit besonderer Berücksichtigung des *Paradise Lost* und des *Messias.* Reichenberg, 1893–95.

Reviewed in *ES*, XXVII, 142–44.

869 J. E. B. Mayor. "Augustine and Milton." *Classical Review,* VIII (1894), 147.

Parallel to *Paradise Lost,* Book I, l. 254: "The mind is its own place."

870 Maria Mitchell. "The Astronomical Science of Milton as Shown in *Paradise Lost.*" *Poet-lore,* VI (1894), 313–23.

Transcribed by Professor Mitchell's sister from notes made about 1857.

Unscientific comments on Milton's astronomy. An appreciation rather than a scientific study.

871 Jonathan Boucher. "Milton and Ariosto." *N & Q,* Ser. VIII, No. VII (1895), p. 505.

Paradise Lost, Book IV, ll. 159–65, compared to *Orlando Furioso,* canto xviii, stanza 138.

872 G. Duflou. "Milton and Vondel." *Acad.,* XLVII (1895), 379–80.

Comment on work of Edmundson, Müller, and Moolhuizen on the problem of Milton's relation to Vondel.

873 Herbert Harris. "Was *Paradise Lost* Suggested by the Mystery Plays?" *MLN,* X (1895), 223.

A question that has strong implications in its favor, particularly in the known ranging of Milton through dramatic literature. The points offered here are cautiously advanced.

874 M. C. Lefferts. "Milton's *Paradise Lost.*" *N & Q,* Ser. VIII, No. VII (1895), p. 447.

A query for originals of the fifth and sixth title-pages, and a complaint that no Milton bibliography gives such data as booksellers need.

875 J. J. Moolhuizen. Vondels *Lucifer* en Miltons *Verlorenes Paradijs.* Kritisch onderzoek. Nyhoff: Gravenhage, 1895. Pp. 128.

Study in part by parallel passages. Some reference study.

876 Lewis F. Mott. [Review of Zumbini's *Studi di Letterature Straniere.*] *MLN*, X (1895), 55–56.

Comments favorably on Zumbini's criticism of *Paradise Lost.*

877 Thomas N. Orchard. The Astronomy of *Paradise Lost.* London, 1896.

Well illustrated. Revised edition, 1913.

878 Paradise Lost. . . . . A Series of Twelve Illustrations Etched by William Strang. London: John Nimmo, 1896. Folio.

Only one hundred fifty copies.

879 A. F. Agard. "Poetic Personifications of Evil." *Poet-lore*, IX (1897), 206–16.

880 Foffano. Ricerche letterarie. Livorno, 1897. Pp. 341.

Pp. 119–23: relation of Milton and Valvasone.

881 W. J. Burnside. "Milton's *Paradise Lost* Considered in Relation to Its Theology." *Lutheran Church Review*, XVII (1898), 327–35.

882 John A. Himes. Milton's *Paradise Lost:* Its Structure and Meaning. New York: Harper, 1898.

Attempts new interpretations of passages. Not valuable.

Review by W. H. Browne, *MLN*, XIII (1898), 226–27. See Himes' reply, *ibid.*, pp. 259–60.

883 Oscar Kuhns. "Dante's Influence on Milton." *MLN*, XIII (1898), 1–6.

Shows influence by citing many parallel passages.

884 C. Alphonso Smith. "Milton-Vondel." *Ibid.*, p. 160.

885 Maud Elma Kingsley. "The First Two Books of *Paradise Lost.*" *Education*, XIX (1899), 570–73.

Methods of presenting *Paradise Lost* to high-school students considered.

886 E. B. N. Dhabar. "The Modern Avista of Milton."

Creation story—Persia > Judaism > Milton. Relies on Addison largely.

In *K. R. Cama Memorial Volume* (essays on Iranian subjects), pp. 79–97. Bombay, 1900.

887 A. M. Scott. Über das Verhältnis von Drydens *State of Innocence* zu Miltons *Paradise Lost.* Halle: C. A. Kaemmerer & Co., 1900. Pp. 67.

888 Th. Vetter. "J. J. Bodmer und die englische Literatur."

In *Bodmer-Denkschrift*, Zürich, 1900, pp. 315 ff.

Estimates the value of Bodmer's 1732 translation.

889 George Dobbin Brown. Syllabification and Accent in the *Paradise Lost*. Johns Hopkins dissertation. Baltimore: John Murphy Co., 1901. Pp. v+73.

A summary of earlier studies of Milton's meters, with new work on syllable division, accents, etc.

890 Albert S. Cook. "*Paradise Lost*, VII, 364–66." *MLN*, XVI (1901), 202–5.

Milton's astronomical information derived from Galileo. A list of passages so influenced indicated.

891 "Who Wrote *Paradise Lost?*" *Macmillan's Magazine*, Vol. LXXXV (March, 1902).

892 Paul Elmer More. "The True Theme of *Paradise Lost*." *Independent*, LIV (1902), 277–80.

Real charm of *Paradise Lost* lies in portrayal of "a garden of innocence, a paradise of idyllic delights." This "pastoral ideal" has haunted the minds of men, especially of poets, from time immemorial.

Reprinted in *Shelburne Essays* (4th Ser., London: G. P. Putnam's Sons, 1907), pp. 239–53.

893 A. Scrocca. Studio critico sul *Paradiso Perduto* del Milton. Naples, [1902]. Pp. 39.

On epic forms of Italian and French literary origin. Decides that *Paradise Lost* is not a true epic because a narrative of defeat, not of victory.

894 Wynne Baxter. [On early editions of *Paradise Lost*.] *Transactions of the Bibliographical Society*, VI (1902), 152–55.

Gives data on Milton's printers and on the 1667 title-pages of *Paradise Lost*.

895 Albert S. Cook. "*Paradise Lost*, III, 7." *JEGP*, V (1903), 32.

Classical parallels to this line.

896 John W. Hales. "Milton and Ovid." *MP*, I (1903), 143–44.

Milton follows Ovid closely in *Paradise Lost*, Book VII, ll. 30–39.

897 G. B. Viles. Comparison of Bodmer's Translation of Milton's *Paradise Lost* with the Original. Leipzig: E. Glausch, 1903. Pp. 127.

898 Friedrich Buff. Miltons *Paradise Lost* in seinem Verhältnisse zur *Aeneide*, *Ilias*, und *Odyssee*. Inaugural dissertation, Munich, 1904. Pp. 77.

Good on epic devices.

899 M. Delines. Le diable et le satanique dans la littérature européenne. "Bibliothèque universelle", September–November, 1904.

900 Albert S. Cook. "Two Notes on *Paradise Lost.*" *MLN*, XX (1905), 125–26.

Possible sources of *Paradise Lost*, Book V, ll. 310–11, found in Chrysostom, Ignatius, and Prudentius. Possible sources of Book VII, ll. 364–66, found in Pliny, Aeschylus, Lactantius, and Martianus Capella.

901 Wilhelm Münch. "Ein italienischer Vorgänger Miltons." *Die neueren Sprachen*, XIII (1905), 321–35.

Thinks Milton copied from, or unconsciously imitated, the *Angeleida* of Erasmo di Valvasone.

Reviewed by S. B. Liljegren in *ES*, LI, 429–30.

902 John H. Shorthouse. "The *Paradise Lost.*"

In *Life and Letters of . . . . edited by His Wife* (London, 1905), II, 123–35.

903 George B. Churchill. "The Relation of Dryden's *State of Innocence* to Milton's *Paradise Lost* and Wycherley's *Plain Dealer:* an Inquiry into Dates." *MP*, IV (1906), 381–88.

Shows that Dryden's work was probably not published until 1677, although Milton gave permission for the paraphrase in 1674. Delay perhaps due to Milton's contract with his publisher. Same conclusion as reached by Ker and Gosse.

904 Wilhelm Münch. "Ein italienischer Vorgänger Miltons." *Die neueren Sprachen*, XIII (1906), 385–401.

Relation of Milton to Erasmo di Valvasone.

905 John S. P. Tatlock. "Milton's Sin and Death." *MLN*, XXI (1906), 239–40.

Possible sources of Sin and Death: Epistle of St. James, 1:15; Hesiod, Vergil, Dante, Spenser (Faerie Queene, Book I, ll. 14–15), and Phineas Fletcher (*Purple Island*, XII, 27–31), last two of whom refer especially to Death; and John Gower's *Mirour de l'omme.*

906 Charles G. Osgood, Jr. "Milton's 'Sphere of Fortune.' " *Ibid.*, XXII (1907), 140–41.

Milton parallels Dante's idea (*Inferno*, Book VII, ll. 73–92) that Fortune controlled her own sphere of activity.

907 J. W. Pearce. "*Paradise Lost*, V, 600–601." *Ibid.*, p. 151.

Parallel in Colossians 1:16; and in Ben Jonson, *Eupheme*, IX: "Elegy on My Muse."

908 Marianna Woodhull. The Epic of *Paradise Lost.* New York: Putnam's Sons, 1907. Pp. xi+375.

Survey of epic treatment. Sources of *Paradise Lost.* Bibliography, pp. 351–68.

909 N. M. J. J. Asa. The *Bundakish* and the *Paradise Lost.* Spiegel Memorial Volume. [In honor of Dr. Friederich Spiegel.] Bombay, 1908. Pp. 136–45.

Compares Milton's Creation with that in Avesta and Pahlavi books. Continues theme of Dhabhar's article in Cama memorial volume. Parallels minute and unconvincing.

910 Edward Chauncey Baldwin. "An Instance of Milton's Debt to Vergil." *JEGP*, VII (1908), 85–86.

Parallel to *Paradise Lost*, Book II, in *Aeneid* xi (scene of infernal council). Vergil probably furnished Milton with a type of Belial.

911 George G. Loane. "Milton and the Brute Creation." *Spectator*, CI (1908), 291–93.

Also in *Living Age*, CCLIX (1908), 244–47.

Milton had no love for any of the brute creation. Nightingale alone was capable of calling out his poetic emotion.

912 Edward Bliss Reed. "Two Notes on Addison." *MP*, VI (1908), 185.

Comments on Addison's desire that his papers on *Paradise Lost* should stand the test of searching criticism.

913 M. A. Woods. The Characters of *Paradise Lost.* London: Ouseley, 1908. Pp. 149.

More religious than literary; no source study.

914 A. R. Benham. "A Note on *Paradise Lost*, I, 351–55." *MLN*, XXIV (1909), 64.

Parallels to Milton's phrases.

915 J. Douglas Bruce. "A Note on *Paradise Lost*, vii, 463–74." *ES*, XLI (1909), 166–70.

These lines probably suggested by classical legends of Cadmus and Medea. Sources not in Ovid, but in Apollonius of Rhodes or Nonnus.

916 Albert S. Cook. [Source of opening lines of *Paradise Lost*, Book III.] *MP*, VI (1909), 469–70.

Suggests Eusebius' writings concerning Constantine.

917 P. T. Forsyth. "Milton's God and Milton's Satan." *Contemporary Review*, XCV (1909), 450–65.

Also in *Living Age*, CCLXI (1909), 519–30.

Milton's God too cold and relentless; his Satan inspires sympathy and admiration. Milton does not at first make much distinction between Lucifer and Christ.

918 Charles Gildon. Vindication of *Paradise Lost* (1694).

Reprinted in J. E. Spingarn's *Critical Essays of the Seventeenth Century* (3 vols.; Oxford, 1909), III, 198.

919 Carl H. Grabo. "Milton and Vondel." *Chautauquan*, LIV (1909), 114–23.

Thinks Milton's debt to Vondel great. No evidence offered except that in Edmundson's work of 1885.

920 Raymond D. Havens. "The Early Reputation of *Paradise Lost.*" *ES*, XL (1909), 187–99.

Early unpopularity of *Paradise Lost* greatly overestimated. Was admired by cultured class, as shown by numerous editions and by comments. *Paradise Lost* so well known that when Addison approved it in *Spectator*, it achieved wide, almost ridiculous, popularity.

921 G. H. Norcross. "*Paradise Lost*, 1667." *Proceedings of the Massachusetts Historical Society, Third Series*, II (1909), 257–59.

922 E. H. Pember. "On the Conception and Treatment of Satan in *Paradise Lost* and the *Inferno*."

In *Milton Memorial Lectures* (Oxford, 1909), pp. 59–82.

923 Emma Schrader. The *Divina Commedia* and *Paradise Lost* Reflect Mediaevalism and the Renaissance, Catholicism and Protestantism. 1909. Pp. 170.

Manuscript thesis, the University of Chicago Libraries.

924 Carey H. Conley. Milton's Indebtedness to His Contemporaries in *Paradise Lost*. 1910.

Manuscript thesis, the University of Chicago Libraries.

925 E. Dick. "La traduction du *Paradis perdu* de Chateaubriand." *RHL*, XVII (1910), 750–67.

Shows that Chateaubriand did not know the language of Milton well enough to make a good translation; yet he compares favorably with Taine as translator of Milton.

926 Orestes Pearl Rhyne. "Conjunction+Participle Group in English." *SP*, IV (1910), 8, 24, 28.

Milton's use of this formation shown from examples in *Areopagitica* and *Paradise Lost*.

927 Helene Richter. [Milton and Tasso.] *ES*, XLI (1910), 145.

In a review of Henry Cloriston's *Later Work of Torquato Tasso*, author tries to prove significant resemblances of Milton to Tasso. Not shown to be definite.

928 Stephen Gajšek. Milton und Caedmon. Wien und Leipzig, 1911. Pp. viii+65.

Sharon Turner, in *History of Anglo-Saxon Literature* (London, 1823), first to suggest relationship of Milton and Caedmon. Surveys critical work on subject of relationship, indicating influence of Caedmon on lyric parts of *Paradise Lost* and *Paradise Regained*, and on the concept of Satan.

Reviews in *ES* (by F. Klaeber), XLV (1912), 314–16; *Archiv*, CXXVII (1911), 480; *Beiblatt* (by K. Jost), XXIII, 270–73.

929 Victor Giraud. "Sur Chateaubriand traducteur de Milton." *RHL*, XVIII (1911), 138–39.

Asserts the excellence of Chateaubriand's translation.

930 C. H. Ibershoff. "A Neglected Klopstock-Milton Parallel." *MLN*, XXVI (1911), 264.

Klopstock's description of Chebar (*Messias*, Canto XII, l. 510) parallel to Milton's description of Raphael (*Paradise Lost*, Book V, l. 278).

931 John M. Robertson. "Form in Poetry." *ER*, VIII (1911), 377–97.

Comments on form of some of Milton's *Minor Poems*. Thinks *Paradise Lost* would have been more popular in rhyme.

932 F. Boillot. "Chateaubriand théoricien de la traduction." *RHL*, XIX (1912), 791–801.

Discusses the theory of translation exemplified in Chateaubriand's translation of *Paradise Lost*.

Reply to Boillot is made by F. Baldensperger in *RHL*, XX (1913), 428–29.

933 Emily Hickey. "Is Satan the Hero of *Paradise Lost?*" *Catholic World*, XCVI (1912), 58–71.

Satan not the hero, because he continues to sink deeper into disgrace. Hero is Adam, who, though temporarily weak, is essentially noble.

934 Ettore Allodoli (ed.). Giambattista Andreini, *L'Adamo*. Lanciano. Carabba, 1913.

Refers to Milton parallels.

935 K. Assman. Miltons epische Technik nach *Paradise Lost*. Berlin, 1913. Pp. viii+90.

Brief bibliography and chapters on Milton's adaptations of classical formulas.

936 J. Douglas Bruce. "Campailla, Berkeley, and Milton." *Nation*, XCVII (1913), 32–33.

Campailla's *L'Adamo* shows Raphael as instructor of Adam, as does *Paradise Lost*. Probably Campailla took idea from apocryphal Book of Tobit.

937 Gustav Hübener. Die stilistische Spannung in Milton's *Paradise Lost*. Halle: Niemeyer, 1913. Pp. 56.

In *Studien zur Engl. Philologie*, LI.

Reviews in *Beiblatt*, XXV, 206–8; *ES* (by W. Franz), LI (1917–18), 132–33.

938 Laura E. Lockwood. "*Paradise Lost*, vii, 15–20." *MLN*, XXVIII (1913), 126–27.

Explains the reference to Bellerophon.

939 Thomas N. Orchard. Milton's Astronomy of *Paradise Lost*. London: Longmans, Green & Co., 1913. Pp. viii+288.

First issued in 1896. Pp. x+338.

Well illustrated. Presents an account of astronomical theory up to Milton's time. Considerable revision and abridgement in the second edition.

Reviewed in *Nation*, XCVIII, 474–75.

940 J. Schmitter. J. J. Bodmer's Übersetzungen von J. Miltons *Verlorenem Paradies*, 1732, 1742, 1754, 1759, 1769, sprachlich verglichen. Inaugural dissertation, Zürich. Zürich: Von Marbach, 1913. Pp. 283.

A studious anatomizing of forms in the successive editions. No conclusions recorded.

941 Elbert N. S. Thompson. "The Theme of *Paradise Lost*." *PMLA*, N.S., XXI (1913), 106–20.

Milton values rebellion of Lucifer and Sin in Eden, not as historical facts, but as symbols of moral truth. Satan not a hero, but symbolizes sin in all its stages. *Paradise Lost* a poetic expression of eternal moral law.

942 H. W. Peck. "The Theme of *Paradise Lost*." *Ibid.*, XXII (1914), 256–69.

Opposes Thompson's ideas. Milton's own tendency was to regard material of *Paradise Lost* as historical. Seventeenth- and eighteenth-century critics so regarded it. Milton's theory of poetic inspiration leads to conclusion that Milton believed he was dealing with historical material.

943 Enrico Pizzo. Miltons *Verlorenes Paradies* im deutschen Urteile des 18. Jahrhunderts. Berlin: Felber, 1914. Pp. 144.

Good bibliographical data in footnotes.

944 W. A. Webb. "Dante and His Influence upon the English Poets." *South Atlantic Quarterly*, XIII (1914), 233–47.

Short comparison of *Paradise Lost* with the *Divina Commedia*.

945 Louis C. Marolf. "A Textual Difficulty in Milton." *Dial*, LVIII (1915), 197–98.

Answers questions asked by W. F. Warren, *Dial*, LVIII, 142. Deals with supposed inconsistency in account of Satan's second interview with Sin and Death.

946 W. F. Warren. The Universe as Pictured in Milton's *Paradise Lost.* New York, [1915]: Abingdon Press. Pp. [79].

Of little value. Far inferior to Orchard's work.

947 Elliot A. White. "Adam's Motive." *MLN*, XXX (1915), 229-31.

Milton brought romance into story of the Fall, by making Adam's chief motive in eating the apple his love for Eve and desire to share her fate.

948 W. B. "Bentley on Milton." *N & Q*, Ser. XII, No. II (1916), p. 107.

Discussion of Bentley's emendation of *Paradise Lost*, Book IX, ll. 62-67, with explanation of passage.

949 Albert H. Daehler. "Adam's Motive." *MLN*, XXXI (1916), 187-88.

Love motive secondary. Adam made so noble because he is protagonist of mankind. Eve is both his foil and the agent of his undoing.

950 "A Line of Milton [*Paradise Lost*, Book VII, l. 121]."

Emendations and interpretations suggested in *Times Literary Supplement* by F. C. Burkitt, XVI (1917), 250; H. H. C., p. 165; William Colgan, pp. 202, 226; E. B. England, p. 153; H. P. Fraser, p. 177; F. C. Hodgson, p. 250; George Hookham, p. 189; D. W. Thompson, pp. 177, 213; A. W. Verity, pp. 189, 237.

951 Raymond M. Alden. "The Lyrical Conceits of the Elizabethans." *SP*, XIV (1917), 133 n.

Conceit of Chesterfield contrasted with one in a passage of *Paradise Lost.*

952 Edward Chauncey Baldwin. "A Note on *Paradise Lost*, IX." *MLN*, XXXII (1917), 119-21.

Identification of serpent of Genesis with Satan, as found in *Paradise Lost*, originated in apocryphal literature, and was used by St. Augustine. Ancients regarded serpent as crafty, not as diabolical. Milton was familiar with both St. Augustine and Aristotle.

953 James A. S. Barrett. "Another Line of Milton." *TLS*, XVI (1917) 393.

Note on *Paradise Lost*, Book V, ll. 799.

954 John Erskine. "The Theme of Death in *Paradise Lost*." *PMLA*, XXXII (1917), 573-82.

Contradiction between earlier and later accounts of death in *Paradise Lost.* Change due to fact that Milton's treatment of Adam and Eve had changed. Theologian had given way to poet.

955 E. B. Greenway. "Another Line of Milton." *TLS*, XVI (1917), 466.

Suggested emendation of *Paradise Lost*, Book V, ll. 794-802.
See also A. W. Verity, *TLS*, XVI, 417, 454.

956 James Holly Hanford. "The Dramatic Element in *Paradise Lost.*" *SP*, XIV (1917), 178–95.

Influence of Elizabethan drama on Milton; his preference for classical drama; psychological and dramatic aspects of *Paradise Lost;* use of elements of Elizabethan tragedy; growth of plan.

957 C. H. Ibershoff. "A Second Note on Klopstock's Indebtedness to Milton." *MLN*, XXXII (1917), 186.

Parallels between *Paradise Lost* and Klopstock's *Messias.*

958 Elbert N. S. Thompson. "A Forerunner of Milton." *Ibid.*, pp. 479–82.

Milton's use of Henry More's *Psychathanasia.* Milton used Ptolemaic system because of its rich imaginative associations and on account of the debated condition of Copernican theory.

959 Augustine Birrell. "Tomkins redivivus." *Living Age*, CCXCVI (1918), 502–5.

Humorous account of Tomkins' probable opinion of *Paradise Lost.* Tomkins was chaplain to the Archbishop of Canterbury, and official reader of the *Paradise Lost* manuscript.

960 R. E. Neil Dodge. "Theology in *Paradise Lost.*"

In "University of Wisconsin Studies in Language and Literature," No. II (September, 1918), pp. 9–21. A comparison of the theology of Milton and Dante. Milton's God is merely a dramatic agent, lacking the aloofness and kindliness of Dante's figure as well as the primitive simplicity of the God of the Old Testament.

961 C. H. Ibershoff. "Bodmer and Milton." *JEGP*, XVII (1918), 589–601.

Milton's influence on Bodmer's epic *Noah.*

962 Olin H. Moore. "The Infernal Council." *MP*, XVI (1918), 186–93.

Scholarly study of Milton's sources of ideas and scenes of infernal council.

963 Elmer Edgar Stoll. "Was Paradise Well Lost?" *PMLA*, XXXIII (1918), 429–35.

Convincing criticism of the ending of *Paradise Lost* as being in harmony with Milton's humanization of Adam and Eve, and with his view of the world.

964 Allan H. Gilbert. "A Parallel between Milton and Seneca." *MLN*, XXXIV (1919), 120–21.

Parallel between *Paradise Lost,* Book XI, l. 549, and Seneca's *Epistles* xxiv. 24, and lxv. 18.

965 F. M. Dill. The Poetical Structure of Milton's *Paradise Lost.* [1920.]

Manuscript dissertation at Cornell University (Ithaca). Pp. 54.

966 A. S. Ferguson. "*Paradise Lost*, IV, 977–1015." *MLR*, XV (1920), 168–70.

Shows that Milton was indebted to the *Aeneid* for many passages usually regarded as of Homeric origin.

967 Allan H. Gilbert. "Milton and the Mysteries." *SP*, XVII (1920), 147–69.

Ramsay (see *SP*, XV, 123–58) made too much of his evidence. Many similarities to *Paradise Lost* noted in *Ludus Coventriae*, Parts I and II, Chester plays, and York plays. Concludes that the Mysteries exerted an influence, indirect if not direct, on Milton.

968 Edwin Greenlaw. "Spenser's Influence on *Paradise Lost*." *Ibid.*, pp. 320–59.

Important study of similarities in thought of Milton and Spenser. Milton's debt to Spenser shown by examination of detailed evidence.

969 William Haller. "Order and Progress in *Paradise Lost*." *PMLA*, XXXV (1920), 218–25.

Theology of *Paradise Lost* is weak. Milton's greatness lies in portrayal of universal humanity and in his political philosophy.

970 Katherine Morse. "Milton's Ideas of Science as Shown in *Paradise Lost*." *Scientific Monthly*, X (1920), 150–56.

Scheme of *Paradise Lost* undoubtedly Ptolemaic; but Milton leaned toward Copernican theory in certain passages. Valuable statements of Milton's ideas of science.

971 Charles G. Osgood. "*Paradise Lost*, IX, 506; *Nativity Hymn*, ll. 133 and 153." *American Journal of Philology*, XLI (1920), 76–80.

Milton's spelling of "Hermione" correct; passage from *Nativity Hymn* paraphrases Lactantius, *Divine Institutes*, V, chaps. v–viii.

972 Hermann Vogel. Über die Behandlung gleichzeitiger Ereignisse in Miltons *Paradise Lost*. Ein Beitrag zur Erzählungstechnik Miltons. Manuscript dissertation, Freiburg i. B., 1921. Pp. 82.

973 Edward Chauncey Baldwin. "The Authorized Version's Influence on Milton's Diction." *MLN*, XXXVI (1921), 376–77.

On the influences seen in *Paradise Lost*, Book VII, ll. 224–31, and in the sonnet on "The Late Massacre in Piemont."

974 Gustav Hübener. "Milton's Satan." *ES*, LV (1921), 136–39.

Paradise Lost follows the tradition of certain mystery plays in making Satan the fallen angel rather than a figure representing evil incarnate.

975 C. A. Moore. "The Conclusion of *Paradise Lost.*" *PMLA*, XXXVI (1921), 1–34.

Final resignation of Adam and Eve not due to a change in the purpose of the poem but to Milton's conception of sin and death. Death is benefit, for it is a means to a better life.

976 Murray W. Bundy. "Milton's View of Education in *Paradise Lost.*" *JEGP*, XXI (1922), 127–52.

Milton expressed a twofold purpose of education. Raphael's commission (*Paradise Lost*, Book V) similar to Milton's own aim as a teacher. Twofold purpose exemplified by instruction given to Adam by Raphael and Michael.

977 G. Sigerson. The Easter Song, Being the First Epic of Christendom, by Sedulius . . . . Including a Schedule of Milton's "Debts." Dublin: Talbot Press, 1922. Pp. viii+269.

Overdrawn. The assumptions of indebtedness are not plausible, inasmuch as nearly all the items could more easily have reached Milton through his reading of the Bible and literary works.

978 "Blake and Milton." *TLS*, XXII (1923), 907.

In a review of Keynes' edition of the *Ode* it is pointed out that Blake by nature was so unlike Milton that his high regard for *Paradise Lost* is more noteworthy. Also, his drawings have an imaginative quality unequaled by any other artist concerned with its scenes.

979 W. Connely. "Imprints of the Aeneid on *Paradise Lost.*" *Classical Journal*, XVIII (1923), 466–76.

Good commentary on structural relationships and on narrative method.

980 Jules Douady. La création et le fruit défendu selon Milton. Paris: Hachette, 1923. Pp. 215.

Expository chiefly.
Review in *RAA*, I, 353–57.

981 Allan H. Gilbert. "Milton's Textbook of Astronomy." *PMLA*, XXXVIII (1923), 297–307.

Milton used *De Sphaera* of Joannes de Sacrobosco as a textbook. This work has so little unique material that one cannot find in it unquestionable sources for passages in Milton's poetry.

982 ———. "The Outside Shell of Milton's World." *SP*, XX (1923), 444–47.

Milton apparently willing to accept Copernican astronomy but employed the Ptolemaic. This he modified freely because of his partial abandonment of the older theory.

983 ———. "The Problem of Evil in *Paradise Lost.*" *JEGP*, XXII (1923), 175–94.

Milton asserts that evil is self-destructive and that good overcomes evil. Evil necessary in present order so that we may know good. Fallen Adam, by conquest of evil, is happier than sinless Adam. Origin of evil lies in man's choice.

984 Geoffrey Keynes. "Blake's Milton." *TLS*, December 13, 1923, p. 875.

985 Arthur Davidson Ficke. "Mr. Milton's *Paradise Lost.*" *Bookman*, LIX (1924), 420–22.

Humorous but sincere appreciation of the epic.

986 Harris F. Fletcher. "Milton and Yosippon." *SP*, XXI (1924), 496–501.

Unlikely that Milton knew the *Zohar*. Striking parallels between *Paradise Lost* and the writings of Yosippon, or the pseudo-Josephus, especially in story of Eden.

987 Heinrich Mutschmann. Studies Concerning the Origin of *Paradise Lost*. Dorpat, 1924. Pp. 72.

Uses Warton's method, whereby *Paradise Lost*, Book IX, ll. 1101–11, is clearly shown a mosaic founded on Gerard's *Herball* (1597), in description of the Indian fig tree. Giving up King Arthur, Milton determined to use gatherings from Hakluyt reading in *Paradise Lost* (reference only to Book IV, ll. 776–96). Puts histories near *Comus* date.

Reviews by Liljegren in *Beiblatt*, XXXVI, 274–75; *ES*, LXI, 89–92.

See *Literaturblatt*, XLVII, 86, for Mutschmann's own comment; and Fischer's reply, *ibid.*, p. 87.

988 [Association Copies.] *Harvard Library Notes*, No. 15 (September, 1925), pp. 43–44.

Mrs. Siddons' manuscript of *Paradise Lost* in the Harvard Library; has four readings for four first Wednesday or Friday evenings in Lent.

989 Edward Chauncey Baldwin. "*Paradise Lost* and the Apocalypse of Moses." *JEGP*, XXIV (1925), 383–486.

Non-biblical embellishments of Genesis story found in *Paradise Lost*, found also in Apocalypse of Moses, which Milton may have used as source.

990 ———. "And on the Left Hand Hell." *MLN*, XL (1925), 251.

Note on *Paradise Lost*, Book X, l. 322.

991 James A. S. Barrett. "Ambiguities in *Paradise Lost.*" *TLS*, October 8, 1925, p. 656.

992 L. J. H. Bradley. "Keats and Milton." *Ibid.*, October 22, 1925, p. 698.

Use of "aloof" in *Paradise Lost*, III, 577, paralleled in "Endymion," Book IV, l. 374, with commentary on Keats's reading of Milton.

993 S. Foster Damon. "Three Generations of One Line." *MLN*, XL (1925), 441.

Paradise Lost, Book VI, l. 350 probably borrowed from Henry More's *Praeexistency of the Soul*, and copied in Shelley's *Queen Mab*.

994 James Hall Pitman. "Milton and the *Physiologus*." *Ibid.*, pp. 439–40.

Certain passages in *Paradise Lost* suggest Milton's familiarity with *Physiologus*, presumably in the English version.

995 Pratt's Great Botanical and Poetical Panorama of the Garden of Eden, as Described in Milton's *Paradise*, an Immense Moving Mirror of Nature, at Cabot Hall (Harvard) in 1850. *Harvard Library Notes*, No. 15 (September, 1925), p. 43.

996 Theodor Spira. "Die Aufgabe der Miltonforschung." *Palaestra*, CXLVIII (1925), 258–80.

The meaning of *Paradise Lost*, Book I, ll. 6–16, in contrast to lines 1–5 discussed. Milton's general purpose in the epic considered, and also the relation of the poem to life of seventeenth-century England.

997 Karel, Štepanik. "Poznámky k Jungmannovu překladu 'Ztracenéhi rdje.'" *Časopis Matice moravskê*, XLIX (1925), 260–80.

Notes on J. Jungmann's translation of *Paradise Lost*.

998 Theodore H. Banks, Jr. "Sir John Denham and *Paradise Lost*." *MLN*, XLI (1926), 51–54.

Attempts to show that it was possible for Denham to have brought into Parliament a freshly printed "sheet" of *Paradise Lost*, which he is said to have praised as "part of the noblest poem that ever was wrote in any language, or in any age."

999 Martin A. Larson. "Milton and Servetus: a Study in the Sources of Milton's Theology." *PMLA*, XLI (1926), 891–934.

Servetus the source of Milton's peculiarly unorthodox conceptions. Teaching of two men compared, especially in regard to Creation, Incarnation, Redemption, and Trinity. Based on assumption that Milton was familiar with *De Erroribus*.

999a Theodore H. Banks, Jr. "Miltonic Rhythm: A Study of the Relation of the Full Stops to the Rhythm of *Paradise Lost*." *PMLA*, XLII (1927), 140–45.

1000 T. W. Baldwin. "Sir John Denham and *Paradise Lost*." *MLN*, XLII (1927), 508–9.

Denham was a member of Parliament at the time when he is alleged to have praised *Paradise Lost*, according to story told by Jonathan Richardson.

See Banks, *MLN*, XLI, 51–54.

1001 Allan H. Gilbert. "Milton and the *Aminta.*" *MP*, XXV (1927), 95–99.

Parallelisms in *Paradise Lost* and *Samson Agonistes* show some semblances of borrowings from the parts of the *Aminta* on the "Age of Gold" and the earthly paradise.

1002 S. B. James. "Milton's Satan." *Catholic World*, CXXVI (1927), 62–65.

1003 J. Michelet. "Caractère d'Adam et d'Ève dans le *Paradis Perdu.* Adam est-il le héros du poème?" *Revue de l'Enseignment des Langues vivantes*, XL (1927), 328–33.

An illustrative examination.

1004 Harris F. Fletcher. Milton and Rashi. *JEGP*, XXVII (1928), 300–317.

Continuing a study of Semitic materials in Milton, the author demonstrates a realistic method of massing details (particularly in *Paradise Lost*, Books VII and VIII) that derived from Rashi's commentary on Buxtorf's *Biblia Hebraica Rabbinorum* (1618–20) and also certain structural formulas of *Paradise Lost* evidently developed under the same influence.

1004a A. L. Keith. "Personification in Milton's *Paradise Lost.*" *EJ*, XVII (1928), 399–409.

1004b Theodore Stenberg. "Sackville's Buckingham and Milton's Satan." *N & Q*, CLIV (1928), 100.

The theory of indebtedness is met by the reply on page 141.

VII. *PARADISE LOST:* SELECTED BOOKS AND ADAPTATIONS

1005 The State of Innocence, and the Fall of Man, Described in Milton's *Paradise Lost.* Rendered into Prose; with Historical, Philosophical, and Explanatory Notes. From the French of the Learned R. de St. Maur. By a Gentleman of Oxford. Trenton: published by William Robinson and John C. Moore; William & David Robinson, printers, 1803.

The Saint Maur translation (1729) was published after 1800 at Avignon, 1810 (5 vols.), 18mo; 1823, 12mo; at Limoges, 1847, 8vo; 1853, 12mo; 1864.

1006 M. P. King. The Intercession. A Sacred Oratorio from Milton's *Paradise Lost.* Performed at . . . . Covent Garden . . . . June 1, 1816. London, [1816]. Pp. 15.

1007 An Abridgement of *Paradise Lost.* By Mrs. Siddons. London: John Murray, 1822. Pp. iv+190.

Issued same year with new title-page: *The Story of Our First Parents; Selected from "Paradise Lost" for the Use of Young Persons.*

1008 Eliza W. Bradburn. The Story of *Paradise Lost* for Children. Portland, Maine, 1830. Pp. 143.

Quotation and summary.

1009 William Forde. The True Spirit of Milton's Versification Developed in a New and Systematic Arrangement of the First Book of *Paradise Lost,* with an Introductory Essay on Blank-verse in Which the New Plan of Arrangement Is Explained and Vindicated. London: Hurst, Chance & Co., 1831. Pp. lxviii+36.

"The language is divided into lines conforming with the sense; and by the place at which a line commences, its degree of connection with other lines, near or remote, is clearly indicated."

1010 The First Four Books of the *Paradise Lost.* With Notes Critical and Explanatory, Selected and Original; for the Use of Schools. By the Rev. J. R. Major. A Critique upon the *Paradise Lost,* by Mr. Addison [abridged]. London, 1835. Pp. 218.

1011 Select Poetical Pieces, with an Introductory Essay; a Logical Arrangement, or Practical Commentary on *Paradise Lost.* By G. A. Marquis. See 2d ed. Paris, 1842. Pp. 140.

Books I, II, and XI used, in part, to develop a method of correct reading by typographical indications of pauses, etc. The standard text form faces the new form on alternate pages.

1012 Charles Eyre. The Fall of Adam, from Milton's *Paradise Lost.* London and Liverpool, [1852]. Pp. v+98.

In four cantos, scattered parts from the entire poem reappear in paraphrase that is to remedy Milton's rough workmanship—due to blindness—and his overplus of learning. Valueless except as a curiosity of literature.

1013 The First Four Books of Milton's *Paradise Lost,* with Copious Notes . . . . by C. W. Connor. London, 1855. Pp. viii+176.

Many footnotes; good Index. Another edition, 1859.
Review in *Athen.,* March 10, 1855, p. 291.

1014 T. Goodwin. The Student's Practical Grammar of the English Language; together with a Commentary on the First Book of Milton's *Paradise Lost.* London, 1855. Pp. 309.

1015 Selections from *Paradise Lost,* with Notes Especially Adapted for Use in Elementary Schools. By R. Demaus. Edinburgh: Oliver & Boyd, 1857. Pp. 180.

Parts of all books, pp. 1–96; Notes, pp. 97–180.
Revised edition, 1859.

1016 Milton's *Paradise Lost.* Books I, II, IV, and VII. London: Christian Knowledge Society, [1859].

1017 The First [to the Fifth] Book of Milton's *Paradise Lost:* with a Prose Translation or Paraphrase, the Parsing of the More Difficult Words, Specimens of Analysis, and Numerous Illustrative Notes. By John Hunter. London, 1861–73.

Separate books issued at intervals for use of students preparing for Oxford.

1018 The First Book of Milton's *Paradise Lost.* With Notes on the Analysis and Parsing, Rules for Analysis, with Examples of Their Application, and a Life of Milton. Edited by C. P. Mason. London, 1861.

Book II, 1862.

1019 Paradise Lost. An Oratorio in Four Parts. The Words Selected from the Works of Milton and Music Composed by J. L. Ellerton. London, [1862]. Pp. 22.

1020 John Milton's *Paradise Lost:* the First and Second, with Part of the Eleventh, Book, with Grammatical and Explanatory Notes by Corréard. Paris, [1865]. Pp. 64.

English text; French footnotes.

1021 Milton's *Paradise Lost* [Books I and II]: with Copious Notes Explanatory and Critical, Partly Selected from Addison, Bentley .... and Partly Original; by J. Prendeville. Les deux premiers livres revus et adaptés à l'enseignement dans les Lycées .... par C. Witcomb. Paris, 1865. 8vo.

1022 R. E. Clark. The First Book of *Paradise Lost* in Rhyme. Lynchburg, Virginia, 1867. Pp. 32.

1023 An Introduction to the Study of Milton. Being the First Book of *Paradise Lost,* with Questions on the Text. By Alexander Monfries. Montrose, 1867. Pp. ii+106.

1024 Milton's *Paradise Lost.* Books I, II, and III. With Life and Glossary. London: Chambers, 1870.

Three parts, of 32 pages each.

1025 The Second Book of Milton's *Paradise Lost,* with Notes on the Analysis and on the Scriptural and Classical Allusions. By C. P. Mason. 2d ed. London, 1871. Pp. 70.

1026 The Third Book of Milton's *Paradise Lost,* with Notes on the Analysis, and on the Scriptural and Classical Allusions, a Glossary .... and a Life of Milton. By C. P. Mason. London, 1872.

1027 The First Six Books of *Paradise Lost,* with Notes by John Bradshaw. Madras, 1873.

Carefully modernized text, notes, and verbal index.

1028 *Paradise Lost,* Books I and II, and *Comus.* Edited by J. G. Davis. London, 1873,

1029 Paradise Lost. Books I [II, X]. .... With Introduction and Notes. Three parts. "Collins' School and College Classics." London, 1874.

1030 *Paradise Lost.* .... Book I. Edited .... by Francis Storr. "English School Classics." London, 1874. Pp. 62.

1031 Milton's *Paradise Lost.* Book I, with Copious Notes. Calcutta: Bose Press, 1879. Pp. 76.

1032 Milton's *Paradise Lost,* Books I and II. With Introduction, Notes, and Diagrams, by Homer B. Sprague. Boston: Ginn & Heath, 1879.

1033 *Paradise Lost*, Book I; with Prefatory and Explanatory Notes by E. F. Willoughby. New York, 1879. Pp. 94.

Contains also Book II with notes by Francis Storr, pp. 64. Published in 1880 in London ("Blackie's School Classics").

1034 Paradise Lost. Book I. . . . . With Notes Compiled by Suresachandra Deva. Calcutta: Bose, 1879. Pp. xxiv+227.

Book II, ll. 1–526, appeared in 1880.

1035 Milton's *Paradise Lost.* Books I and II. Edited by H. B. Sprague. Boston: Ginn & Heath, 1880. Pp. xxxii+113.

Reissued, with "Lycidas," in 1898.

1036 Paradise Lost. Oratorio in Three Parts, from the Poem of Milton. English Version by Josiah Pittman; Music by Rubinstein. London and Paris [printed, 1880]. Pp. 27.

1037 *Paradise Lost*, Book I. Edited . . . . by F. Storr. New Edition, [1883]. Pp. 64.

1038 Paradise Lost. . . . . The Numerous Mutilations of the Text Emended, and the Obnoxious Punctuation Entirely Revised, and Presented, All Collectively, with Notes and Preface; Also a Short Essay on the Intellectual Value of Milton's Works, and Some Remarks on the Origin of Mutilations. By Matthias Mull. London, 1884. Pp. cxxx+160.

The first six books, done by a Bentley without scholarship.
Reviews in *SR*, LVIII (1884), 570–71; *Spectator*, December 6, 1884, pp. 1635–36.

1039 Milton. *Paradise Lost*, Book I. Edited by H. C. Beeching. Oxford: Clarendon Press, 1887. Pp. 153.

Has Bridges' essay on the "Elements of Milton's Blank Verse." Notes.

1040 Milton's *Paradise Lost*, Books I and II. Edited, with Introduction and Notes, by M. Macmillan. London: Macmillan, 1887. Pp. xxix+141.

Reissued, 1891, 1893.
Review in *Athen.*, II (1887), 243.

1041 The First Book of Milton's *Paradise Lost*, with Notes . . . . a Glossary . . . . and a Life of Milton. By C. P. Mason. Fourth Edition. London: Bell & Sons, 1887. Pp. xviii+76.

"References in the notes have been corrected to make them suit the latest edition of my Latin Grammar."

1042 Milton: *Paradise Lost*, Book VII. Edited, with Introduction, Notes, and Questions for Examination by L. J. Woodroffe. London, 1888. Pp. 48.

1043 Milton. *Paradise Lost*, Book I. London: Nelson & Sons, 1889. Pp. 47.

1044 Milton's *Paradise Lost*, Books V–VIII. With Notes for the Use of Schools by C. M. Lumby. Cambridge: Deighton Bell & Co., 1892. Pp. 120.

1045 Milton's *Paradise Lost*, Books XI and XII. With Introduction, Notes, Glossary, and Index by A. W. Verity. Cambridge: Cambridge University Press, 1892. Pp. lxviii+106.

1046 Milton's *Paradise Lost.* Book II. Edited by E. K. Chambers. Oxford: Clarendon Press, 1893. Pp. 118.

Beeching's text.

1047 Milton's *Paradise Lost.* The Text Reduced. With Introduction and Notes by H. Millicent Hughes. London, 1894. 2 vols.

Prose summaries used to connect selected passages.

1048 *Paradise Lost*, Book III. Edited with Life, Introduction and Notes by F. Gorse. London: Blackie & Son, 1895. Pp. 64.

Book I, by the same editor, also out in 1895; Book II, 1897.

1049 *Paradise Lost* (Books I and II). . . . . "Eclectic English Classics." New York: American Book Co., [1895]. Pp. 90.

1050 Milton's *Paradise Lost.* Books III and IV. With Introduction and Notes by R. G. Oxenham. London: Bell & Sons, 1895. Pp. x+76.

1051 *Paradise Lost*, Books III and IV. Edited by J. Sargeaunt. London: Arnold, [1895]. Pp. xxxix+72.

The same editor brought out Books I and II in an undated volume, probably in 1896.

1052 Milton's *Paradise Lost.* Books I and II. Edited with Introduction and Notes by Albert S. Cook. Boston: Leach, Shewell & Sanborn, [1896]. Pp. xi+201.

Review by K. D. Bülbring, *Beiblatt*, VII, 306–7.

1053 Milton's *Paradise Lost.* Books I and II. Edited with Notes and an Introduction by Edward Everett Hale, Jr. New York: Longmans, Green & Co., 1896. Pp. 112.

Reprinted 1897 and 1898.

1054 Milton's *Paradise Lost.* Book III. Edited with Introduction and Notes by M. Macmillan. London: Macmillan & Co., 1896. Pp. xxxi+83.

Review in *Athen.*, February 8, 1896, p. 180.

1055 Paradise Lost. Books I–III . . . . with Introduction and Notes. "Riverside Literature Series." Boston: Houghton Mifflin Co., [1896].

From Moody's edition.

1056 Milton's *Paradise Lost*, Books VII and VIII. With notes by A. M. Trotter. London: Chambers, [1896].

1057 Paradise Lost. Books I and II. Edited by Henry W. Boynton. Boston: Allyn & Bacon, 1897. Pp. 124.

There is a prose summary of the remaining books.

1058 Milton's *Paradise Lost*. Books I and II. Edited with Introduction and Notes by Alexander S. Twombly. New York: Silver, Burdett & Co., 1897.

1059 Selections from *Paradise Lost*, including Books I and II Entire, and Portions of Books III, IV, VI, VII, and X. With Introduction, Suggestions for Study, and Glossary. Edited by Albert Perry Walker. Boston: D. C. Heath & Co., 1897. Pp. xi+270.

1060 Paradise Lost. Books I and II. With Introduction and Notes. Boston: Educational Publishing Co., [1898].

1061 Milton's *Paradise Lost*, Books I and II, Edited for School Use by Frank Edgar Farley. Chicago: Scott, Foresman & Co., 1898. Pp. 160.

1062 *Paradise Lost*. . . . . Books I and II. Edited . . . . by T. Page. London: Moffatt, 1899. Pp. 180.

1063 *Paradise Lost*, Books I and II, by John Milton; Edited for High School Use by William I. Crane. New York: Macmillan, 1900.

1064 Evans's Edition of Milton's *Paradise Lost*, Book III. Edited by E. H. Moreton . . . . and A. Howes. Redditch: Evans, [1900]. Pp. 76.

1065 *Paradise Lost*, I–IV. Edited with Introduction and Notes by J. L. Robertson. London: Blackwood, 1900. Pp. xi+179.

Review in *Athen.*, July 14, 1900, p. 55.

1066 Milton's *Paradise Lost*, Books I and II, with Introduction, Notes, etc. Edited by A. P. Walker. Boston: D. C. Heath & Co., 1900. Pp. 270.

1067 Milton's *Paradise Lost* [Books I–IV]. Edited by A. E. Ikin. London: Normal College Press, [1901].

Published as separate books; also, Volumes I and II together. Introduction and notes. Book IV issued in 1902; Book VI, in 1904.

1068 Milton: *Paradise Lost*. Book III, with Introduction and Notes by Thomas Page. London: Moffatt & Paige, 1901. Pp. 60.

1069 Milton's *Paradise Lost.* Book III. Edited by T. W. Berry and T. P. Marshall. Newport and London, [1901]. Pp. 109.

Text: prose paraphrase; notes.

1070 Helps to the Study of Milton's *Paradise Lost.* Book III, with Introduction and Notes by T. E. Margerison. London: Holland & Co., 1901. Pp. 87.

Interleaved for notes. Has full apparatus of helps.

1071 *Paradise Lost,* Book III. Edited by Alfred L. Cann. London: Waddington & Jackman, [1901]. Pp. 154.

A good school text.

1072 Milton's *Paradise Lost.* Book III. A Complete Paraphrase by E. E. Denney and P. L. Roberts. London, [1901]. Pp. 25.

Another pamphlet issue of Book III, by these editors, in 1901, gave the text "parsed and analysed."

1073 Milton's *Paradise Lost,* Book III. Edited by A. T. Flux. London: Nelson & Sons, 1901.

Notes; interleaved.

1074 Cusack's Edition of *Paradise Lost,* Book III, with Copious Explanatory Notes . . . . by W. R. Lever. London, 1901. Pp. 125.

1075 Milton's *Paradise Lost.* Books V and VI. With Notes and Introduction by Flora Masson. London: Dent & Co., [1902]. Pp. 84.

1076 Helps to the Study of Milton's *Paradise Lost,* Book VI, and Milton's "Lycidas." By A. L. Cann. London: Holland & Co., 1904.

Interleaved. Full notes; index to notes; specimen examinations.

1077 Milton: *Paradise Lost,* Book VI. With Introduction and Notes by H. B. Cotterill. London: Macmillan & Co., 1904. Pp. xxxvi+70.

Chronological table and good notes.

1078 Milton's *Paradise Lost,* Book VI. A Complete Paraphrase by Jean F Terry. "Normal Tutorial Series." London, [1904]. Pp. 23.

Published by the same press, edited by A. E. Ikin, 1905.

1079 Milton's *Paradise Lost,* Book VI. Parsed and Analysed by M. K. A. Beisiegel. London, [1905]. Pp. 100.

1080 *Paradise Lost,* Book V. Edited by A. E. Roberts. London: Blackie & Son, [1905]. Pp. xvi+84.

Review in *Athen.,* September 9, 1905, pp. 331–32.

1081 *Paradise Lost*, Book I. . . . . With a Short Biography by D. Salmon. London: Longmans, 1905. Pp. xi+34.

1082 *Paradise Lost*, Books I and II. By John Milton. With Introduction and Notes. New York: Educational Publishing Co., [1906]. Pp. 101.

1083 Paradise Lost. Books I and II. Edited . . . . by A. L. Cann. London: Holland, 1906. Pp. lxiv+100.

Elaborate notes and maps.

1084 Paradise Lost. A Drama in Four Acts, by Walter Stephens. London: Simpkin, Marshall, Hamilton, Kent & Co., [1906]. Pp. 48.

The right of production was refused on the ground that a "scriptural" text was ineligible for public license. Based on the poem and Milton's notes for the dramatic plan.

1085 *Paradise Lost*, Books I and II. Edited by A. F. Watt. London: University Tutorial Press, [1906]. Pp. xxiv+88.

1086 *Paradise Lost*, Book IV. Edited . . . . by Albert E. Roberts. London: Blackie, 1907. Pp. 84.

Book VI also issued the same year.

1087 Milton: *Paradise Lost*, Books IV and V. Edited by S. E. Goggin. London: University Tutorial Press, [1907]. Pp. 116.

1088 *Paradise Lost:* a Compendium of Milton's Twelve Books. Boston: Educational Publishing Co., [1907].

1089 *Paradise Lost*, I and II. . . . . Edited . . . . by W. I. Crane. New York: Macmillan, 1908. Pp. xxiii+118.

Well edited, with charts. Often reprinted.

1090 Milton's *Paradise Lost*. First edition. [London, 1908.]

A pamphlet of sixteen pages showing six title-pages and variants in the text. See Sandys' collation in the Pickering facsimile edition.

1091 The Story of Milton's *Paradise Lost*. Narrated for the Most Part in the Words of the Poet, by George Carter. London: Methuen, 1909. Pp. 148.

A good paraphrase, with some selections.

1092 Milton's *Paradise Lost*. Books V and VI. Edited by A. J. F. Collins and S. E. Goggin. London: University Tutorial Press, 1910. Pp. 114.

Books III and IV followed in 1912.

1093 *Paradise Lost*, Books I and II. Edited by C. F. Gregory. London: Bell, 1915. Pp. 93.

1094 Paradise Lost. Books I and II. With Introduction and Notes by J. C. Scrimgeour. London: Macmillan & Co., 1915. Pp. 186.

Good notes; Index.

1095 Milton: *Paradise Lost*, Book III. Edited by C. B. Wheeler. London. Oxford University Press, 1915. Pp. x+50.

1096 Milton's *Paradise Lost.* Books I and II. Edited for School Use by Frank Edgar Farley. Chicago: Scott, Foresman & Co., [1919].

1097 Milton's *Paradise Lost*, Abbreviated and Edited by D. C. Somervill. "The King's Treasuries of Literature." London, [1920]. Pp. 192.

Books I and II entire; short selections from the other books. A school reader.

1098 *Paradise Lost*, Book I. Edited with Life, Introduction, and Notes by F. Gorse. London: Blackie & Son, [1924]. Pp. 88.

VIII. *PARADISE REGAINED* AND OTHER POEMS

1099 *Paradise Regained*, a Poem. In Four Books, to Which Is Added *Samson Agonistes* and *Poems upon Several Occasions*. With a Tractate of Education. The Author, John Milton. H. Fenwick. [N. d.]

1100 Paradise Regained. New York: Mershon, [1800]. Pp. 192.

1101 Paradise Regained. New York: Caldwell, [1800]. Pp. 387.

1102 *Paradise Regained* . . . . with Notes of Various Authors, by Charles Dunster. London: G. Stafford, [1800]. Pp. vi+280.

A revised edition with new cuts and added notes. Dated Preface, April 12, 1800, refers to first edition and to copies of *Paradise Regained* used by the Wartons and Thyer.

1103 Paradise Regained. With the Life of the Author. London: J. Sharpe, 1809.

1104 *Paradise Regained*, by John Milton, with Select Notes Subjoined; to Which Is Added a Complete Collection of His Miscellaneous Poems Both English and Latin. London: Printed for F. C. and J. Rivington, 1817. Pp. 384.

1105 *Paradise Regained;* and Other Poems. London: J. Jones & Co., 1823. Pp. xvii+201.

Introductory study of literary qualities and origin. Contains also *Comus, Samson Agonistes*, and the English *Minor Poems*. Reissued, 1832.

1106 *Paradise Regained, Samson Agonistes, Comus*, and "Arcades." (*Poems on Several Occasions*.) [With Westall's plates.] London: J. Sharpe, 1827. 2 vols.

1107 *Paradise Regained* and Other Poems. Philadelphia: Perry, 1855. Pp. 479.

1108 *Paradise Regained* and Other Poems by John Milton. London: T. Nelson & Sons, 1825. Pp. xvii+201.

All the English poems except *Paradise Lost*.

1109 Milton's *Paradise Regained* and Other Poems. London: Bell & Daldy, 1861. Pp. vii+328.

Minor Poems; Samson Agonistes.

1110 Paradise Regained. . . . . Edited with an Introduction and Notes by C. S. Jerram. London, 1877. Pp. lii+193.

Notes, glossary, maps.

1111 Paradise Regain'd. A Poem in Four Books. To Which Is Added *Samson Agonistes*. Edited by C. S. Jerram. London, 1882.

1112 *Paradise Regained*, and *Samson Agonistes*. [With an Introduction by Henry Morley.] London: Cassell, 1886. Pp. 192.

Reissued 1889, the same year as their Addison criticisms, and again in 1905.

1113 *Paradise Regained*, *Samson Agonistes*, and the Minor English Poems. London: Religious Tract Society, 1886. Pp. 192.

1114 *Paradise Regained* and Other Poems. New York: Caldwell, [1890]. Pp. iv+387.

1115 *Paradise Regained* and Other Works. New York: Stokes, 1892. Pp. 221.

1116 *Paradise Regained*, "L'Allegro," "Il Penseroso," "Lycidas," *Comus*, *Samson Agonistes* and "Christmas Hymn." Boston: Perkins Institution and Massachusetts School for the Blind, 1892.

Raised type for the blind.

1117 Milton's *Paradise Regained*. With Introduction and Notes by K. Deighton. London: Bell & Sons, 1894. Pp. xiv+112.

1118 *Paradise Regained*, *Samson Agonistes*, and Other Poems. Edited by W. H. D. Rouse. London: Dent, [1898]. Pp. viii+371.

Based on Masson. Glossary; no notes.

1119 Milton. Paradise Regained. Edited by A. J. Wyatt. London: University Corr. College Press, [1898]. Pp. xxiii+96.

1120 Paradise Regain'd. A Poem in IV Books to Which Are Added *Samson Agonistes* & Poems Both English and Latin Compos'd on Several Occasions. The Author John Milton. Hammersmith: Doves Press, 1905. Pp. 344.

The 1645 text with added English poems from the 1673 edition, excepting the metrical versions of the Psalms and the four sonnets then unpublished. Slight corrections made and an alteration of the sonnet arrangement.

1121 John Milton. Paradise Regained. Decorated by Thomas Lowinsky. London: Fleuron, 1924. Pp. 80.

Only 350 copies, 3 on Japan vellum.
Published at the Cambridge University Press.
Review in *SP.*, XXII (April, 1926), 551.

1122 Milton. Paradise Regained. Edited by L. C. Martin. Oxford: Clarendon Press, 1925. Pp. xx+67.

Review in *Beiblatt*, XXXVI (1925), 337–38.

CRITICISM

1123 Gerald Donnelly. "Milton's *Paradise Regained.*" *Antiquary*, I (April, 1880), 190.

Question as to value of copy of *Paradise Regained* published by Johnson in 1765.

1124 On the Prosody of *Paradise Regained* and *Samson Agonistes*. Being a Supplement to the Paper "On the Elements of Milton's Blank Verse in Paradise Lost," Which Is Printed in the Rev. H. C. Beeching's Edition of *Paradise Lost*, Bk. I. Oxford: privately printed by Blackwell, 1889. Pp. 12.

By Bridges.

1125 R. D. Miller. "Milton's Conception of the Temptation as Portrayed in *Paradise Regained.*" *MLN*, XV (1900), 202–5.

Agrees with Stopford Brooke that Milton did not understand the Temptations. Hence the lack of unity in *Paradise Regained*. Milton right in regarding the second temptation as objective. Subjective temptations were those which took into account Christ's mental state.

1126 E. Traeger. Milton's *Paradise Regained.* Prog. Werdau. 1900. Pp. 53.

1127 Edward Dowden. Paradise Regained. [In] *Milton Memorial Lectures.* Oxford, 1909. Pp. 191–210.

1128 Allan H. Gilbert. "The Temptation in *Paradise Regained.*" *PMLA*, XXX (1915), xiii–xiv.

Brief summary of paper read before the Association, December 30, 1914. Milton followed Biblical narrative closely. Banquet scene belongs to second, not to first temptation.

1129 ———. "The Temptation in *Paradise Regained.*" *JEGP*, XV (1916), 599–611.

Milton's work characterized by excellence of structure, compressed diction, and respect for exact details.

Milton expanded Luke's account of temptations by developing incidents already provided, not by adding new material. The banquet belongs to the second temptation, not to the first, and is one of the glories Satan offers.

IX. *SAMSON AGONISTES* AND ADAPTATIONS

1130 *Samson Agonistes:* a Tragedy. "Select Plays," Vol. VI, No. 3. Baltimore, 1804.

In verse; one act.

1131 Handel's Oratorio, *Samson.* The Words Chiefly from Milton. Composed in the Year 1742. The Additional Accompaniments by Mr. Perry. London: J. Hart, [1840]. Pp. 16.

1132 *Samson Agonistes* by John Milton. London: Christian Knowledge Society, [1869].

1133 Milton's *Samson Agonistes.* With Notes. London and Edinburgh: Chambers, [printed] 1870. Pp. 64.

1134 Milton's *Samson Agonistes* and "Lycidas." With . . . . Illustrative Notes . . . . by J. Hunter. London: Longmans & Co., 1870. Pp. xiii+92.

1135 Milton's *Samson Agonistes.* With Notes by . . . . A. J. Church. London: Seeley, Jackson & Halliday, 1872. Pp. 95.

1136 Milton's Imitation of a Greek Tragedy. *Samson Agonistes,* with Notes . . . . and a Glossary. . . . . By I. P. Fleming. London: Longmans & Co., 1876. Pp. x+139.

1137 Samson Agonistes. A Dramatic Poem . . . . with Introduction and Notes by W. Collins. London: Collins, 1873.

1138 Samson. [An oratorio by H. M. Schletterer.] Breitkopf and Hartel's *Textbibliothek,* No. 32 [1879].

1139 *Samson Agonistes,* Edited, with Introduction and Notes by John Churton Collins. Oxford: Clarendon Press, 1883. Pp. 94.

Reprinted in 1906 and 1915.

1140 Samson Agonistes. Edited, with Introduction and Notes, by C. S. Jerram. London: Rivington, 1890. Pp. xvi+106.

Review in *Athen.,* April 5, 1890, p. 434.

1141 Milton's *Samson Agonistes.* With Introduction and Notes by H. M. Percival. London: Macmillan & Co., 1890. Pp. xlvii+202.

Masson's text. Historical study of the diction.

1142 Milton's *Samson Agonistes.* With Introduction, Notes, Glossary, and Indexes by A. W. Verity. "Pitt Press Series." Cambridge: Cambridge University Press, 1892. Pp. lxvi+171.

Reprinted several times. Very full notes, with a glossary and index to the notes appended. The text is based on the two seventeenth-century editions.

1143 Milton's *Samson Agonistes*, with Church's Introduction and Milton's Preface. Edited by J. M. D. Meiklejohn. New York, [1892]. Pp. 82.

Reprinted, 1893.

1144 Samson Agonistes. Edited by A. J. Wyatt. London: W. B. Clive & Co., [1892].

1145 *Samson Agonistes* by John Milton. Edited with Life, Introduction, Notes . . . . by T. Page. London: Moffatt & Paige, 1896. Pp. 184.

1146 Samson Agonistes. Edited by E. K. Chambers. London: Blackie & Son, 1897. Pp. 146.

1147 Milton: *Samson Agonistes.* Edited by E. H. Blakeney. Edinburgh and London: Blackwood & Sons, 1902. Pp. xxxiv+129.

1148 *Samson Agonistes*, a Dramatic Poem by John Milton. [New Rochelle, New York: Elston Press, 1904.] Pp. 65.

One hundred and twenty copies printed.

1149 *Samson Agonistes* by John Milton. With Introduction, Notes, and Glossary. Edited by A. J. Grieve. London: Dent & Co., [1904]. Pp. xiv +90.

1150 Milton. Samson Agonistes. Edited by C. T. Onions. London: Horace Marshall & Son, 1905. Pp. 84.

Few, but excellent, notes. Bibliography.

1151 Samson Agonistes. . . . . Edited by H. M. Percival. London: Macmillan & Co., 1916. Pp. xlvii+202.

CRITICISM

1152 O. Ilbert. Senarii Graeci [from *Samson Agonistes*]. Marlborough College prolusiones, 1863.

1153 A. Schmidt. Miltons dramatische Dichtungen, eine Vorlesung. Königsberg, 1864.

1154 [Change in the 1678 edition of *Samson Agonistes.*] *GM*, N.S., II (September, 1866), 332.

A change from the 1671 edition, made on account of the handwriting of Milton's secretary.

1155 Wolff. On Milton's *Samson Agonistes* Both as a Drama and an Illustration of the Poet's Life. Göttingen, 1871.

1156 On the Prosody of *Paradise Regained* and *Samson Agonistes*. Being a Supplement to the Paper "On the Elements of Milton's Blank Verse in Paradise Lost," Which Is Printed in the Rev. H. C. Beeching's Edition of *Paradise Lost*, Bk. I. Oxford: privately printed by Blackwell, 1889. Pp. 12.

By Bridges.

1157 H. V. Ross. *Samson Agonistes:* Its Autobiographical Character and Its Relation to Greek Drama. Manuscript dissertation at Cornell University. Pp. iv+237.

1158 Athen., April 4, 1900, p. 475.

An account of the first-known dramatic production of *Samson Agonistes*, presented by the Elizabethan Stage Society.

1159 Max Beerbohm. "*Samson Agonistes* and Zaza." *SR.*, LXXXIX (April, 1900), 489.

Comments on the production of Milton's work by the Elizabethan Stage Society. Play lacks dramatic quality.

1160 Ludwig Fränkel. "Klassisches (Shakespeare, Milton) auf der heutigen Londoner Bühne." *ES*, XXVIII (1900), 479–80.

Comment on *Samson Agonistes*, "a poem of sentiment and impressions, not a drama."

1161 R. Garnett. [On an emendation by M. W. Sampson of *Samson Agonistes*, l. 218.] *Athen.*, December 28, 1901, p. 878.

See also W. A. Craigie, *Athen.*, January 18, 1902, p. 84.

1162 George Sampson. "Emendation in Milton's *Samson.*" *Ibid.*, January 11, 1902, p. 50.

Rejects emendation as made by M. W. Sampson and accepted by Garnett.

1163 Robert Bridges. "Extraordinary." *Ibid.*, July 18, 1903, pp. 93–94.

Comment on *Samson Agonistes*, l. 1383.

1164 Ernest Dupuy. "Les origines littéraires d'Alfred de Vigny." *RHL*, X (1903), 373–412.

Milton, pp. 391–401.
Milton's influence strong in Éloa; Vigny's Samson very different from Milton's.

1165 Macmillan Brown. The *Samson Agonistes* of Milton. New Zealand and London, 1905.

The personal picture of Milton in *Samson Agonistes* his theme.

1166 Jeanne Stengers. "Le *Samson* de Milton et de Vondel." *Revue de l'université de Bruxelles*, X (1905), 261–84.

Puts *Samson* in 1671. Indicates that Vondel and Milton were not well known in France; author is trying to arouse interest in their works.

1167 F. C. L. Van Steenderen. "Vondel's Place as a Tragic Poet." *PMLA*, XX (1905), 546–66.

Vondel's influence on Milton and others is epical and lyrical rather than dramatic. This fact is due to his mistaken conception of tragedy.

1168 Albert S. Cook. "*Samson Agonistes*, ll. 1665–66." *MLN*, XXI (1906), 78.

Parallels to Horace *Odes* iii. 24. 6; to Aeschylus *Prometheus*, ll. 1076–79; to Sophocles *Antigone*, ll. 343–47.

1169 G. C. Moore Smith. "Milton, *Samson Agonistes*, 373." *MLR*, III (1907), 74.

The definition of the word "appoint": prescribe or determine the course of; pin down to a fixed course.

1170 X. "Samson Agonistes." *Athen.*, December 19, 1908, p. 799.

An account of an excellent presentation by the British Academy.

1171 Programme of Performance of *Samson Agonistes* at the Theatre, Burlington Gardens, on December 15, 1908. Produced by W. Poll under Invitation of the British Academy. Pp. 8.

Printed with summaries of papers read.

1172 Sir R. C. Jebb. *Samson Agonistes* and the Hellenic Drama. London: published for the British Academy by H. Frowde, [1908]. Pp. 8.

Published also in *Proceedings of the British Academy, 1907–8*, pp. 341–48. Greater as a poem than as drama: not Hellenic, but Hebraic in spirit.

1173 Sir Walter Raleigh. "Milton's Last Poems." *Living Age*, CCLX (1909), 251–53.

Milton is his most mature self in his last poems. Sense of loneliness and remoteness from human sympathy conveyed by these is unparalleled in literature.

1174 Allan H. Gilbert. "*Samson Agonistes*, 1096." *MLN*, XXIX (1914), 161–62.

"With" or "wish"?

1175 P. H. Epps. "Two Notes on English Classicism." *SP*, XIII (1916), 190–96.

Study of Milton's classicism in *Samson Agonistes*.

1176 Edward J. Thompson. "Samson Agonistes." *LQR*, CXXV (1916), 244–54.

Samson is almost a perfect drama of its kind. Lack of real artistic perception in modern times responsible for its obscurity. Milton a poet's poet, one not popular among critics.

1177 James Waddell Tupper. "The Dramatic Structure of *Samson Agonistes*." *PMLA*, XXXV (1920), 375–89.

Supports Johnson's attack on *Samson Agonistes* as a drama. Points out faults in dramatic structure of the work.

See refutation by P. F. Baum, *PMLA*, XXXVI, 354–71.

1178 Paull Franklin Baum. "*Samson Agonistes* Again." *Ibid.*, XXXVI (1921), 354–71.

Defends dramatic structure of *Samson Agonistes* as in accord with Aristotle's requirements. Chief fault is in theme. Samson not a true tragic hero. Hebraic conception of divine justice antithetical to true tragic spirit.

1179 E. C. Knowlton. "Causality in *Samson Agonistes*." *MLN*, XXXVII (1922), 333–39.

Answers Baum, *PMLA*, XXXV, 375–89. Chief fault of *Samson Agonistes* as drama is that it lacks a middle.

1180 Walter Clyde Curry. "*Samson Agonistes* Yet Again." *Sewanee Review*, XXXII (1924), 336–52.

Not a Greek drama but a Christian drama of the highest order, with great tragic beauty.

1181 J. W. Kilgo. "Hebrew Samson and Milton's Samson." *Methodist Quarterly Review*, LXXIII (1924), 312–16.

Milton's Samson great because copied from the Hebrew Samson.

1182 James Holly Hanford. *Samson Agonistes* and Milton in Old Age. *Studies in Shakespeare, Milton, and Donne*. New York: Macmillan, 1925. Pp. 232.

Pages 167–89. A significant unifying of materials that shows Milton's intellectual and spiritual changes, particularly the enunciation through Samson of his final acceptances of divine law.

Reviews in *RES*, II, 475–79; *MLN*, XLI, 264–68; *ES*, LXIII (1928), 114–19; *JEGP*, XXV (1926), 426–27; *ibid.*, XXVII (1928), 93–96.

1183 E. E. Kreipe. Milton's *Samson Agonistes*. Halle: Niemeyer, 1926. Pp. ix+69.

Studien zur englischen Philologie, Heft 70.

Bibliography, pp. vii–ix.

A search for personal revelations through *Samson Agonistes* that fails to make it a sustained allegory. Sympathetic study, but too definite in conclusions.

Reviews in *Beiblatt*, XXXIX (1928), 364–67; *RES*, IX, 117–18.

1184 Chilton L. Powell. "Milton Agonistes." *Sewanee Review*, XXXIV (1926), 169–83.

1185 W. Brewer. "Two Athenian Models for *Samson Agonistes*." *PMLA*, XLII (1927), 910–20.

Uses Aeschylus' *Prometheus Bound* and Sophocles' *Oedipus at Coloneus* for good parallels.

1186 Grace Faulks Fretz. "*Samson Agonistes:* an Appreciation." *Methodist Review*, CX (1927), 103–8.

1186a E. M. Clark. Milton's Conception of Samson. *University of Texas Studies in English*, VIII (1928), 88–99.

X. THE PROSE WORKS

1. COLLECTED PROSE WORKS

1187 The Prose Works of John Milton; with a Life of the Author, Interspersed with Translations and Critical Remarks, by C. Symmons. London: J. Johnson, 1806. 7 vols.

The standard edition until the "Bohn Library" edition appeared.

1188 The Prose Works of Milton, Containing His Principal Political and Religious Pieces, with New Translations and an Introduction by George Burnett. London: Miller, 1809. 2 vols.

Review in *Monthly Review*, LXV (1811), 247–48.

1189 The Prose Works of John Milton; with an Introductory Review by R. Fletcher. London, 1833. Pp. xliii+963.

Published by Westley & Davis.
Frequently reprinted in stereotype (1834, 1835, etc.).
Index added in the edition published by William Ball, 1838.

1190 Milton. I. Prose Works. II. Poetical Works. Paris: A. and W. Galignani, [*ca.* 1836].

From the London edition of Westley & Davis; two volumes in one.

1191 The Prose Works of John Milton, with a Biographical Introduction. Edited by R. W. Griswold. Philadelphia: Hooker, 1845. 2 vols. Pp. xii+548+550.

Same plates used by Wiley & Putnam, New York, 1847, and by J. W. Moore, Philadelphia, 1851 and 1853.

The editor takes Brydges to task for blaming Milton for his opinions on kingship, adding that "in the United States, where the divine right of any man to oppress his fellows is not held, we think differently."

1192 The Prose Works of John Milton. . . . . With a Preface, Preliminary Remarks, and Notes, by J. A. St. John. "Bohn's Standard Library." London: Bell & Son, [1848]–1881. 5 vols.

Original issues, only Volume V by Bell & Son.

Volume IV has a revised edition of Sumner's translation of *De doctrina*. Frequently reprinted.

Reviews in *Literary World*, IV (1849), 350–51; *New Monthly Magazine*, XLVI (1836), 509.

193 The Works of John Milton in Verse and Prose, Printed from the Original Editions with a Life of the Author by the Rev. John Mitford. London: Pickering, 1851. 8 vols.

Lacks *De doctrina* and some minor items.

194 The Prose Works of John Milton. New York: Hurst & Co., [1865].

195 The Prose Works of John Milton. Philadelphia: Caxton Press, 1864. 2 vols.

2. INDIVIDUAL PROSE WORKS AND SELECTIONS

196 Milton's *Treatise on Education. To Master Samuel Hartlib.* Boston: Directors of the Old South Work, [1800].

197 Occasional Essays on Various Subjects, Chiefly Political and Historical. London: Wilks, 1809. Pp. 607.

Contains *Areopagitica*, pp. 189–246, and *Of True Religion*, pp. 416–30. Some interesting evidences of religious toleration appear in the notes.

198 "Mr. J. Milton's *Character of the Long Parliament.*" *Harleian Miscellany*, V (1810), 576–79.

The part of *The History of Britain*, Book III, that was excised by the licenser in 1670.

199 *Thoughts on True Religion, Heresy, Schism, and Toleration* by John Milton. . . . To Which Are Added Remarks on Essentials in Religion, Charitableness and Uncharitableness, Extracted from the Writings of Isaac Watts. Edited by B. Fowler. Harlow: Fowler, 1811. Pp. 32.

An attempt to discredit sectarianism.

200 "Reflections on the Civil War in England." [In] *Select Tracts Relating to the Civil Wars in England in the Reign of King Charles the First.* London: R. Wilks, 1815. 2 vols.

See Vol. II, pp. 805–15. From *The History of Britain*, Book III; edited by F. Maseres.

201 The History of Britain, That Part Especially Now Call'd England, from the First Traditional Beginning, Continu'd to the Norman Conquest. London: R. Wilks, 1818. Pp. xliii+408.

Phillips' life. Edited by F. Maseres.

Preface; index to text. *The Tenure of Kings and Magistrates* (pp. 297–342) has, in inverted commas, Milton's 1650 additions as "omitted in every former edition of the author's works." *The Ready and Easy Way* and *Brief Notes upon a Late Sermon* are also included.

1202 Areopagitica. With Prefatory Remarks, Copious Notes and Excursive Illustrations by T. Holt White. To Which Is Subjoined a Tract *Sur la Liberté de la Presse, imité de l'Anglois de Milton par le Comte de Mirabeau.* London: R. Hunter, 1819. Pp. cxlix+311.

Extensive footnotes and illustrative parallels. A list of editions.

1203 Milton's Plan of Education, in His Letter to Hartlib (Now Very Scarce), with the Plan of the Edinburgh Institution Founded Thereon [by William Scott]. Edinburgh: W. Laing, 1819. Pp. 47.

A school proposed for the study of electricity, animal chemistry, and experimental philosophy; also the publication of books on Gothic and Anglo-Saxon.

Republished in the *Pamphleteer* (London), XVII (1820), [121]-56.

1204 *The Doctrine and Discipline of Divorce:* in Two Books: also *The Judgment of Martin Bucer; Tetrachordon;* and an Abridgement of *Colasterion.* With a Preface Referring to Events of Deep and Powerful Interest at the Present Crisis; Inscribed to the Earl of Liverpool. By a Civilian. London: Sherwood, 1820. Pp. xv+430.

Review in *Monthly Review,* XCIII (1820), 144-58.

1205 Joannis Miltoni Angli *De Doctrina Christiana* libri duo posthumi, quos ex schedis manuscriptis deprompsit et typis mandari primus curavit C. R. Sumner. Cantabrigiae: Typis Academicis, 1825.

The first issue. Translated by Sumner in the same year.

Reviews in *North American Review,* XXII, 364-73; *Monthly Review,* CVII (1825), 273-94.

1206 A Selection from the English Prose Works of John Milton. Edited by F. Jenks. Boston: Bowles & Dearborn, 1826. 2 vols.

Review in *North American Review,* XVI (1827), 73-89.

1207 The Poetry of Milton's Prose; Selected from His Various Writings; with Notes and an Introductory Essay [by C.]. London, 1827. Pp. lxvi+138.

Introductory essay. Advertisement dated at Huntingdon, January 29, 1827.

Review in *GM,* XCVII (1827), 621; *Monthly Review,* N.S., V, 463-64.

1208 Joannis Miltoni Angli *De Doctrina Christiana* libri duo posthumi, quos ex schedis manuscriptis deprompsit et typis mandari primus curavit C. R. Sumner. Brunsvigiae: Typis Academicis, 1827. Pp. viii+544.

1209 John Milton's Last Thoughts on the Trinity. Extracted from His Posthumous Work, *A Treatise on Christian Doctrine.* London: R. Hunter, 1828. Pp. xii+90.

210 Milton's Familiar Letters. Translated from the Latin, with Notes by John Hall. Philadelphia: E. Littell, 1829. Pp. 120.

Brief footnotes and Index, 6 pages. Many small errors of dating and in grammar. Reviews in *American Quarterly Review*, V (1829), 301–10; *Revue encyclopédique* (by Louise Sw. Belloc), September, 1829, p. 637; *Southern Review*, VI (1830), 198–206.

211 Considerations Touching the Likeliest Means To Remove Hirelings out of the Church. London: J. Cleave, [1834]. Pp. 47.

A note in the British Museum copy quotes the *Times* for November 11, 1834, praising the edition.

212 *Areopagitica:* a Speech for the Liberty of Unlicensed Printing, to the Parliament of England. London: J. Cleave, [1834]. Pp. 48.

213 Select Prose Works of Milton. . . . . With a Preliminary Discourse and Notes by J. A. St. John. "The Masterpieces of English Prose Literature." London, 1836. 2 vols.

Includes selections headed "Account of His Own Studies," "Apology for His Early Life and Writings," "Tractate on Education," *Areopagitica*, "Tenure of Kings," *Eikonoklastes*, "Divisions of the Commonwealth," "Delineation of a Commonwealth," "Mode of Establishing a Commonwealth," "Familiar Letters."

214 Extracts from the Prose Works of John Milton, Containing the Whole of His Writings on the Church Question. Now First Published Separately. Edinburgh: Tait, 1836. Pp. vii+316.

215 The Schoolmaster. Essays on Practical Education Selected from the Works of Ascham, Milton, Locke, and Butler. London: Knight, 1836. 2 vols.

Of Education, pp. 106–21.

216 Considerations Touching the Likeliest Means To Remove Hirelings out of the Church. Aberdeen: Murdoch, 1839. Pp. ii+35.

217 Tracts for the People. No. 1. London, 1839. Pp. 36.

Has *A Treatise of Civil Power*, part of *A Treatise of True Religion*, and the sonnets to Cromwell and to Sir Henry Vane. Two editions in 1839.

218 Tracts for the People. No. 10. London, 1840. Pp. 48.

Areopagitica.

219 On the Civil Power in Ecclesiastical Causes. The author J. M. With a Historical Sketch and Notes [by C. R. E.]. *Buried Treasures*, Part II, London, 1851. Pp. xii+1–28.

220 Considerations Touching the Likeliest Means To Remove Hirelings out of the Church. *Buried Treasures*, Part II. London, 1851. Pp. 29–68.

1221 John Milton's Last Thoughts on the Trinity Extracted from His Posthumous Work Entitled *A Treatise on Christian Doctrine.* New Edition. London: Whitfield, 1859.

See Item 1209.

1221a W. Douglas Hamilton. Original Papers, Illustrative of the Life and Writings of John Milton, Including Sixteen Letters of State Written by Him, Now First Published. London: Camden Society, 1859.

Reviews in *Edinburgh Review,* CXI (1860), 312–47; *Athen.,* December 17, 1859, pp. 810–11.

1222 Selections from the Prose Writings of John Milton. Edited, with Memoir, Notes, and Analyses, by the Rev. S. Manning. "Bunyan Library." London, 1862. Pp. lxv+309.

1223 Treasures from the Prose Writings of John Milton. Boston: Ticknor & Fields, 1866. Pp. viii+486.

Review in *Nation,* III (1866), 471.

1224 John Milton. *Areopagitica,* 24 November 1644. Preceded by Illustrative Documents. Carefully edited by Edward Arber. "English Reprints." London, 1868.

Other issues in 1869, 1895, 1903.

1225 Britain under Trojan, Roman, Saxon Rule. By John Milton.—England under Richard III. By Sir T. More.—The Reign of Henry VII. By F. Bacon. . . . . Verbatim reprint from Kennet's England, Ed. 1719. [Edited by A. Murray.] London: A. Murray & Son, 1870. Pp. 424.

Milton text, pp. 9–192. Footnotes correcting Milton; final note stating that many other corrections might be added from Sheringham's *De Gentes Anglorum* and Langhorne's *Antiquitates Albionenses.* A stereotype reprint (1878) by Ward, Locke & Co.

1226 Selections from the Prose Works of John Milton. With Critical Remarks and Elucidations. Edited by James G. Graham. London: Hurst & Blackett, 1870. Pp. 338.

Chronological order, with preliminary chapters. Appendix, a prose "transversion" of Lord Lytton's poem on Milton.

1227 A Modern Version of Milton's *Areopagitica:* with Notes, Appendix, and Tables. By S. Lobb. Calcutta: Thacker, Sprinker & Co., 1872.

In simple English, for Bengalese students.

1228 Autobiography of John Milton; or Milton's Life in His Own Words. Edited by J. J. G. Graham. London: Longmans, Green & Co., 1872. Pp. viii+181.

Review in *Athen.,* July 13, 1872, pp. 42–43.

229 Milton's *Areopagitica:* . . . . with Notes for the Use of Schools. By T. G. Osborn. London: Longmans & Co., 1873. Pp. 109.

Review in *LQR*, XL (1873), 236–37.

230 Milton's *Areopagitica*. Edited with Introduction and Notes by J. W. Hales. Oxford: Clarendon Press Series, 1866. Pp. xliv+159.

Still a standard edition in the revised edition of 1882. Reprinted 1886, 1898, 1917. Review in *Athen.*, March 20, 1875, pp. 387–88.

231 Georg Weber. "John Miltons prosaische Schriften über Kirche." [In] *Geschichte des Reformations-Zeitalters*, Leipzig, 1874. Pp. 398–616.

Also in *Historisches Taschenbuch*, Dritte Folge, 3 and 4. *See* Item 1288.

232 A Common-place Book of John Milton. Reproduced by the Autotype Process from the Original Manuscript in the Possession of Sir Frederick J. U. Graham. . . . . With an Introduction by A. J. Horwood. London: privately printed, 1876. 87 sheets, folio.

Only 100 copies printed.

233 A Common-place Book of J[ohn] Milton, and a Latin Essay and Latin Verses Presumed To Be by Milton. Edited . . . . by A. J. Horwood. "The Camden Society," N.S., Vol. XVI. Westminster, 1876. Pp. xx+69.

Revised edition (1877), pp. xxvi+68.
Reviews in *Acad.*, March 25 and April 1, 1876, p. 308; *Athen.*, September 9, p. 331.

234 A Small Tractate of Education. By John Milton. Written about the Year 1650. Syracuse, New York: C. W. Bardeen, 1882.

235 Milton's Tractate on Education. A Facsimile Reprint from the Edition of 1673. Edited . . . . by Oscar Browning. "Pitt Press Series." Cambridge: Cambridge University Press, 1883. Pp. xxv+43.

Excellent notes. Reprinted, 1890, 1897.

236 Selected Prose Writings of John Milton, with an Introductory Essay by E. Myers. London, 1883. Pp. xxx+253.

Only 50 copies printed. Light criticism and some unauthenticated assertions in the essay. Reissued, 1884, and published by Appleton & Co. (New York), 1889.
Reviews in *Athen.*, September 20, 1884, pp. 359–60; *Nation*, November 20, p. 444.

237 Milton's *Areopagitica*. Edited by Henry Morley. "Morley's Universal Library." London, 1886.

238 The English Prose Writings of John Milton. . . . . Edited by Henry Morley. "Carisbrooke Library," Vol. V. 1889.

Selections.

1239 *Areopagitica;* a Speech of Mr. John Milton for the Liberty of Unlicensed Printing, to the Parliament of England. With an Introduction by James Russell Lowell. New York: Grolier Club, 1890.

1240 Prose of Milton. Selected and Edited, with an Introduction, by Richard Garnett. "The Scott Library." London, [1894]. Pp. xxii+256.

1241 Tractate of Education. Edited with an Introduction and Notes by Edward E. Morris. London: Macmillan, 1895. Pp. xlv+50.

Careful introductory study.

Review in *Athen.*, August 31, 1895, p. 287.

1242 A Free Commonwealth, by John Milton. The Ready and Easy Way To Establish a Free Commonwealth, and the Excellence Thereof, Compared with the Inconvenience and Dangers of Readmitting Kingship in This Nation. [First published in 1660.] Boston: Directors of the Old South Work, [1896]. Pp. 24.

1243 John Milton. Areopagitica. Edited by Ernest Rhys. "Literary Pamphlets," Vol. II. London, 1897.

1244 An Introduction to the Prose and Poetical Works of John Milton, Comprising All the Autobiographic Passages of His Works . . . . *Comus*, "Lycidas" and *Samson Agonistes.* With Notes and Forewords by Henry Corson. New York: Macmillan Co., 1899. Pp. xxxii+303.

1245 *Areopagitica* and Other Tracts. Edited by C. E. Vaughan. "Temple Classics." London: Dent, 1900.

Of Education and selections from four other pamphlets. Reprinted, 1907.

1246 Selections, Chiefly Autobiographical, from the Pamphlets and Letters, with the Tractate on Education and *Areopagitica.* New York: Doubleday, Page & Co., 1901. Pp. xii+211.

1247 H. Fernow. Milton's Letters of State. Hamburg: Lütcke & Wulff, [1903]. Pp. 51.

Literae pseudo-senatus anglicani.

1248 Areopagitica. Border and Initial Letters Designed by Lucien Pissarro and Engraved on Wood by Esther Pissarro. Hammersmith: Eragny, 1904.

Of the 226 copies on handmade paper, all but 40 were destroyed by fire. A fresh issue of 160 copies was made.

1249 Milton's *Areopagitica.* Edited by J. E. B. Allen. London: Normal Tutorial Series, [1904]. Pp. xii+96.

1250 Milton: *Areopagitica.* Edited with Notes by H. B. Cotterill. New York: Macmillan Co., 1904. Pp. xlii+118.

251 *Areopagitica: a Speech for the Liberty of Unlicenc'd Printing, to the Parlament of England.* [London: Eragny Press, 1904.] Pp. 40.

Original text and spelling.

252 Milton's *Areopagitica.* Hammersmith: Doves Press, 1907. Pp. 73

Limited edition.

253 Milton on the Son of God and the Holy Spirit, from his *Treatise on Christian Doctrine;* with Introduction by Alexander Gordon. London: British and Foreign Unitarian Association, 1908. Pp. xvi+136.

254 *Reason of Church Government, an Apology for Smectymnus, Of Education,* Preface to *Paradise Lost,* Preface to *Samson Agonistes.* [In] J. E. Spingarn, *Critical Essays of the Seventeenth Century* (3 vols.). Oxford, 1908. Vol. I.

255 John Milton's Treatise on Education. Edited with Preface by Paul Chauvet. Paris, 1909.

Contains a zinc reproduction of Milton's list of pamphlets given to the Bodleian. The 1664 text; footnotes; new punctuation and paragraphing. No deep understanding of Milton shown in criticism.

256 *Essays, Civil and Moral* and *The New Atlantis,* by Francis Bacon; *Areopagitica* and Tractate on Education, by John Milton; *Religio Medici,* by Sir Thomas Browne, with Introductions, Notes and Illustrations. "Harvard Classics," Vol. III. New York: P. F. Collier & Son, [*ca.* 1909]. Pp. 347.

257 *The Tenure of Kings and Magistrates,* by John Milton; edited with Introduction and Notes by William Talbot Allison. "Yale Studies in English." New York: Holt & Co., 1911. Pp. liii+185.

Reviews in *Beiblatt* (by Th. Mühe). XXV, 208–10; *Archiv,* CXXVII (1911), 480.

258 *Of Education; Areopagitica; The Commonwealth,* by John Milton; with Early Biographies of Milton, Introduction, and Notes. Edited by Laura E. Lockwood. Boston: Houghton Mifflin Co., [1911]. Pp. lxxxvi+205.

An excellent school text. English edition (Harrap), 1912.

259 Areopagitica. The Preface [by Mr. Thomson] and Milton's Arms Are Here Reproduced from an Edition Dated 1780. Printed for [and edited by] Sidney Humphries. London, 1911.

Issued in 1911, 500 copies. Unsold copies with addenda reissued in 1912. In 1913, with Saxo's *Amleth,* as translated by Oliver Elton, and Shakespere's *Hamlet,* 10 copies only bound together. Unusually able editing.

Review in *Athen.,* July 22, 1911, p. 107.

1260 *The Ready and Easy Way To Establish a Free Commonwealth*, by John Milton; Edited with Introduction, Notes, and Glossary, by Evert Mordecai Clark. "Yale Studies in English." New Haven: Yale University Press, 1915. Pp. lxxi+198.

Review in *AHR*, XXV (1920), 743–44; *ES*, LIV (1920), 432–37.

1261 *Of Reformation Touching Church Discipline in England*, by John Milton. Edited with Introduction, Notes, and Glossary by Will Taliaferro Hale. "Yale Studies in English." New Haven: Yale University Press, 1916. Pp. lxxxix+224.

Reviews in *ES*, LII (1918), 385–90; *Archiv*, CXXXV (1916), 469, and CXLV (1923), 160; *AHR*, XXII (1917), 145–46; *Beiblatt*, XXVIII (1917), 115–17; *MP*, XV (1917), 60–63.

1262 Animadversions upon the Remonstrant's Defence against Smectymnuus. Cambridge: Norman McLean, 1919.

1263 *Areopagitica*, with a Commentary by Sir Richard C. Jebb, and with Supplementary Material. "Pitt Press Series." Cambridge: Cambridge University Press, 1918. Pp. xl+130.

Reviews in *Athen.*, January, 1919, p. 35; *SR*, CXXVII, 65.

1264 Milton. Poetry and Prose, with Essays [abridged] by Johnson, Hazlitt, Macaulay. With an Introduction by A. M. D. Hughes and Notes by Various Scholars. Oxford: Clarendon Press, 1920. Pp. xii+224.

Edited by Beatrice G. Madan. Portraits and facsimile title-pages.
An excellent selection for school purposes. Notes, pp. 189–224.

1265 The Digression [in Milton's *The History of Britain*, Book III]. Manuscript of the XVIIth Century, Clearly Written upon Six Leaves of Paper. Catalogue No. 215 (1923) of Messrs. Ellis, London.

Now in Harvard Library.

1266 Milton's Prose Selected and Edited with an Introduction by M. M. Wallace. Oxford: Oxford University Press, 1925. Pp. xxix+476.

American edition, 1926. An excellent Introduction. Old punctuation; modern spelling.

Reviews in *RAA*, IV (1926–27), 241–42; *Beiblatt*, XXXIX (1928), 362–64. In *TLS*, December 2, 1925, the review covers press censorship from Sixtus IV to present times.

1267 J. Milton. Areopagitica. "The Noël Douglas Replicas." London: Noël Douglas, 1927. Pp. 40.

1268 *Areopagitica* and Other Prose Works of John Milton. "Everyman's Library." London: Dent, 1927. Pp. xv+306.

Introduction by C. E. Vaughan. Selections also from *Of Education, Of Reformation, An Apology, The Ready and Easy Way, The Doctrine and Discipline, Meditations upon Divine Justice,* and autobiographical extracts.

1269 William Haller. *Areopagitica,* and Other Prose Writings. "Modern Readers' Series." New York: Macmillan, 1927. Pp. xvii+170.

1270 Areopagitica. [In] *British Poetry and Prose, a Book of Readings,* edited by P. R. Lieder, R. M. Lovett, and R. K. Root. Boston: Houghton, Mifflin Co., 1928. Pp. xxxvi+1346+xvi.

Footnotes of interest; text, pp. 399–423.

1271 Milton on Education. The Tractate *Of Education* with Supplementary Extracts from Other Writings of Milton. "Cornell Studies in English," Vol. XII. New Haven: Yale University Press, 1928. Pp. xiv+369.

Introduction, notes on the tractate, and selections that present Milton's theories in reference to contemporary ideas.

CRITICISM

1272 James Harrington. The Censure of the Rota upon Mr. Milton's Book Intituled *The Ready and Easy Way To Establish a Free Commonwealth.* Printed at London by Paul Giddy, printer to the Rota, at the sign of the Windmill in Turn-again lane, 1660.

In *Harleian Miscellany,* IV (1809), 188–95.

1273 Archibald Bruce. A Critical Account of the Life, Character and Discourses of Mr. Alexander Morus. Edinburgh, 1813. Pp. 352.

The Salmasius controversy recounted. Appended is Diodati's letter to Salmasius from Geneva.

1274 T. Holt White. A Review of Johnson's Criticism on the Style of Milton's English Prose: with Strictures on the Introduction of Latin Idioms into the English Language. London: R. Hunter, 1818. Pp. 87.

1275 Monthly Review, XCIII (1820), 144–58.

Milton's ideas on divorce discussed in a review of an 1820 edition of *The Doctrine and Discipline of Divorce.*

1276 "Milton's History of England." *Retrospective Review,* VI (1822), I, 87–100.

Extracts of the most interesting paragraphs in *The History of Britain.*

1277 [A Latin manuscript believed to be by Milton.] *GM*, XCIV (February, 1824), 165.

Description of a manuscript in Latin discovered at the State Paper Office. Believed to be in handwriting of Milton's nephews.

1278 "Milton's *Areopagitica*." *Retrospective Review*, IX (1824), 1–19.

Ideas summarized, with extracts to furnish the casual reader a knowledge of the work.

1279 Edinburgh Review, XLII (1825), 304–46.

A comment on *De doctrina;* also a history of the manuscript. Favorable survey of Milton's poetry and his political views.

1280 [Bibliographical account of Milton's *Prose Works*.] *Retrospective Review*, XIV (1826), 282–305.

Likewise in *Museum*, XI (August, 1827), 114–23.
Based on Preface to Pickering's edition.

1281 Gentleman's Magazine, XCVI (1826), 609–12.

A review of the treatise *On True Religion*, by Thomas Burgess, with a prefatory note on "Milton's Religious Principles and Unimpeachable Sincerity."

1282 William Ellery Channing. Remarks on the Character and Writings of John Milton; Occasioned by the Publication of His Lately Discovered *Treatise on Christian Doctrine*. Boston: Butts & Co., 1826 Pp. 51.

Reprinted from the *Christian Examiner*, III (1826); type reset and called therefore the "second edition." Reprinted for E. Rainford (London), 1826; 2d ed., 1828; 3d ed., 1828; another ed., 1830. The 1826 edition has Jenks's proposals for publishing selections from Milton's prose works.

Reviews in *Edinburgh Review*, L (1829), 125–44; *Monthly Review*, CXV, 471–78; *Edinburgh Review*, LXIX (1839), 214–30, of 3d ed.; *Fraser's Magazine*, XVII (1838), 627–35.

1283 Willard. Milton on Christian Doctrine. *North American Review*, XXII (1826), 364–73.

Milton's *De doctrina* valuable only for reader who wishes general survey of scriptural teachings. Critic is contemptuous of Milton's motives.

1284 "Milton's *Prose Works*." *Colburn's New Monthly Magazine*, XL (1834), 39–50.

Appreciative.

1285 Anonymous. Opinion de Milton sur la Trinité. Paris, 1842.

1286 F. W. P. Greenwood. The Miscellaneous Writings of F. W. P. Greenwood. Boston, 1846.

Criticism of Milton's prose works, pp. 208–26.

1287 Auguste Geoffroy. Étude sur les pamphlets politiques et religieux de Milton. Paris, 1848. Pp. 295.

Discussion of Milton's value as a defender of liberty. Questions the validity of his views in *Eikonoklastes*. Detailed bibliographical record of his prose works.

Review in *Athen.*, October 7, 1848, p. 1000.

1288 Georg Weber. John Miltons prosaische Schriften über Kirche, Staat und öffentliches Leben seiner Zeit. Ein literarisches und publizistisches Charakterbild aus der englischen Revolution. Erste Abtheilung, pp. 321–479. (Die zweite Abtheilung dieses Aufsatzes im nächsten Jahrgang.) Zweite, pp. 391–531.

In *Historisches Taschenbuch* (F. von Raumer). Dritte Folge. Dritter Jahrgang. Leipzig: Brockhaus, 1852–53.

See Item 1231.

1289 J. Zelle. Remarks on the Translation of Milton's Treatise *Of Education*. Coeslin: Budack, [1858]. Pp. 18.

1290 Milton's Prophecy of Essays and Reviews, and His Judgement on Prosecution of Them. London: 1861. Pp. iv+48.

Extracted from *Areopagitica*, to which is added an extract from the charge delivered to his clergy in 1861, by Walter Kerr, Bishop of Salisbury, on unity with the Bishop of Rome.

Preface quotes Symmons on freedom of press and for religious tolerance.

1291 The Right Hon. Mr. Justice Keogh. Milton's Prose.

In *The Afternoon Lectures on Literature and Art Delivered in the Theater of the Museum of Industry*, St. Stephen's Green, Dublin, in April and May, 1865. London: Bell and Daldy, 1866. Pp. 224.

Milton paper, pp. 131–51. Used as topic for expression on freedom. Rhetorical and general.

1292 E. H. Gillette. [Newly discovered prose writings of Milton.] *Hours at Home*, IX (October, 1869), 532–36.

Two pamphlets supposed to be Milton's dated 1642 and 1643.

1293 R. C. Jebb. Milton's *Areopagitica*. A Commentary. Privately printed, [1872]. Pp. xvi+32.

Arber's 1868 text is used for references. Gives the orders concerning licensing, an analysis of the text, and notes.

1294 [On the discovery of the *De doctrina* manuscript.] *Acad.*, VI (August 22, 1874), 205.

1295 [On the discovery of Milton's *Commonplace Book.*] *Ibid.*, VI (October 3, 1874), 374.

On A. J. Horwood's find. Description of the manuscript. See also the issue of October 10, 1874, p. 402.

1296 Jean Chapelain. Lettres 1652–1672. Paris, 1880–83. 2 vols.

Vol. II, pp. 103, 110. Unfavorable comments on Milton.

On the *Defence:* "Malheureux champion de l'iniquité."

To Heinsius: He had read with anger what Salmasius the elder said against Heinsius in unpublished reply to Milton brought out by Salmasius' son after his death.

1297 John W. Hales. "Milton's Divorce Pamphlets." *Athen.*, January 29, 1881, p. 163.

A letter of James Howell attacks Milton for his stand on divorce.

1298 Joseph Mazzini Wheeler. "Milton's Tract on Divorce." *Ibid.*, May 29, 1886, p. 715.

First reference to Milton's tract said to have appeared in *Heresiography* by Ephraim Pagitt, published May 8, 1645.

Calls Milton an atheist for his attitude on divorce.

1299 Theodore W. Hunt. Representative English Prose and Prose Writers. New York, 1887.

Milton's prose style, pp. 246–64.

1300 John G. R. McElroy. "Matter and Manner in Literary Composition." *MLN*, III (1888), 29–33, 56–66.

Criticism of the style of *Areopagitica.*

1301 P. Jörss. Grammatisches und Stilistisches aus Miltons *Areopagitica.* Leipzig, 1890. Pp. 31.

Published also in 1893.

1302 W. Kahle. Miltons Pädagogische Grundsätze, vorzugsweise nach seiner Abhandlung *Of Education*, vom Seminarlehrer W. K. Cöthen: Schettler, 1890. Pp. 48.

1303 J. B. Meyer. Miltons *Pädagogische Schriften und Äusserungen* mit Einleitung und Anmerkungen. Langensalza, 1890. Pp. xvi+64.

1304 R. H. Quick. Essays on Educational Reformers. London, 1890. Pp. 560.

"Greatly enlarged and in part rewritten." First edition, 1868; second, 1887.

Milton, pp. 23, 150, 212, 213, 215, 510. Not significant.

1305 J. H. Allen. "John Milton and the Commonwealth." *Unitarian Review*, XX (1891), 242.

1306 F. C. Birkbeck Terry. "Icon Basilike." *N & Q*, Ser. VII, No. XII (1891), p. 235.

Note on the spelling "Icon" instead of "Eikon."

1307 Jules Vodoz. An Essay on the Prose of John Milton. Dissertation at Zurich, 1895. Pp. vii+105.

Good analysis in light of rules set forth by Mulcaster, Butler, and Hodge. Study of accidence. Pronounciation as well as etymology in Milton's mind.

Reviewed by W. Franz in *ES*, XXV (1898), 302–3.

1308 G. di Laghi. Il pensiero pedagogica di Giovanni Milton. Milano, [190–]. Pp. 130.

1309 Edward Dowden. Puritan and Anglican: Studies in Literature. New York: Holt, 1900. Pp. xii+341.

Milton, pp. 133–97. On his ideas of liberty, chiefly as seen in his prose. A standard presentation of the outstanding points. Second edition, 1901.

1310 C. B. Wheeler. "Milton's Doctrine and Discipline of Divorce." *Nineteenth Century*, LXI (1907), 127–35.

Short summary of Milton's ideas on divorce. Writer in sympathy with them; predicts that reform Milton advocated will be carried out.

1311 C. H. Firth. "Milton as an Historian." *Proceedings of the British Academy*, III (1907–8), pp. 31.

Read November 25, 1908.

Milton aimed at research and criticism. Prejudice against women shown in comment on Boadicea, "a distracted woman with a mad crew at her heels." Earlier books more carefully finished; in Books IV and V, weary of task. Failed to realize value of research into monastic antiquities. Used history as means of edification.

1312 M. M. Kleerkooper. "Some Milton Papers." *Athen.*, December 19, 1908, p. 790.

Quotes letter written January 19, 1677, urging prevention of printing of a book at Leyden. This book supposed to be a surreptitious edition of Milton's state letters.

1313 Sir Oliver J. Lodge. Milton and the Education Controversy. Birmingham, 1908. Pp. 7.

Says that Milton would doubtless speak today, when "education of future generations . . . . seems to be at the mercy of rival sects."

1314 W. G. Tarrant. Milton and Religious Freedom. London: Green, 1908. Pp. 28.

Used Milton's writings for unitarian values only, but produced an excellent sketch.

1315 William E. A. Axon. "Milton and the Liberty of the Press." [In] *Milton Memorial Lectures*. Pp. 39–58. Oxford, 1909.

1316 Foster Watson. "A Suggested Source of Milton's Tractate *Of Education*." *Nineteenth Century*, LXVI (1909), 607–17.

Milton's ideas of education, especially his academy and curriculum, founded on Vives.

1317 Martin Visser. Miltons Prosawerken. Rotterdam: Brusse, 1911. Pp. 192.

Good in relating the political writings to events. Chapters on life, on church, on divorce, on state, political writings, *De doctrina*.

1318 L. March Phillips. "Modern Thought and the Renaissance." *ER*, XVI (1913), 43–58.

Comment on formlessness of Milton's prose style (pp. 49–50).

1319 Edward Bensly. "Two Passages Explained." *N & Q.*, Ser. XI, No. IX (1914), p. 272.

Of Reformation discussed. See also pp. 150, 198, 216, 234, 333.

1320 John T. Curry. [Answers to Milton queries.] *Ibid.*, Ser. XI, No. IX (1914), p. 216.

Sources of Milton's references in *Of Reformation* presented. See also pp. 150, 272.

1321 R. S. Loomis. "A Note on the *Areopagitica*." *MLN*, XXXII (1917), 437–38.

Source of simile of the eagle.

1322 Chilton L. Powell. English Domestic Relations, 1487–1653. New York, 1917.

On Milton, pp. 225–31; attempt to remove the divorce pamphlets from any bearing on Milton's first marriage.

1323 Elbert N. S. Thompson. "Milton's *Of Education*." *SP*, XV (1918), 159–75.

A discursive study of current educational theories at the time when Milton wrote his essay.

1324 William A. Webb. "Milton's Views on Education, Their Present Significance and Value." *Educational Review*, LV (1918), 137–48.

Summary of Milton's views.

1325 Allan H. Gilbert. "Martin Bucer on Education." *JEGP*, XVIII (1919), 321–45.

Influence of Bucer on Milton's ideas of education. Milton probably used Bucer's *Scripta Anglicana* as source for his tractate *Of Education*.

1326 Harry Glicksman. "Lowell on Milton's *Areopagitica.*" *MLN*, XXXV (1920), 185–86.

Shows that invective against Long Parliament was omitted from all editions of *The History of Britain* before Birch's (1738).

1327 ———. "The Sources of Milton's *History of Britain.*" *University of Wisconsin Studies in Language and Literature, 1920*, No. 11, pp. 105–44.

Study of Milton's formidable list of sources.

Reviewed by Thornton S. Graves in *South Atlantic Quarterly*, XX, 372.

1328 James Holly Hanford. "The Date of Milton's *De Doctrina Christiana.*" *SP*, XVII (1920), 309–18.

Concludes from study of handwriting of manuscript that it was completed in the early sixties. This is supported by comparison of theology with that of *Paradise Lost*, and by consideration of the general scheme of Milton's prose writings.

1329 A. W. Harrison. "Milton's Prose Works." *LQR*, CXXXIV (1920), 213–25.

Appreciative evaluation of Milton's prose works.

1330 James Holly Hanford. "Milton and Ochino." *MLN*, XXXVI (1921), 121–22.

Discussion of Milton's indebtedness to Ochino for heretical conception of Trinity, and for his doctrine of polygamy embodied in *De doctrina.*

1331 ———"Milton and the Art of War." *SP*, XVIII (1921), 232–66.

Milton read widely in military literature, both ancient and modern. A careful analysis of his use of military material in his writings. It is unlikely that he served in the army.

1332 E. Lehmann. Tendenz und Entstehungsgeschichte von Miltons *History of Britain.* (Dissertation.) Berlin: Mayer & Müller, 1921. Pp. 39.

1333 Warren H. Lowenhaupt. "The Writing of Milton's *Eikonoklastes.*" *SP*, XX (1923), 29–51.

Shows a use of three earlier pamphlets of the same year and demonstrates Milton's habit of using his reading at once for composition.

1334 F. F. Madan. Milton, Salmasius and Dugard (with Facsimiles). London: Oxford University Press, 1923. Pp. 29.

Reprinted from the *Library*, IV (1923), [119]–45.

Has definite evidence on the part taken by Dugard in the printing of their controversial works.

1335 Oliver M. Ainsworth. "Milton as a Writer on Education." *Transactions of the Wisconsin Academy of Sciences, Arts, and Letters*, XXI (1924), 41–50.

Valuable survey of Milton's statements on education.

1336 S. J. Crawford. "Milton and Aldhelm." *TLS*, September 24, 1925, p. 619.

Cites a parallel between *Reason of Church Government* and Aldhelm's poem *De Virginitate*.

1337 J. P. Pritchard. The Influence of the Fathers upon Milton, with Especial Reference to Augustine. Manuscript dissertation at Cornell University, 1925. Pp. iii+213.

Bibliography.

1338 Frederic E. Faverty. "A Note on the *Areopagus*." *PQ*. V (1926), 278–80.

1339 William Haller. "Before *Areopagitica*." *PMLA*, XLII (1927), 875–900.

A good survey of Milton's place in the current controversies.

1340 Elbert N. S. Thompson. The Seventeenth Century English Essay. Iowa City: University of Iowa, 1927.

Reviews in *MLN*, XLII (1927), 563–64; *MLR*, XXIII (1928), 77–78.

1341 Milton on Education. The Tractate *Of Education* with Supplementary Extracts from Other Writings of Milton . . . . by Oliver M. Ainsworth. "Cornell Studies in English." New Haven: Yale University Press, 1928. Pp. xiv+369.

The critical apparatus and comment cover the materials of the text thoroughly.

1342 G. A. Bonnard. "Two Remarks on the Text of Milton's *Areopagitica*." *RES*, IV (1928), 434–38.

Hale's text contains errors because he followed too closely the faulty Arber reproduction of the 1644 text. Holt White's 1819 edition more accurate. Critic asserts that the Pitt Press edition (1918) is a reliable text.

1343 Thomas O. Mabbott. "On Milton's Letters." *TLS*, February 16, 1928, p. 112.

Notice of the discovery of letters of Oldenburg. Full details to be given in the Columbia edition.

XI. SELECTIONS FROM THE PROSE AND POETICAL WORKS

1344 Poems by John Milton: Containing Extracts from *Paradise Lost*, *Samson*, "L'Allegro," "Il Penseroso," and "Lycidas," with the Author's Life. [In] G. Nicholson, *Literary Miscellany*, Vol. I, No. 5. Poughnill, 1803.

1345 Selections from the Works of Taylor, Hooker, Milton, Hall, Barrow, and Bacon. . . . . By B. Montagu. London, 1805. 2 vols.

Second edition, 1807; third edition (1829) has additional names.

1346 "Milton's History of England." *Retrospective Review*, VI (1822), 87–100.

Extracts of the most interesting parts.

1347 The Beauties of Milton; Consisting of Selections from His Poetry and Prose, by Alfred Howard. London, [1834]. Pp. 188.

1348 The Flowers of Milton by Jane Elizabeth Giraud. London, [1846].

Twenty-nine colored plates with mottoes.

1349 The Poetical Works of Milton, Young, Gray, Beattie, and Collins. Philadelphia: Lippincott, Grambo & Co., 1850.

Five parts in one volume.

1350 *Paradise Lost* (I and II). *Comus*, "Lycidas," "Il Penseroso," and "L'Allegro," . . . . [Edited by] J. G. Davis. London: Collins Sons & Co., 1874. Pp. 120.

1351 The Milton Anthology. Selected from His Prose Writings. Preface by F. Hurd. New York: Holt, 1876. Pp. viii+486.

1352 Thomas A. Ward. The English Poets; Selections with Critical Introductions, etc. London, 1880. 4 vols.

Milton selections and sketch by Mark Pattison, II, 293–379.

1353 Readings from Milton. New York: Phillips & Hunt; Cincinnati: Walden & Stowe, [1883].

1354 Shakespeare and Milton Reader: Being Scenes and Other Extracts from the Writings of Shakespeare and Milton. London, [1883].

1355 Readings from Milton. With an Introduction by H. W. Warren. Boston: Chautauqua Press. 1886. Pp. xii+308.

1356 *Areopagitica*, Letter on Education, Sonnets and Psalms. [With an Introduction by Henry Morley.] "Cassell's National Library," Vol. CXXI, 1886. Pp. 192.

Other editions, 1904, 1906.

1357 Milton's *Minor Poems* and Three Books of *Paradise Lost*. Cambridge: Houghton Mifflin Co., 1896. Pp. 112.

1358 Henry Corson. An Introduction to the Prose and Poetical Works of John Milton. London: Macmillan, 1899. Pp. xxxii+303.

Selections of prose and poetry arranged chronologically to give an autobiographic record of Milton's life and thought.

1359 Selections from the Poetical Works of John Milton; with Introduction, Suggestions for Study, Notes, and Glossary. Edited by A. P. Walker. Boston: D. C. Heath & Co., 1900. Pp. xiv+395.

1360 Helps to the Study of Milton's *Areopagitica* and English Sonnets. By C. W. Crook. London: Ralph Holland & Co., 1904. Pp. xxxii+98.

Footnotes; interleaving for school use.

1361 Milton: *Areopagitica*, *Paradise Lost*, Book VI, "Lycidas," and Sonnets. Specially Edited for the Certificate Examination of 1906. London: University Tutorial Press, 1904. Pp. xi+172.

1362 The Prose Works of John Milton [selections]. London: Methuen, 1905. Pp. viii+174.

Passages from *Eikonoklastes*, *Tenure of Kings and Magistrates* (1650 ed.). Edited by Sir Sidney Lee.

1363 A Day Book of Milton. By Richard F. Towndrow. London: Methuen, 1905. Pp. xvi+366.

A good selection of poetry and some prose passages.

1364 Milton and His Poetry. Edited by W. H. Hudson. London: Harrap & Co., 1912. Pp. 184.

A good introductory text from the *Minor Poems* and selections from *Paradise Lost*.

1365 Poems by John Milton. London: Bell, 1913. Pp. vi+128.

No notes. *Paradise Lost* (Books I and II); the chief *Minor Poems;* seven sonnets.

1366 Milton. Edited by R. Lawson. Melbourne, [1919]. Pp. 128.

Questions and notes on selections from *Paradise Lost*, *Samson*, and the chief *Minor Poems*.

1367 Milton: Poetry and Prose; with Essays by Johnson, Hazlitt, Macaulay. Edited by Beatrice G. Madan, with an Introduction by A. M. D. Hughes and Notes by Various Scholars. Oxford: Clarendon Press, 1920. Pp. xi+224.

Excellent texts of all the shorter poems commonly read; also selected passages of *Paradise Lost*, of *Areopagitica*, and *Reason of Church Government*. Notes from Hales, Browne, and Firth.

1368 Selections from the Prose and Poetry of John Milton. Edited by James Holly Hanford. "Riverside College Classics." Boston: Houghton Mifflin Co., [1923]. Pp. vi+310.

An excellent textbook for preparatory schools. Notes.

XII. TRANSLATIONS

1. POETICAL WORKS IN GERMAN AND ITALIAN

1369 Traduzione delle Opere poetiche di Giovanni Milton. [By G. Polidori.] Stampato presso il traduttore. Londra, 1840. 3 vols.

The "Angeleida" of E. di Valvasone is appended to the second volume. Another edition appeared in 1842. Lowndes lists a three-volume edition of 1812.

Review by D. Ancona, *Varietà*, I, 149.

1370 Milton, Sämmtliche poetische Werke, deutsch von Adolf Böttger. Leipzig, 1843.

Lacks the poems in other languages than English and the shorter *Minor Poems.*

1371 Miltons poetische Werke. Deutsch von Adolf Böttger. Neue Ausgabe. Leipzig, 1846.

Paradise Lost and *Paradise Regained.* Third edition, 1869 (xiv+423); fourth, [1873]; fifth, 1878; sixth, [1880]; seventh, with new Preface as the only change, 1894.

1372 Miltons poetische Werke . . . . Übersetzt von Bernhard Schuhmann, Alexander Schmidt, Immanuel Schmidt und Hermann Ullrich. Herausgegeben mit biographisch-literarischen Einleitungen und vollständigem Kommentar. Leipzig: Heffes, [1909]. Pp. 744.

Contains a bibliography of German translations of Milton. Notes of merit.

Review in *Archiv*, CXXIX (1912), 520.

2. LATIN AND ITALIAN WORKS IN ENGLISH

1373 [The Familiar Letters Translated by Robert Fellowes. In] Symmons, *Prose Works* (1806), I, i–xliii.

1374 The Second Defence of the People of England. [In] Symmons, *Prose Works* (1806), III, 103–18.

A translation ascribed by Toland to Mr. Washington, a gentleman of the Inner Temple.

1375 "On the Sonnets of Milton, with a Translation of One of His Italian Sonnets." *Censura literaria*, VI (1908), 414–17.

Translates "Diodati, io te'l diro. . . . ."

1376 Latin and Italian Poems of Milton Translated into English Verse, and a Fragment of a Commentary on *Paradise Lost* by the "Late William Cowper, Esqr., with a Preface by the Editor [W. Hayley] and Notes of

Various Authors. [Chichester printed.] London: J. Johnson and R. H. Evans, 1808. Pp. xxvii+328.

The complimentary poems are included. The English versions are followed by the originals, these by notes on line of *Paradise Lost*, and finally are many original notes from contemporary works bearing on Milton's lines as well as borrowings from standard editors. Finely printed in large quarto sheets, with three Flaxman engravings.

1377 [Translations of the Latin and Italian poems. In] Milton's Life and Poetical Works with Notes by William Cowper. Edited with a Life of Milton by W. Hayley. Chichester, 1810. 4 vols.

See Volume III.

1378 The Latin and Italian Poems of Milton. Translated into English Verse, by Jacob George Strutt. London: J. Conder, 1814. Pp. viii+144.

Preface shows the work to have been done independently, without use of Cowper or Symmons.

1379 Milton's *Second Defence of the People of England*. . . . . Translated by Archdeacon Francis Wrangham. London: C. Baldwin, 1816. Pp. 199.

Only 50 copies printed, but included in his *Sermons* (1816), Vol. III.

1380 A Treatise of Christian Doctrine, Compiled from the Holy Scriptures Alone by John Milton. Translated from the Original by Charles R. Sumner. Cambridge: Cambridge University Press, 1825. Pp. xlii+711.

Occasioned Macaulay's famous essay in the *Edinburgh Review* of August, 1825. Published at the same time as the original text in its first issue.

1381 A Treatise of Christian Doctrine, Compiled from the Holy Scriptures Alone. . . . . Translated from the Original by C. R. Sumner. Boston, 1825. 2 vols.

1382 Familiar Letters. Translated from the Latin, with Notes, by John Hall. Philadelphia: E. Littell, 1829. Pp. vi+120.

Professes this to be the first translation. Brief footnotes and an Index. There are minor errors in dating and in grammar.

Reviews in *American Quarterly Review*, V (1829), 301–10; *Southern Review*, VI (1830), 198–206.

1383 Horace Translated by Philip Francis. With . . . . Translations of Various Odes . . . . by . . . . Milton. London: Valpy, 1831. 2 vols.

1384 The Second Defence of the People of England. Translation by Dr. R. Fellowes.

In Griswold's edition of the prose works (1845), II, 477–527; and in St. John's edition (1848–53).

1385 Milton's *Epitaphium Damonis*, A.D. 1639. Done into English by Arthur Compton Auchmuty. Leominster: Orphans' Printing Press, [1884]. Pp. 27.

1386 Milton's Earlier Poems, Including the Translations of W. Cowper of Those Written in Latin and Italian. [With an Introduction by Henry Morley.] London: Cassell, 1886. Pp. 192.

1387 The Shorter Poems of John Milton, Including the Two Latin Elegies and Italian Sonnet to Diodati and the *Epitaphium Damonis* Arranged in Chronological Order. With Preface, Introduction, and Notes by Andrew J. George. New York: Macmillan, 1898. Pp. xxvi+299.

Translations of the Latin and Italian pieces.

1388 The Italian Poems of Milton and the *Pervigilium Veneris* Translated by John Clark. Cape Town: Darter Bros. & Co., 1911.

Text only.

1389 W. MacKellar. The Latin Poems of John Milton: an Annotated Edition. Manuscript dissertation at Cornell University, 1923. Pp. lxxxvi+468.

Translation, bibliographical notes, and text notes.

3. THE MINOR POEMS

1390 Uppinghamiensis. [Latin translation of "L'Allegro."] *GM*, LXXVII (June, 1807), 556–57; LXXVIII, 145, 241–42.

Reader of the *Gentleman's Magazine* requests that his translation be printed and promises to continue verses if they are favorably received.

1391 "Il Licida," "L'Allegro," ed "Il Penseroso" di Giovanni Milton. Tradotti da Gaetano Polidori. Londra: Presso l'autore, 1814. Pp. 60.

1392 Œuvres choisies de Milton. *Comus*—"L'Allegro"—"Il Penseroso"—*Samson Agonistes*—"Lycidas"—Sonnets—Poésies Latines. Traduction nouvelle [in prose, by M. G. Kervyn] avec le texte en regard. Paris, 1839. Pp. xxxii+377.

Notes with each selection. F. Henry in *Les petits poèmes* (1909): ". . . . serait excellente sans un certain nombre de contresens fâcheux. Le lecteur qui désirerait la consulter, devra se résigner, comme moi, à aller à la Bibliothèque Nationale."

1393 Milton. Gedicht auf Shakespeare, von Friedrich Bodenstedt. Berlin, 1861.

"Bei Bodenstedt fehlen von den 16 Zeilen des Originals zwei Zeilen" (Ullrich).

1394 Sonnets on Fairfax and Cromwell.

Translated into German in *Rose und Distel Poesien aus England und Schottland übertragen von Gisbert Freiherrn Bincke.* Pp. 144–45. Zweite vermehrte Auflage. Weimar: Bohlau, 1865.

1395 Milton. Sonett an den Lord General Cromwell. Von Moritz Carriere.

In Die Kunst im Zusammenhange der Kulturentwicklung und die Ideale der Menschheit (5Bde.; Leipzig, 1873–80), IV, 639.

1396 Miltons Gedicht auf Shakespeare. Übersetzt von Max Koch. [In] *Shakespeare* (Stuttgart, 1885), p. 12.

1397 Religion et libre pensée (contient une imitation du Paradis reconquis et une traduction du XIXe sonnet). Genève, 1886.

1398 Langue anglaise. Auteurs anglais. Poésies: par Milton (extraits) et par Longfellow (extraits). Avec notices biographiques et annotations par F. Aigre. 1891.

1399 Extraits des œuvres poétiques de Milton, à l'usage des aspirants au baccalauréat, par J. M. Laughlin. Paris, 1892.

1400 Immanuel Schmidt. Miltons Jugendjahre und Jugendwerke. Hamburg, 1896.

German translations of "An Epitaph on Shakespeare," "On the University Carrier," and Sonnet I.

1401 "Miltons Sonett." *Preussische Jahrb.*, LXXXV (1896), 324–43.

Omits first of Divorce sonnets "On the detraction," etc., and the caudata sonnet.

1402 H. Fernow. Miltons Sonnett auf seine Blindheit an seinen Freund Cyriack Skinner. *ES*, XXXIV (1904), 446.

Translated into German verse.

1403 On Time. On Shakespeare. [Translated by E. Wülker. In] Richard Wülker, *Geschichte der englischen Literatur.* Zweite Auflage, 2 Bde. Leipzig, 1906.

1404 Les petits poèmes de John Milton [Sonnets—"L'Allegro"—"Il Penseroso"—"Lycidas"]. Traduits en vers avec texte Anglais et notes par Fernand Henry. Paris: E. Guilmoto, 1909.

English texts and French translations on opposite pages. Ten of the sonnets included. Interesting comments on earlier French translations of these poems and some remarks on Mareuil's translation of the three title poems included in this work. Mareuil first put them and *Paradise Regained* into French in 1730, and thereafter they were often printed with St. Maur's *Paradise Lost.*

Introduction by Edmund Gosse.

1405 Walter Thomas. "Les sonnets de Milton et sa vie intime." *RELV*, XLI (1924), 252–58, 289–96.

Selected sonnets included.

4. *COMUS*

1406 *Il Como*, favola boschereccia di Giovanni Milton . . . . tradotta da G. Polidori. Londra: Dulau, 1802.

Review in *Monthly Review*, XXXVIII (1802), 102–4.

1407 Traduction en vers français de *Comus*. Par M. de Bintinaye, avec une traduction italienne [Polidori's]. Paris, 1806.

Reprinted in 1812 and 1815.

1408 *Como*, dramma con maschere. . . . . Traduzione sostenuta ad litteram. *Comus*, masque . . . . traduction littérale. [Edited by F. H. Egerton, Earl of Bridgewater.] Paris: Chapelet, 1806. Pp. xiii+85.

Italian translation on left pages, French on right. Prefatory note, errata, texts, and critical comments on *Comus*. Reissued in 1812, in spite of the poor quality of the Italian translation.

1409 Il Como. Favola boschereccia di Giovanni Milton, tradotta in Italiano da Gaetano Polidori. Seconda edizione migliorata, corretta, e di note corredata dal traduttore. Londra, 1809. Pp. xiv+88.

1410 Il Como. Favola boschereccia di Giovanni Milton tradotta in Italiano da Gaetano Polidori. Terza edizione, migliorata e corretta. Paris: Didot, 1812. Pp. xii+80.

Included in the 1840 edition of his works.

1411 F. C. *Il Como* tradatto da. . . . . Venezia, 1831.

Allodoli remarks that this reads like melodrama.

1412 *Comus* . . . . de anglais, 1634. [In] *Bibl. étrangère*, Vol. II, par M. Aignan. Paris, 1823.

1413 Fabulae *Samson Agonistes* et *Comus* Graece. E. Greswell. Oxon, 1832. Pp. 133.

1414 John Miltons dramatische Werke. *Comus*. *Simson Agonistes* . . . . von H——h [Hirsch?]. Berlin, 1840. Pp. viii+152.

1415 Milton's *Comus* übersetzt und mit einer erläuternden Abhandlung begleitet von Dr. Immanuel Schmidt. (Beilage zum Programm . . . .). Berlin, 1860. Pp. 47.

Another edition, same year, 69 pages.

1416 Miltoni *Comus*. Graece reddidit Georgius, Baro Lyttelton. Cantabrigiae et Londini: Macmillan et Soc., 1863. Pp. 121.

English and Greek texts on alternate pages.
Revised edition, 1885.

1417 Umfangreiche Stücke aus Miltons *Comus* und *Samson Agonistes*. Übersetzt von Alexander Schmidt in dessen Vorlesung: Miltons dramatische Dichtungen. Königsberg, 1864.

Also in his collected works, Berlin, 1889.

1418 Comus. Paris, 1890.

Telleen notes a French translation by MacFautrie, with notes, in this year.

1419 The Gaisford Prize. 1901. Milton's *Comus*, Lines 244–330, in Theocritan Verse, by Frederick Lewisohn. Oxford: Blackwell, 1901.

English and Greek texts on opposite pages.

1420 *Komus* of Milton. Oversat of Uffe Birkedal. Copenhagen: Tillge, 1908. Pp. 53.

5. "L'ALLEGRO" AND "IL PENSEROSO"

1421 "L'Allegro" di Milton ed il Tragitto di San Gotardo di Madama la Duchessa di Devonshire a' suoi figli, tradotti e d'alcune note corredati da Gaetano Polidori. Londra: Didier & Tebbett, 1805.

Review in *Monthly Review*, L (1806), 99–100.

1422 "Il Penseroso" . . . . tradotto da G. Polidori. Londra: G. Schulze & Co., 1809. Pp. 19.

1423 L'Allegro. Miltoni poema, Latine redditum a C. M. Olim Cantab [i.e., Charles Marsh]. Londini: T. Payne, 1811.

1424 Milton: der Frohsinn—Der Tiefsinn ["L'Allegro" and "Il Penseroso"] von Johann Baptist Rupprecht. [In] *Dichtungen der Britten in metrischen Übersetzungen* (Wien, 1812), I, 129–39.

1425 "Allegro" und "Penseroso." Von Johann Heinrich Voss. [In] *Sämmtliche poetische Werke* (Leipzig, 1835), pp. 267–73.

"L'Allegro" translated, 1789; "Il Penseroso," 1792.

1426 Milton, "L'Allegro." [In] O. L. Heubner, *Englische Dichter*. Leipzig: Wigand, 1856. Pp. 181–93.

1427 "L'Allegro" und "Il Penseroso," oder Lebenslust und Weihe. Eine Doppel-Ode von John Milton. Gotha, 1859.

Translation of H. A. Werner.

1428 Milton. "L'Allegro": "Il Penseroso." Übersetzt von Alexander Schmidt. [In] Scherr, *Bildersaal der Weltliteratur*. Stuttgart: Kroner, 1869.

Second edition.
Third edition, in Volume III of the 1884–85 edition.

1429 Milton's "L'Allegro" and "Il Penseroso" Translated into French, by John Roberts. London, Cambridge [printed], 1874. Pp. 53.

English text on pages opposite an excellent French version. Privately printed. Review in *Athen.*, August 15, 1874, p. 210.

1430 Milton's "Il Penseroso" Rendered into Greek Verse by F. E. Gretton, Rector of Oddington, Gloucestershire. Cambridge: Cambridge University Press, 1878. Pp. ii+15.

Done as a benefit for "poor desolated" colliers and sent out with a request for two shillings in stamps. Greek and English on opposite pages.

1431 ["L'Allegro" in French prose.] *RELV*, 1889.

A translation by Émile Legouis, with excellent notes.

1432 ["L'Allegro" and "Il Penseroso" in French translations.] Versailles: M. B. Charpentier, 1898.

1433 W. Thomas. [French translation of "L'Allegro."] *RELV*, XXXIV (1917), 102–4, 106–9.

1434 "Allegro": "Il Penseroso." Leipzig. 1921.

The German paraphrases of Otto Heinrich reprinted, with illustrations.

6. "LYCIDAS"

1435 "Licida." . . . . monodia, per la morte del naufragato E. King tradotta dall'inglese da T. J. Matthias. Londra: [privately printed], 1812. Pp. iv+34.

Some copies of same year in quarto. English text follows the Italian. Ninth edition published in Naples, 1830 (Lowndes).

1436 "Licida" di Giovanni Milton monodia per la morte del naufragato Eduardo King, tradatto dall'inglese da T. J. Matthias. Londra, 1816.

1437 C. S. Calverley. [Latin translation of "Lycidas." In] *Verses and Translations*. London, 1862.

A second edition, 1862; also, 1865, 1866, 1871, 1874, 1881.

1438 Milton's "Lycidas" Translated into Latin Hexameter Verse by W. C. Green. Rugby, 1874. Pp. 15.

Had not seen Calverley's version. He evidently refers to Paley in comments on the version of "a well-known scholar."

1439 Milton's "Lycidas," Lines 15–84; in Theocritean Verse by H. Sidebotham. (Gaisford Prize, 1893.) Oxford: B. H. Blackwell, 1893. Pp. 13.

1440 C. S. Calverley. [Latin translation of "Lycidas."]

In *The Complete Works of .... with a Biographical Notice by Sir Walter J. Sendall.* London: Bell, 1901. Pp. 514. See pp. 428–33.

1441 "Lycidas" de John Milton. Traduction lyrique avec une introduction et des notes par Émile Le Brun. Paris: Didier, 1917. Pp. 31.

Amply annotated. First issued in *RELV*, XXXIV (1917), 16–21, 52–66.

1442 Robert F. Arnold. "Miltons 'Lycidas' deutsch." *Z. f. franz. u. engl. Unterricht*, XXI (1922) 241–53.

Comments on former German translations; new translation given.

1443 ———. "Miltons 'Il Penseroso' deutsch." *Ibid.*, XXII (1923), 252–64.

7. *PARADISE LOST*

FRENCH

1444 *Le Paradis perdu* de Milton. Traduction nouvelle. Paris, [1800]. 2 vols. Pp. viii+303+280.

Prose translation of Monseron, first published in 1787; appeared later in 1804 (2 vols.), 1811, 1832, 1840, and 1841.

1445 Choix des plus beaux morceaux [*Paradise Lost*] traduit en vers par Louis Racine et Nivernois, avec une notice sur la vie de Milton et l'analyse d'Addison sur son poème .... traduit en vers par G. M. Bontemps. Paris: Langlois, 1803.

See Item 1831 for another French translation of selected passages.

1446 Invocation à la lumière. Fragment de la traduction du *Paradis perdu*, Livre III, par. J. de Lille. Paris, 1804. 3 vols.

In two forms, 8vo and 4to.

See *Almanach des muses*, XL (1804), 77–79.

1447 *Le Paradis perdu*, traduit par J. de Lille [Preface by L. G. Michaud]. Remarques d'Addisson sur *Le Paradis perdu.* [In] *Œuvres de J. de Lille*, 3 vols., Paris, 1805.

In nine formats. Reprinted in 1818 (2 vols.), 1820, 1820, 1822, 1823, 1832, and in his complete works after 1824.

Reviewed in *Almanach des muses*, XLII (1806), 266; *ER*, VIII (1806), 167–90.

1448 [Dialogues from *Paradise Lost*, in French. In] Hennet, *Poëtique anglaise* (3 vols.; Paris, 1806), III, 34–39.

1449 *Le Paradis perdu*, par B. Salgues. Paris, 1807.

A prose translation.

1450 *Le Paradis perdu* de Milton [prose] par Louis Racine. Fifth Edition, 2 vols. Paris, 1808. Pp. xxxv+500+602.

First edition, 1775; in his complete works after 1806. The notes and criticism are supplemented by discourses on epic and on Addison's observations on Milton.

1451 L'Esprit de Milton, un traduction en vers français du *Paradis perdu*, dégagée des longueurs et superfluités qui déparent ce poème. Par l'auteur des traductions en vers français des *Odes* d'Horace et de *L'Éneide* de Virgile [C. de Loynes d'Autroche]. Orléans, 1808. Pp. xvi+314.

An abridgment of De Lille's excellent translation (Lanson); the advertisement defends such editing and attacks Mosneron's translation.

1452 Le Paradis perdu. . . . . [Translation of Dupré de Saint Maur]. Avignon, 1810. 5 vols.

First published in 1729, this translation was issued after 1800 also in the following editions: at Avignon, 1823, 12mo; 3 vols., 1864, 16mo; at Limoges, 1847, 8vo; 1853, 12mo; 2 vols., 1883, 32mo; at Paris, 1879, 1881, 8vo; 2 vols., 1882, 32mo; 2 vols., 1892–94; 1894, 16 mo; 1899, 32mo; likewise in many undated editions.

In 1803 the Saint Maur version was turned into English prose.

1453 *Le Paradis perdu* de Jean Milton, traduit de l'anglais par J. Mosneron. Quatrième édition, revue et corrigée avec le plus grand soin, précédée de la vie de Milton. Paris, 1811.

The first edition, in 3 volumes, appeared in 1787.

1454 *Le Paradis perdu* traduit en vers par J. V. A. Delatour de Pernes. Paris, 1813.

1455 *Le Paradis perdu*, poème en six chants, traduit de l'Anglais en vers français par Eugene Aroux. Études sur Milton. Paris, 1830.

1456 *Le Paradis perdu* de Milton. Traduction nouvelle, par M. de Chateaubriand. Paris: Gosselin & Cie, 1836. 2 vols.

Prose. Critical commentary. Telleen's list of Chateaubriand editions: Paris, 1836, 2 vols. 12mo, two editions of 2 vols. 8vo; 1837, 2 vols. 18mo; 1841, 12mo; 1850, 8vo; 1850, folio with Lamartine's criticism and illustrations; 1857, 18mo; 1861, 8vo; 1862, 8vo; 1863, 4to; 1866, 12mo; 1867, 8vo; 1868, 18mo; 1870, 8vo, 4to with Lamartine's criticism; 1871, 18mo; 1872, 12mo; 1873, 18mo; 1875, 12mo; 1877, 12mo; 1881, 2 vols. folio; many editions without date. Also, Poissy, 1862, 8vo; Limoges, 1867, 8vo. Desrez published in 4 vols. (Paris), 1835–37.

Review by Villemain, *Journal des savants*, 1837, p. 215.

1457 Le Paradis perdu. Pantheon Littéraire. Paris: A. Desrez, 1837.

De Lille's version.

French text on upper half page; English on lower half. Notes and critical estimates for each book.

1458 *Le Paradis perdu* de Milton, traduit en Français [prose], texte anglais en regard, par le Vicomte de Chateaubriand. Édition monument, illustrée par 55 dessins originaux composés par Flatters, gravés au burin sur Acier, par les artistes les plus célèbres de la France et de l'étranger. Paris, [1837].

Books I and II, the text being printed on large sheets margined by pictures illustrating the text of the page. English text in left column; French prose in right.

1459 *Le Paradis perdu* de Milton. . . . . Traduction nouvelle, précédée d'une notice, par De Pongerville. Paris, 1838. 8vo.

Prose. In addition to undated editions, 1841, 18mo; two in 12mo; 1843, 1847, 1853, 1858, 1861, 1865, 1870, 1875, and 1881 in 12mo. The 1838 edition has D. O'Sullivan's *Un aperçu sur Milton*.

1460 A Poem by John Milton [left title-page] *Le Paradis perdu* de J. Milton [right title-page] par J. Mosneron. Cinquième édition, avec le texte en regard. Paris, 1841.

1461 Le Paradis perdu. Paris, 1842. 2 vols.

The verse translation by E. Aroux.

1462 Le Paradis perdu. Paris, 1850.

Pongerville's version.

1463 Le Paradis perdu. Paris, 1850.

Chateaubriand's version.

1464 Le Paradis perdu. Paris, 1850.

Prenderville's version, with a memoir.

1465 Le Paradis perdu. Limoges, 1853.

Ronsier's revision of Saint Maur.

The first edition of Saint Maur, 3 volumes, appeared in 1729. Others noted by Lanson are 1755, 1772, 1823.

See Item 1452.

1466 Le Paradis perdu. Traduction de Chateaubriand, précédé de réflexions sur la vie et les écrits de Milton, par Lamartine; et enrichi de vingt-cinq magnifiques estampes originales gravées au burin sur acier. Paris: Bigot & Voisvenel, 1855. Pp. xxxi+157.

1467 Le Paradis perdu. Paris, 1857.

Translation of Paul Guerin.

1468 *Le Paradis perdu* de Milton traduit par De Pongerville. Nouvelle édition, revue, corrigée et précédée de considérations sur Milton, son époque et ses ouvrages par le traducteur. Paris: Charpentier, 1861. Pp. 356.

The same as the 1858 edition.

1469 La Perte d'Eden. Paris, 1863.

Translated by Jean de Dieu.

1470 La Perte d'Eden. *Le Paradis perdu* de Milton. Traduction linéaire, métaphrastique et littérale par Jean de Dieu. Paris: Hachette, 1864.

French and English texts on opposite pages. New title-page, 1865. Review in *Athen.*, April 30, 1864, p. 609.

1471 Le Paradis perdu. Paris, 1865.

Translated by Corréard; Books I, II, and part of XI: notes.

1472 Le Paradis perdu. Paris, 1865.

Books I and II, with notes; translated by A. Beljame.

1473 Le Paradis perdu. Paris, 1866.

Books I and II of the English text, with notes in French by A. Elwall.

1474 Milton. *Le Paradis perdu*, livres I et II. Nouvelle édition, publiée avec une notice, un argument analytique de tout le poème et des notes en Français par Auguste Beljame. Paris: Hachette, 1866.

English text. Another edition, 1875.

1475 *Le Paradis perdu* de Milton; traduction de F. de Chateaubriand, précédée d'une de M. John Lemoinne. Paris: Michel Lévy frères, 1866.

Collection Michel Lévy. Œuvres choisies de F. de Chateaubriand.

1476 J. Dessiaux. Traduction du *Paradis perdu* en vers français, précédée d'une notice sur Milton et son poème et d'un discours sur la traduction en vers. Paris, 1867.

1477 Le Paradis perdu. Poème en douze livres. . . . . Traduit en vers français par André Tasset. Chartres, 1867. Pp. 450.

Literally translated, in verse suited to the heroic style of the original. Another edition, 1868.

1478 *Le Paradis perdu*, suivi de *Essai sur la littérature anglaise* par Chateaubriand. Paris: Garnier frères, [1872]. Pp. xx+579.

A new edition, the text based on a study of early English editions.

1479 *Le Paradis perdu*, I et II. Paris, 1874.

Translated by E. Sedley. English text given also.

1480 *Le Paradis perdu* avec traduction pour des écoles [Marie]. Toulouse, 1875.

Another edition, 1878.

1481 Fallet. Traduction du *Paradis perdu.* Paris, 1875.

1482 *Le Paradis perdu,* I et II, expliqués littéralement traduit en français et annotés par A. Legrand. Paris, 1875.

Other editions, 1880, 1881, 1887.

1483 *Le Paradis perdu,* drame-oratorio en quatre parties, musique de M. Théodore Dubois, exécuté le 27 Nov. 1878 aux Concerts du Chatêlet, par Edouard Blau. 1878.

No reference to publisher given by Telleen.

1484 Les Auteurs anglais expliqués d'après une méthode nouvelle par deux traductions françaises, l'une littérale et juxtalinéaire . . . . l'autre correcte et précédée du texte anglais, avec des sommaires et des notes par une Société de Professeurs et d'Anglais. Milton. *Le Paradis perdu.* Livres I et II expliqués littéralement, traduits en Français et annotés par M. A. Legrand. Paris, 1880. Pp. 220.

See Item 1482. This (1880) edition has a prose paraphrase in English beneath the original text; the latter is arranged line by line opposite the French version.

1485 Le Paradis perdu. Paris, 1881.

Books I and II in English, with French notes by A. Julien.

1486 Le Paradis perdu. Rouen, 1884.

Translated by Paul Baudry.

1487 Le Paradis perdu. Traduction de Dupré de Saint Maur. Paris: Librairie de la Bibliothèque nationale, 1886–85.

1488 *Le Paradis perdu,* précédé de *réflexions sur la vie et les écrits de Lamartine.* Paris: Guerin, 1901–3. 3 vols.

A new edition; 30 engravings. Chateaubriand's text.

1489 *Paradise Lost* (extraits) illustrée . . . . avec une introduction et des notes par P. Chauvet. Paris: Hachette, [1924]. Pp. 109.

GERMAN

1490 Morgenhymne. Poesien, Neueste Auflage. Berlin, 1803.

From *Paradise Lost.* Translated by Ludwig Gotthard Rosengarten (Leipzig, 1788).

1491 Erster Gesang des *Verlorenen Paradies* von J. F. Pries. Rostock, 1807. Pp. 47.

1492 [*Paradise Lost*, Book II, ll. 378–628. In] *Neue Berlinische Monatschrift*, XVIII (December, 1807), 320 ff.

Translated by J. F. Pries.

1493 [*Paradise Lost*, Book III, ll. 416–590.] *Neuer Teutscher Merkur*, December, 1807, pp. 282–93.

Translated by J. F. Pries.

1494 Miltons *Verlorenes Paradies* übersetzt von J. F. Pries. Rostock und Leipzig: Stiller, 1813.

Johnson's *Life* and a sketch of the characters in *Paradise Lost*.

1495 Johann Miltons *Verlorenes Paradies*. Neu übersetzt von Samuel Gottlieb Bürde. Breslau, 1822. 2 vols.

First published in Berlin, 1792.

1496 Morgenhymne. Dichtungen. Greifswald, 1824. Pp. ix+138+144.

See Item 1490.

1497 Johann Miltons *Verlorenes Paradies*. Neu übersetzt von Samuel Gottlieb Bürde. Wien, 1826. 2 vols. in 1.

Cheap printing of the 1822 edition.

1498 Johann Miltons *Verlorenes Paradies*. Aus dem Englischen neu übersetzt [in prose] by Friedrich Wilhelm Bruckbräu. München, 1828. 2 vols.

1499 Miltons *Verlorenes Paradies* in deutschen Hexametern. Übersetzer: Carl Friedrich von Rosenzweig. 4 Bändchen. Dresden und Leipzig, 1832.

1500 Miltons *Verlorenes Paradies*. Aus dem Englischen neu übersetzt von Friedrich Wilhelm Bruckbräu. Wohlfeile Ausgabe. 5 Bändchen. München, 1835.

1501 Miltons *Verlorenes Paradies*. Aus dem Englischen übersetzt von Dr. Kottenkamp. Nebst einer Biographie Miltons, vom Übersetzer verfasst. Mit 2 Stahlstichen. Pforzheim, 1841. Pp. 410.

Reprinted, 1842, in same form.

1502 Milton. *Verlorenes Paradies* [Book IV, ll. 598–688) . . . . von Louise von Plönnies. [In] *Britannia. Eine Auswahl englischer Dichtungen alter und neuer Zeit. Ins Deutsch übersetzt mit beigedrucktem Originaltext*. Frankfurt: Schmerberschen, 1843.

Pp. 34–41.

1503 *Das verlorene Paradies. Das wiedergewonnene Paradies*, von John Milton. Übersetzt von Bernhard Schuhmann. Stuttgart und Augsburg [printed], 1855. Pp. 466.

1504 Miltons *Verlorenes Paradies.* Übersetzt von Dr. Kottenkamp. Zweite unveränderte Ausgabe. Stuttgart, 1858. Pp. 410.

1505 Gustav Liebert. Milton. Studien zur Geschichte des englischen Geistes. Hamburg, 1860.

Contains 8 lines of *Paradise Lost* "in eigener vorzüglicher (auch in metrum durchaus treuer) Übersetzung."

1506 *Das verlorene Paradies,* Episches Gedicht von John Milton. Übersetzt von Karl Eitner. 1867. [In] *Bibliothek ausländischer Klassiker.* Bde. LIX, LX, (1865).

Excellent edition, with biography and an analysis of the poem. Another edition, 1886. The British Museum has an edition dated [1890?] that is doubtless the same, but comparison has not been made.

1507 John Milton und *Das verlorene Paradies.* Dr. Baumgarten, Oberlehrer. Coburg, [1875].

Critical comments on *Paradise Lost* and a few letters; English text and translation on opposite pages.

1508 Miltons *Verlorenes Paradies.* Eine Auswahl aus dem Texte mit erklärenden Anmerkungen von Dr. Wilh. Münch. Neue Ausgabe. Salzwedel, [1875].

1509 *Das verlorene Paradies.* Oratorium in drei Theilen. Text frei nach J. Milton. Musik von Anton Rubenstein. Op. 54. Leipzig: B. Senff, [1875].

Printed also with an 1876 title-page.

1510 *Das verlorene Paradies* und *Das wiedergewonnene Paradies* von John Milton. Übersetzt von B. Schuhmann. Zweite Auflage. Stuttgart, 1877. Pp. viii+412.

First edition, 1855.

1511 Milton. Das verlorene Paradies. Deutsch von Adolf Böttger. [Engravings by Gustav Doré.] Leipzig: Bach, 1879.

1512 Paradise Lost. Das verlorene Paradies. Oratorio. (Part II.) English Version by D. C. Addison. Composed by Anton Rubenstein. [1879.]

German words after Milton by Julius Rodenberg. The location of this volume did not make it possible to compare with it the 1875 oratorio.

1513 John Miltons *Verlorenes Paradies.* Erstes Buch. Ins Deutsche übertragen von Isaak Molenaar. . . . . London, 1881. Pp. 38.

Review by Max Koch, *ES,* VI (1883), 282–85.

1514 Das verlorene Paradies. . . . . Übersetzt von F. W. Zachariä mit Einleitung von Ludwig Pröscholdt. Stuttgart, 1883.

Translated in 1760. Another edition, 1891.

1515 Johann Milton. Das verlorene Paradies. Deutsch von Samuel Gottlieb Bürde. Halle: Hendel, 1894. 2 vols.

See Item 1495.

1516 Milton. Das verlorene Paradies. Deutsch von Adolf Böttger. Berlin: Neufeld-Henius, 1899.

Second edition of the 1879 text.

1517 Milton, *Paradise Lost*, I–VI . . . . herausgegeben von Luise Spies. 1920.

School edition; many errors.
Reviews in *ES*, XXXIII (1904), 436–38; *Die neueren Sprachen*, XII (1905), 617–21.

1518 Das verlorene Paradies. Episches Gedicht. Aus dem Englischen von Karl Eitner. Leipzig und Wien: Bibl. Institut, [1905].

Has the same plates as the 1894 edition.

ANGLO-SAXON

1518a James Ingram. A Translation into Anglo-Saxon of the Exordium of *Paradise Lost.*

The translation was used in his address "On the Utility of Anglo-Saxon Literature." Reviewed in the *Monthly Review*, LXIII (1810), 76–83.

DUTCH

1519 *Het verloren Paradijs* van Milton. Het Engelsch gevolgd door J. H. Reisig, Stukje 1, 2; door J. B., Stukje 3; door P. J. Witsen Geysbeek, Stukje 4. Zutphen: Stukje 1 & 2, Eldik, Stukje 3 & 4, Thieme, 1791–1811. 4 vols.

Vol. I (Books I–III), 1791; Vol. II (Books IV–VI), 1792; Vol. III (Books VII–IX), 1801; Vol. IV (Books X–XII), 1811.

1520 *Het verloren Paradijs* door John Milton. In het Nederduitsch overgebragt door J. F. Schimsheimer. Met platen. Amsterdam: H. Höveker. 1856.

Prose. Two pages of notes.

1521 Het verloren Paradijs. J. J. L. ten Kate. Leiden, 1875.
Illustrated.

1522 Milton's *Verloren Paradijs*. Heldendicht in twaalf zangen, overgebracht door J. J. L. ten Kate. Leiden: A. W. Sijthoff, [1891]. Pp. xxii+272.

1523 Het verloren Paradijs. Heldendicht in twaelf zangen, overgebracht door J. J. L. ten Kate. Leiden: A. W. Sijthoff, [1904]. Pp. xxiv+320.

Verse translation, with the Doré illustrations. No notes.

SWEDISH

1524 *Det Förlorade Paradiset*, Poem i tolf sånger af Milton. Öfversättning af Joh. G. Oxenstierna. Stockholm, 1815. Pp. xi+452.

1525 Milton's Poetiska Verk. *Det Förlorade Paradiset* och *Det Återvunna Paradiset*. Öfersatta af V. E. Öman. Upsala, 1862. Pp. 450.

NORWEGIAN

1526 Det tabte Paradis. Paa Dansk ved Uffe Birkedal. Andet Oplag. Kristiania, 1914. Pp. xxiv+405.

Footnotes. Masson's text as basis.

ICELANDIC

1527 Ens Enska skálds, J. Miltons, *Paradísar missir*. . . . . [Edited with a Preface by Th. Guðmundsson and Th. Helgason.] Kaupmannahöfn, 1828.

Published by the Islenzka Bókmentafèlag, at the expense of Mr. J. Heath. No notes.

ITALIAN

1528 *Il Paradiso perduto* di Giovanni Milton tradotto da Girolamo Silvio Martinengo. Venezia, 1801. 3 vols.

English and Italian texts on opposite pages, with a few notes at the end of each book. A life in Italian and Addison's observations, in both languages, conclude the final volume.

1529 *Il Paradiso perduto* di Milton, versione di Luc' Antonio Corner. 1803.

1530 *Il Paradiso perduto* di Giovanni Milton tradotto da Lazarro Papi. 3 tom. Lucca, 1811.

Reprinted, 1817; Milan, 1851. Preface, brief notes, and an Addison paper on *Paradise Lost*.

1531 Il Paradiso perduto. . . . . Tomo IV. Tradatto da Carlo Tirelli. 1811.

Noted by Allodoli.

1532 Il primo canto del *Paradiso perduto* . . . . recato in ottava rima, version libera di Vicenzo Petrobelli. Lendinara: Michelini, 1831. Pp. 326.

1533 *Il Paradiso perduto* di Giovanni Milton tradotto in verso italiano da Felice Mariottini col testo inglese a rincontro. Roma, 1813–14. 3 vols.

Italian and English texts on opposite pages. Notes and Addison's critical essays.

1534 *Il Paradiso perduto* di Giovanni Milton, versione di Luc' Antonio Corner. Venice, 1815. 2 vols.

1535 *Il Paradiso perduto,* poema . . . . recato in versi italiani da Michele Leoni. Pisa, 1817. 3 vols.

A free paraphrase but notable for use of texts, for study of sources, and for biography.

1536 *Il Paradiso perduto* di Giovanni Milton tradotto da Lazarro Papi. Edizione seconda. Lucca, 1817. 2 vols.

Preface, biography, and Addison's essays. General notes on each book. Reprinted at Milan, 3d ed., 3 vols., 1827; 4th ed., 1829; 5th ed., 1833.

1537 *Il Paradiso perduto* di Milton, versione italiana di G. Sorelli. Londra: Dulau, [1820].

Reviews in *Monthly Magazine,* LVIII (1824–25), 516–18; LIX, 419.

1538 *Il Paradiso perduto* di Giovanni Milton tradotto dal padre Giovanni Francesco Cuneo d'Ornano . . . . con prefazione e note di Mr. C. D'O. editore. Roma, 1822. 2 vols.

In ottava rima.

1539 Il Paradiso perduto. . . . . Versione italiana di Guido Sorelli. Seconda edizione. Londra: Dulau, 1827.

Reprinted, 1832. Review by S. Uzielli, *Antologia,* XXX (1828), 27 ff., praises the edition.

1540 *Il Paradiso perduto* di Milton riportato in versi italiani da G. Sorelli da Firenze. Terza edizione, rivista, corrètta, e Toscanemente accentuata. Londra: J. Murray, 1832.

A subscription edition.
Review in *Athen.,* December 15, 1832, p. 807.

1541 Il Paradiso perduto. Tradotto da Lazarro Papi. Firenze, 1836. 2 vols. in 1.

1542 La Creazione, libro settimo del *Paradiso perduto* di Giovanni Milton, voltato dalla sciolto inglese nell'ottava rima italiana da Lorenzo Mancini, etc. Firenze, 1839.

Notes. Reprinted in 1842 (2 vols.).

1543 *Il Paradiso perduto,* recato dallo sciolto inglese nella nostra ottava rima da Lorenzo Mancini. Firenze, 1841.

1544 *Il Paradiso perduto* di Giovanni Milton, recato dallo sciolto inglese nella nostra ottava rima da Lorenzo Mancini. Firenze, 1842. 2 vols.

Translator has omitted anti-Catholic passages.

1545 Il Paradiso perduto. Naples, 1843. 2 vols.

Seventh edition of Lazarro Papi's translation.

1546 A New Edition of Milton's *Paradise Lost* with a New Translation into Italian Poetry, Verse by Verse, by Domenico Arnaldi. *Paradiso perduto* di Milton. Nuova edizione, con una nuova traduzione in poesia italiana verso a verso. The Life of Milton with Criticisms on His Works by Dr. Johnson. A General Critique upon the *Paradise Lost*, by J. Addisson. Genoa, 1852. 2 vols.

Poorly done. Revised, 1856.

1547 *Il Paradiso perduto;* traduzione di Antonio Bellati. Milano, 1856. Pp. 595.

The biography is based on Prendeville. Second edition out in the same year.

1548 *Il Paradiso perduto;* poema . . . . traduzione del cavaliere Andrea Maffei. Torino, 1857.

Has Chateaubriand's commentary on English literature and an Italian version of a canto of Klopstock's *Der Messias*.

1549 *Il Paradiso perduto* . . . . traduzione del Andrea Maffei. Prima edizione Fiorentina. Firenze, 1863.

Contains four sonnets written at various stages of the work (in 1846, 1853, 1854, 1857).

1550 Satana. Sceni infernali, terrestri e celesti del *Paradiso perduto*, tradotte nel metro e col ritmo dell'originale. Milano, 1876.

Contains a sonnet on Milton's blindness, dedicated to Gladstone.

1551 *Il Paradiso perduto* di Giovanni Milton. Traduzione del Andrea Maffei. Edizione fiorentino rivista dal traduttore. Firenze: Successori le Monnier, 1880.

1552 *Il Paradiso perduto* . . . . tradotto da Lazarro Papi. Con illustrazioni di G. Doré. Milano, 1881. Pp. xii+282.

1553 *Il Paradiso perduto* di Giovanni Milton tradotto da Lazarro Papi. Milan, 1901. Pp. 279.

Cheap edition of the old text; Doré illustrations.

1554 Giovanni Milton. Il Paradiso perduto. Poema. Traduzione di Andrea Maffei. Torino, 1924. Pp. xxxix+383.

The 1857 translation.

1555 *Paradise Lost*, con introduzione e note di G. Ferrando. Firenze: F. le Monnier, 1925. Pp. 109.

Translation of extracts from *Paradise Lost*. The collection includes parts of the *Minor Poems* and extracts from works of other English writers.

Review in *RC*, XCII (1925), 194.

1556 [Manuscript of an Italian translation of *Paradise Lost*.]

Fragments of a translation of *Paradise Lost* are preserved among Salvini's papers, in the Biblioteca Ricardiana, Florence. See C. Cordaro, *A. M. Salvini* (Piacenza, 1906), p. 44.

SPANISH

1557 *El Paraiso perdido*, poema de Milton traducido en verso castellano por Don J. de Escoiquiz. Bourges: Gilles, 1812. 3 vols.

The same translation was printed in Madrid, 3 volumes (1844) and in Barcelona (1862 and 1883). Has a prefatory comment, Addison's criticism, and notes.

The 1883 edition has Lamartine's *Life*, and Chateaubriand's study, translated by Juan Cortada.

1558 *El Paraiso perdido* de J. Milton, poema ingles, traducido al castellano por D. Benito Ramon de Hermida y dado a luz por su hija la marquesa de Santa Coloma. Madrid, 1814. 2 vols.

1559 *El Paraiso perdido* . . . . par Don J. de Escoiquiz. Madrid, 1844. 3 vols.

1560 El Paraiso perdido. Traducido en prosa por Santiago Angel Saura Mascaró. Barcelona: Pujol, 1849. 2 vols.

1561 [*Paradise Lost*, Book I.]

Translation into Spanish by G. M. de Jovellanos, in *Bibl. de Autores Españoles*, XLVI (1858), 26 ff.

1562 El Paraiso perdido. Traduccion en verso par Don J. de Escoiquiz, precedida de una sucinta biografia de Milton por Lamartine, y de un estudio histórico y literario acerca del mismo por Chateaubriand, traducidos aquella y este por D. J. Cortada. Adornan esta obra 24 laminas magnificas. Barcelona, [1862].

Same text as in The Madrid edition (1844) in 3 volumes. Reprinted, 1883.

1563 El Paraiso perdido. . . . . Con notas de Addisson, Saint-Maur y otros. Traducida al Castellano por D. Dionisio San Juan. Barcelona: Tasso, 1868.

Prose; a few footnotes.

También, Id. Jepús, 1883. Pp. 487.

Esta misma corre con portade de Barcelona, Riudor: Llondachs, 1883. Pp. 487.

1564 *El Paraiso perduto* di Milton. Traducido del Ingles por Anibal Galindo. Gante, 1868. Pp. xxvii+501.

English and Spanish texts on opposite pages, the latter in prose. The translator asserts that he selected *Paradise Lost* as being the best seventeenth-century document on religious liberty. Notes.

1565 El Paraiso perdido. Traducido en prosa por Demetrio San Martin. Barcelona: Jané hermanos, 1873. Pp. 301.

Second edition, 1873. The same text printed in Madrid, by Calleja, in 1882. Pp. 381.

1566 El Paraiso perdido. Nueva traduccion del Inglés anotada y precedida de la vida del autor por D. Cayetano Rosell. Barcelona: Montaner & Simón, 1873. Pp. 293.

1567 El Paraiso perdido. Madrid, 1882. 2 vols.

This translation is a part of *La Biblioteca Clásica*. Other editions in 1905, 1906, 1909, and 1913.

1568 *El Paraiso perdido* . . . . con notas de Addisson, Chateaubriand, Saint-Maur y otros: traducida al castellano por D. Demetrio San Martin. Madrid, 1882.

Prose translation.

1569 El Paraiso perdido. . . . . Traducida al Castellano por D. Dionisio Sanjuan. Milton, estudio biográfico y critico, por M. de Chateaubriand. Barcelona, 1883. Pp. 487.

In *Los Grandes Poemas . . . . publicados bajo la direción literaría de F. J. Orellana.* A prose translation.

1570 *El Paraiso perdido:* poema . . . . E. A. Bonilla. Bogota, 1897. 2 vols.

1571 [Translation of parts of *Paradise Lost* into Spanish prose. In] Menéndez y Pelayo, *Historia de las ideas estéticas en España.* 2d ed. Madrid, 1903. Pp. 29 and 175.

Noted that Ignacio de Luzan was the first Spaniard to draw attention to Milton.

1572 El Paraiso perdido. Traducida literal con biografia, prólogo y notas por Juan Mateos. Ornamentada por Coll Salieti. Barcelona: Editorial Ibérica (Puges), 1914. Pp. 353.

PORTUGUESE

1573 *O Paraiso Perdido*, poema epico de João Milton traduzido em verso Portugez por Francisco. Bento Maria Targini. Pariz, 1823. 2 vols.

1574 *Paraiso Perdido*, poema heroico de J. Milton. Traduzido em vulgar pelo Padre Jose Amara da Silva. . . . . Com o *Paraiso Restaurado*. . . . .

Notas . . . . de M. Racine; e as Observacoes de M. Addisson sobre o *Paraiso Perdido.* Nova edicao. Lisboa, 1830. 2 vols.

Many footnotes. First edition, 1789.

1575 O Paraïso Perdido. Epopea de João Milton; vertida do original inglez pâra verso portuguez por Antonio José de Lima Leitão. Lisboa, 1840. 2 vols.

Frontispiece portrait wrongly asserted to be from an original miniature. Notes.

1576 A. J. de Lima Leitão . . . . revista por Xavier da Cunha *O Paraiso perdido.* Lisboa, 1880.

Doré illustrations.

GREEK

1577 Miltoni *P*[*aradisi*] *A*[*missi*] Graecae metaphraseos specimen integrum. [In] Ricardi Dawesii, *Miscellanea Critica.* Cantabrigiae: Thomas Kidd, 1817.

Paradise Lost, Book I, ll. 250–64, given in Greek and English on opposite pages, with Latin footnotes. The Appendix sets forth proposals for printing by subscription the entire book.

1578 Proposal for Printing . . . . *Paradisi Amissi* . . . . liber primus Graeca versione donatus una cum annotationibus a R. Dawes. [In] *ibid.*, editio secunda. 1827.

1579 Milton's Invocation to Light. [*Paradise Lost*, Book III, ll. 1–55, translated into Greek iambics. London, 1849.] Pp. 4.

1580 Milton's *Paradise Lost* Now for the First Time Translated into Greek Accentual Dactylic Hexameters by Alexander S. Casdagli. With Illustrations by Gustave Doré. London, Leipzig printed, 1887. Pp. vii+170.

Published by the translator. Out also with an 1888 title-page.

1581 Gaisford Prize, 1887. Hexameter Verse. [A Greek translation of *Paradise Lost*, Book VI, ll. 746–85.] By F. W. Hall. Oxford: Blackwell, 1887. Pp. 7.

LATIN

1582 Concilium Infernorum e libro secundo *Paradisi Amissi* Johannis Miltoni carmine latino donatum. (Epistola Ambrosii Philips.) Auctor P. F. Bromptonae, 1831.

HEBREW

1583 Milton's *Paradise Lost*, in Hebrew Blank Verse. [By Isaac Eliezer Salkinson]. Vienna, 1871. Pp. 351.

1584 [Hebrew translation of *Paradise Lost*, by] Samuel Raffalovich. Jerusalem, 1892. Pp. 63.

Selections, in prose; footnotes.

RUSSIAN

1585 [Russian translation of *Paradise Lost;* greatly abridged.] Moscow, 1859. 2 vols.

1586 [*Paradise Lost*, translated into Russian verse by] S. T. Pisarev. St. Petersburg, 1871. Pp. lxx+430.

1587 [*Paradise Lost* and *Paradise Regained* translated into Russian prose, by] Borodin. Moscow, 1888. Pp. 335.

1588 [*Paradise Lost* and *Paradise Regained*, in Russian.] St. Petersburg, [1895]. Pp. 332.

An octavo volume of prose paraphrases of the two poems appeared in Moscow in the same year.

1589 [*Paradise Lost* and *Paradise Regained* translated into Russian prose by] Kanshin. St. Petersburg, 1905. Pp. 420.

Crude illustrations.

POLISH

1590 Sąd ostateczny. Poema Edwarda Yunga Anglika. Z przydaniem pierwszey jego nocy, i kilku ulomkow Miltona [from *Paradise Lost*]. Przez F. Dmochowskiego, etc. Warsaw, 1803.

Selected passages from Young and Milton.

1591 Jana Miltona. Raj utracony. [Translated by W. Bartkiewicza.] Warsaw, 1902. Pp. x+423.

Brief notes following each book. In verse.

CZECH

1592 J. Miltona *Ztracený Ráj přeložený* . . . . od J. Jungmanna. Prague: Společnost Vlastenského Museum v Cechách, 1841. Nowo česka Biblioteka. Gslo 3.

HUNGARIAN

1593 [Hungarian translation of *Paradise Lost.*] O. Wigand. Kassann, 1817. 2 vols.

This translation was first published in 1796.

1594 [Hungarian translation of *Paradise Lost*], Ford. Bessenyei Sánder. K. L. Kötve. 1874. 2 vols.

1595 [Hungarian translation of *Paradise Lost.*] G. Jánosi. Olesó Könyvtár, 1875. Pp. 447.

A clear and accurate translation. Reprinted, 1890.

LETTISH

1596 [*Paradise Lost,* in Lettish.] Leepaja, 1893, 1899. 2 vols.

Translated by Dünsberga Ernsts, Sr.

ARMENIAN

1597 [*Paradise Lost,* translated into Armenian prose by Haroutiun Aukerian; with a biographical notice of Milton]. [Venice], 1819.

Another edition, 1824. Pp. 503.

1598 [*Paradise Lost* in Armenian.] Pascal Aucher. Venice, 1824. Pp. 503.

WELSH

1599 *Coll Gwynfa,* cyfieithiad gan W. Owen Pughe. Llundain: W. Marchant, 1819. Pp. 371.

Another printing appeared in the same year, with a slightly different title-page and with a dedication in Welsh instead of English. Brief footnotes and a glossary.

Review in *Monthly Magazine,* XLVII (1819), 225–26.

1600 Coll Gwynfa. Cyfieithiad o *Paradise Lost,* John Milton. Gyda chofiant, a sylwadau ar ei athrylith, yn nghryda nodiadau eglurhaol, gan John Evans. Wrexham: Hughes aï Fab., [1871].

Second edition, 1891.

MANX

1601 *Paradise Lost:* a Poem by John Milton. Translated into the Manks Language by Thomas Christian. 1872.

"Publications of the Manx Society." Selections from *Paradise Lost.*

TONGAN

1602 [*Paradise Lost,* in Tongan.] London: Walker & Co., 1892. Pp. 116.

Selections.

ESPERANTO

1603 [*Paradise Lost,* Book IV, ll. 32–114, in Esperanto.] Parolado de Satano al la Suno el *Paradizo Perdita.* Tradukita de Charles Stewart, [1908].

Typed manuscript, in the British Museum.

8. *PARADISE REGAINED*

1604 Johann Miltons *Wiedererobertes Paradies.* Aus dem Englischen neu übersetzt von Friedrich Wilhelm Bruckbräu. München, 1828. Pp. 100.

In prose.

1605 Johann Miltons *Wiedererobertes Paradies*. Aus dem Englischen neu übersetzt von Friedrich Wilhelm Bruckbräu. Wohlfeile Ausgabe. München, 1835.

1606 Das verlorene Paradies. Das wiedergewonnene Paradies. Übersetzt von Bernhard Schuhmann. Stuttgart und Augsburg [printed], 1855. Pp. 466.

1607 *Le Paradis reconquis*, ou le tentation de Jésus au désert. Poème de Milton. Traduit de l'Anglois par Louis Vaucher. Paris, 1859.

In prose.

1608 Milton's Poetiska Verk. Det *Förlorade Paradiset* och Det *Atervunna Paradiset*. Ö fersatta af V. E. Oman. Upsala, 1862. Pp. 450.

1609 *Das verlorene Paradies* und *das wiedergewonnene Paradies* von John Milton. Übersetzt von B. Schuhmann. Zweite Auflage. Stuttgart, 1877. Pp. viii+412.

First edition, 1855.

1610 [*Paradise Lost* and *Paradise Regained* translated into Russian prose by Borodin.] Moscow, 1888.

1611 [*Paradise Lost* and *Paradise Regained* in Russian.] St. Petersburg: Marcks, [1895]. Pp. 332.

An octavo volume of prose paraphrases of the two poems appeared in Moscow in the same year.

1612 J. Milton. Het herwonnen Paradijs. Utrecht, 1901. Pp. 76.

Translated by H. Van Dijk. A metrical version of *Paradise Regained*, each book being preceded by an "argument." No notes.

1613 [Russian translations in prose, of *Paradise Lost* and *Paradise Regained*.] St. Petersburg, 1905. Pp. 420.

9. *SAMSON AGONISTES*

1614 Fabulae *Samson Agonistes* et *Comus*, Graece. E. Greswell. Oxon, 1832. Pp. 133.

1615 John Miltons dramatische Werke. *Comus*. *Simson Agonistes* . . . . von H——h [Hirsch?]. Berlin, 1840. Pp. viii+152.

1616 Traduction de *Samson Agonistes* de Joseph d'Avenel. Paris, 1860.

1617 O. Ilbert. Senarii Graeci [from *Samson Agonistes*]. Marlborough College prolusiones, 1863.

1618 Umfangreiche Stücke aus Miltons *Comus* und *Samson Agonistes.* Übersetzt von Alexander Schmidt in dessen Vorlesung: *Miltons dramatische Dichtungen.* Königsberg, 1864.

Also printed in his *Gesammelten Abhandlungen.* Berlin, 1889.

1619 Miltoni *Samson Agonistes.* Graece reddidit Georgius, Baro Lyttelton. Londini: Macmillan et Soc., 1867. Pp. [v]+189.

English and Greek on opposite pages.
Review in *Athen.*, February 15, 1868.

1620 Milton's *Samson Agonistes* in metrischer Übertragung, mit Vorwort und Anmerkungen von E. C. Eddelbüttel. [In] *Programm.* . . . . Düsseldorf, [1869].

1621 F. A. P[aley]. Iambici trimetri. Scripsit F.A.P. Cambridge: J. Palmer, [1888]. Pp. 7.

Samson Agonistes, ll. 1596–1659, and a Greek version on opposite pages.

1622 [*Samson Agonistes* in Hebrew. Translated by] J. Massel. Manchester: privately printed, 1890. Pp. [iv]+108.

Done to demonstrate the flexibility and beauty of Hebrew as equal to the possibilities of modern languages. On the whole a poor translation.
Review in *Athen.*, II (1890), 583–84.

1623 Gaisford Prize, 1892. Milton's *Samson Agonistes,* Lines 1570–1660, Translated into Tragic Iambic Verse, by W. D. Bailey. Oxford: Blackwell, 1892. Pp. 15.

English and Greek lines on opposite pages.

1624 [*Samson Agonistes* in Russian. Translated by N. A. Briansky.] St. Petersburg, 1911. Pp. v+57.

No notes.

1625 [Swedish translation of *Samson Agonistes*] in verse, by U. Lindelöf]. Helsingfors: Scheldt, 1918. Pp. 80.

Brief biographical preface and notes.

10. PROSE WORKS

1626 A. B. E. "Letter of Milton." *Monthly Magazine*, XXIV (1807), 565–66.

Translation of his letter to Leonard Philaras, dated September 28, 1654. The letter was included in Aylmer's edition of the *Familiar Letters*, 1674.

1626a Die Schutzrede von Johann Milton für das englische Volk. [Translated by I. P. V. Troxler. In] *Fürst und Volk nach Buchanans und Miltons Lehre.* Aurau, 1821. Pp. 142.

Introduction, pp. 1–16.

I. Das Gespräch zwischen Buchanan und Metellan über das Recht zu herrschen, pp. 17–76.

II. Die Schutzrede. . . . , pp. 81–141.

Refers to Buchanan's (1576) *De Jure Regni apud Scotos* as related also to the freedom of the people in England.

1627 *Aréopagitique* . . . . de anglais, 1644; *De l'éducation* . . . . de anglais, 1650; *Comus* . . . . de anglais, 1634. [In] *Bibliothèque étrangère,* par M. Aignan. Paris, 1823.

Volume II has notes and texts of the three pieces at pages 1, 87, and 117.

1628 [*Eikon Basilike* in French translation. In] F. Guizot's *Collection des mémoires relatifs à la révolution d'Angleterre.* Paris: Pichon-Béchet, 1827. 25 vols.

Volume IX contains the Milton item.

1629 Areopagitica. Übersetzt von Dr. Richard Koeppell. Berlin, 1851.

1630 Miltons *Rede über Pressfreiheit.* Berlin, 1852.

In 1858 J. Zelle referred to this as one of two pieces of Milton's prose then available in German translation.

1631 Johann Miltons Abhandlung über Lehre und Wesen der Ehescheidung mit der Zueignung an das Parlament vom Jahre 1644. Nach der abgekürzten Form des George Burnett. Deutsch von Franz von Holtzendorff. Berlin, 1855. Pp. v+45.

Presumably the second item referred to by Zelle.

1632 Remarks on and Translation of Milton's Treatise *Of Education.* By Dr. J. Zelle. [In] *Beilage zum Programm des Königl. und Stadt-Gymnasium* zu Cöslin. 1858.

English Preface, German text, and an uncritical commentary.

1633 John Miltons Politische Hauptschriften. Übersetzt und mit Anmerkungen versehen von Wilhelm Bernhardi. Berlin, 1874, 1876, 1879. 3 vols.

Volumes made up of gathered pamphlets bearing dates between 1871 and 1879. Review by A. Stern, *RC,* IX (1875), 76–78.

1634 [Russian translation of Milton's *History of Moscovia.*] Published by the Imperial Society of Russian History and Antiquities, at the Moscow University. Pp. ii+83.

1635 Miltons pädagogische Schriften und Äusserungen. Jürgen Bona Meyer. Langensalza, 1890. Pp. xvi+64.

Of Education, parts of *Areopagitica*, passages from the church pamphlets, and four letters. Notes.

1636 John Milton. Über Erziehung. [In] *Neue Jahrbücher für Philologie und Pädagogik.* II. Abteilung (1890), pp. 81–105.

Translated by Hermann Ullrich.

1637 John Milton's Essay *Of Education.* Englischer Text und deutsche Übersetzung mit Einleitung und erklärenden Erläuterungen. Von Dr. Joseph Reber. *Beilage zum Programm der höheren weiblichen Bildungsanstalt zu Aschaffenburg.* [1893.] Pp. 46.

1638 Milton. *De educación*, traducido por Natalia Cossío. Madrid: Acabo, 1916. Pp. 54.

A school text, with Introduction and footnotes. The work was done twenty years before publication.

1639 Areopagitica. . . . . Ausgewählt und mit Anmerkungen versehen von R. Ritter. 1925. Pp. 32.

XIII. BIOGRAPHY

1640 "Milton's Will." *Monthly Magazine*, X (1800), 535.

Extract from Milton's will, to show his attitude toward his daughters. The will appears in full in the second (1791) edition of the *Minor Poems* by Warton and in Todd.

1641 Theatrum poetarum Anglicanorum. Containing the Names and Characters of All the English Poets, from the Reign of Henry III to the Close of the Reign of Queen Elizabeth, by Edward Phillips, the Nephew of Milton. First Published in 1675, and Now Enlarged by Additions to Every Article from Subsequent Biographers and Critics. Canterbury: Simmons & Kirby, 1800. Pp. lxxix+336+4.

Edited by Sir Egerton Brydges. Has added names and sketches. Interesting chiefly as evidence of an interest in Milton and in the earlier poets, in the year 1800.

1642 Henry J. Todd. Life of Milton. London, 1801.

Prefixed to his edition of the *Poetical Works*. Revised for the 1809 and 1826 editions, *q.v.*

Reviews in the *Monthly Review*, CXI (1826), 258–73; *Congregational Magazine*, X, 33; *Monthly Mirror*, XIII (1802), 249–50.

1643 J. P. Malcolm. Londinium redivivum, or an Ancient History and Modern Description of London Compiled from Parochial Records, Archives of Various Foundations, the Harleian MSS., and Other Authentic Sources. London: John Nichols & Son, 1803. 4 vols.

Vol. III, p. 300: "Lordship; John Milton *Gentleman*, buried Nov. 12th 1674: consumption: *Chancel.*"

Vol. IV, p. 128: "Mrs. Catherine Milton, wife to John Milton, Esq. buried Feb. 10, 1657."

1644 [Samuel Johnson.] Vies de Milton et d'Addison . . . . trad. par A. M. H. Boulard. 1804. 2 vols.

1645 J. Mosneron. Vie de Milton. Paris, 1804.

1646 [Sir William Jones and Forest Hill.

In a review of Lord Teignmouth's *Memoirs of the Life, Writings, and Correspondence of Sir William Jones* in] *Monthly Review*, XLV (1804), 338–39.

Jones described the house at Forest Hill where he vaguely supposed Milton wrote "L'Allegro." Called Milton "the most perfect scholar, as well as the sublimest poet, that our country ever produced."

1647 [Review of Lord Teignmouth's *Memoirs of the Life, Writings, and Correspondence of Sir William Jones* in] *Edinburgh Review*, V (1805), 329–46.

Gives Sir William's account of Milton's residence at Forest Hill. Asserts that Milton wrote "L'Allegro" there. As in the preceding item, the critic accepts the assertion.

1648 D. H. "Milton's Academic Punishments." *GM*, LXXVI (April, 1806), 320–21.

Attempts to show that Milton suffered corporal punishment at Cambridge. Unimportant evidence.

1649 J. N. "Milton's Second Tutor." *Ibid.*, LXXVI (May, 1806), 420–21.

1650 Charles Symmons. Life of Milton. London, 1806. Pp. xxxv+645.

In his edition of Milton's *Prose Works*. Second ed., 1810; 3d ed., 1822.

Preface defends first assertions that Milton did not lose a term at Cambridge; that January, 1629, was the probable time of his degree. Ten terms required plus entry and degree terms.

1651 Mark Noble. "The Pedigree of Milton." *Monthly Mirror*, N.S., VI (1808), 201–5; VII (1810), 17–20; 89–95.

Begins with poet's grandfather, a native of Oxfordshire. Inaccurate in details. Accepts John Phillips' statement that Milton's mother was a Caston of Wales. Gives 1656–57 as date of elder Milton's death.

1652 W. P. "The Tendency of a Note of Mr. Thomas Warton upon Milton Refuted." *GM*, LXXX (March, 1810), 220–21.

Deals with the character of Milton.

1653 John Aubrey. Lives of Eminent Men. London, 1813.

1654 Gentleman's Magazine, LXXXIV (1814), 4.

A note by "Laicus" on Milton at Cambridge.

1655 *Ibid.*, LXXXV (1815), 292.

T. G. C. presents documents on Milton's third marriage and some data on the writing of *Paradise Lost*.

1656 William Godwin. Lives of Edward and John Philips Including Various Particulars of the Literary and Poetical History of Their Times. To Which Are Added: I. Collections for the Life of Milton by John Aubrey, FRS, Printed from the Manuscript Copy in the Ashmolean Museum at Oxford; II. The Life of Milton. By Edward Philips. Printed in the Year 1694. London: Longmans, etc., 1815. Pp. viii+410.

Contains much unique material. Reprinted, 1911.

Review by J. Mackintosh in *Edinburgh Review*, XXV, 485–501; *Monthly Review*, LXXVIII, 414–24; *Monthly Magazine*, XL, 614–24.

1657 Gentleman's Magazine, LXXXV (1815), 22–25.

C. Torrens shows the facts regarding the Powells, disproving Todd's statements regarding another family of the same name as origin of Milton's first wife.

1658 David Bertolotti. [Milton's Italian maiden.] *Il Raccoglitore*, VI (1819), 60.

Presumably the source of the story to the effect that Milton was found sleeping under a tree near Cambridge by two young Italian girls; that one left a note in his hand; and that the incident motivated his Italian journey. Artists have used the notion in designing plates for editions of Milton.

1659 "Milton's House at Chalfont." *Monthly Magazine*, LI (1821), 493.

Description of the house, accompanied by an engraving showing Milton dictating to his amanuensis.

1660 "Milton's House in Petty France." *Ibid.*, LIV (1822), 97.

Description and engraving.

1661 Theatrum poetarum Anglicanorum: Containing Brief Characters of the English Poets down to the Year 1675. By Edward Phillips, the Nephew of Milton. The Third Edition. Reprinted at the Expense, and with the Notes, of Sir Egerton Brydges. Geneva: Bonnant, 1824.

One hundred copies printed. Interesting for the lists of writers added by the editor, and for his brief comments on their works.

1662 "Milton." *New Monthly Magazine*, XV (1825), 209.

Notes the discovery by Lemon of new Milton materials, in addition to the manuscript of *De doctrina*.

1663 Henry John Todd. Some Account of the Life and Writings of John Milton, Derived Principally from Documents in His Majesty's State Paper Office, Now First Published. London: C. and J. Rivington, 1826. Pp. 370.

A new biography as Volume I of the 1826 edition of the *Poetical Works*. Appendix containing an "Inquiry into the Origin of *Paradise Lost*."

1664 "Milton's Retreat during the Plague." *Saturday Magazine*, I (1832), 28–29.

On the length of Milton's residence at Chalfont. Engraving of his house.

1665 John Mitford. Life of Milton.

In his edition of Milton's *Poetical Works*. London: Pickering, 1832. Review in *Colburn's New Monthly Magazine*, XXXIV, 581–82.

1666 Joseph Ivimey. John Milton, His Life and Times, Religious and Political Opinions with an Appendix Containing Animadversions upon

Dr. Johnson's *Life of Milton.* . . . . London: E. Wilson, 1833. Pp. xvi+397. New York: Appleton & Co. Pp. xiv+300.

Contents: pp. 1–343, biography; pp. 343–82, attack on Johnson; pp. 383–97, royal proclamations and extracts from *Council Order Book* (from Todd).

Reviews in *GM*, CIII, i, 242–45; *New Monthly Magazine*, XXXVIII, 102–3.

1667 Sir Edgerton Brydges. Milton. London: J. Macrone, [1835]. Pp. xxix+303.

Frontispiece portrait, refined drawing. Text, pp. 1–276; Appendix I, memoranda relating to Powell family of Forest-Hill, Oxfordshire; Appendix II, descendants of Milton; Appendix III, Milton's agreement with Symmons; Appendix IV, Cowley's Preface to his *Poems*.

1668 Gentleman's Magazine, N.S., VI (1836), 451–68.

Review of recent editions of Milton and survey of his life.

1669 "Youth of Milton." *North American Review*, XLVII (1838), 56.

1670. "Local Memories of Great Men: Milton." *Penny Magazine*, March 6, 1841, pp. 97–100.

Engravings of Milton, of Ludlow Castle, Chalfont, Christ's College, Cambridge, and the Church of St. Giles, Cripplegate. Biographical sketch, accompanied by a brief history of each of Milton's residences.

1671 John Mitford. Life of Milton.

In Mitford's edition of *Poetical Works* . . . . , I, [xix]–cvii. Boston, 1841.

1672 "Milton's Blindness." *Chamber's Edinburgh Journal*, III (1845), 392–94.

Shows difference in Milton's poetry after blindness. Tries to prove that only a blind man could have written *Paradise Lost*.

1673 E. Taylor. "Some Unrecorded Passages in the Life of John Milton." *Christian Reformer*, 1846.

1674 G. F. Holmes. "Domestic Life of Milton." *De Bow's Review*, N.S., III (1847), 12, 113.

1675 "Milton's Widow." *Athen.*, September 22, 1849, pp. 953–54.

Biographical note on Elizabeth Minshull.

For date of her death, see *Athen.*, October 20, 1849, p. 1065. For discussion of her character, see *ibid.*, September 29, 1849, pp. 984–85.

1676 [Sale of Milton's *Arati solensis phaenomena et diosemea*, etc., 1519.] *Ibid.*, January 19, 1850, p. 76.

Contains Milton's autograph.

1677 Joseph Hunter. Milton. A Sheaf of Gleanings after His Biographers and Annotators: I. Genealogical Investigation; II. Notes on Some of His Poems. London: J. R. Smith, 1850. Pp. 72.

Biographical notes on Richard Milton and John Milton, Sr.

Baptism records of John, Sarah, Tabitha, and Christopher Milton.

Milton owned Fitz-Herbert's *Natura Brevium*, 1584. Assumes Milton started to study law, on this evidence.

Reviews in *Athen.*, August 3, 1850, p. 812; *GM*, XXXIV (October, 1850), 405–8; by H. A. Whitney, *North American Review*, LXXXII, 388–404.

1678 Cyrus R. Edmonds. John Milton: A Biography Especially Designed To Exhibit the Ecclesiastical Principles of That Illustrious Man. London: Cockshaw, 1851. Pp. vii+251.

1679 John Fitchett Marsh. Papers Connected with the Affairs of Milton and His Family. Chetham Society Miscellanies, Vol. I. Manchester: 1851. Pp. 46.

See also his contributions to the *Transactions of the Historic Society of Lancashire and Cheshire.*

Edited by J. F. M. from the original documents in his possession.

Frontispiece of signatures.

Papers sold from library of James Boswell (second son of Johnson's biographer): (1) will of Elizabeth Milton, probated October 10, 1727; and (2) Anne Milton, Mary Milton, and Deborah Clarke: receipts of £100 each as portions of estate.

1680 John Mitford. The Life of John Milton. London: Pickering, 1851.

One of 10 copies printed separately; compare the 6-volume edition.

Has Mitford's poem on Milton advertisements, a partial pedigree, and a copy of the *Paradise Lost* agreement.

1681 "Milton." *National Magazine*, I (July, 1852), 9–13.

Biographical sketch based on one in the *North British Review.*

1682 John Fitchett Marsh. Notice of the Inventory of the Effects of Mrs. Milton, Widow of the Poet. Liverpool, 1855.

Extracted from the *Proceedings of the Historic Society of Lancashire and Cheshire.* Read February 22, 1855.

Itemized, total value £38 8*s.* 4*d.*

1683 "Miltonian Relics at Cambridge." *Chamber's Edinburgh Journal*, N.S., XXVIII (1857), 319–20.

Mulberry tree and Milton manuscripts.

1684 [Biographical notes on Milton.] *GM*, N.S., II (March, 1857), 261, 336, 356.

On his religion, the relics belonging to Milton, and the character of his third wife.

1685 [Milton autographs.] *Athen.*, September 17, 1859, p. 375; October 1, 1859, p. 432; October 15, 1859, p. 499; February 11, 1860, p. 208.

Disputed Milton autographs discussed.

1686 Hyde Clarke. "Milton's Genealogy." *N & Q*, VII (1859), 232, 489.

Biographical note on Milton's father, based on Guildhall and Scriverner's records of freedom.

See also *Athen.*, March 19, 1859, pp. 389–90.

1687 W. Douglas Hamilton. Original Papers Illustrative of the Life and Writings of John Milton, Including Sixteen Letters of State Written by Him Now First Published from Manuscripts in the State Paper Office. With an Appendix of Documents Relating to His Connection with the Powell Family. Collected and Edited with the Permission of the Master of the Rolls. London: Camden Society, 1859.

Reviews, in *Edinburgh Review*, CXI (1860), 312–47; *Athen.*, December 17, 1859, pp. 810–11.

1688 Thomas Keightley. Life, Opinions, and Writings of John Milton. London: Chapman & Hall, 1859.

Reviews by H. A. Whitney, *North American Review*, LXXXII, 388–404; *Living Age*, LXIII, 226–29; *Athen.*, September 17, 1859, pp. 360–61.

1689 "Youth of Milton." *Edinburgh Review*, CXI (1860), 312.

1690 "Youth of Milton." *Blackwood's Magazine*, LXXXVII (1860), 673.

1691 John Fitchett Marsh. On the Engraved Portraits and Pretended Portraits of Milton. . . . . Liverpool: T. Brakell, 1860.

From the *Transactions of the Historic Society of Lancashire and Cheshire*, XII (1860). Read May 3, 1860.

Had catalogue of 164 portraits; 150 on exhibition.

1692 W. L. Nichols. "Milton at Chalfont." *N & Q*, Ser. II, No. IX (1860), pp. 397–98.

Biographical note. Refers to Dunster's notable essay on Milton's early reading.

1693 Samuel Leigh Sotheby. Ramblings in the Elucidation of the Autograph of Milton. London: T. Richards, 1861. Pp. xxviii+263.

In folio; presents many valuable reproductions of manuscript pages, etc. Little definitive judging of evidence.

1694 "Home, School, and College Training of John Milton." *American Journal of Education*, XIV (1864), 159–90.

Cursory notes on seventeenth-century methods.

695 A. D. Gridley. "Milton's Early Life." *American Presbyterian Review*, XIV (1865), 360–64.

A summary from Masson.

696 Nation, III (1866), 82.

On Milton's copy of *Lycophron* (Geneva, 1601) with his autograph and marginal notes.

697 R. L. Dabney. "John Milton." *Land We Love*, II (1867), 445–58; III, 38–108, 199–203.

Biographical sketch; extremely sympathetic.

698 John Ward Dean. "Milton, Ward, and Drake." *Historical Magazine* (Dawson's), XV (February, 1869), 128–30.

See also *Athen.*, November 7, 1868.
Record pertaining to Milton's mother.

699 Richard Owen. "Milton and Galileo." *Fraser's Magazine*, LXXIX (1869), 678–84.

Letters of Milton relative to his acquaintance with Galileo. No opinion as to their genuineness.

700 John W. Hales. "Did Milton Serve in the Parliamentary Army?" *Acad.*, VI (October 31, 1874), 485–86.

Negative conclusions.

701 "John Milton, the Scrivener." *Ibid.*, VI (November 21, 1874), 560–61.

Record of lawsuit involving elder Milton.

702 Joseph Lemuel Chester. [Name of Milton's mother.] *Ibid.*, VII (April 3, 1875), 346.

Chester claims the discovery of her name and the locale of her family. His assertions substantiated.

703 Academy, VIII (December 11, 1875), 600.

A note on 19 York St., Westminster, at that date the only remaining structure among those in which Milton had lived.

704 Charles Matthew Clode. Memorials of the Guild of Merchant Tailors. London: privately printed, 1875.

On the transfer of property, including house where Milton was born, No. 61 Bread Street, to Merchant Tailors' Company by John Treswell, March 1, 1518–19.

1705 Charles Cook. "The Hollis Bust of Milton." *Scribner's Monthly*, XI (1876), 472–76.

List of paintings of Milton, and a history of the Hollis bust in Christ's College. This bust is authentic.

1706 A. von Reumont. "Milton e Galileo." *Archiv. stor. ital.*, XXVI, (1877), 427–43.

1707 Edward Scott. "Milton's Blindness." *Athen.*, May 18, 1878, p. 633.

On Morus' attack on Milton, 1652–54.

1708 T. E. Sharpe. "Milton, Minshull, and Gouldsmyth." *Genealogist*, II (1878), 309–15.

Pedigree of Dr. Nathan Paget and Elizabeth Minshull, third wife of Milton. Shows him her great-uncle: she, the grand-daughter of Ellen Gouldsmith and Richard Minshull, and great-granddaughter of Nicholas Gouldsmith of Nantwich.

Completes speculations in *N & Q*, Ser. I, Nos. VIII and IX.

Richard Minshull's Letters, Harl. MS 2039, fol. 16.

1709 Joseph Lemuel Chester. "Milton's Mother and Grandmother." *Athen.*, October 18, 1879, pp. 496–97.

On the financial status of the Jefferys.

See also Hyde Clarke, *Athen.*, October 11, 1879, pp. 464–65.

1710 Hyde Clarke. "Milton's Divorce." *Ibid.*, September 20, 1879, p. 366.

On Milton's politics and the Powell family.

1711 Edward Scott. "Milton's Divorce." *Ibid.*, September 13, 1879, p. 337.

New light on cause of Milton's separation from Mary Powell.

1712 Mark Pattison. Milton. "English Men of Letters Series." London, 1879.

Reviews listed in Item 2105. Frequently reprinted in London and New York by Macmillan and by Harper's.

1713 "Milton Notes." *Athen.*, May 1, 1880, pp. 565–66.

Biographical notes relating to the poet's father and to Richard Milton.

1714 [Portraits of Milton.] *Nation*, XXX (January 1, 1880), 10.

On Jonathan Richardson's etching and Munkacsy's picture of Milton dictating *Paradise Lost*.

1715 [Cotton *versus* John Milton and Bower.]

Athen., July 3, 1880, p. 15, has an item on the lawsuit in question. Earlier items of small value on the same matter are: *N & Q*, Ser. II, No. X (1860), pp. 341–42; *Standard*, November 12, 1874; *Acad.*, VI (1874), 560–61. The *Cottonian Charters* (I, 5) show the case from an unusual angle.

1716 Joseph Lemuel Chester. "Milton Notes." *Athen.*, May 29, 1880, pp. 695–96.

Biographical note on Milton's mother.

1717 Hyde Clarke. "Milton Notes: Cousin Blackborough." *Ibid.*, April 24, 1880, pp. 536–37.

This cousin was Hester Jeffery, at whose house the reconciliation between Milton and Mary Powell took place. Gives John Jeffery's will.

1718 Hyde Clarke. [Biographical notes on Milton.] *Ibid.*, March 13, 1880, pp. 760–61; *ibid.*, June 12, 1880, pp. 343–44.

Notes on Milton's father and Richard Milton.
See also George F. Warner, *Athen.*, March 20, 1880, p. 375.

1719 Thomas Ellwood. Relations with John Milton.

See Arber's *English Garner*, III (1880), 473–86, for selections from Ellwood's autobiography.

1720 Henry Foley. Records of the English Province of the Society of Jesus. Vol. VI. London, 1880.

Shows "Pilgrim book" records, 1588–1656.
John Milton dined in the college in October, 1638, at the time when he was spending two months at Rome.
Review in *Genealogist*, IV (1880), 211.

1721 David Masson. [Biographical note on Milton.] *Athen.*, July 3, 1880, pp. 15–16.

Note on lawsuit brought by Thomas Cotton against Milton's father in 1637.
Date of birth of John Milton the elder fixed as 1563.

1722 Geo. F. Warner. [House on Bread Street.] *Ibid.*, March 20, 1880, p. 376.

Gives data on house in Bread Street, from Lansdowne MSS.

723 A. H. "Melton or Milton." *Ibid.*, April 30, 1881, p. 592.

Milton not the Melton who in 1659 was studying law in Temple.
See *Athen.*, April 23, 1881, p. 560.

724 E. Scott. "Melton=Milton." *Ibid.*, April. 23, 1881, p. 560.

Is Milton the John Melton who sold Hardwick Manor to Sir Edward Nicholas for £2,000? This John Melton was of Middle Temple, and held a mortgage on the property in 1658/9.

725 Edward Walford. "The Unknown Portrait of John Milton." *Antiquarian Magazine* and *Bibliographer*, II (1882), 1–4.

Description of portrait owned by Mrs. Morrison. Thought to be from Milton's own hands. List of known portraits given.

1726 W. Denton. Records of St. Giles' Cripplegate. London: Bell & Sons, 1883. Pp. viii+205.

Items on Milton, pp. 27, 31, 39, 53, 159.

Page 159. "Nearly opposite Bridgewater House, and fronting the open country was a house occupied for a time by John Milton. This has been destroyed only within the last few years. The poet removed here in 1645 from the 'pretty garden house' in Aldersgate."

1727 Thomas Sinclair. "Milton's Father." *Athen.*, December 22, 1883, pp. 814–15.

A signature of the elder Milton in 1638, when he was seventy-five years old, reported.

1728 Thomas Kerslake. "Milton's Bible." *Ibid.*, January 5, 1884, pp. 19–20.

Description of a Milton Bible and its inscriptions.

1729 A. Ademollo. La Leonora di Milton e di Clemente IX. Milano, [1885]. Pp. 16.

Portrait of Leonora. Records events of her life: born at Mantua, 1611; married G. C. Castellano, May 27, 1640; died, April 6, 1670.

1730 J. Q. A. [A Milton Bible.] *N & Q* (Manchester, New Hampshire), II (1885), 606.

Bristol bookseller catalogued a Bible containing a Milton signature and a portrait profile of "Myself 1640."

1731 "Milton's Bed." *N & Q*, Ser. VII, No. III (1887), pp. 247, 372–73.

Query and reply on the possibility of Akenside's having died on Milton's bed.

1732 "The Milton Bible." *N & Q* (Manchester, New Hampshire), IV (1887), 266.

Bible purchased by British Museum was first Mrs. Milton's, but Milton himself wrote in it the dates of births of his children.

1733 [Tablet recording Milton's baptism.] *N & Q*, Ser. VII, No. IV (1887), pp. 309, 378, 434.

Query and replies on location of tablet; formerly at All Hallows Church.

1734 John Ashton. "Milton's Bones." [Pages 55–82 in] *Eighteenth Century Waifs*. London: Hurst & Blackett, 1887. Pp. 353.

Refers to article in *N & Q*, V (April 17, 1852), 369.

Quotes LeNeve's article in full and a refutation from *St. James' Chronicle*, September 4–7, 1790, and the *European Magazine*, XVII (September, 1790), 206–7.

Quotes Aubrey, III, 450: "His stone is now removed. About two years since (1681), the two steppes to the communion-table were raysed."

735 "The Milton Window." *Critic*, XII (1888), 94–95.

Account of unveiling of the memorial window in St. Margaret's Church, Westminster.

736 J. W. Allison. "Milton-Baptismal Font." *N & Q*, Ser. VII, No. VI (1888), p. 324.

Note on location of font at which Milton was baptized. See also note by Edmund Venables, p. 454.

737 J. J. Baddeley. An Account of the Church and Parish of St. Giles, without Cripplegate, in the City of London. London: privately printed, 1888. Pp. 220.

Illustrated. Only work wherein notice of Richard Powell's burial place is printed, so far as is known, and best source of parish data regarding the church structure.

738 Daniel Hipwell. "John Milton's Bible." *N & Q*, Ser. VII, No. VI (1888), p. 253.

Description of the Milton Bible in the British Museum.

739 Eugene Schuyler. "Milton's Leonora." *Nation*, XLVII (October 18, 1888), 310–12.

Account of life of the Leonora to whom Milton addressed three Latin epigrams.

740 "Milton in Westminster." *Bookworm*, II (1889), 173–76.

Biographical notes on Milton taken from Public Record Office and parish register.

741 Charles W. Dilke. "Milton's Bones." *N & Q*, Ser. VII, No. IX (1890), p. 361.

Account of disinterment of Milton's remains in St. Giles' Cripplegate, one hundred years after burial.

See also *N & Q*, pp. 396, 473.

742 Carolus. "Milton an Alleged Papist." *Ibid.*, Ser. VII, No. XI (1891), p. 306.

Gives sources of statement that Milton died a Roman Catholic.

743 John Bradshaw. "The Descendants of Milton." *Athen.*, November 26, 1892, pp. 740–41.

Traces descendants of Caleb Clarke, son of Milton's daughter Deborah. These descendants died out at Madras before 1750.

744 David Masson. "Local Memories of Milton." *Good Words*, 1893, pp. 39–44, 130–81, 170–75, 232–41.

Illustrated. On Milton's residences in Cambridge, Horton, and London.

1745 W. D. Pink. John Milton, *N & Q*, Ser. VIII, No. VII (1895), p. 489.

Refer to *Commons Journals* for September 25, 1647, for name of "John Milton, Junr.," as among those indicted for high treason "for aiding and abetting the late Force upon the Houses of Parliament."

1746 Ernest G. Atkinson. "John Milton, Senior." *Athen.*, July 31, 1897, pp. 160–61.

Account of recently discovered bill of complaint against John Milton, Sr., and his answer.

1747 William P. Trent. "John Milton." *Sewanee Review*, V (1897), 1–16.

1748 H. B. Wheatley. "Milton and London." *Acad.*, LIV (1898), 201–2.

Same article in *Living Age*, CCXIX, 194–96.

List and description of Milton's ten London residences. Favors proposal of turning graveyard of St. Giles' Church into a public garden.

1749 "Milton in the Market Place." *Ibid.*, LIX (1900), 385–86.

A review of Sir Walter Raleigh's Milton.

1750 [Portrait of Milton.] *Scribner's Magazine*, XXVII (1900), 315.

Portrait from crayon drawing by Faithorne.

1751 John Morley. "Oliver Cromwell." *Century Magazine*, N.S., XXXVII (1900), 570.

On portrait of Milton from miniature by Samuel Cooper.

1752 [A Milton Autograph.] *Athen.*, February 9, 1901, p. 177; February 16, 1901, p. 213.

A ninth autograph of Milton discovered in a Bible to be sold at Sotheby's. Milton's signature and date "ffeb. 24: 1654" pasted in. Contains signature of "Elizabeth Milton, 1664," and her signature before marriage, "Elizabeth Minshull."

1753 Eugene Schuyler. Italian Influences. New York: Scribner's, 1901. Pp. x+435.

Milton's "Leonora," pp. 156–72.

Originally published in the *Nation* (New York).

1754 "A Site in Moorfields." *Living Age*, CCXXXIII (1902), 181–84.

Account of erection of tablet over door of house in Bunhill Row, marking site of house where Milton is supposed to have completed *Paradise Lost* and to have died.

1755 John Fiske. "Life and Writings of Milton." *Cosmopolitan*, XXXIV (1902), 41–53.

Biographical sketch based on Masson; short appreciation of Milton's poems; several pictures, including portraits of Milton at ages of ten, twenty-one, forty-two, and sixty-two.

756 T. Hopkins. "Milton's Cottage at Chalfont St. Giles." *Leisure Hour*, L (1902), 856.

757 P. W. Phipps. Chalfont St. Giles; Past and Present: with the Parish Church, Milton's Cottage, and Jordan's, the Quakers' Burial Ground. Third Edition. London: Macmillan, 1902. Pp. 63.

On Cottage: 1709–37, a public house; 1887, bought by public subscription; put under three trustees and committee.

On Milton; pp. 42–46. No new values.

758 Edward J. L. Scott. "Miltoniana." *Athen.*, November 29, 1902, p. 722.

Copy of a deed signed by John Milton, Sr., on October 22, 1628. Supports Masson's surmise that Milton, Sr., did not move from Bread Street, Cheapside, to Horton until second quarter of seventeenth century.

759 [On Milton's father.]

Review of *The Bernards of Abington and Nether Winchendon*, by N. Higgins (2 vols.; London, 1903), in the *Ancestor*, VII (October, 1903), 153.

Robert Bernhard's name associated with Milton's by reason of his moving in the court of requests, as counsel for Sir Thomas Cotton, that an attachment should be issued of the goods of John Milton, the elder, "the poet's old and infirm father."

760 Beverley Chew. "Portraits of Milton." *Bibliographer* (New York), II (1903), 92–101.

761 Edward S. Parsons. The Earliest Life of Milton. Colorado Springs, 1903.

Reprinted from the *English Historical Review*, January, 1902. Reprinted by L. E. Lockwood, Boston, 1911. Reviewed by C. G. Osgood, *JEGP*, VI (1904), 1 ff.

762 B., R. W. "The Fleetwoods and Milton's Cottage." *N & Q*, Ser. IX, No. IX (1902), p. 261; Ser. X, No. I (1904), p. 422.

763 Goldwin Smith. "English Poetry and English History." *AHR*, X (1904–5), 31–32.

Not important. Brief mention of Milton's political career.

764 Charles G. Osgood, Jr. [Review of *The Earliest Life of Milton*, edited by Edward S. Parsons.] *JEGP*, VI (1906), 133–39.

Account of recently discovered manuscript, chief source of Wood's *Life* (1691), containing unknown anecdotes of Milton. This manuscript probably the earliest biography of Milton.

765 J. B. McGovern. "Cromwell and Milton; a Famous Picture." *N & Q*, Ser. X, No. VIII (1907), pp. 22, 158, 375.

1766 A. M. Burke. Key to the Ancient Parish Registers of England and Wales. London: Sackville Press, 1908.

Supplement, 1909.

1767 N. C. Carson. "Homes of Milton." *Book News*, XXVII (1908), 241.

1768 Edward Dowden. "Portraits of Milton." *Bibliophile*, II (1908), 167.

1769 Eugarps. "A Note on Foresthill (Oxon)." *Christ's College Magazine*, XXIII (1908), 92–94.

Notes on the architecture of the church and on the Powell dwelling, with some statements regarding the parish records.

1770 John W. Hales. "Milton and His College." *Ibid.*, pp. 8–16.

Discredits Johnson's story of whipping at Cambridge as a mere partisan legend. Uses Milton's own statements concerning his popularity at college. "Old Damœtas" of "Lycidas" considered possibly a senior fellow or praelector.

1771 George F. Matthews. Contemporary Index to Printed Parish (and Non-Parochial) Registers (1908), with a Supplementary List of Manuscript Transcripts To Be Found in the Public Libraries of England and Wales. London: privately published, 1908. Pp. 109.

Valuable index to parish records.

1772 John Peile. "Milton and His College." *Christ's College Magazine*, XXIII (1908), 16–29.

Says Milton entered 12 February, 162$\frac{4}{5}$, matriculated April 9, and without a break resided until June 1632—even in long vacations. Away only short vacations.

Has some of Joseph Mead's account books (1614–36), giving books provided for his pupils.

Description of old college forms. One-third of students lived in halls then; many lived outside in Petty Cury under care of Troilus Atkinson, college factotum.

Fellows on first floor; ground floor rooms and attics held three or four men each. All slept in the sitting room. Milton "could never have been a sole occupant anywhere." Toward end of time, may have been senior occupant of "chamber assigned to him by tradition."

1773 S. W. G. "The Milton Exhibition." *Ibid.*, pp. 94–99.

The Janssen portrait unearthed again as plans were being made from the centenary exhibition. Copy of Onslow portrait, from Nuneham, included.

1774 George C. Williamson. The Portraits, Prints, and Writings of John Milton, Exhibited at Christ's College, Cambridge, 1908, with an Appendix and Index by C. Sayle. Cambridge, 1908.

Contains facsimiles of early title-pages, etc., as well as data regarding the Williamson collection, now dispersed. Issued in large quarto and small, the latter being printed first on June 12 and reprinted on July 8. The Huntington Library holds the greatest collection of Milton portraits and prints, largely acquired from this collection. The Janssen portrait, however, is in the Morgan Library.

775 Maurice W. Brockwell. "Cornelius Janssen's Portrait of Milton." *Athen.*, January 16, 1909, p. 81.

A note on Janssen, with reference to his residence in London, and his Milton portrait.

776 George C. Williamson. Portraits of Milton. [In] *Milton Memorial Lectures*. Oxford, 1909.

Pp. 1–10.

777 John Peile. Biographical Register of Christ's College, 1505–1905, and of the Earlier Foundation, God's House, 1448–1505. Edited by J. A. Venn. Cambridge: University Press, 1910–13. 2 vols.

Vol. I (1448–1665), pp. viii+620; Vol. II (1666–1905), pp. vi+954.
John Milton, I, 363; Christopher, I, 406.

778 J. C. Whitebrook. London Citizens in 1651: Being a Transcript of Harleian MS 4778. London: Hutchings & Romer, [1910]. Pp. 42.

The Milton item is the following unsupported assertion (p. 4): "The presence of John Milton's name among the membership of the Company of Coopers was of the nature of a surprise. It would be strange if any other of his name, a contemporary, wrote a hand so similar to that of the poet; yet, on the other hand, neither Masson, nor any other biographer, ... alludes to the episode in Milton's life which is indicated by the signature."

779 Chautauquan, LXI (1911), 423.

Gives a reproduction of the Nuneham portrait.

780 Laura E. Lockwood. Selected Essays. *Of Education*, *Areopagitica*, the Commonwealth by John Milton. With Early Biographies of Milton, Introduction, and Notes. Boston: Houghton, Mifflin Co., 1911. Pp. lxxxvi+205.

Contains "The Earliest Life of Milton," Aubrey's "Collections for the Life of Milton," a selection from Wood's *Fasti Oxoniensis*, and Phillips' *Life*.

781 S., J. S., and Others. "Milton's Bibles." *N & Q*, Ser. XI, No. III (1911), pp. 1, 70, 109.

782 I. G. Sieveking. "Chalfont St. Giles and Milton." *Home Counties Magazine*, XIII (1911), 284–89. See also *ibid.*, VII (1906), 99.

Brief description of the village and a record of the Milton house.

783 [On a lock of Milton's hair.] Sotheby's *Browning Sale Catalogue*, May, 1913, p. 157.

Note on a lock of Milton's hair owned by Addison, Leigh Hunt, and Browning.

1784 John S. Smart. "Milton in Rome." *MLR*, VIII (1913), 91.

Account of Milton's attendance at an opera that may have influenced his work.

1785 Douglas Macleane. "Milton's Youngest Daughter." *SR*, CXIX (1915), 114–15.

Note on Deborah Milton penciled by Robert Harley, Earl of Oxford, in his copy of Wood's *Athenae Oxoniensis*.

1786 "Portraits of Milton." *Connoisseur*, XLVI (1916), 17, 126.

1787 H. J. C. Grierson. "John Milton." [In] Hasting's *Encyclopedia of Religion and Ethics*. New York: Scribner's. 12 vols.

See VIII (1916), 641–48.

1788 "Milton's Portrait." *Bellman*, XXIV (1918), 629.

1789 G. G. L. "Milton's Oak." *N & Q*, Ser. XII, No. IV (1918), p. 299.

Asks Lamartine's authority for statement that Milton composed famous apostrophe to light under an oak on slope of Hampstead Hill.

1790 A. G. Seymour. "The Poet Milton's Wives." *TLS*, XVII (1918), 644.

Tries to show that Milton had married once before his marriage to Mary Powell. A. W. Verity discredits this theory in *TLS*, XVII, 657.

1791 Henry Broadbent. "The Poet Milton's Wives." *Ibid.*, XVIII (1919), 10.

Shows Seymour's conjecture as to Milton's first marriage to be wrong.

1792 Raymond D. Havens. "Mr. Dryden Meets Mr. Milton." *Review* (New York), I (1919), 110.

Record of Dryden's visit found in *Monitor*, April 6–10, 1713.

1793 J. G. M. "Milton's Assistant Editor." *TLS*, XVIII (1919), 56.

Relations of Milton and John Hall; their collaboration in *Mercurius Politicus*.

1794 A. E. H. Swaen. "Een japansch Portret van Milton." *Neophilologus*, V (1920), 46–48.

List of known portraits, and description of one in Japan (with photograph of it).

1795 Joseph M. Beatty, Jr. "John Milton and the Milburns." *N & Q*, Ser. XII, No. VIII (1921), p. 131.

Unsuccessful attempt to prove the Milburns of London descendants of Milton.

1796 S. B. Liljegren. "A Fresh Milton-Powell Document." *ES*, LV (1921), 40–45.

Add. MS 34,326, recently discovered to contain documents relating to Anne Powell. Probable cause of quarrel between Milton and Mrs. Powell set forth on this evidence.

97 R. S. M. "Christopher's Milton's Descendants." *N & Q*, Ser. XII, No. XI (1922), p. 31.

Owns Bible containing autographs of descendants.

98 Edward Bensly. "Christopher Milton: Descendants." *Ibid.*, Ser. XIII, No. I (1923), p. 118.

Answer to inquiry of Chamberlain brothers (*N & Q*, Ser. XIII, No. I, p. 71) as to descendants of Christopher Milton. Quotes Masson.

99 M.L. Toynbee. "An Attempt To Identify the Subject of the So-called 'Milton' Miniature at Rokeby." *Connoisseur*, LXVI (July, 1923), 151.

00 G. F. R. B. "Daniel Skinner, Amanuensis to Milton." *N & Q*, CXLVI (1924), 291.

Daniel Skinner, amanuensis to Milton in 1673–74, was elected a major fellow o Trinity College, Cambridge, May 23, 1679.

01 R. Stewart-Brown. "A Milton Monument." *Ibid.*, p. 329.

Error in Manchester inscription to Elizabeth Mynshull: date of her death confused with date of her will. The 1662 date is of her marriage to Milton.

02 Dorothy Gardiner. "The '3rd and Best' and Her Uncle Thomas." *North American Review*, CCXIX (1924), 372–83.

Biographical data on Elizabeth Mynshull and Thomas, her uncle, from an inscription over a shop in Manchester.

03 William H. Hulme (editor). "Two Early Lives of Milton." *Western Reserve University Bulletin*, N.S., Vol. XXVII. Cleveland, Ohio, 1924. Pp. 94.

Life of Milton by Toland, and *Life* by Elijah Fenton. Errors in the reprinting are partly compensated for by the provision of a convenient edition of Toland's work.

04 J. B. McGovern. "A Milton Monument." *N & Q*, CXLVI (1924), 405.

Answer to note of R. Stewart-Brown in *N & Q*, CXLVI, 329, concerning the Elizabeth Mynshull inscription.

05 D. Angeli. "L'amore romano de Milton." *Gior. d' Italia*, September 2, 1925.

06 Raymond D. Havens. "Dryden's Visit to Milton." *RES*, I (1925), 348–49.

Refers to his article in *Review* (New York), I, 110.
Evidences faith in Aubrey's account.

1807 Denis Saurat. "Note sur la date du mariage de Milton, d'après les recherches de J. S. Smart." *RAA*, August, 1925, pp. 515–23.

Restates the query put as a footnote in his volume of the same year, but does not give any valid proof that Milton and Mary Powell were married earlier than is supposed from the statement of his nephew. Based on unpublished notes of John S. Smart.

1808 ———"Milton and the King's Prayer." *RES*, I (1925), 385–91.

Effectually destroys Liljegren's assumption of Milton's connivance and shows the carelessness of his reference to Charles I as plagiarist; also demonstrates the unreliability as a witness of Henry Hills.

Review, Liljegren, *Beiblatt*, XXXVII (1926), 91–94.

1809 A. Sorani. "Milton a Vallombrosa." *Marzocco*, September 15, 1925.

See *SRL*, II (1925), 318.

1810 Ruth S. Grannis. "The Beverley Chew Collection of Milton Portraits." *Bulletin of the New York Public Library*, XXX (1926), 3–6.

1811 Marjorie H. Nicolson. "Milton's 'Old Damœtas.'" *MLN*, XLI (1926), 293–300.

Suggests identity of Milton's Damœtas and Henry More's Mnemon with Joseph Mead.

1812 D. Angeli. "Milton e Leonora Baroni." *Marzocco*, XXXI (1927), 27.

1813 David H. Stevens. Milton Papers. Chicago: University of Chicago Press, 1927. Pp. x+46.

Proof through deeds to London property that the poet owned part title to a valuable Covent Garden holding in 1627 and that between 1619 and 1629 his father had other important real estate transactions. Further facts regarding the Powell family, the will of Edward King, and critical papers on *Comus* are followed by printings of four Milton deeds.

Review in *TLS*, December 15, 1927.

1814 Burns Martin. "The Date of Milton's First Marriage." *SP*, XXV (October, 1928), 457–62.

"Since the question is merely the relative reliability of two inaccurate writers—one of whom, however, has fewer mistakes—let us see what will result if we take the year 1642 for that of Milton's marriage." On this possibility, hinted at by J. S. Smart, the author erects a circumstantial framework for 1642 that has merit for cautious approach and suggestion of ways toward new evidence.

XIV. GENERAL CRITICISM

1815 [Milton and Du Bartas.] *Monthly Mirror*, X (1800), 155–56.

Dunster's method favorably contrasted with that of Lauder. Milton's debt to Du Bartas a "general obligation."

1816 "Milton Gallery, Pall-Mall." *Ibid.*, IX (1800), 176.

Appreciative comment on Fuseli's exhibition of pictures from Milton's poems.

1817 Charles Dunster. Considerations on Milton's Early Reading and the Prima Stamina of His *Paradise Lost;* together with Extracts from a Poet of the Sixteenth Century [Du Bartas, in Sylvester's translation]. In a Letter to William Falconer, M.D., from Charles Dunster. London: John Nichols, 1800. Pp. 249.

Parallels from Sylvester's 1621 *Du Bartas*, words and phrases.

Page 69, "Il Penseroso": "Among the various works which compose the folio edition of Sylvester's Du Bartas (as it is commonly called), are the *Trophies and Tragedy of Henry the Great,* translated from the French of Pierre Mathiew. The part termed the Tragedy, which describes the death of the King, opens with the following exclamation:

> Hence, hence, false pleasures, momentary joys!
> Mock us no more with your illuding toys."

Page 109, "Lycidas": "I cannot forbear here referring to the Elegy on Dame Helen Branch, ... entitled "*Monodia.*" [Among Sylvester's *Posthumi* in 1633 edition.]

Page 118, "To Cromwell": Close parallel to Du Bartas' first sonnet to Henry IV of France.

Much significant material gathered at a time when such source work on Milton was not common.

Reviews in *Monthly Review*, XXXIV (1801), 234–39; *Monthly Mirror*, X (1800), 155–56.

1818 Edward Phillips. Theatrum poetarum Anglicanorum; Containing the Names and Characters of All the English Poets, etc., Enlarged by Additions to Every Article from Subsequent Biographers and Critics [by Sir S. E. Brydges]; Vol. I. London; Canterbury: J. White, 1800. Pp. lxxix+336.

Another edition privately printed at Geneva, 1824; limited to 100 copies.

1819 R. Rosières. La littérature anglaise en France, de 1750 à 1800. *Revue bleue*, August 19, 1882.

1820 Mme de Staël. De la littérature considérée dans ses rapports avec l'état moral et politique des nations. Paris, 1800.

1821 "Milton's Early Reading." *Monthly Magazine*, XI (1801), 43, 237.

Suggests a number of Italian authors possibly read by Milton on his Italian journey: Tasso, Soranzo, Valvasone, for material used in *Paradise Lost;* Nizzoli, for its structure; Arthurian romances by Fossa, Agostini, Alamanni, and Valvasone, for proposed Arthurian epic.

1822 [Milton's early reading. Review of Dunster's *Considerations. . . .*] *Monthly Review*, XXXIV (1801), 234–39.

Milton referred to as "our first poet." Many similarities between expressions of Milton and of Du Bartas are due to the fashion of the age and are not to be regarded as borrowings.

1823 [Tonson's *Paradise Lost.*] *Monthly Mirror*, XII (1801), 100.

Reprint of Tonson's edition necessary because of great demand for Todd's edition.

1824 "Polidori's Translation of *Comus* (1802)." [Review in] *Monthly Review*, XXXVIII (1802), 102–4.

The translator has failed to catch the beauty of Milton's imagery, and his melody. The rendering of the song *Sweet Echo* "is no more happy than Henry Lawes' melody." Arne's melody for this song furnished a model to Handel, when he composed "Sweet Bird" in "Il Penseroso."

1825 [Todd's Milton.] *Monthly Mirror*, XIII (1802), 249–50.

"We can assure the admirers of Milton, who, in course, are a numerous class, that their favourite never has been introduced to the British nation in so advantageous and satisfactory a manner."

1826 Brutus and Mortimer. "A Survey of the Political Life of the Illustrious Patriot, John Milton." *Ibid.*, XIV (1802), 165–69, 303–5, 373–75.

Valuable for contemporary opinion. Milton no longer regarded as a stern and rigid puritan but as a conscientious patriot. The survey is at times conjectural, as in tracing the results of the alleged visit to Galileo, but is keenly appreciative of Milton's defense of liberty.

1827 O. G. Gilchrist. [Annotations on passages in *Comus* and *Paradise Regained.*] *Monthly Magazine*, XIII (1802), 346–49.

Valuable suggestions as to Milton's use of Scripture, of Fletcher, Shakespeare, Drayton, Quarles, and Jonson. Parallel passages given.

1828 "Essay on Milton." *Monthly Mirror*, XVI (1803), 86–89.

Defends Milton's part in the "Eikon" controversy. Asserts his innocence in the interpolation of the Pamela prayer, as indicated by the fact that *Eikon Basilike* was edited three times before Milton's answer appeared.

1829 [Miltoniana.] *Monthly Magazine*, XIV (1803), 532.

Announcement of a proposed volume of biographical notes, on the same order as *Walpoliana*, *Addisoniana*, already published.

1830 E. R. "Cantabrigiana." *Ibid.*, XVI (1803), 133–34, 527.

An account of Milton's college career.

1831 [Grandmaison's translation of *Paradise Lost.*]

Review of *Les amours épiques* (1804), in the *Monthly Review*, XLV (1804), 511–15, contains fragments in translation. In the 1806 edition Grandmaison ranked Milton next to Homer and discredited the attacks of Voltaire. See the *Monthly Review*, LVII (1808), 509–11.

1832 [Milton criticized.] J. F. La Harpe. *Lycée*, Vols. XIII and XIV. Paris; London: De Boffe, 1804.

Review in *Monthly Review*, XLV (1804), 515–28.

La Harpe thus attacks *Paradise Lost:* "No man of taste, notwithstanding some sublime passages, and some beautiful conceptions, will ever compare a shapeless production, which swarms with faults the most offensive, to Virgil and Tasso; a poem which has neither course nor plan. . . . ."

1833 "Milton's 'Il Penseroso.' " *Monthly Mirror*, XVII (1804), 164.

Gives lines, first published in 1647, which may have suggested the subject to Milton.

1834 [Spanish controversy over Milton's style.] *Correo literario y económico de Sevilla*, IV (1804), 177 ff., 201 ff., 209 ff., and 217 ff.

Blanco White attacks M. J. de Quintana's study of Milton in spirit of French classicism, based upon imitation of *Paradise Lost* by Felix José Reinoso (1799): *La inocencia perdida.*

1835 Critique on *Paradise Lost*, by . . . . Joseph Addison. With Remarks on the Versification of Milton, by Samuel Johnson. London: J. Sharpe, 1805.

"The Works of the British Poets," collated by T. Park.

1836 C. B. "Milton's Cipher, and Harleian Library." *Censura Literaria*, I (1805), 438.

Says cipher used by Milton in government communications is contained in Clarendon collection.

(From Oldys.)

1837 Laocoon. "Milton." *Monthly Mirror*, XX (1805), 221–22.

Proposes *Aeneid* ii. 274, as source of "Lycidas," ll. 84 ff.

1838 Charles Edward Mortimer. An Historical Memoir of the Poetical Life of John Milton. London, 1805. Pp. 82.

Frontispiece—Liberty contemplating the tomb of Milton.

Announces fair-minded view of Milton. Deals at random with his Italian journey; political and biographical writings after return seem to him related to arguments over religion in Rome. Discusses *Areopagitica* and state service.

1839 Monthly Review, XLVIII (1805), 330–31.

Reviews Mortimer's work disparagingly and so reflects the high place given Milton in 1839 for recognized patriotic services.

1840 Emanueli Bava S. Paolo. "Dialogo tra Dante e Milton . . . . ." *Mémoires de l'Académie des sciences et littérature de Turin*, Vol. XVII (1805–8).

Allodoli notes this as a poor critique on Dante and Milton.

1841 [Polidori's translation of "L'Allegro." *Monthly Review*, L (1806), 99–100.

Polidori has not translated Milton's poem so well as he has the Duchess of Devonshire's *Tragedy of San Gotard* (bound with the translation of "L'Allegro").

1842 M. Hennet. Poétique anglaise. Paris, 1806. 3 vols.

Vol. I. Elaborate discussion of all types under separate heads. Milton, *passim*.
Vol. II. Chronological list of English poets.
Vol. III. Selections—English with translations; Milton, pp. 38–39.

1843 J. Thelwall. "Milton Vindicated." *Monthly Magazine*, XXII (1806), 211–13.

Milton's word order and versification in *Paradise Lost*, Book I, ll. 44 ff., defended against criticism of M. N., *Monthly Magazine*, XXI, 392.

1844 "Biographical Memoirs of the Late Bishop of Salisbury." *GM*, LXXVII (May, 1807), 475–77.

Defends Milton against a charge of plagiarism.

1845 "Milton, Voltaire, and Johnson." *Monthly Mirror*, N.S., IV (1808), 151–52.

Voltaire's criticism of *Paradise Lost* ingenious; his remarks on Milton's prose style unjust. Possibly Voltaire thought *Pro populo Anglicano defensio* was written in English with a Latin title—a mistake, the converse of one made by Johnson in supposing that *Theatrum Poetarum* was originally composed in Latin.

1846 [Milton notes.] *Monthly Magazine*, XXVI (1808), 15.

On copy of Bentley's Milton, annotated by Pope; and on Milton's contract with Simmons for *Paradise Lost*.

1847 [Warburton, Lauder, and Milton. In] *Letters from a Late Eminent Prelate to One of His Friends*. Second Edition. 1809.

Review in *Monthly Review*, LX (1809), 1.

Speaking of Lauder's "silly and knavish book," Warburton adds: "However, in one view it does not displease me; it is likely enough to mortify all the silly adorers of Milton, who deserve to be laughed at."

1848 Mark Noble. "The *Icon Basilike*." *Monthly Mirror*, N.S., V (1809); 77.

Asserts Dr. Gauden incapable of writing such a work.

1849 Percival Stockdale. Lectures on the Truly Eminent English Poets. London: Longman, 1809. 2 vols.

Ranks Milton above Shakespeare because he displays "more rare and august talents of . . . . mind." Criticisms of Milton's versification are ill-founded.

Review in *Monthly Review*, LIX (1809), 141–44; *Edinburgh Review*, XII (1809), 62–82.

1850 Henry J. Todd. Some Account of the Life and Writings of John Milton. London, 1809. Pp. 217+Index (unpaged).

This forms Volume I of the 1809 edition of Todd's *Milton*, a certain number of copies being printed off with a distinct title-page.

Issued with additions and with a verbal index to the whole of Milton's poetry.

1851 [A source for *Paradise Lost.*] *Monthly Magazine*, XXIX (1810), 145–46.

Text of a Latin oratorio containing the temptation story, performed at Milan while Milton was there.

1852 L. L. "Milton's Sublimity." *Monthly Mirror*, N.S., VIII (1810), 23–25.

Defend's Milton's style against adverse criticisms (*ibid.*, VII, 335).

1853 James Ingram. An Inaugural Address on the Utility of Anglo-Saxon Literature.

A review in the *Monthly Review*, LXIII (1810), 76–83, refers to his translation of the exordium of *Paradise Lost* into Anglo-Saxon as a demonstration of its reliance upon Anglo-Saxon words for its "majestic simplicity."

1854 "The Devil's Dinner." *Monthly Magazine*, XXXI (1811), 448.

Suggestion that description of dinner in *Paradise Regained* is of cabinet dinner which Milton attended as Latin secretary.

1855 W. Bilderdijk. "De Echt." *Dichtwerken*, Vol. VII (1856–59).

1856 Capel Lofft. "Coincidence between Milton and Shakespeare." *Monthly Magazine*, XXXIII (1812), 211.

Milton borrowed from *As You Like It* the proverb "Forbearance no acquittance" used in *Paradise Lost*.

1857 John Nichols. "The Author of *Eikon Basilike*." *Literary Anecdotes*, I, 522–29. London: Nichols, Son, & Bentley, 1812.

1858 [Miss Seward on Milton. In a review of Scott's edition of the *Poetical Works of Miss Seward*.] *Monthly Review*, LXIX (1912), 29.

Milton and Johnson inferior to Shakespeare because they lack "that universally acceptable ingredient, humor."

1859 E. H. Barker. "Error in Milton's Latinity Noticed and Passages in Milton, Sophocles, and Aeschylus Explained by the Doctrine of the Association of Ideas." *Classical Journal* (London), VII (1813), 393 ff.

1860 I. B. J. Breton. Nouveaux éléments de littérature. Paris, 1813. 6 vols.

Milton discussed IV, 157–92.

1861 A. H. [Milton on the consciousness of the human soul.] *GM*, LXXXIV (June, 1814), 548.

1862 "Milton's Emendations of Euripides." *Monthly Magazine*, XXXVII (1814), 397–99.

Emendations made by Milton in copy of P. Stephens' edition of Euripides. Milton's notes used by Barnes in his edition and transcribed in full by Porson in copy of Brubach's edition.

First published in *Museum criticum*.

1863 J. M. Gutch. [Milton's use of Latin.] *GM*, LXXXIV (June, 1814), 533.

Refers to Milton's use of Latin while secretary to the Council of State.

1864 C. Symmons. "Observations on Milton's Latin Poetry." *Classical Journal* (London), IX (1814), 338–45.

1865 [Biographical notes in review of Godwin's *Lives of Edward and John Philips, etc.*] *Monthly Magazine*, XL (1815), 614–24.

A good summary of the Milton materials in Godwin.

1866 "Milton and Lauder." *Portfolio*, 3d. Ser., VI (1815), 388–91.

Condemns Lauder, but shows insufficiency of John Douglas' defense of Milton.

1867 Sir J. Mackintosh. [Review of William Godwin's *Lives of Edward and John Philips, etc.*] *Edinburgh Review*, XXV (1815), 485–501.

Gives history of Milton's descendants, traces his reputation, and discusses his views on civil liberty.

1868 Henry Neele. [Literary character of Milton.] *Monthly Magazine*, XL (1815), 493–94.

Milton distinguished by mastery of blank verse, sublimity, and propriety of sentiment. Comment on imitators.

1869 ["Atticism."] *Portfolio*, 4th Ser., II (1816), 420–21.

Milton's use of word in *Apology for Smectymnuus* is an allusion to words of Demosthenes to Aeschines (*De corona*, par. 80).

1870 "Winstanley and Milton." *Ibid.*, p. 115.

Comments on Winstanley's erroneous prediction of Milton's reputation.

1871 [Character and writings of Milton. In review of John Nichols' *Illustrations of the Literary History of the Eighteenth Century*.] *GM*, LXXXVII (December, 1817), 523–25.

1872 "Character of Chaplains." *Monthly Magazine*, XLIV (1818), 526.

Quotes Milton to show how much he disliked the clergy. Compares Milton with Dryden in this respect.

1873 "Lycidas." *Ibid.*, p. 234.

Notes George Turberville's elegy on the drowning of Arthur Brooke (1567) as a possible source.

1874 "Letter in English History by a Distinguished Scholar at Cambridge to a Young Nobleman." *GM*, LXXXVIII (1818), 291.

Milton favorably criticized in contrast with Sir William Temple.

1875 [Milton's views on religion. In review of *The Protestant Catechism*, by the Bishop of St. David's.] *Ibid.*, LXXXVIII (1818), 332.

1876 William Hazlitt. [On Shakespeare and Milton. In his] *Lectures on the English Poets*. London, 1818–19.

1877 T. Holt White. A Review of Johnson's Criticism on the Style of Milton's English Prose. London: Hunter, 1818.

Attempts to refute Johnson's statement that Milton endeavored to write English prose with a foreign idiom. Quotes and refutes Earl of Orrery's criticism. Includes selections from Milton's prose works.

Review in *Monthly Review*, LXXXV (1818), 446–47.

1878 [Fame of Milton.] *Edinburgh Review*, XXXI (1819), 462–97.

Incidental to a review of Campbell's *Specimens of the British Poets*.

1879 The History of St. Paul's School. London: R. Ackerman, 1819. Pp. 34.

Plates, large folio. Includes the charter of the school and a list of early scholars.

1880 Richard Attwood. Parody of *Paradise Lost*. *Monthly Magazine*, XLVII (1819), 334.

Begins:

"Of woman's disobedience, and the fruit
"Of list'ning hazardous, ..."

1881 John Jones. [A Welsh translation of Milton.] *Ibid.*, pp. 225–26.

A favorable criticism of Owen Pughe's translation, with comments on the adaptability of Welsh to Milton's "majestic style."

1882 W. Shanahan, M.D. [Estimate of Milton's genius.] *GM*, LXXXIX (August, 1819), 122.

Milton ranked among world's twelve greatest poets.

1883 [Milton and Cromwell. In a review of *Memoirs of the Protector, Oliver Cromwell, and of His Sons, Richard and Henry. . . .* By *Oliver Cromwell; a Descendant of the Family* (London: Longman, 1820. Pp. 773).] *Monthly Review*, XCV (1821), 1–16, 126–36.

Milton represented as opposing Cromwell's imperialistic ambition.

1884 "Milton's *Doctrine of Divorce.*" *Monthly Review*, XCIII (1820), 144–58.

Recent edition of the divorce pamphlets (1820) used as propaganda to bring about revision of canon and civil codes. The editor advanced Milton's suggestion as a much-needed remedy, using contemporary high regard for Milton as a means to favor.

Reviewer condemns Milton's arbitrary use of Scripture.

1885 "Milton and Shakespeare." *Scots Magazine*, N.S., LXXXV (1820), 241–48.

Says Milton is less known, but more generally read and more passionately admired by the learned among our nation.

1886 John Macdiarmid. Lives of British Statesmen. London, 1820. 2d ed. 2 vols.

Volume II, page 368, discusses authorship of *Eikon Basilike.*

1887 [Review of T. C. L. Simonde de Sismondi's *Histoire des Français.*] *Edinburgh Review*, XXXV (1821), 488–509.

Milton characterized as the first of our general historians to discredit legends which for centuries had been regarded as history.

1888 John Chipchase. [Ellwood's *History.*] *Monthly Magazine*, LII (1821), 308–10.

Extracts which contain Milton materials, made because of contemporary interest in Milton.

1889 A. F. Villemain. "Milton." *Biographie universelle ancienne et moderne*, XXIX (1821), 59–72.

1890 [Milton's knowledge of Randolph's poems in] "Philosophy of Contemporary Criticism." *Monthly Magazine*, LIV (1822), 223–24.

Brief comment, accompanied by note on Milton as a historian.

1891 [Milton's prose style.] *Ibid.*, pp. 427–28.

Milton's prose exemplifies simplicity of style combined with "strong feelings of a liberal mind." Quotations from the prose.

1892 "On Milton's Sonnets." *New Monthly Magazine*, IV (1822), 238–43.

Superior to Wordsworth's. Appreciative comment on Milton's character as revealed in his sonnets.

1893 Edinburgh Review, XXXVII (1822), 350–79.

Milton's descriptions of the Anglican bishops and his prayer for their deliverance used in a review of the *Trial of John Ambrose Williams.*

1894 "Stephensiana." *Monthly Magazine*, LIII (1822), 143.

Milton's *Defence* was burned at Paris and Toulouse by the common hangman. Milton's political activities defended. Marvell referred to as a "protector of Milton."

1895 Nathan Drake. Evenings in Autumn. London: Longman, 1822. 2 vols.

Milton, II, 1–23, 170–96, 252–86.

Review in *Monthly Review*, XCIX (1822), 302–12. This review contains quotation of the most valuable of the Milton materials in the book.

1896 "Milton at Chalfont." *Museum*, III (1823), 548–51.

Imaginary conversations between Milton and Ellwood.

1897 Y. J. "Milton's *Comus.*" *New Monthly Magazine*, VII (1823), 222–29.

Minor poems not so popular as they deserve to be.

"Milton's object in *Comus* was to personify virtue by characters superior to impulses prompted by common passion." This explains the unreality of the poem, as well as the purity of its thought.

Notes Erycius Puteanus as possible source.

1898 M. Villemain. Discours et mélanges littéraires. Paris, 1823.

Contains a fine historical essay on Milton.

See *Mélanges historiques et littéraires*. Paris, 1827. 3 vols.

1899 [Milton's *Areopagitica.* In review of Ancillon's *Nouveaux essais de politique et de philosophie* (Paris, 1824).] *Monthly Review*, CIII (1824), 487–88.

Ancillon's work ridiculous in comparison with Milton's. Milton anticipated and refuted every argument used by Ancillon to defend censorship of press.

1900 [Paulding's notice of Milton corrected.] *QR*, XXX (1824), 537–38.

Paulding, in his *Sketch of Old England*, asserts that *Paradise Lost* is neglected because Milton was a republican. Reviewer shows the inconsistency of this argument.

1901 C. Wordsworth. Who Wrote *Eikon Basilike?* Considered and Answered, in Two Letters, Addressed to His Grace the Archbishop of Canterbury. London: John Murray, 1824. Pp. v+413.

Documentary supplement to this work, by the same author, appeared in 1825.

Review in *QR*, October, 1825, pp. 467–505. See also Sir James Mackintosh, *ER*, June, 1826, pp. 1–47.

1902 "L'ape Italiana." *Monthly Magazine*, LVIII (1824–25), 516–18.

Sorelli's translation of *Paradise Lost* superior to Mariottini's, but contains errors due to want of familiarity with resources of the Italian language.

Sorelli's reply, *Monthly Magazine*, LIX (1825), 419.

1903 Walter Savage Landor. Imaginary Conversations. London, 1824–29, 5 vols.

"Milton and Andrew Marvell." "Southey and Landor." "Andrew Marvell and Bishop Parker." "Galileo, Milton, and a Dominican."

1904 [A critical estimate of Milton's poetry.] *Edinburgh Review*, XLII (1825), 31–64.

Immoderate praise of Milton, especially of poetic beauty and sublimity. His debt to Dante discussed.

1905 [Milton's debt to Longinus.] *Ibid.*, pp. 241–54

Milton charged with borrowing conception of liberty from Longinus without acknowledging his debt.

1906 [Milton's theology. In review of Sumner's translation of *De doctrina.*] *Monthly Review*, CVII (1825), 273–94.

Milton was in doctrine an Arian, in discipline an Independent. *De doctrina* indispensable as an auxiliary to understanding *Paradise Lost.*

1907 "Milton's Treatise on Christian Doctrine." *New Monthly Magazine*, XIV (1825), 185–90.

Survey of contents, with particular notice of Milton's heresies.

1908 [Milton and sacred poetry.] *QR*, XXXII (1825), 228–29.

Tried to rescue religion from pollution by earthly passions; but *Paradise Lost* defective as a religious poem. Indicates Milton's position as a sacred poet. Contrasted with Spenser.

1909 "Originality of Milton's Use of Proper Names." *New Monthly Magazine*, XIV (1825), 387–92.

Asserts Milton's originality in forming sonorous proper names, against Black's assertions (in his *Life of Tasso*) that Milton imitated Tasso's method.

1910 Thomas B. Macaulay. Milton. *Edinburgh Review*, LXXXIV (1825), 304–46.

Constantly reprinted. Several significant issues are noted elsewhere. Occasioned by the appearance of Sumner's translation of *De doctrina.*

1911 Henry J. Todd. Letter to His Grace the Archbishop of Canterbury Concerning the Authorship of *Eikon Basilike.* London, 1825.

1912 Milton Contrasted with Milton and with the Scriptures. London, 1826.

Anonymous pamphlet.

1913 "Milton on Theology." *Boston Monthly Magazine*, I (1826), 489–91.

1914 W. G. Broughton. A Letter to a Friend, Touching the Question "Who Was the Author of *Eikon Basilike?*" London: C. and J. Rivington, 1826. Pp. 92.

Argues for Dr. Gaudens' authorship.
Elaborated his arguments in an additional volume, in 1829.
Todd also wrote supporting this view, in a 72-page argument, 1829.

1915 Thomas Burgess [Bishop of Salisbury]. Protestant Union. A Treatise of True Religion, Heresy, Schism, Toleration, and What Best Means May Be Used against the Growth of Popery. To Which Is Affixed a Preface on Milton's Religious Principles and Unimpeachable Sincerity. London: F. and C. Rivington, 1826. Pp. lviii+56.

A defense of Milton as being a Church of England man and Trinitarian. Denies his authorship of the *De doctrina*. Appendix, Lord Monboddo's "Origin and Progress of Language" quoted regarding Milton's language.

1916 J. B. Shenston. The Authority of Jehovah Asserted, ... with Some Free Remarks on the Article on "Milton's Essay on the Sabbath and the Lord's Day," Which Appeared in the *Evangelical Review* for September, 1826. London, 1826. Pp. 47.

Uses Milton's idea that we ought to follow the biblical injunction to observe the seventh day.

1917 A Milton Anecdote.

Translated from a foreign journal in the *Monthly Review*, N.S., V (1827), 599.
Of the two ladies who saw him sleeping under a tree and left with him verses which inspired his Italian journey. Unfounded.

1918 "Milton's Poetical Works." *Museum*, XI (1827), 114–22.

Reprinted from the *Retrospective Review*. A bibliographical account of first editions.

1919 F. W. P. Greenwood. "Milton's English Prose Works." *North American Review*, XXV (1827), 73–89.

On the reception of Milton's prose works in America. Survey and criticism.

1920 [Milton's prose.] *Monthly Review*, N.S., V (1827), 463–64.

Milton's prose neglected because of his pedantic style and the nature of his purposes, which were limited to contemporary events.

1921 J. J. Blunt. "John Milton." *QR*, XXXVI (1827), 29–61.

Same article in the *Museum*, XI (1827), 385–99.
Biographical and critical; based on Todd. Special emphasis on Milton's theology.

1922 Monthly Review, N.S., VII (1828), 471–78.

Review of Channing's essay; a defense of Johnson's criticism. "Those who quarrel with Johnson's critique of Milton, should be condemned to read . . . . Milton's prose writings, and no other book."

1923 *Ibid.*, N.S., IX (1828), 474–89.

On Milton and Cromwell, Godwin wrote: "There is no improbability in the supposition, that Milton, in describing the person of our first parent, had that of Cromwell in his recollection." See his *History of the Commonwealth of England* (1828) and this review.

1924 Southern Review, I (1828), 31.

Iliad, Book II, l. 297, noted as source of a simile in *Paradise Lost*, Book II, l. 486.

Milton noted as possessor of "the most multifarious learning that ever fell to a poet's lot."

1925 Nathan Drake. "Milton and Galileo." *Mornings in Spring*, II, 313–38. London, 1828.

1926 Christopher Wordsworth. King Charles I the Author of *Eikon Basilike* Further Proved. London: John Murray, 1828. Pp. 256.

Replies to objections of Lingard, Todd, Broughton, and others.

1927 "Milton's Letters." *American Quarterly Review*, V (1829), 301–10.

An appreciative essay on Milton's literary career, occasioned by the appearance of Hall's translation of the letters.

1928 "Milton and Women." *The Loves of the Poets*. London: Colburn, 1829. 2 vols.

Milton, Vol. I. Author tries to combat the opinion of Milton as an austere puritan, by showing that he was an ardent lover. Makes use of the Leonora episode and of the three marriages of Milton. Not persuasive.

Review in *Monthly Review*, N.S., XII (1829), 25–26.

1929 "Shades of the Dead." *Athen.*, July 15, 1829, p. 441.

Shakespeare, Newton, Bacon, and Milton named as four great Englishmen. Milton's greatness lies not in his art but in his moral teachings and in his defense of liberty. A Hebrew in faith, a Greek in knowledge and culture.

See also *Athen.*, July 29, 1829, pp. 474–75.

:930 Finn[r] Magnúsōn. Herra Jons Heath fra Íslendíngum. Minnis-Ljodum Jón Milton ok Jón þorláksson: The memory of John Milton and John Thorlakson to John Heath, M.A., in the name of Iceland. Kaukmannahöfn, 1829. Pp. 7.

Icelandic and English verses, in 8-line stanzas.

1931 The Literary Remains of the Late Henry Neele. London: Smith, Elder, 1829. Pp. 543.

Refutes the common error that *Paradise Lost* was received with indifference on its first publication. Shows that Milton was indebted for idea and rhythm of "Il Penseroso" and "L'Allegro" to song in Beaumont and Fletcher.

Review in *Monthly Review*, N.S., X (1829), 141–54.

1932 "Milton and Byron Compared." *Southern Review*, V (1830), 496, 518.

In a review of *Moore's Letters and Journals of Lord Byron . . . .* (1830).

1933 W. B. O. Peabody. "Villemain's Estimate of Milton." *North American Review*, XXXI (1830), 101–3.

Conclusion reached is that Villemain undervalues the works of Milton, especially the sonnets and *Minor Poems*.

1934 [Hall's translation of Milton's *Familiar Letters*.] *Southern Review*, VI (1830), 198–206.

Translation welcomed because of lack of an adequate edition of Milton's prose. Quotes from a review of Hall, by Louise Belloc, in *Revue encyclopédique*, September, 1829, p. 637.

1935 "Milton and Sir Humphrey Davy." *New Monthly Magazine*, XXXI (1831), 186–87.

Condemns Dr. Paris for ranking Davy's usefulness above Milton's. *Paradise Lost* noted as the "grandest manifestation of the power of our language."

1936 [Dupin's misuse of Milton.] *QR*, XLVI (1832), 466.

Dupin shown to have attributed to Milton epigrams against the governments of England, Italy, Germany, and France that are not to be found in *Paradise Regained*.

1937 Penny Magazine, December 8, 1832, pp. 359–60.

Biographical sketch.

1938 [Milton and Hesiod.] *QR*, XLVII (1832), 13, 24–27.

The storm scene in *Paradise Regained* and the battle of the angels taken from Hesiod's *Theogony*.

1939 "A New Life of Milton." *New Monthly Magazine*, XXXIV (1832), 581–82.

Commends Mitford's *Life* and suggests possible sources of other new materials.

1940 John Dove. The Life of Andrew Marvell. London: Simpkin & Marshall, 1832.

Traces the friendship of Milton and Marvell. Inaccurate in dates.

Review in *Monthly Review*, N.S., III (1832), 193–206.

1941 "Milton and His Biographers." *Museum*, XXII (1833), 173–83.

Reprinted from the *British Critic*. The author gives a survey of biographies of Milton by Richardson, Johnson, Hayley, Todd, Symmons, and Mitford.

1942 New Monthly Magazine, XXXVIII (1833), 102–3.

Review of Ivimey's work. Indicated that Ivimey was wholly unable to do justice to Milton. Robert Hall noted as the only nonconformist of modern times who could do justice to such a theme.

1943 "Violation of Milton's Tomb." *Museum*, XXIII (1833), 455–56.

An extract from General Murray's unpublished diary bearing on the disinterment of Milton's remains in 1790.

1944 Henry Acton. Religious Opinions and Example of Milton, Locke, and Newton. A Lecture with Notes. London: Hunter; [Boston: American Unitarian Society], 1833. Pp. 47.

1945 J. Paillet. Milton mourant: discours en vers, prononcé en séance publique de l'Athénée des arts, le 5 août 1833. [Paris], 8.

1946 Edinburgh Review, LIX (1834), 174–75.

In a review of Lyte's *Poems*, Milton is discussed with special regard to his use of poetry and drama for religious themes.

1947 Sir Egerton Brydges. Imaginative Biography. London: Saunders & Otley, 1834. 2 vols.

Milton, I, 123–52.

Appreciative; in dialogue form, Milton and Lord Brackley speaking.

1948 A. H. Everett. [Milton's tomb.] *North American Review*, XXXVIII (1834), 243–46.

Reprints from the *Monthly Magazine* the story of the opening of Milton's tomb. Quotes Milton's opinion as to his posthumous fame.

1949 Charles Augustus Hulbert. On the Genius of Milton; a Declamation. Shrewsbury, 1834. For private circulation. Pp. ii+23.

Delivered at Sidney Sussex, November 20, 1832, in reply to one on *The Transcendent Mind of Newton*. Again in 1833. Received annual prize, December 17, 1833.

Milton, "like the bird of morn, mounts soaring out of sight, amid the music of his grateful piety."

1950 A. H. Everett. "Criticism of Channing's Essay on Milton." *North American Review*, XLI (1835), 378–82.

Channing undervalued Johnson's criticism, but exhibited correctness of taste in his estimate of Milton's poems.

1951 "Milton's Estimate of His Own Poems." *Southern Literary Messenger*, II (1836), 501.

Noted as exception to the rule that a great poet is able to form a correct opinion of his own work. Ventures the assertion that Milton preferred *Comus* to his epics.

1952 New Monthly Magazine, XLVI (1836), 509.

Commends St. John for undertaking an edition of Milton's prose, a work greatly needed.

1953 William Carpenter. The Life and Times of John Milton. London: Wakelin, [1836]. Pp. 177.

Preface is written to stress Milton's political service. Discredits Brydges and Symmons as biographers.

Almost no comment on his poetry; first-hand comment on affairs.

1954 Samuel Taylor Coleridge. "Milton." *The Literary Remains of Samuel Taylor Coleridge*. London, 1836.

1955 Benjamin Hérisson. "Une entrevue de Corneille et Milton." *Annales de l'École de Sorèze*, Vol. I (1836).

1956 Gentleman's Magazine, N.S., VII (March, 1837), 271–72.

Praises Milton's orthography.

1957 Stanhope Busby. "The Poetry of Milton and Some of His Contemporaries." *Lectures on English Poetry*. London: Whittaker, 1837.

Good survey of the "Miltonian era." Criticizes *Comus* adversely because it is lofty where it should be familiar and is less dramatic than imaginative; *Paradise Lost*, because it is too episodic in structure. On the whole, a sympathetic appreciation of Milton's mental, moral, and political character.

Review in *Monthly Review*, CXLIV (1837), 166–80.

1958 Ralph Waldo Emerson. Milton. *North American Review*, XLVII (1838), 56–73.

Appreciative and critical. Mainly a commentary on Milton's character.

1959 Alfred A. Fry. A Lecture on the Writings, Prose and Poetic, and the Character, Public and Personal, of John Milton, Delivered at Several Metropolitan Institutions. London: Hooper, 1838. Pp. 55.

Apologizes for trying to follow Channing and Macaulay; attempts to interest the general reader.

Some original notes on law cases regarding divorce.

Summary and quotation of prose passages.

Says the Cripplegate bust is from a cast taken in 1793, "when his remains were disturbed and found in a state of great preservation, having been evidently embalmed." Made by Bacon: done by "the late Mr. Whitehead at his own expense."

1960 Thomas Keightley. "Milton's Use of Mythology." *The Mythology of Ancient Greece and Italy*. London: Whittaker, 1838.

Milton's practice, even at an early age, was to resort to materials not generally known. *Comus*, ll. 95–101, traced to an obscure passage in Athenaus.

Review in *Monthly Review*, CXLVIII (1839), 20–24.

1961 Isaac D'Israeli. Curiosities of Literature. [1839.] 7 vols.

Milton items, *passim*. First edition, 1791–1834; twelfth, 1841.

Volume III contains an account of the publication of Milton's *Character of the Long Parliament*.

1962 Thomas De Quincey. Life of Milton. 1839.

Published in *Blackwood's Magazine* for December, 1839, and included in all collected editions of De Quincey's works. See David Masson's 14-volume edition (1896–97), for the scattered allusions to Milton and for the sketches, "Questions as to Actual Slips in Milton," "On Johnson's Life of Milton," and "Dryden's Hemistich on Milton."

1963 Henry Hallam. Introduction to the Literature of Europe.

Regards "Ode on the Nativity" as "perhaps the finest in the English language." *Comus* contains "nothing prosaic or feeble, no false taste in the incidents. . . . ."

Review in *Monthly Review*, CL (1839), 93–101.

1964 "Lord Grenville's Letter to Dr. Burgess." *GM*, XIV (1840), 352–53, 471.

In review of Harford's *Life of Thomas Burgess* . . . . ; argues that religious opinions in Milton's other works are directly opposite those in *De doctrina*.

1965 Saturday Magazine, XVI (1840), 159.

Comment on Milton's belief in the necessity of inspiration; quoted from his widow.

1966 Quarterly Review, LXV (1840), 190–91.

Milton as a republican discussed. Unknown author of *Ernest* charged with desecrating Milton's name by linking it to the absurd political scheme of poem dedicated to him. Milton's political views defined.

1967 Saturday Magazine, XVI (1840), 148.

On Milton's accuracy of observation.

Mrs. Piozzi shows that Milton was correct in speaking of "autumnal leaves that strow the brooks in Vallombrosa." Critics had objected that all trees there were evergreens.

1968 George D'Oyly. Life of William Sancroft, Archbishop of Canterbury. London, 1840. Pp. viii+464.

Second edition, revised.

Volume I, page 47, asserts Dr. Gauden's authorship of *Eikon Basilike*.

1969 "Rural Scenes of Pope and Milton." *Fraser's Magazine*, XXIII (1841), 519–28.

Description of scenes Milton knew at Cambridge, Horton, and Chalfont St. Giles.

1970 Thyer. [The moral of *Paradise Lost.*] *Saturday Magazine*, XIX (1841), 96.

Suffering of fallen angels regarded as natural consequence of sin. Milton never forgets "the main end of all good writing, the recommendation of virtue and religion."

1971 T. N. Talfourd. [Shelley's *Queen Mab* compared with *Paradise Lost.*] *Speech for the Defendant in the Prosecution of the Queen v. Moxon, for the Publication of Shelley's Works.* London: Moxon, 1841.

Defends Shelley by comparing his language and Milton's. Poetic imagination should be regarded as a divine gift; as in Milton, so in Shelley.

Review in *Monthly Review*, CLV (1841), 545–52.

1972 [Macaulay on Milton's copyrights.] *QR*, LXIX (1842), 209–11.

In his speech on Talfourd's bill (1840), Macaulay makes an unworthy use of the case of Milton as the holder or seller of copyrights. Conditions of copyright in Milton's time indicated as not to be judged by standards of the nineteenth century.

1973 "Milton's Resignation on the Loss of His Sight." *Saturday Magazine*, XXI (1842), 188.

Quotations from Milton.

See also pp. 37, 54.

1974 Monthly Review, CLXI (1842), 48–61.

Defense of Milton as religious thinker and poet. An answer to vague slurs of J. B. Morris in his poem *Nature a Parable* (1842) on Milton's irreverence in *Paradise Lost.*

1975 Edward Jones Donoughue. Milton, a Lecture. London, 1843. Pp. 23.

Oratorical; not critical.

1976 "On the Intellectual Qualities of Milton." *Saturday Magazine*, XXV (1844), 235.

Breadth of culture his distinguishing quality. Used as example of a poet whose imagination was not restricted by his scholarship.

1977 A. G. H. Hollingsworth. The History of Stowmarket. London, 1844.

On Milton's supposed visit to Young, see pp. 187–95.

1978 Thomas Babington Macaulay. "Milton, sa poésie et sa politique." *Revue britannique*, XXII (1844), 5–60.

French translation of the 1825 essay.

1979 James Nichols (ed.). Sermons Preached at Cripplegate, St. Giles in the Fields, 1659–89. London: T. Tegg, 1844–45. 6 vols.

1980 S. Roberts. Milton Unmasked. London (Sheffield), 1844. Pp. x+136.

Only 50 copies printed.

Abusive, assailing him for sacrilege in describing God in real style, with devils.

His character criticized for pride and unkindness; the worst implied of his first marriage—that after losing the love of his first wife he tried to seduce another woman before Mary Powell regained his favor.

1981 "Milton's Blindness." *Chambers' Journal*, III (1845), 392–94.

Conception of scenes in *Paradise Lost* possible only to a blind man whose fancy is unrestricted by concrete imagery.

1982 Galileo's Dream. By the Author of "Job." London, 1846.

The supposed meeting with Galileo treated imaginatively in verse.

1983 Thomas De Quincey. Milton vs. Southey and Landor. 1847.

Works of De Quincey, XI (1896–97), 453–74. First published in *Tait's Magazine*, April, 1847.

1984 R. Richard. Zoilomastix: or, a Vindication of Milton, from All the Invidious Charges of Mr. William Lauder. With Several New Remarks on *Paradise Lost*. London: M. Cooper, 1847.

1985 John Sterling. Essays and Tales Edited with a Memoir of His Life, by J. C. Hare. London, 1848. 2 vols.

Milton, I, 73–86.

Religious appreciation. Defends Milton's anger by comparing his situation and that of Christ.

1986 "Milton and the Commonwealth." *British Quarterly Review*, X (1849), 224–54.

1987 "Milton's *Prose Works*." *Literary World*, IV (1849), 350–51.

Review of J. A. St. John's edition for the "Bohn Library."

1988 Edinburgh Review, XC (1849), 410–13.

A presentation of Shakespeare and Milton as leaders in two national schools of English poetry.

1989 Gentleman's Magazine, XXXII, Part II (1849), 344–46.

Milton continued to gain knowledge in remarkable fashion after his blindness. Admitted that he made some errors in describing natural phenomena.

1990 "Effect of Vagueness in Milton." *Chambers' Journal*, XIV (1850), 342–44.

Milton awakens awe and admiration by the indefiniteness of his images, as in his descriptions of Death, the realms of Chaos, and the journey of fallen angels.

1991 George Gilfillan. A Second Gallery of Literary Portraits. Edinburgh: Hogg, 1850.

A social rather than a literary study of Milton, pp. 1–39.

1992 Jane E. Giraud. Flowers of Milton. London, 1850.

1993 "Milton and Wordsworth." *Harper's Magazine*, II (1851), 201.

1994 "The New Library Edition of Milton." *Literary World*, IX (1851), 86–87.

A favorable criticism of Pickering's edition.

1995 North British Review, XVI (1852), 295–335.

A review of Pickering's edition that contains useful critical material.

1996 Clara Lucas Balfour. Sketches of English Literature from the Fourteenth to the Present Century. London, 1852.

Milton and his literary contemporaries, pp. 151–73. Author has list of about 30 stories for children, and some critical sketches.

1997 E. P. Hood. John Milton: The Patriot and Poet. London, 1852. Pp. x+235.

1998 "A Triad of Great Poets: Milton, Dante, and Aeschylus." *Tait's*, N.S., XX (1853), 513–25, 577–87, 641–50.

1999 Edward Everett. Orations and Speeches. New York, 1853. 2 vols.

On Milton, II, pp. 221–22.
First published in 1836. A 4-volume collection appeared in 1850–68.

2000 Walter Savage Landor. "Shakespeare and Milton." *Last Fruit off an Old Tree*. London, 1853.

2001 K. W. Bouterwerk. Caedmons des Angelsachsen *Biblische Dichtungen*, I, cxli, ccxxviii. Gütersloh, 1854.

Asserts that Milton did not know Caedmon's *Genesis*.

2002 Thomas Babington Macaulay. "Milton." *Critical and Historical Essays*. 1854.

Reprint of the famous review among the collected works.

2003 Thomas De Quincey. Theological Essays. Boston, 1854. 2 vols.

On Milton, II, 97–112.

2004 D. McBurnie. Mental Exercises of a Working Man. London, 1854.

Dante, Tasso, and Milton compared in an essay.

2005 S. Osgood. "Milton in Our Day." *Christian Examiner*, LVII (1854), 323–39.

2006 "Lamartine on Milton." *Living Age*, XLIV (February 24, 1855), 497–99.

Lamartine's memoir not satisfactory to English readers.

2007 John Keightley. An Account of the Life, Opinions and Writings of John Milton. London, 1855.

A work of scholarly value, having a strong collection of selected and original comments. Another edition, 1859.

2008 John Payne Collier (ed.). Seven Lectures on Shakespeare and Milton by the Late Samuel Taylor Coleridge. A List of All the Manuscript Emendations in Mr. Collier's Folio, 1632; and an Introductory Preface. London: Chapman & Hall, 1856. Pp. cxx+275.

Collier's defense against charges of literary forgery. Of doubtful authenticity. Notes taken in 1811, on 15 Coleridge lectures: not found until 1854.

Wild reference to poem in 1632 folio signed "J. M. S." which some said = "John Milton, student." Collier has Coleridge say he accepts it as Milton's because no one else then was capable of such appreciation. Two pages of rimed couplets.

2009 A. de Lamartine. "Milton (1608–1674. de Jesus Christ)." *Vies des grands hommes*, III, 177–222. Paris, 1856.

Also in *Memoirs of Celebrated Characters*, Vol. III. London: R. Bentley, 1854–56.

2010 David Masson. Essays, Biographical and Critical: Chiefly on English Poets. Cambridge: Macmillan & Co., 1856. Pp. 475.

On Milton's youth, pp. 37–52 (reprinted from *North British Review*, February, 1852, as a review of Mitford's 8-volume edition of 1851).

"The Three Devils: Luther's, Milton's, and Goethe's," pp. 53–87 (reprinted from *Fraser's Magazine*, December, 1844).

2011 H. A. Whitney. North American Review, LXXXII (1856), 388–404.

On the works of Keightley, Hunter, and Mitford. Traces history of Milton's reputation. Calls attention to lectures on Milton delivered before the Lowell Institute (Boston) by G. S. Hillard and by Lowell; and to Charles Knight's essay "Milton the Londoner" in his *Once upon a Time*.

2012 "Miltonian Relics at Cambridge." *Chambers' Journal*, VIII (1857), 319–20.

Mulberry tree; manuscript of *Comus*, in Trinity College.

2013 William Dowling. Poets and Statesmen; Their Homes and Haunts in the Neighborhood of Eton and Windsor. Second Edition. London, 1857. Pp. xvi+312.

Milton, pp. 1–39. Engravings of Chalfont St. Giles and of Horton Church.

2014 William Howitt. Homes and Haunts of the Most Eminent British Poets. London, 1857. Third Edition. 2 vols. in 1. Pp. 703.

Milton, pp. 46–68.

On Milton's residence at Horton, see p. 54: "I am informed that several papers, in Milton's own hand, were found by the gentleman who was last in possession of the estate."

2015 Max Ring. John Milton und seine Zeit. Historischer Roman. Frankfurt a. Main, 1857. Pp. 562.

Volume XII of *Deutsche Bibliothek.*

2016 H. Taine. "Milton: son génie et ses œuvres." *Revue des deux mondes,* IX (1857), 818–54.

Discussion of Milton's character, prose works, and poetry. A comprehensive review of his work.

2017 B. "A Friend of Milton." *Athen.*, November 13, 1858, pp. 617–18.

Sketch of the life of Alexander Gill.

2018 "John Milton and Thomas Hollis." *Historical Magazine,* II (1858), 230–33.

On Hollis' memoranda in an edition of Milton's works, including his account of the existing effigies of Milton.

2019 North British Review, LX (1859), 155–70.

Chiefly a review of Masson, but adds a good general criticism of Milton's poetry.

2020 "John Milton." *Chambers' Journal,* XI (1859), 117–19.

Biographical; based on Masson.

2021 H. Ahn. De Bentleio Miltoni editore. Dissertation at Bonn, [1859]. Pp. 57.

2022 A. D. Barber. "The Religious Life and Opinions of Milton." *Biblio. sacra,* XVI (1859), 557–603; XVII (1860), 1–43.

Tries to prove that *De doctrina* was completed by 1641: that Milton was then a sublapsarian. *Paradise Lost* used as an argument for predestination. Remarks on early commentators on Milton. Illogical.

2023 Chambers' Journal, II (1859), 117–19.

A review of the first three volumes of Masson, published in Boston in 1859.

2024 David Masson. The Life of John Milton: Narrated in Connexion with the Political, Ecclesiastical, and Literary History of His Time. Cambridge and London: Macmillan, 1859–94. 7 vols.

Volume I, greatly improved by revision, reissued in 1881.

Volume I issued in Boston by Gould & Lincoln, etc., same year; Vols. II and VII issued in London and New York by Macmillan, 1871–94; Vols. III–VI, in London by Macmillan, 1873–80.

Index added in 1894.

Reviews (of separate volumes), *North British Review,* XXX (1859), 155–70; *Living Age,* LXI (1859), 731–47; *Athen.*, January 1, 1859, pp. 13–16; *GM,* N.S., VI (1859), 132–40; *Dublin University Magazine,* LIII (1859), 609–23; *Chambers' Edinburgh Journal,* XXXI (1859), 117–19; *British Quarterly Review,* XXIX (1859), 185–214; *Edin-*

burgh Review, CXI (1860), 312–17; *Living Age*, LXV, 579; *QR*, CXXXII (1872), 393–423; *Nation*, XVII (1873), 165–66; *International Review*, January, 1874, pp. 131–35; *Nation*, XXXI (1880), 15–16; *Colburn's New Monthly Magazine*, CXV, 163; *Nation* (by J. L. Deman), XXVI (1878), 342–44; *Acad*. (by S. R. Gardiner), XIII (1878), 276–77; *North American Review*, CXXVI (1878), 537–42; *Eclectic Review*, CIX, 1; *International Review* (by Henry C. Lodge), IX (1880), August, 1880, pp. 125–35; *Westminster Review*, CXIII (1880), 365–85; *Athen.*, March 6, 1880, pp. 303–4; *American Church Review* (by E. H. Washburn), XII, 545.

2025 Thomas De Quincey. The Logic of Political Economy, and Other Papers. Boston, 1859.

See pages 221–55 for his sketch of Milton's life. In his *Works* (16 vols., 1835–60), the Milton material is in IV, 31–52 and X, 79–98. Based on material published in *Blackwood's Magazine* in 1842.

2026 Preussische Jahrbücher, VI (1860), 419–48.

Essay on Milton's political and social values.

2027 G. Fitzhugh. "Milton and Macaulay." *De Bow's Commercial Review*, XXVIII (June, 1860), 667–79.

2028 ———. "Milton, Byron, and Southey." *Ibid.*, XXIX (October, 1860), 430–40.

Bitter attacks on Milton for his "injurious effect on morals, religion, and prosperity of mankind."

2029 Gustav Liebert. Milton, Studien zur Geschichte des englischen Geistes. Hamburg: O. Meissner, 1860. Pp. viii+396.

Biographical plan used throughout the main part of the volume. See pages 335 ff. for comments on the characters in *Paradise Lost*.

2030 Ferdinand Lotheissen. Studien über John Miltons poetische Werke. Budingen, 1860. Pp. 37.

2031 Arthur Lloyd Windsor. Ethica, or Characteristics of Men, Manners, and Books. London: Smith Elder & Co., 1860.

"Milton, His Politics, Writings, and Biographers," II, 51–111.

Acute study. Insists on studying Milton's youthful work apart from any feeling toward his later career: his youthful mind original while imitative. Excellent study of parliamentary conditions under Cromwell. Acute denial of Johnson as a critic; says Masson suggests "inharmonious uniformity of a lumber room."

2032 Anon. The Life of John Milton. London: Christian Knowledge Society, [1861]. Pp. 72.

2033 Alfred A. Fry. Milton: Patriot and Poet. A Lecture Delivered before the British Literary and Scientific Institute, Pera. Constantinople, 1860. Pp. 30.

2034 A. Mézières. "La jeunesse de Milton." *Review nationale*, Vol. II (1861).

2035 J. Tulloch. English Puritanism and Its Leaders. Edinburgh and London, 1861.

2036 F. H. Ahn. John Miltons Leben und poetische Werke. Eupen: Lechner, [1862]. Pp. 26.

2037 Antiquitatis historicae studiosus. A Milton Memorial. A Sketch of the Life of John Milton, Compiled with Reference to the Proposed Restoration of the Church of St. Giles', Cripplegate (where he was buried). London: Woodley, 1862. Pp. 32.

Brief biographical sketch of Milton and a history of Cripplegate Church from the year 1099. Statement of the plan for restoring the structure.

2038 W. Dodd. Familiar Explanation [alphabetical] of the Poetical Works of Milton. London, 1862.

2039 J. W. Morris. John Milton, a Vindication, Specially from the Charge of Arianism. London: Hamilton Adams & Co., [1862]. Pp. vii+118.

Review in *Athen.*, May 10, 1862, p. 627.

2040 Edmond Scherer. Études critiques sur la littérature contemporaine. Paris, 1863–95.

On Milton, Vol. VI.

Praise given the "unfailing level of style" and the "equilibrium" of Milton in his early poems.

Translated by Saintsbury and published in 1891 as *Milton and "Paradise Lost."* Reviews in *QR*, CXLIII (1877), 186–204; *Living Age*, CXXXII, 579–89.

2041 H. Taine. Histoire de la littérature anglaise. Paris, 1863–64.

2042 "Bibliomania." *North British Review*, XL (1864), 38–40.

It is asserted that Milton attempted to introduce a regular and systematic orthography.

2043 North British Review, XLII (1865), 236–37.

Milton, more than Shakespeare, wrote for his own times. Modern taste fails to appreciate Milton because his imagery "magnifies a set of ideas whose vividness is of the past."

2044 Heinrich von Treitschke. Milton. Historische und politische Aufsätze. Leipzig, 1865.

See pp. 69–122.

Also in his *Historische und politische Aufsätze. Fünfte vermehrte Auflage*, Bd IV. Leipzig: S. Hirzel, 1886–97.

2045 Nation, II (March 22, 1866), 372.

Comparison of Arnold's monody with "Lycidas."

2046 L. Gidley. "Milton's Spelling." *GM*, N.S., I (February, 1866), 238.

Emendation of "sow'd" to "sew'd" in *Paradise Lost*, Book IX, l. 1110.

2047 Victor Lamy. Quelques héros des luttes religieuses aux XVIe et XVIIe siècles. Paris, 1866. Pp. 242.

Milton, pp. 75–114.

Macaulayesque creations of dramatic incidents. Dialogue between the jailers and Deborah before she goes to Davenant to inquire regarding her father.

2048 W. C. Martyn. Life and Times of John Milton. New York: American Tract Society, [1866].

Emphasizes church questions. Calls Masson too bulky, then incomplete.

2049 F. da Costa Braga. Comedia em um acto. [Lisboa], 1867.

Character of Milton in action.

2050 Alexander Monfries. An Introduction to the Study of Milton. Montrose, 1867. Pp. ii+106.

Book I of *Paradise Lost*. Footnotes and notes, pp. 53 ff.

2051 Gentleman's Magazine, N.S., V (1868), 192–97.

A comment on the purity and sublimity of Milton's character by way of a review of E. W. Farrar's *Epochs of English Poetry*.

2052 E. de Guerle. Milton, sa vie et ses œuvres. Paris: Michel Lévy Frères, 1868. Pp. viii+398.

On page vi he calls Masson's work "monument peut-être un peu massif et de proposition demesurée, mais imposant et d'une structure aussi ingénieuse que solide." Praises Keightley.

An important study.

2053 F. Jordan (tr.). John Milton and His Times. An Historical Novel by Max Ring. New York: Appleton & Co., 1868. Pp. 308.

2054 Thomas Babington Macaulay. Cowley and Milton. A Conversation between Mr. Abraham Cowley and Mr. John Milton Touching the Great Civil War. Set Down by a Gentleman of the Middle Temple. Reprinted, 1868, from Charles Knight's *Quarterly Magazine*, in "Crocker's British Classics," pp. 71–96.

2055 ———. An Essay on the Life and Works of John Milton, together with the Imaginary Conversation between Him and Abraham Cowley. London: Crocker, 1868. Pp. 96.

2056 The Poems of Phineas Fletcher . . . . for the First Time Collected and Edited, with Memoir, Essay, and Notes, ... by A. B. Grosart. Blackburn: C. Tiplady, 1869. 4 vols.

Grosart raises a query regarding relationship of Milton: from the poems themselves one might presume that Milton knew Fletcher's *Locustae* before writing *In Quintum Novembris*, but the dating seems to discredit this idea completely.

2057 George Gilfillan. Modern Christian Heroes: a Gallery of Protesting and Reforming Men, Including Cromwell, Milton, the Puritans, Covenanters, First Seceders, Methodists, etc. London: E. Stock, 1869. Pp. vi+312.

Milton, chap. iii, pp. 81–118.

A rhetorical biographical account; chief interest of the author is in religion. Relates him to Puritans and new thought: "In his views of church and state, few now will deny that he shot far before his days, and that ours have only of late, and very tardily, come up to him."

2058 R. Pauli. Aufsätze zur englischen Geschichte. Leipzig, 1869.

Milton, pp. 348–91. Chiefly a biographical sketch.

2059 J. R. Seeley. "Milton's Poetry." *Macmillan's Mag.*, XIX (1869), 407.

2060 John Tomlinson. Three Household Poets; viz. Milton, Cowper, Burns. With an Introduction on Poetry and Song. London: W. Freeman, 1869. Pp. 174.

"A Conversation about Milton," pp. 39–85. A family discussion in which "Mr. Benson" tells his two children of Milton's life and works.

2061 John Robert Seeley. Lectures and Essays. Macmillan, 1870.

On Milton's political opinions, pp. 89–119; on his poetry, pp. 120–54.

2062 [Republicans of the Commonwealth.] *Westminster Review*, N.S., XL (1871), 106–36.

Reviews of John Forster's *The Debates on the Grand Remonstrance, November and December, 1641, with an Introductory Essay on English Freedom under Plantagenet and Tudor Sovereigns* (London, 1860); and of C. R. Markham's *Life of the Great Lord Fairfax* . . . . (London, 1870).

Milton, *passim;* follows Guizot, on relations of Milton and Cromwell.

2063 Emmanuel des Essarts. De veterum poetarum tum Graeciae, tum Romae apud Miltonem imitatione. Paris, 1871. Pp. 158.

"De Miltonis poetae tirociniis," pp. 1–40; "De Paradiso Amisso," pp. 41–130; "De novissimis Miltonis poematibus imitationibusque ceteris," pp. 131–52; "Conclusio," pp. 152–58.

Indicates the great importance of Milton among users of classical stanzas and ideas.

2064 John Robert Seeley. Roman Imperialism, and Other Lectures and Essays. Boston: Roberts Bros., 1871. Pp. iv+335.

Another edition, 1889.

2065 Thomas Warton's *History of English Poetry* with a Preface by Richard Price and Notes Variorum. Edited by W. Carew Hazlitt . . . . with Indexes of Names and Subjects. London: Reeves & Turner, 1871. 4 vols.

Milton, Vols. II–IV, *passim.*

2066 London Quarterly Review, XXXVIII (1872), 30–32.

Milton's religious views reviewed, with a final suggestion that *De doctrina* represents the unsettled opinions of his youth.

2067 Nation, XIV (1872), 218–19.

A comparison of Milton and Lord Byron that gives the former the advantage.

2068 Edward Dowden. "The Idealism of Milton." *Contemporary Review,* XIX (1872), 198–209.

A contrasting study of Milton's aims in poetry and prose. A detailed comparison of his characterizations of woman.

2069 Alfred Stern. John Milton und der Calvinismus. Gotha: Perthes, 1872. Pp. 32.

Taken from *Jahrbücher für deutsche Theologie.*
Review in *RC,* VI (1872), 394–95.

2070 Charles Duke Yonge. Three Centuries of English Literature. London: Longmans, Green & Co., 1872. Pp. 649.

Milton, pp. 185–210. Biographical sketch; author applies no life-data to poetry. An estimate of the beauties and ethical effect of Milton's poetry.

2071 Peter Bayne. "John Milton." *Contemporary Review,* XXII (1873), 427–60.

Reprinted in the *Eclectic Magazine,* LXXXI (1873), 565–85, and in *Living Age,* CXVIII (1873), 643–62.
Useful for its summary of critical writings on Milton's prose.

2072 Thomas De Quincey. "Richard Bentley" and Other Essays. Boston, 1873.

Milton, pp. 311–25.
Also in his *Theological Essays and Other Papers,* II, 97–122. Boston, 1854.

2073 L. Scharf. John Milton und Jean Jacques Rousseau. Eine vergleichende Studie. Programm des Realgymnasiums in Freudenthal (Schlesien), 1873. Pp. 39.

2074 Max Schlicht. On the Influence of the Ancients To Be Traced in Milton's Style and Language. Dissertation at Rosenberg, 1873. Pp. 21.

A grammatical study.

2075 Academy, VI (1874), 234.

Milton's autograph in the volume sent to Patrick Young mentioned, the volume being at Trinity College, Dublin.

2076 Emmanuel des Essarts. Les prédécesseurs de Milton. Clermont: Ferrand, 1874. Pp. 30.

2077 Malcolm Maceuen. Celebrities of the Past and Present. Philadelphia, 1874.

Milton and his poetry, pp. 195–202.

2078 David Masson. The Three Devils: Luther's, Milton's, and Goethe's, with Other Essays. London: Macmillan, 1874. Pp. 327.

Milton, pp. 1–58. *See* Item 2010.
Review in *Nation*, XX (1875), 114–15.

2079 F. D. Maurice. The Friendship of Books, and Other Lectures. Edited with a Preface by T. Hughes. London: Macmillan, 1874. Pp. xxxvi+392.

Essays on "Milton," pp. 244–70, and "Milton Considered as a Schoolmaster," pp. 271–303.
Good critical sense; no new facts. Other editions are noted.

2080 H. Mouron. John Milton, conférence faite à Strasbourg et à Mulhouse. Strasbourg, 1874. Pp. 61.

Biographical details and civil history. Insignificant.

2081 H. A. Taine. History of English Literature. Translated by H. Van Laun. Edinburgh, 1873–74. 4 vols.

Milton, II, 239–318.

2082 "The Three Great English Poets, Spenser, Shakespeare, Milton." *Victoria Magazine*, XXV (1875), 856–68.

An early literary outline of Milton's relation to Spenser.

2083 Milton. Irta Macaulay T. B. Angolból forditotta B. P. Olesó Könyvtár. 1875.

2084 J. De Morgan. John Milton Considered as a Politician. "Men of the Commonwealth," No. 1. [1875].

A small pamphlet; an ignorant performance.

2085 Mark Pattison. "Milton." *Living Age*, CXXV (1875), 323–29.

2086 J. C. Shairp. "Keble's Estimate of Milton." *Macmillan's Magazine*, XXXI (1875), 554–60.

2087 Alfred Stern. Milton und Cromwell.

In R. Virchow and Fr. von Holtzendorff's *Sammlung gemeinverständlicher wissenschaftlicher Vorträge, etc.* Serie X, Hft. 217–40, pp. 681–710. Berlin, 1875.

2088 Quarterly Review, CXLII (1876), 24–27.

Summary of Macaulay's essay. Notes that Macaulay in 1843 regretted its "gaudy and ungraceful" style.

2089 H. Carpenter. "Theism of *Paradise Lost.*" *Unitarian Review*, V (1876), 302–12.

2090 James Russell Lowell. Milton. [In] Among My Books. Second Series, 1876.

A review (1872) of Masson's first two volumes exposing faults in perspective, taste, and logic. Lowell put his own nature more adequately into such comments as those on *Samson Agonistes* in the essay on "Swinburne's Tragedies" (1866), etc.

2091 M. Monnier. "Milton, poète aveugle." *Biblioth. univ. et rev. suisse*, n. pér., LXI (1876), 193–218.

2092 Thomas Babington Macaulay. Essay on Milton. Boston: Osgood & Co., 1877. Pp. 104.

Other American editions: Harper, 1878; Maynard, Merrill & Co., [1892]; American Book Co., [1901]; Sanborn & Co., [1902]; etc. The Sanborn edition is fully annotated and has considerable comment.

2093 "A French Critic on Milton." *QR*, CXLIII (1877), 186–204.

Occasioned by Scherer's "Milton et le *Paradis perdu*" in *Études critiques de littérature*. Supports Scherer's unfavorable criticism.

2094 Alfred Stern. Milton und seine Zeit. Leipzig, 1877–79. 2 vols.

Reviews in *Acad.* (by S. R. Gardiner), XI (1871), 156–57; *ES* (by J. Caro), IV (1881), 326–35; *RC* (by J. J. Jusserand), N.S., IX (1880), 474–77.

2095 American Journal of Education, XXVIII (1878), 383–400.

A summary of Milton's views on education, with an account of his Cambridge period.

2096 "Milton's Poems for Students." *SR*, XLVI (1878), 723–25.

Comments adversely on Bradshaw's Introduction to his edition of Milton's poems, and asserts that the notes lack originality.

2097 Peter Bayne. The Chief Actors in the Puritan Revolution. London: J. Clarke, 1878. Pp. 512.

Milton, pp. 297–346. Author asserts that Milton was sympathetic with his environment and religious circumstances. Says Milton had no children after 1653. Reworked from articles in *Spectator* and *Academy*.

2098 William Michael Rossetti. Lives of Famous Poets. London: Ward, Locke & Co., [1878]. Pp. xii+406.

Antiquated as biography, and not good criticism.
Milton, pp. 65–79.

2099 Wilhelm Windelband. Die Geschichte der neueren Philosophie in ihrem Zusammenhange mit der allgemeinen Kultur und den besonderen Wissenschaften. Leipzig: Breitkopf & Härtel, 1878–80. 2 vols.

Volume I, from the Renaissance to Kant.

2100 Opinions of the Continental Press on Munkácsy and His Latest Picture, "Milton Dictating *Paradise Lost* to His Daughters." (Now exhibited at 168 New Bond St., London.) With a Biography and an Engraved Portrait of the Artist. Paris: Sedelmeyer, 1879. Pp. 100.

Frontispiece portrait.

2101 Matthew Arnold. A French Critic on Milton.

In *Mixed Essays*, pp. 237–73. London, 1879. Also in *Collected Works* (1904), X, 227–60. Points out faults in criticisms of Milton by Addison, Johnson, Macaulay, and especially by Scherer.

2102 W. Bagehot. Literary Studies. London, 1879. 2 vols.

Milton, I, 173–220. Third edition, 1884; fourth, 1891.

2103 Stopford A. Brooke. Milton. London: Macmillan & Co., 1879. Pp. 168.

In the series "Classical Writers," edited by J. R. Green. Other editions, 1881, 1902, 1909, 1911, 1914, 1915, 1916.
Review in *Nation*, XXIX (1879), 101.

2104 Edward Dowden. "Milton's 'Rivers arise.'" *Acad.*, XV (1879), 54–55.

Note on George Rivers, fellow-student of Milton at Christ's College and author of *The Heroinae*.

2105 Mark Pattison. Milton. "English Men of Letters Series." London, 1879.

The most widely read essay on Milton and perhaps the most finely constructed. Now displaced by studies revising many older limited opinions of Milton's character and work.

Published in many later editions, as: Harper, 1880; "Acme Library" 2d Ser., 1880; Morley's, 1906.

Reviews in *Nation*, XXX (1880), 30–32; *Beiblatt*, VII, 79–80. *See* Item 1712.

2106 Allen Thorndike Rice. Essays from the *North American Review*. New York, 1879.

John Milton, by Ralph Waldo Emerson, pp. 99–122.

2107 "Milton and Wordsworth." *Temple Bar*, LX (1880), 106–15.

2108 George H. Clark. "Contemporary Men of Letters on Their Predecessors." *Contemporary Review*, XXXVIII (1880), 338–52.

Covering eight volumes in the "English Men of Letters Series," among which the critic finds Pattison's work most badly marred by "the over-informed quality which we too frequently find in modern literature which is not imaginative."

2109 C. B. Huet. Litterarische Fantasien en Kriticken. Haarlem, 1880.

Milton, 12th Deel, pp. 150–220.

Biographical and literary survey, with comment on Macaulay, Ten Kate, and Masson.

2110 Mark Pattison. "Milton." Ward's English Poets. 1880. 4 vols.

Introductory essay for selections. Milton, II, 293–305.

2111 Ludwig Scharf. John Milton und Jean Jacques Rousseau, eine vergleichende Studie. Braunschweig, 1880. Pp. ii+39.

Progr. d. K. K. Staatsgymnasiums zu Freudenthal, 1873.
In *Studien und Skizzen*. Braunschweig, 1882.
Absolute contrast in private lives of two men.
Compared as to literary, political, and social thought.

2112 [Damrosch's production of "L'Allegro," "Il Pensieroso," ed "Il Moderato."] *Nation*, XXXII (March 3, 1881), 150–51.

Libretto taken from Milton and from Jennens' addition to Milton's work.

2113 Nation, XXXII (March 3, 1881), 151.

Critic asserts that opponent made J. O. Halliwell-Phillips the victim of epithets borrowed from Milton's divorce pamphlets, in controversy with New Shakespeare Society.

2114 H. New. "John Milton." *Living Age*, CXLVIII (1881), 515–25.

2115 F. G. Stephens. Notes on a Collection of Drawings, Paintings, and Etchings, by the late Samuel Palmer; with an Account of the Milton Series of Drawings by Their Possessor, L. R. Valpy. London, 1881. Pp. 53.

Discusses pictures to illustrate English poetry. Done during life in London suburbs.

2116 Sylvanus Urban. [Swinburne and Milton.] *GM*, CCL (1881), i, 125.

On Swinburne's appreciation of Milton's grandeur and musical values.

2117 R. Wülcker. "Cædmon und Milton." *Anglia*, IV (1881), 401–5.

Evident that Milton had little or no knowledge of Anglo-Saxon, for he always uses the Latin chronicles and virtually admits ignorance of the language. Used Wheloc's Latin translation of Cædmon, not the original.

2118 W. G. Black. "Milton's Animadversions." *N & Q*, Ser. VI, No. III (1881), p. 112; No. IV, p. 154.

2119 "English Poets and Oxford Critics." *QR*, CLIII (1882), 234–35.

Summary of Milton's qualities as discovered in recent criticisms.

2120 Anna Buckland. The Story of English Literature. London: Cassell, 1882. Pp. ix+519.

Milton, pp. 230–96.

2121 Henricus Schmidt. Über Miltons politische Schriften. Halle, 1882. Pp. 66.

Sketchy, but offers exact references to Milton's text for evidence. Not well grounded in period.

2122 Charles Symmons. The Life of John Milton. 3d ed. London, 1882. Pp. viii+490+ Index.

Appendix, pp. 450 ff., has much data on Lauder, Todd, and other critics.

2123 Sylvanus Urban. "Milton on Education." *GM*, CCLIII (1882), ii, 638.

2124 John Dennis. Heroes of Literature: English Poets. A Book for Young Readers. London: C. K. S., 1883. Pp. vii+406.

Milton, pp. 114–47.

2125 A. MacLeod. "The Shadow of the Puritan War in Milton." *Catholic Presbyterian*, IX (1883), 169–76, 321–30.

Insignificant.

2126 David Masson. "John Milton." *Encyclopaedia Britannica*, XVI, 324–40. London, 1883.

Substantially the same essay in later editions. The 1929 edition has a very limited presentation of the new Milton scholarship since Masson's day.

2127 E. Myers. Selected Prose Writings of Milton. London, 1883.

Slight critical value in his introductory essay and some unauthenticated assertions.

2128 Henry J. Nicoll. Landmarks of English Literature. New York: Appleton, 1883. Pp. vi+482.

John Milton, pp. 112–25.

2129 Georges Pelissier. La vie et des œuvres de Du Bartas. Paris, 1883.

On literary relationships.

2130 [Johnson's *Life of Milton*, in German.] Edited by C. Böddeker. Berlin, 1884.

2131 "The Three Poems 'In Memoriam.'" *QR*, CLVIII (1884), 163–83.

Excellent criticism of "Lycidas," "Adonais," and "In Memoriam."

2132 Samuel Andrews. Our Great Writers; or, Popular Chapters on Some Leading Authors. London: Stock, 1884. Pp. iv+275.

Milton, pp. 84–112.

2133 L. C. Holloway. Mothers of Great Men and Women. New York, 1884.

Contains a section on Milton's wives, pp. 457–78. Well told; based entirely on Masson.

2134 Alexander Mackie. Macaulay's Milton, Edited To Illustrate the Laws of Rhetoric and Composition. London, 1884.

2135 Gentleman's Magazine, CCLVII (1884), 204.

Review of emendations and notes in editions of Milton's poetry. Not important except as a reflection of limited understanding of Milton.

2136 Dictionnaire des Littérateurs. Paris, 1884.

Article on Milton by G. Vapereau.

2137 Theodore W. Hunt. "John Milton: Doctrinal Errors of His Later Life." *Bibliotheca Sacra*, XLII (1885), 251–69.

2138 Laurence Hutton. Literary Landmarks of London. 1885.

Milton, pp. 210–16.

2139 Mark Pattison. Memoirs. London: Macmillan, 1885. Pp. vi+334.

Compares Milton's experiences after 1660 and his own disappointments (p. 332).

2140 Religion et libre pensée (contient une imitation du *Paradis reconquis* et une traduction du XIXe sonnet.) Genève, 1886.

2141 George Dawson. Biographical Lectures. London, 1886.

Milton, pp. 82–88.

2142 Albert Hamann. A Sketch of the Life and Works of John Milton. Berlin, 1886. Pp. 35.

Based on course of lectures. Much of it a summary of Milton's works.

Review by G. Boyle, *Archiv*, LXXVI (1886), 477.

2143 [R. L'Estrange] "No Blinde Guides, in Answer to a Seditious Pamphlet of J. Milton's, Intituled, Brief Notes upon a Late Sermon Titl'd, the Fear of God and the King, Preach'd and Since Publish'd by Matthew Griffith, etc." [In] *A Collection of . . . . Historical Tracts, etc.*, No. 5. Edinburgh: privately printed, 1884. Pp. 374.

Each tract numbered separately.

First published, April 20, 1660.

2144 B. Zumbini. Sulle poesie di Vincenzo Monti. Florence, 1886.

On Milton's influence, pp. 3 ff., 107 ff.

2145 O. Faulde. Stellung und Bedeutung Miltons in der Geschichte der Pädagogik. Programm. Ratisbon, [1887]. Pp. 15.

2146 George Saintsbury. A History of Elizabethan Literature. London: Macmillan, 1887. Pp. xiv+471.

Milton, pp. 315–29.

2147 W. Willis. John Milton: His Life and Writings; a Lecture Delivered in the Primitive Methodist Chapel, Chalfont St. Giles, May 17, 1887. London: privately printed, 1887. Pp. 45.

2148 W. M. Harris. "Carlyle on Milton." *N & Q*, Ser. VII, No. IV (1887), p. 429; No. V (1888), p. 33.

Harris replies to Bouchier's query, that Carlyle called Milton "the moral king of authors," in *Life of Schiller*, II, 59.

2149 "The Milton Window." *Critic*, IX (1888), 94–95.

Account of the dedication, and of the sermon preached by Archdeacon Farrar, at St. Margaret's.

2150 Matthew Arnold. Essays in Criticism. 2d Ser. London: Macmillan, 1888. Pp. vii+331.

Milton, pp. 56–68.

2151 ———. "John Milton." *Century*, N.S., XIV (1888), 53–55.

Address delivered at St. Margaret's Church, Westminster, February 13, 1888. Milton praised for refining influence, and for the "grand style" of poets of antiquity. See also *GM*, CCLXIV (1888), I, 623–24.

2152 Arthur Benson. "Henry More, the Platonist." *Contemporary Review*, LIV (1888), 393–407.

Valuable in the light of recent research into the background of Milton's thoughts.

2153 Edward Dowden. Transcripts and Studies. London, 1888.

The idealism of Milton, pp. 454–73.

2154 O. Faulde. Stellung und Bedeutung Miltons in der Geschichte der Pädagogik. Ratisbon, 1888.

2155 C. H. Firth (ed.). Johnson's *Lives of the Poets: Milton*. Oxford: Clarendon Press, 1888. Pp. xii+144.

Review in *LQR*, LXXI (1888), 188.

2156 S. S. Laurie. Occasional Addresses on Educational Subjects. Cambridge, 1888. Pp. 215.

Milton, pp. 164–89.

2157 Spare Moments with Milton. Selected and arranged by Gertrude B. Mosher. Albany, New York: Brandon, 1888. Pp. 29.

2158 J. Bass Mullinger. History of the University of Cambridge. London: Longmans, Green & Co., 1888. Pp. xvi+232.

Has seventeenth-century background material of interest.

2159 John Phelps Fruit. "Completeness in Literary Art Illustrated from Shakespeare and Milton." *MLN*, IV (1889), 144–45.

That Shakespeare is a greater descriptive artist than Milton is the conclusion.

2160 J. T. Y. "Milton." *N & Q*, Ser. VII, No. VIII (1889), pp. 67, 236.

Query and reply on Milton's idea of immortality.

2161 John Jefferson (tr.). John Milton and His Times. A Historical Novel in Three Parts, by Max Ring. Manchester and London: Heywood, 1889. Pp. 472.

2162 Robert Newman. John Milton: a Lecture. London, 1889.

2163 W. J. C. Ross. "Translations of Dryden's Epigram on Milton." *Scottish Notes and Queries*, II (1889), 59.

On Johnson's and Cowper's translations.

2164 "Milton's Last Days." *Literary News*, N.S., XI (1890), 143–44.

Reprinted from Mitchell's *English Lands, Letters, and Kings*.
An account of Milton's habits, his religious views, and his death.

2165 Samuel Taylor Coleridge. Lectures and Notes on Shakespeare and Other English Poets: Now First Collected by T. Ashe. London: Bell, 1890. Pp. xi+552.

The same editor in 1885 had issued the *Miscellanies: Aesthetic and Literary*. In the lectures (1808–19), which were imperfectly recorded, Coleridge used Milton, as in his essays, to exemplify points of diction and figurative language and as his contrast—"compeer not rival"—to Shakespeare.

2166 L. Clarke Davis (ed.). The Story of the Memorial Fountain to Shakespeare at Stratford-upon-Avon; also Accounts of the Herbert and Cowper Window, St. Margaret's Church, Westminster; the Milton Window, St. Margaret's Church, Westminster; and the Bishop Andrewes and Ken Reredos, St. Thomas's Church, Winchester, England. Gifts of George W. Childs. Cambridge, Massachusetts: Riverside Press, 1890.

2167 Richard Garnett. Life of John Milton. London: W. Scott, 1890. Pp. 205+xxxix (bibliography).

Better in summary and exposition than in its literary estimates. Contains a very useful bibliography by J. P. Anderson. See especially the list of articles on Milton in periodical publications. The criticism is adequately concerned with the work of Stern, Masson, and Keightley and also is based on a knowledge of the political background of Milton's writings. Another edition in 1900.

Review in *Athen.*, February 22, 1890, p. 242.

2168 Vincent Minutoli. [Letter to Bayle, December 15, 1690. In] E. Gigas. Choix de la correspondance inédite de P. Bayle. Copenhagen, 1890. Pp. 579.

Shows high opinion the English then had of Milton.

See also Spingarn, *MLN*, XXII (1907), 232.

2169 Donald G. Mitchell. English Lands, Letters, and Kings from Celt to Tudor (from Elizabeth to Anne). London and New York: Sampson, Low & Co., 1890. 2 vols.

General criticism and background material.

2170 Sir Frederick Pollock. "John Milton." *Fortnightly Review*, LIV (1890), 510–19.

Milton's poetic powers; his versification; his prose. Asserts that Landor's commentary on Milton's poetical workmanship is the best yet produced.

2171 Fred N. Scott. "Simple, Sensuous, and Passionate." *MLN*, V (1890), 230–31.

Milton's use of these adjectives to characterize poetry made in a comparison of poetry with logic and rhetoric.

See also J. B. Henneman, *MLN*, VI, 124.

2172 Augustine Birrell. Obiter Dicta. Second Series. New York: Scribner's, 1891.

Milton, pp. 1–51.

2173 J. G. Croswell, (ed.). Macaulay's Essays on Milton and Hastings. Boston, 1891.

In raised letters for the blind.

2174 L. Cl. Delfour. La Bible dans Racine. Paris: Laroux, 1891. Pp. 261.

Chapter viii, pages 233–57, deals with Lamartine, Vigny, Hugo, Milton, and Racine, as inspired by the Bible.

2175 John W. Hales. "Milton's Macbeth." *Nineteenth Century*, XXX (1891), 919–32.

See also *Beiblatt*, II (1892), 278. Milton's consideration of subject of Macbeth; probable reasons for choosing, instead, the theme of *Paradise Lost*.

Also in *Folia Literaria*, pp. 198–219. New York: Macmillan, 1893.

2176 Walter Savage Landor. Imaginary Conversations. London: J. M. Dent, 1891.

Edited by C. G. Crump. Milton and Marvell, III, 332–41; Galileo, Milton, and a Dominican, IV, 384–93; Milton and Marvell, V, 33–40, 40–49.

2177 Percy Bysshe Shelley. Defense of Poetry. 1821. Edited by A. S. Cook. Boston, 1891.

The 1891 edition has a valuation of the Milton materials.

2178 Johnson's *Lives of the Poets. Milton.* With an Introduction and Notes, by K. Deighton. London: Macmillan & Co., 1892.

2179 The Six Chief Lives from Johnson's *Lives of the Poets*, with Macaulay's *Life of Johnson.* Edited with a Preface and Notes, by Matthew Arnold. London and New York: Macmillan & Co., 1892. Pp. xxvii+463.

2180 John W. Hales. "Milton's Macbeth." *Beiblatt*, II (1892), 278.

See also *Nineteenth Century*, XXX (1891), 919–32.

Relation of Milton to Shakespeare and to the Romantic Movement. Comparison of characters of *Macbeth* and *Paradise Lost.*

2181 George Hempl. "Milton and Plautus." *Nation*, LIV (June 2, 1892), 412.

Milton followed Plautus (*Aulularia* i. I), in expressing his advice to Salmasius to hang himself.

2182 James Russell Lowell. Latest Literary Essays and Addresses. Boston and New York: Houghton Mifflin, 1892.

Contains the material on *Areopagitica.*

2183 Allan Schlesinger. Der Natursinn bei John Milton. Leipzig, 1892. Pp. 127.

Scant bibliography. Divides uses into naïve, subjective, objective, *geo-topographische, mystische, wissenschaftliche, moralische, religiöse.*

2184 "Milton's Houses." *Review of Reviews*, VII (1893), 396.

Description and engraving of Milton's house at Chalfont. Based on Masson.

2185 Phillips Brooks. "Milton as an Educator." *New England Magazine*, N.S., VIII (1893), 385–92.

Reprinted from *New England Journal of Education*, March 6 and 13, 1875. Sketch of Milton's life and ideas of education. His three great principles of education are said to be naturalness, practicalness, and nobleness.

2186 John W. Hales. Folia Literaria. New York: Macmillan, 1893.

Milton's Macbeth, pp. 198–219; Milton's and Gray's Inn Walks, pp. 220–30; Milton notes, pp. 231–45.

2187 F. McElfresh. "The Theology of Milton." *Methodist Review*, LXXV (1893), 69–73.

2188 F. Hübler. Milton und Klopstock mit besonderer Berücksichtigung des *Paradise Lost* und des *Messias*. Reichenberg, 1893–95.

Review by M. Koch, *ES*, XXVII (1900), 142–44.

2189 Phillips Brooks. Essays and Addresses, 1858–92. New York, 1894.

Contains the essay on "Milton as an Educator."

2190 David Masson. In the Footsteps of the Poets. New York, 1894.

Milton, pp. 13–104.

2191 Johnson's *Life of Milton*. With Introduction and Notes, by F. Ryland. London: Bell & Sons, 1894.

2192 Vernon P. Squires. "Milton's Treatment of Nature." *MLN*, IX (1894), 227–37.

Milton's descriptions of nature derived mostly from books, not from first-hand observation.

2193 S. R. Gardiner. History of the Commonwealth and Protectorate. London, 1894–1901. 3 vols.

2194 W. J. Courthope. History of English Poetry. London: Macmillan, 1895–1910. 6 vols.

Milton, III, 378–451. A second edition, 1903.

2195 Thomas Babington Macaulay. Essay on Milton. Edited by J. G. Croswell. London: Longmans, Green & Co., 1895. Pp. lii+89.

Reissued 1903, 1907, 1915.

2196 Isaac Taylor. "Milton's Estotiland." [*Paradise Lost*, Book X, l. 686.] *N & Q*, Ser. VIII, No. VII (1895), pp. 461–62.

A tracing of this ghost-name to its first appearance, on a map, of 1558. See also the same volume, p. 421, and Gilbert's book on the geographical allusions in Milton.

2197 C. Fisher. "A Triad of Elegies." *Temple Bar*, CVIII (1896), 388–96.

2198 Immanuel Schmidt. "Miltons Jugendjahre und Jugendwerke." *Sämml. Gemein.*, N.S., XI (1896), 99–134.

Review by G. Sarrazin, *Beiblatt*, VII (1897), 304.

2199 A. S. Twombly. The Masterpieces of Michelangelo and Milton. New York: Silver Burdett, 1896. Pp. 172.

Illustrated.

2200 Thomas Babington Macaulay. Critical and Historical Essays. Edited by Lady Trevelyan. New York, 1897. 8 vols.

Milton, Vol. V.

2201 J. H. B. Masterman. The Age of Milton. London: Bell & Sons, 1897.

A standard survey of the literature of the period. Sixth edition, 1911.
Reviews in *ES* (by Schnabel), XXIV (1897), 443 ff.; *Athen.*, July 10, 1897, p. 64.

2202 Edward Payson Morton. [Review of F. T. Palgrave's *Landscape in Poetry from Homer to Tennyson.*] *MLN*, XII (1897), 207–9.

Criticism of Palgraves' classification of Milton with Homer, Sophocles, Vergil, Dante, and Tennyson, in their use of landscape.

2203 Augustus H. Strong. The Great Poets and Their Theology. Philadelphia. American Baptist Publication Society, 1897. Pp. xvii+531.

2204 Francis Thompson. "John Milton." *Acad.*, LI (1897), 357–58.

Comments favorably on the sublimity of *Paradise Lost*, and on its union of "Gothic richness" and "classic form." Calls Milton "The great lapidary of Latin splendours in the English tongue."

2205 A. Clark (ed.). John Aubrey's *Brief Lives*. Oxford, 1898. 2 vols.

Milton, II, 60–72.

2206 Gustave Derudder. Étude sur la vie et les œuvres de Cato. Calais, 1898. Pp. 478.

Part II, chapter iv, deals with Milton.

2207 F. W. Farrar. Great Books: Bunyan, Shakespeare, Dante, Milton, the Imitation. London, 1898. Pp. 235.

Milton, pp. 181–217.
Appreciative; not new.

2208 A. A. H. Kraeger. Der Byronsche Heldentypus. München: C. Haushalter, 1898. Pp. vi+139.

Essay on Milton included.

2209 René Samuel. "Milton." *Le Grande Encyclopédie*, XXIII, 1003–4. Paris, 1898.

2210 Ernest Zyromski. De A. Chenerio poeta, quonam modo Graecos poetas sit imitatus et recentiorum affectus expresserit. Paris: G. Maurin, 1898.

Part II, chapter ii, deals with Milton.

2211 "England's Debt to Milton." *Living Age*, CCXXIII (1899), 845–47.

Same article in *Spectator*, LXXXIII (1899), 746. Asserts that modern England and America need the chastening influence of Milton to counteract the perils of materialism.

2212 Henry Corson. An Introduction to the Prose and Poetical Works of John Milton. London: Macmillan, 1899. Pp. xxxii+303.

Selections that constitute an autobiography.
Reviews in *Dial*, XXVIII (1900), 204–5; *Nation*, LXX, 248–49.

2213 [Carl Theodor] Rudolf Kirsten. Studie über das Verhältnis von Cowley und Milton. Meiningen: Keyssnersche Buchdr., 1899. Pp. viii+125.

2214 A. H. Millar. "William Lauder, the Literary Forger." *Blackwood's Edinburgh Magazine*, September, 1899, pp. 381–96.

Summary of Lauder's work, and replies to his assertions.

2215 E. S. Nadal (ed.). "The Warner Classics " New York: Doubleday, Page & Co., 1899.

Milton, III, 131–56.

2216 Modern Language Notes, XIV (1899), 24–28.

C. Alphonso Smith's review of Van Noppen's translation into English of Vondel's *Lucifer*. An able estimate of Milton's indebtedness and of the validity of Van Noppen's views.

2217 William P. Trent. John Milton: a Short Study of His Life and Works. New York: Macmillan, 1899. Pp. xii+285.

Review in *Nation*, LXX (1900), 249.

2218 Johnson's Lives of Milton and Addison. Edited by J. Wright Duff. Edinburgh: Blackwood & Sons, 1900.

2219 Edward Dowden. Puritan and Anglican: Studies in Literature. New York: Holt, 1900. Pp. xii+341.

Milton, pp. 133–97. On his ideas of liberty.
Second edition, 1901.

2220 Thomas Ellwood. The History of the Life of. . . . . London: Methuen, 1900. Pp. xlviii+225.

Refers to the life of Milton at Chalfont St. Giles.
Another edition, 1906, by W. H. Summers.

2221 Edmund Gosse. "The Milton Manuscripts at Trinity." *Atlantic Monthly*, LXXXV (1900), 586–93.

Quotes Lamb's reflections upon seeing the manuscripts in 1799 or 1800. Traces history of the manuscripts and describes them.

2222 Elbert Hubbard. Little Journeys to the Homes of English Authors. East Aurora (New York): Roycrofters, 1900.

Essay on Milton's country places of residence.

2223 Laurence Hutton. Literary Landmarks in London. New York, 1900.

On sites and streets associated with Milton, *passim*.

2224 Thomas Babington Macaulay. Essays on Addison and Milton. Edited with notes by Herbert Augustine Smith. Boston: Ginn, 1900.

2225 Charles G. Osgood. The Classical Mythology of Milton's English Poems. New York: Holt, 1900. lxxxv+111.

An excellent interpretation of Milton's classical allusions and source materials.

Reviews in *Beiblatt* (by Rudolf Fischer), XIII (1902), 361–63; *RC* (by Ch. Bastide), L (1900), 240–43.

2226 Sir Walter A. Raleigh. Milton. New York and London, 1900. Pp. xx+286.

Among the best appreciations of Milton's poetry.

Reviews in *Nation*, LXXI (1900), 451; *QR*, CXCIV (1901), 102–25; *Acad.*, LIX (1900), 385–86; *Athen.*, December 1, 1900, pp. 716–17.

2227 Leverett W. Spring. "Milton on Education." *Education*, XX (1900), 598–602.

Asserts that in educational objectives Milton's main ideal was that of good citizenship.

2228 Thomas Babington Macaulay. Essay on Milton. New York: American Book Co., [1901]. Pp. 85.

2229 Charles G. Osgood. "Milton's Classical Mythology." *MLN*, XVI (1901), 141–43.

Source of *Paradise Lost*, Book I, ll. 508–21, is pointed out in Lactantius. Evidently Milton followed the patristic account, since that fits in with his identifying of the Greek gods with fallen angels.

2230 B. Scheifers. On the Sentiment for Nature in Milton's Poetical Works. Eisleben, 1901.

2231 Leslie Stephen. "New Lights on Milton." *QR*, CXCIV (1901), 103–25.

Lists recent works on Milton, and reviews in particular Raleigh's *Milton*.

2232 James Weller. "Christian Mythology." *Westminster Review*, CLVI (1901), 577–79.

Disapproves of Milton's theology. Denies that Satan was ever in Heaven.

2233 College Requirements in English for Careful Study, for the Years 1903–1908. Boston and New York: Houghton, Mifflin Co., [1902].

Biographical note and texts of some of the *Minor Poems*.

2234 Quarterly Review, CXCVI (1902), 98–99.

Milton's prose reveals the defects of Latinized diction; is not important in the history of English prose. His style contrasted with Marvell's.

2235 "Two Passing Notices of Shakespeare and Milton in the Eighteenth Century." *Athen.*, April 5, 1902, pp. 434–35.

Robert Balle in a letter dated July 11, 1721, tells of meeting in Italy Antonio Saliuni, "esteemed the most learned man in Florence, if not in all Italy," who had started to translate *Paradise Lost* into Italian.

2236 H. K. Milton's Organ, and Other Tewkesbury Sketches. Tewkesbury: Gardner, [1902]. Pp. 62.

Illustrated. Really a guide book. Trivial; no evidence for assertion that the Tewkesbury organ has any Milton association.

2237 Ewald Pommrich. Miltons Verhältnis zu Torquato Tasso. Halle, 1902. Pp. viii+79.

On Milton's relation to Italian speech and literature. It is asserted that he gained Italian qualities of style and ideas on his Italian journey, and from reading Fairfax's translation of Tasso.

Review in *Archiv*, CXXIV (1910), 433.

2238 Sir Walter Raleigh. "Milton, a Critical Study." *Critic*, XXXVII (1902), 408–12.

Appreciation of Milton's character and style; based on his *Milton*, 1900.

2239 Edward J. L. Scott. "A Notice of Milton in Italian." *Athen.*, April 26, 1902, p. 531.

Quotes letter of Lord Chancellor Sommers (Sloane MS 4061, fol. 33), who writes that Count Lorenzo Magalotti has made great progress in translating *Paradise Lost* into Italian verse.

2240 Leslie Stephen. Studies of a Biographer. New York, 1902.

His essay "New Lights on Milton" included; republished from *QR*, CXCIV (1901), 103–25.

Review of recent works on Milton by Beeching, Bridges, Verity, and Raleigh is the basis of the essay.

2241 George A. Wood. "The Miltonic Ideal." *Historical Essays by Members of the Owens College, Manchester. . . .* Edited by T. F. Tout and James Tait. London: Longmans, Green & Co., 1902.

Pp. 357–76. Keynote: liberty in activity. "A life of active virtue, free from external control, save that of God and conscience."

2242 Stopford A. Brooke. Milton. New York: Appleton, 1903. Pp. 167.

See Item 2103.

2243 [Fanny Byse.] "The Young Milton?" *Acad.*, LXIV (1903), 79.

2244 John Downing. Testimonies and Criticisms Relating to the Life and Works of John Milton. St. Austell: W. B. Luke, 1903. Pp. 297.

A valuable compilation from Stebbing (*Memoir and Analysis of Milton's Life and Writings*, 1841), Jas. Montgomery, Th. Cooper, Coleridge, Burke, Shelley, Hazlitt, De Quincey, Swinburne, etc. Valuable also for bibliography, especially of periodical material.

2245 Thomas Ellwood. Relations with John Milton.

Reprinted in *An English Garner*, V, 135–48. Westminster, 1903.

2246 S. S. Laurie. Educational Opinion since the Renaissance. Cambridge, 1903.

Milton treated as a transmitter of Renaissance ideas.

2247 W. L. Liebknecht. [Hebrew study of Milton.] London: Nathauson 1903. Pp. 8.

British Museum copy has this note: "Die Spinnen und Fliegen von W. Liebknecht."

2248 Thomas Babington Macaulay. Essays on Milton and Addison. Edited with Introduction and Notes, by James Arthur Tufts. New York: Holt, 1903.

2249 ———. Essay on Milton. Edited by Edward Leeds Gulick. New York: American Book Co., [1903].

2250 Lucia Ames Mead. Milton's England. London and Boston, 1903. Pp. 311.

Portrait; well illustrated with maps and portraits.

Reviews in *Athen.*, October 31, 1903; pp. 575–76; *Literary World*, XXXIII (1902), 177–78.

2251 Pietro Raveggi. L'Idealità spirituale in Dante, Milton, Klopstock, Goethe, Mickiewicz. Florence: O. Paggi, 1903. Pp. 100.

Pages 27–64 on Dante, Milton, and Klopstock.

2252 E. N. S. Thompson. The Controversy between the Puritans and the Stage. "Yale Studies in English," No. 20. New York: Holt, 1903. Pp. 275.

2253 Sylvanus Urban. "Reviving Appreciation of Milton." *GM*, CCXCV (1903), 414.

Comments on an increasing interest in Milton. Criticizes Fanny Byse's argument that "L'Allegro" and "Il Penseroso" were influenced by Milton's foreign travels, but does not sufficiently indicate the unscholarly character of her book.

2254 Richard Garnett and Edmund Gosse. [In] *English Literature, an Illustrated Record*. New York, 1903–4.

2255 J. M. Hart. "Milton and Shakspere." *Nation*, LXXIX (July 7, 1904), 9.

Parallel between *Paradise Lost*, Book II, ll. 1–4, and *Love's Labors Lost*, IV, iii, ll. 22–24. Star mentioned in *Comus*, l. 93, is not Venus, or the evening star.

2256 Joseph Spencer Kennard. De deo lapso commentarius. Dissertation at Paris. Florence: Barberanis, 1904. Pp. 63.

Latin and Italian on opposite pages, each with separate paging.

2257 Thomas M. Parrott. "Autobiography of John Milton." [In his] *Studies of a Book-lover*. New York, 1904.

2258 Margaret Kyffin Roberts. John Milton: an Appreciative Monograph. London: Burleigh, 1904. Pp. iv+75.

Popular lecture; not particularly valuable.

2259 Barrett Wendell. The Temper of the Seventeenth Century in English Literature. New York: Scribner's, 1904. Pp. viii+360.

Milton, pp. 267–326. Skilfully phrased lectures dealing most adequately with the rhetorical values of Milton. The series has an appeal to readers through its statement of facts and traditional ideas. No fresh research behind the lectures, but skill in selection and arrangement.

2260 H. O. Boas. [Mrs. Frederick Boas.] With Milton and the Cavaliers. London: Nisbet, 1905. Pp. viii+336.

Slight critical value. Twelve sketches. Milton, pp. 313–36.

2261 John Churton Collins. Studies in Poetry and Criticism. London: Bell & Sons, 1905.

"Miltonic Myths and Their Authors," pp. 167–203, is an excellent essay in review of early scholarly efforts and some misconceptions.

2262 R. P. Downes. Seven Supreme Poets. London: Aylesbury, [1905]. Pp. 336.

Milton, pp. 269–336. Sketchy and dogmatic.

2263 Tudor Jenks. In the Days of Milton. New York: A. S. Barnes & Co., 1905. Pp. x+306.

Sketches of life and customs of the seventeenth century. Brief bibliography, pp. 293–96.

2264 Samuel Johnson. Lives of the Poets. Edited by G. B. Hill. Oxford: Clarendon Press, 1905.

Milton, Vol. I.

2265 George C. Williamson. Milton. London: Bell & Sons, 1905. Pp. 113.

Excellent data on portraits. "General account for young students."

Review in *Athen.*, July 1, 1905, pp. 7–8.

2266 G. E. Woodberry. The Torch. Eight Lectures on Race Power, ... London and New York: McClure, Phillips & Co., 1905.

"Milton as a Race Exponent," pp. 139–61.

Reprinted three times; in 1920 by Harcourt, Brace & Co. (New York).

2267 George Buchanan. Tyrannical Government Anatomized; or, a Discourse concerning Evil-Councellors; Being the Life and Death of John the Baptist, and Presented to the King's Most Excellent Majesty by the Author.

In George Buchanan, *Glasgow Quartercentenary Studies* (1906–7), pp. 61–173, an argument for crediting the translation to Milton.

2268 Lane Cooper. "The Abyssinian Paradise in Coleridge and Milton." *MP*, III (1906), 327–32.

Relation of Coleridge to Milton with reference to their use of Purchas' *Pilgrimage* (1617).

2269 The History and Life of Thomas Ellwood, Written by His Own Hand, with Extracts from Joseph Wyeth's Supplement, Appendices, and Biographical Notes. Edited by S. Graveson with Historical Introduction by W. H. Summers. Illustrated. London: Headley Bros., 1906. Pp. xxx +372.

First published in 1714; second edition the same year. The text of the 1906 (thirteenth?) edition was used in the Pocket Edition of "Quaker Classics," 1906.

Gives a bibliography of Ellwood's writings. On Milton, pp. 121–23, 125, 174, 198, 199.

2270 Laura E. Lockwood. "A Note on Milton's Geography." *MLN*, XXI (1906), 86.

Comment on location of the "Nyseian Isle," *Paradise Lost*, Book IV, l. 275.

2271 Ettore Allodoli. Giovanni Milton e l'Italia. Prato: C. & G. Spighi, 1907. Pp. xiv+170.

A useful survey that gives incidental material on editions and translations. By indirect evidence the conclusion is reached that Milton wrote his Italian sonnets before going to Italy, a view held by others who have given special study to the sonnets recently.

2272 John Churton Collins. Milton.

In Andrew Lang's *Poet's Country*, pp. 116–26. London, 1907.

2273 C. H. Firth (ed.). Johnson's *Lives of the Poets. Milton.* Edited with Notes. Oxford: Clarendon Press, 1907. Pp. xii+144.

2274 John G. Robertson. "Notes on *Giovanni Milton e l'Italia.* (Prato Tipografia Succ. Vestri, 1907) by Sig. Ettore Allodoli." *MLR*, II (1907), 376.

Praises account of influence of Italy on Milton, and also the chapters on Italian criticism and translation of Milton's works. Regrets that the author had not studied more closely the Italian periodicals of the beginning of the eighteenth century, in order to attend to the extraordinary enthusiasm for Milton which characterized the little band of cosmopolitan Italians settled in London about that time.

2275 Wilhelm Schmidt. Der Kampf um den Sinn des Lebens. Von Dante bis Ibsen. Berlin, 1907. 2 vols.

Milton, I, 95–188.

Volume I, Dante, Milton, Voltaire; Vol. II, Rousseau, Carlyle, Ibsen.

2276 J. E. Spingarn. "Milton's Fame." *MLN*, XXII (1907), 232.

Vincent Minutoli, a Swiss scholar, in 1690 wrote to Bayle of dictionary fame a significant and disinterested reference to *Paradise Lost.*

2277 B. Zumbini. Studi di letterature straniere. Second Edition. Florence, 1907.

See "Il Messia del Klopstock," pp. 153 ff.

2278 Johnson's *Life of Milton. QR*, CCVIII (1908), 89–90.

Summary of the criticisms of Johnson's critique.

2279 "Milton." *SR*, CVI (1908), 74.

Asserts that Milton's political and religious opinions largely resulted from his arrogance of mind. He belonged to the Middle Ages rather than to his own generation.

2280 Milton, 1608–1674. Facsimiles of Autographs and Documents in the British Museum. 1908.

The items are:

Milton's *Commonplace Book*, purchased in 1900 from Sir Richard James Graham of Netherby. (Add. MS 36354.)

Entries 1637?–1646?

Signature of Milton in the *Album Amicorum* of Christopher Arnold. Dated "London, 19 Nov., 1651."

Warrant.

Bible.

2281 "The Milton Tercentenary." *SR*, CVI (1908), 723–24.

Condemns those who regard Milton merely as a nonconformist prophet of liberty rather than as "the one great classic poet whom England can claim." Milton is blamed because he is thought to have desired "Arianism in the church, polygamy in the home, and a Venetian oligarchy in the state."

2282 Tercentenary Anniversary of the Birth of John Milton. Ithaca, New York, [1908]. Pp. 4.

2283 "John Milton." *Spectator*, CI (1908), 933–34.

Discussion of Milton's character.

2284 "Milton." *Ibid.*, pp. 9–10.

Milton held the greatest artist in English literature. Even his egotism is pleasing to this critic.

2285 "Milton after Three Centuries." *Outlook*, XC (1908), 813–15.

Brief biographical sketch and praise of his character.

2286 "The Milton Celebration at Cambridge." *Athen.*, July 18, 1908, p. 70.

Account of the dinner at Christ's College and of the performance of *Comus*.

2287 "The Music in *Comus*." *Christ's College Magazine*, XXIII (1908), 64–80.

Notes on sources of the music and scores for the tercentenary revival of *Comus*.

2288 "Notes on the Milton Tercentenary." *Athen.*, July 18, 1908, p. 70; October 24, 1908, p. 514; November 14, 1908, p. 609; November 28, 1908, p. 685; December 5, 1908, pp. 723, 724; December 12, 1908, pp. 761, 763, 769.

These are accounts of meetings held and of papers read.

2289 Christ's College Magazine, Vol. XXIII (1908), No. 68.

Milton tercentenary number. Contains contributions by Austin Dobson, C. R. Fay, John W. Hales, J. W. Mackail, J. W. Peile, J. C. Sayle, W. W. Skeat, and others. The list of guests at the college dinner on July 10 has special interest.

Review in *Archiv*, CXXXI, 478.

2290 [Milton tercentenary newspaper clippings (from English journals) in the Harvard Library.]

Large collection; pages not numbered.

2291 "Some Reflections Suggested by the Milton Tercentennial." *Century Magazine*, LXXVII (1908), 314–16.

Praises Lowell's essay on Milton's prose, and Arnold's address on his poetry. Author considers Milton a stimulating example in an age when "geniuses" seek excuses for lack of control in their lives.

2292 "The Story of Satan in the Earliest English Poetry." *Christ's College Magazine*, XXIII (1908), 39–51.

2293 Sir Frederick Bridge. "Milton and Music." *Proceedings of the British Academy*, III (1907–8), pp. 349–52.

Tells of Milton's musical training, and of his father's musical gift.

Illustrations. Elder Milton's famous madrigal and selections from *Comus* are discussed.

2294 British Academy. "The Tercentenary of Milton's Birth." *Ibid.*, pp. 1–31.

Lines by George Meredith; oration by A. W. Ward; summary of an address on Milton and music by Sir Frederick Bridge; program of music.

2295 Phillips Brooks. "Milton as an Educator." *Journal of Education*, LXVIII (1908), 533–35.

See also the *New England Magazine*, VIII (1893), 385–92.

Address to the Massachusetts Teachers' Association, 1874; reprinted.

2296 J. Brown. "Milton as a Puritan." *Book News*, XXVII (1908), 235.

2297 C. G. Child. "Milton's Place Today in Literature." *Ibid.*, p. 225.

2298 John Cooke. John Milton, 1608–1674. A Lecture Delivered in the Parochial Hall, St. Bartholomew's, Dublin . . . . on Dec. 9, 1908. Dublin: Hodges, Figgis & Co., [1908]. Pp. 56.

Pleasing; a blend of biography and criticism.

2299 Lane Cooper. "Dryden and Shelley on Milton." *MLN*, XXIII (1908), 93.

Both classified Milton as among the three greatest epic poets.

2300 W. J. Courthope. "A Consideration of Macaulay's Comparison of Dante and Milton." *Proceedings of the British Academy*, III (1907–8), pp. 259–74.

Macaulay used Dante and the *Divine Comedy* to set off the professed perfection of *Paradise Lost.*

2301 C. R. Fay. "The Political Philosophy of John Milton." *Christ's College Magazine*, XXIII (1908), 81–92.

Read before the Christ's College Historical Society in 1908.

2302 John W. Hales. "Milton and His College, I." *Ibid.*, pp. 8–16.

2303 John A. Hamilton. The Life of John Milton, Englishman, Partly in His Own Words. London: Congregational Union of England and Wales, 1908. Pp. 72.

2304 Alice Law. "The Tercentenary of John Milton." *Fortnightly Review*, XC (1908), 947–63.

Biographical sketch of Milton and a study of his later poems.

2305 A. F. Leach. "Milton as Schoolboy and Schoolmaster." *Proceedings of the British Academy*, III (1907–8), pp. 295–318.

Read December 10, 1908.

Sketch of Milton's schooldays, subjects studied, and books read. Discussion of his views on education and his suggested curriculum.

Review by S. Blach, *Archiv*, CXXIII (1909), 419–20.

2306 John W. Mackail. "The Memory of John Milton." *Christ's College Magazine*, XXIII (1908), 30–35.

Address delivered at the tercentenary dinner at Christ's, expressing high regard for Milton in comparison to various other poets.

2307 Massachusetts Historical Society. The Commemoration of the Tercentenary of the Birth of John Milton, at the First Church in Boston, on December Ninth, 1908. Pp. 31.

Program. Reproduction of title-pages. Text of introductory remarks by C. F. Adams and address by William Everett.

2308 J. E. G. de Montmorency. "Milton and Modern Men." *Contemporary Review*, XCIV (1908), 693–704.

Also in *Living Age*, CCLX (1909), 72–90. Account of Milton's productive period and of his qualities in comparison to those of Shelley, Wordsworth, Beethoven, Swinburne, and Ruskin.

2309 Paul Elmer More. "Milton after Three Hundred Years." *Nation*, LXXXVII (December, 1908), 542–45.

Milton the victim of the conflict of his times. This resulted in an exaggeration of tendencies that kept him from fulfilling his natural genius. For example, *Paradise Lost* is marred by the poet's political experiences.

2310 John Peile. "Milton and His College, II." *Christ's College Magazine*, XXIII (1908), 16–29.

2311 Sir Walter Raleigh. "Milton's Last Poems." *SR*, CVI (1908), 757–58.

Milton's supposed preference of *Paradise Regained* to *Paradise Lost* credited to a feeling that it contains more of his own feelings and beliefs.

2312 Whitelaw Reid. London Commemorations. Winter of 1908–09. Remarks by the American Ambassador. London: Harrison & Sons, 1909. Pp. 35.

"The Milton Tercentenary. Mansion House, December 9, 1908."

2313 J. G. Robertson. "Milton's Fame on the Continent." *Proceedings of the British Academy*, III (1907–8), 319–40.

Read December 10, 1908.

Milton first known abroad as a secretary of the Commonwealth. Popular in Germany; attempt made in 1682 to translate *Paradise Lost* into German. Voltaire awakened French interest. Some adverse criticism in Italy in early eighteenth century. Influence greatest in France.

Review in *Beiblatt*, XXII (1911), 364.

2314 S. W. G. "The Milton Exhibition." *Christ's College Magazine*, XXIII (1908), 94–99.

Sketch regarding the volumes brought together for the tercentenary by Dr. Williamson and Charles Sayle, Esq.

2315 Charles Sayle. "Comus." *Ibid.*, pp. 57–63.

Critical estimate of the stage technique needed as discovered through the tercentenary revival of *Comus.*

2316 Walter W. Skeat. "Manners of the English in the Days of Milton." *Ibid.*, pp. 37–38.

General; based on Aubrey.

2317 Jane A. Stewart. "Milton Exercise [for tercentennial]." *Journal of Education*, LXVIII (1908), 486–87.

School exercises for the occasion.

2318 J. T. Stoddard. "Foreign Criticisms of Milton." *Bookman* (London), XXXV (1908), 126.

2319 E. M. Thompson. "The Tercentenary of Milton." *Athen.*, May 30, 1908, p. 671.

Note of the program arranged in London.

2320 W. R. "Miltoniana in America." *Ibid.*, March 21, 1908, p. 354.

List of Miltoniana collected for the exhibition at Columbia University to celebrate the tercentenary.

2321 W. T. D. "Milton's Theology." *LQR*, CX (1908), 315–19.

Milton's work discussed as it illustrates his theological ideas. His greatness lies in his imaginative treatment of theological material, in his art rather than in any system.

2322 R. W. Wallace. "Milton; Puritan, Patriot, Poet." *Journal of Education*, LXVIII (1908), 564–65.

Biographical.

2323 A. W. Ward. "Tercentenary of the Birth of John Milton." *Proceedings of the British Academy*, III (1907–8), 213–25.

Read December 8, 1908.

Biographical sketch, and an appreciation of Milton's genius.

2324 William Hayes Ward. [John Milton.] *Independent*, LXV (1908), 1159–64.

Critic asserts that only Spenser and Tennyson approach Milton in melody. Not the greatest poet, but of English poets he is the greatest personality. List of portraits given.

2325 Wilfred Whitten. "The Milton Tercentenary." *Putnam's Magazine*, V (1908), 321–34.

Brief biographical sketch, with portraits and other illustrations.

2326 Athenaeum, January 2, 1909, pp. 18–20.

Composite review of papers read before British Academy by Jebb, Dowden, Robertson, Leach, and Courthope.

2327 *Ibid.*, January 16, 1909, p. 77.

A record of items in the exhibition held by the Grolier Club in New York; includes 324 portraits of Milton.

2328 "Moral Genius of Milton." *Current Literature*, XLVI (1909), 186–88.

Author contends that in all tercentenary tributes to Milton, one of two attitudes predominates: one praising him as a poet, the other praising his moral qualities.

Brief discourse on Milton's purity of life concludes the essay.

2329 W. F. Alexander. "Milton." *Contemporary Review*, XCVI (1909), 668–83.

Milton unsuccessful as theologian; takes mystery out of religion. As a poet he has majestic harmony, intense perception of beauty, and is purely of the Renaissance. His best poetry is human and personal.

2330 Milton Memorial Lectures, 1908. Read before the Royal Society of Literature. Edited with an Introduction by Percy W. Ames. London: Oxford University Press, 1909. Pp. xiii+222.

Lectures by G. C. Williamson, W. H. Hadow, E. H. Coleridge, W. E. A. Axon, E. H. Pember, E. B. Saintsbury, H. G. Rosedale, E. Dowden, Sir Edward Brabrook.

Contents noted, *Archiv*, CXXII (1909), 451.

2331 Alfred Austin. "Milton and Dante: a Comparison and Contrast." *QR*, CCX (1909), 157–70.

Also in *Living Age*, CCLX (1909), 588–96.

Milton does not have such hold upon our affections as Dante because he had no Beatrice; his relations with women lacked romance.

Both were erudite, loved music, and engaged in political conflicts. Dante more human, but lacked lyrical exhilaration shown by Milton in early poems.

2332 W. Grinton Berry. John Milton. London: Jarrold & Sons, [1909].

Used Masson, Macaulay, Pattison.

2333 Sir Edward Brabrook. "The Royal Society of Literature and the Study of Milton." *Milton Memorial Lectures, 1908*, pp. 211–20. Oxford, 1909.

2334 Paul Chauvet. La religion de Milton. Dissertation. Paris: Didier, 1909. Pp. 276.

Brief bibliography. Professes that Milton's treatise held the same theory as his poems—that finally all Protestant sects are arrayed against Roman Catholicism. Author unconvincingly asserts that Neilson failed to discredit Walter Begley's attribution of *Nova Solyma* to Milton. In other respects the work traces methodically the known shifts of Milton's point of view in religion.

Review by Liljegren in *Beiblatt*, XXIX (1915), 13–16.

2335 G. K. Chesterton. "Milton and His Times." *Oxford and Cambridge Review*, VII (Midsummer, 1909), 3–13.

2336 Edward Dowden. Milton in the Eighteenth Century, 1701–50. Oxford, [1909].

2337 Roman Dyboski. Milton i iego wiek ["and his age"]. Kraków, 1909. Pp. vi+131.

Biographical account of current ideas influencing Milton, with some social background material.

2338 George A. Gordon. "Milton." *Atlantic Monthly*, CIII (1909), 8–25.

Biographical sketch. Appreciative analysis of Milton's character.

2339 W. H. Hadow. "Milton's Knowledge of Music." *Milton Memorial Lectures, 1908*. London, 1909.

2340 W. M. Harris. John Milton: Puritan, Patriot, Poet. London, 1909.

2341 Raymond D. Havens. "Seventeenth Century Notices of Milton." *ES*, XL (1909), 175–86.

First printed mention of Milton by Edward Phillips in 1689; followed by Poole, Woodford, Slater, Oldham, Hare, Temple, Atterbury, etc. Early praise limited almost entirely to *Paradise Lost.* Pope the first to praise Milton's lyrics.

2342 W. H. Hudson. Milton and His Poetry. London: Harrap & Co., 1909. Pp. 184.

Brief bibliography and much quotation of texts. Another edition, 1912.
Review by Theo. Mühe, *Beiblatt*, XXX (1919), 125–27.

2343 A. J. Huffel, Jr. "Milton in the Netherlands." *De Boekzaal*, III (January, 1909), 1.

2344 Charles Joseph Little. John Milton; a Paper Read before the Chicago Literary Club, ... Dec. 7, 1908. Chicago, 1909.

2345 J. W. Mackail. The Springs of Helicon. London, 1909.

On Milton's classical sources, *passim.*

2346 W. Morison. Milton and Liberty. Edinburgh and London: Green, 1909. Pp. 152.

Moral and ethical ideas stressed in an interesting and valuable essay.

2347 Richard Green Moulton. "Milton as the Greatest of Englishmen." *University of Chicago Magazine*, I (1909), 88–95.

Address at the University of Chicago on December 9, 1908. Indicates the points of excellence in Milton's work, stressing his political, poetical, philological, journalistic, and theological contributions.

2348 Wilfred P. Mustard. "Later Echoes of the Greek Bucolic Poets." *American Journal of Philology*, XXX (1909), 245–83.

On uses by Milton and others of the Greek bucolic poets.

2349 E. S. Parsons. Johnson and Milton on Shakespeare. "Colorado College Language Series." Colorado Springs, 1909. Pp. [116]–17.

Reprinted from the *Nation*, November 12, 1908.

2350 Herbert Paul. "Milton." *Nineteenth Century*, LXV (1909), 65–73.

A discussion of the Puritan and Renaissance elements in Milton. Estimate of Milton's character and poetry.

2351 Whitelaw Reid. "The Milton Tercentenary, Mansion House, Dec. 9, 1908." *London Commemorations, Winter of 1908–09*. London: Harrison & Sons, 1909. Pp. 35.

2352 H. G. Rosedale. "Milton: His Religion and Polemics." *Milton Memorial Lectures, 1908*, pp. 109–90. Oxford, 1909.

2353 George E. B. Saintsbury. "Milton and the Grand Style." *Ibid.*, pp. 83–108. Oxford, 1909.

2354 A. A. Van Schelven. Nederduitsche. Uluchtelingskerken der XVIe Ewu in England. s'Gravenhage, 1909.

2355 Paget Toynbee. Dante in English Literature from Chaucer to Cary (c. 1380–1844). London: Methuen, 1909. 2 vols.

Review in *Contemporary Review*, XCVI (1909), 4–7.

2356 Foster Watson. "Milton as Schoolmaster." *School World*, II (1909), 11–13.

2357 William Willis. John Milton: Political Thinker and Statesman. Address Delivered to an Assembly of Free Churchmen, at Cambridge, Dec. 9, 1908. London: W. H. Bartlett Co., 1908. Pp. 30.

Prefers Milton's prose to his poetry. Discredits Macaulay, and a professor of history (unnamed) who edited Macaulay and showed a dislike of Milton. Ends with a strong defense of *Eikonoklastes*.

2358 "Milton's Identification of Druid and Bard." *QR*, CCXII (1910), 370–71.

Milton's association of "druid" with "bard" contributed, in the eighteenth century, to the use of "druid" as a synonym for poet.

2359 Chautauquan, LX (1910), 429–33.

Reprint of Mathew Arnold's address delivered on February 13, 1888, at St. Margaret's Church, Westminster.

2360 C. W. Beers. "Milton Tercentenary: Address before the Modern Language Club, Yale University." *Revue germanique*, 1910.

2361 Percy Holmes Boynton. "Milton's London." *Chautauquan*, LX (1910), 356–83.

Popular account, with many illustrations.

2362 Gilbert K. Chesterton. "Milton and His Age." *Living Age*, CCLXIV (1910), 556–62.

See also *Catholic World*, CIV (1917), 463–70.

2363 R. Eibach. "John Milton." *New Schaff-Herzog Religious Encyclopedia*, VII, 382–83. New York, [1910].

2364 C. G. Griffenhoofe: Celebrated Cambridge Men, A.D. 1390–1908. Cambridge: Dixon, 1910.

Milton, pp. 74–75. No new facts.

2365 F. Hamel. "English Books in the *Indexes Librorum prohibitorum et expurgatorum*." *Library*, Ser. III, No. I (1910), p. 368.

Covers Milton's place on the *Index* records.

2366 George Lyman Kittredge. "Milton and Roger Williams." *MLN*, XXV (1910), 159.

Shows that Milton was not indebted to Williams for translation of Salmasius. Refutes E. J. Carpenter's assertion that Williams translated Salmasius because he knew "Dutch."

2367 Orestes Pearl Rhyne. "Conjunction + Participle Group in English." *SP*, IV (1910), 8, 24, 28.

Instances in *Areopagitica* and *Paradise Lost* of this formation.

2368 W. P. Trent. Longfellow and Other Essays. New York: Crowell, [1910].

"Milton after Three Hundred Years," pp. 121–38.

2369 Roland G. Usher. Reconstruction of the English Church. London, 1910. 2 vols.

Contains comment on Milton's theology. Not an analytic summary of the successive steps in his thinking.

2370 John C. Bailey. "The Grand Style." *Essays and Studies by Members of the English Association*, II (1911), 104–33.

2371 Charles Bastide. Les gazettes françaises de Londres au XVIIe siècle. [Paris: L. Cerf, 1911.] Pp. 15.

No title-page.

2372 Alfred W. Benn. "Milton's Etnics." *International Journal of Ethics*, XXI (1911), 422–47.

Milton as philosopher is asserted to be a truer representative of Graeco-Roman than of Christian and Protestant traditions. Identified by Benn as possessing scriptural Christianity with anarchic individualism of a metaphysical nature-worship.

2373 A. Clutton-Brock. "Description in Milton." *Essays and Studies by Members of the English Association*, II (1911), 99–102.

An interesting sketch on a difficult topic.

2374 H. Buxton Forman. "The Dilke 'Endymion' and Milton." *Athen.*, June 17, 1911, pp. 687–88.

Raises the question whether the Dilke copy of Milton really belonged to Keats. See also a note by H. K. Hudson, *Athen.*, June 24, 1911, p. 717.

2375 Allan H. Gilbert. "Milton's China." *MLN*, XXVI (1911), 199–200.

Allusions to China in *Paradise Lost*, Book XI, ll. 385–90, are pointed out.

2376 Theron Wilbur Haight. "Milton and Du Bartas." *Nation*, XCII (1911), 59.

Repeats Dunster's (1880) assertion of Milton's borrowings from Du Bartas.

2377 N. W. Hill. "Milton on Plagiarism." *N & Q*, Ser. XI, No. III (1911), p. 191.

2378 Richard Green Moulton. World Literature. New York, 1911. Pp. ix+502.

Offers an extended comparison of Dante and Milton.

2379 George Saintsbury. "Milton." *Cambridge History of English Literature*, VII (1911), 108–57.

2380 Walter Thomas. "Le sentiment de la nature dans Milton." *Revue germanique*, VII (January, 1911), 29–49.

Milton's attitude toward nature shows a gradual evolution, analogous to a change from freedom and grace of romanticism to the severity of classicism.

2381 Christopher Welch. Six Lectures on the Recorder and Other Flutes in Relation to Literature. London: H. Frowde, 1911. Pp. xvi+457.

The fourth lecture deals with this phase of Milton's allusions.

2382 Louis Aubrey Wood. The Form and Origin of Milton's Antitrinitarian Conception. Dissertation at Heidelberg. London, Ontario, Canada, 1911. Pp. 96.

Heavy English; not exact in meanings. The author makes much of Chauvet's study; credits Ochino as a source of Milton's ideas. Notes on the "Dialogue on Polygamy," published in 1657, translated (London) with added section on divorce. No direct evidence, internal or external. Credits Milton with authorship of *Nova Solyma*. Brief bibliography.

Review by S. B. Liljegren in *Beiblatt*, XXVIII (1917), 296–98.

2383 "Milton as a Journalist." *Oxford and Cambridge Review*, XVIII (1912), 73.

2384 W. H. S. Aubrey. "Puritanism: Its Merits and Mistakes." *LQR*, CXVIII (1912), 66–83.

Milton, *passim*. Bibliography of writings on the general subject of English puritanism.

2385 H. W. Boynton. The World's Leading Poets: Homer, Vergil, Dante, Shakespeare, Milton, Goethe. New York: Henry Holt, 1912.

Milton, pp. 184–256.

2386 Paul Chauvet. "Milton et la Bible." *RELV*, XXIX (1912), 290–91.

Note on Milton's feeling in regard to the value of the Bible.

2387 Albert S. Cook. "Milton's Views of the Apocalypse as a Tragedy." *Archiv*, CXXIX (1912), 74–80.

A presentation of the view of Pareus, on whom Milton relied in regarding the Apocalypse as a tragedy. Milton used *In Divinam Apocalypsin S. Apostoli et Evangelistae Johannis Commentarius*.

2388 Herbert E. Cory. Spenser, the School of the Fletchers and Milton. "University of California Publications," 1912.

A discursive study of forms, allusions, and imitations.

2389 Oliver Elton. Milton and Party. Cambridge: Cambridge University Press, 1912.

Noted in the *English Association Bulletin*, No. 18 (November, 1912).

2390 Allan H. Gilbert. "A 'Mystical Man' at Sturbridge Fair." *N & Q*, Ser. XI, No. V (1912), pp. 503–4.

On the possibility that Milton visited Thomas Young.

2391 Frank P. Graves. Great Educators of Three Centuries. New York: Macmillan, 1912. Pp. 289.

See pages 1–9 on "John Milton and His Academy." "Humanistic realism" as relief from "classical Ciceronianism" the Miltonic aim.

2392 Frederic Harrison. "Among My Books,—Poets That I Love, Pt. III." *ER*, X (1912), 425–41.

Appreciative but inaccurate. Notes the use of Milton in English schools during the middle of the nineteenth century in interesting fashion.

2393 Émile Legouis. "Milton (1608–1674)." *RCC*, XX (1912), 314–20, 394–400, 447–53, 604–12, 701–9, 728–33, 796–802; XXI (1912–13), 39–45, 142–50, 384–89.

2394 [Macaulay's *Essay on Milton* in Russian translation.] 1912. Pp. 187.

2395 Henry Newbolt. "A New Study of English Poetry. Poetry and Personality." *ER*, XI (1912), 373–90.

Milton's personality as shown in his poetry (p. 386).

2396 Watson Nicholson. "Notes on Milton." *MLN*, XXVII (1912), 252–53.

Biographical notes, and notes on Milton's fame.

2397 E. O'Rourke. The Use of Mythological Subjects in Modern Poetry. Hobbes memorial essay, University of London. London: University of London Press, 1912. Pp. 63.

Milton, *passim*.

2398 J. E. C. Weldon. "The Theology of Milton." *Nineteenth Century Magazine*, LXXI (1912), 901–18.

Discussion of points of theology in which Milton differed from orthodox beliefs.

2399 J. B. Williams. "John Milton, Journalist." *Living Age*, CCLXXIV (1912), 169–76.

Account of Milton's connection with *Mercurius politicus*, and of John Hall's association with Milton.

2400 George Edward Woodberry. Great Writers: Cervantes, Scott, Milton, Virgil, Montaigne, Shakespeare. New York: Macmillan, 1912. Pp. 216.

2401 Quarterly Review, CCXIX (1913), 244–46.

Milton and Robert Bridges compared as to musical power and sublimation of scholarship through poetic genius.

2402 F. W. Robertson Butler. Puritanism in the Poetical Works of Milton. London: Hunter & Longhurst, 1913. Pp. 102.

2403 Floris Delattre. "La conception politique de Milton." *RELV*, XXX (1913), 65–74.

Milton's conception of liberty an imprtacicable idealism. Not wholly a Puritan, but he represented fully the revolution taking place in church and state.

2404 Edwin Durning Lawrence, and Others. [Milton's epitaph on Shakespeare.] *N & Q*, Ser. XI, No. VII (1913), p. 456; No. VIII, pp. 141, 196, 232, 294, 317, 320; No. IX, pp. 11, 73, 114, 172, 217, 237, 294, 353.

See also *Dial*, LV (1913), 349–50; LVI (1914), 53.

Discussion of Milton's use of the form "starre-ypointing," and its bearing on authorship of Shakespeare's plays. Used in a broadcast pamphleteering campaign to make a basis for the Baconian case. Completely answered by Smith's (1928) pamphlet on the Second Folio.

2405 Professor Rémond. "The Sexual Correlations of Poetic Genius." *ER*, XIV (1913), 575–88.

Brief comment on the inspiration of Milton, which is exceptional in that it is due, not to love passion, but to political and religious passion.

2406 Adam Reusse. Das persönliche Geschlecht, unpersönlicher Substantiv bei John Milton und John Dryden. Pp. viii+124. Dissertation at Kiel. Darmstadt, 1913.

Details *ad infinitum* to show entry of forms into common use.

2407 S. G. Spaeth. Milton's Knowledge of Music. Its Sources and Its Significance in His Works. Dissertation. Princeton, New Jersey: printed, Sohn, Weimar, 1913. Pp. vi+186.

Well-written narrative on the musical conventions and Milton's originality in lyric for accompaniment; on his interest in varied instruments; and on the ethical appeal of music to his nature. Appendixes give the classical origins of his ideas and definitions of his terminology, with references to passages of his works.

Reviews in *Revue germanique* (by Dauchin), XI (1920), 100–101; *JEGP* (by Baldwin), XIV, 310–12; *Archiv*, CXXXI (1913), 497; *ibid.*, CXXXVII (1918), 130.

2408 William Stebbing. Five Centuries of English Verse. Oxford: University Press, 1913. 2 vols.

Milton, I, 113–27; chiefly quotations.

2409 Roland G. Usher. Rise and Fall of the High Commission. Oxford, 1913.

Discusses Milton's political service.

2410 M. L. Bailey. Milton and Jakob Boehme; a Study of German Mysticism in Seventeenth-Century England. Thesis (Ph.D.), University of Illinois, 1912. New York: Oxford University Press, 1914. Pp. 256.

Reviews in *JEGP* (by L. Cooper), XIV, 290–96; *Nation*, C, 712; *Archiv* (by A. Brandl), CXLIII, 288–89; *MLN* (by Preston A. Barba), XXX (1915), 60–61; *Beiblatt* (by S. B. Liljegren), XXIX (1918), 11–13, and XXXVI (1925), 7–8, 172–78.

2411 W. Dilthey. [Estimate of Milton. In] *Gesammelte Schriften*, Vol. II, 1914.

2412 Louise Imogen Guiney. "Milton and Vaughan." *QR*, CCXX (1914), 353–64.

Notes some references and parallels to Milton in Vaughan's writings, and especially some that prove Vaughan's later distaste for Milton's political views.

2413 R. W. G. Hunter. "Milton and the Liberties of England." *LQR*, CXXII (July, 1914), 52–67.

Milton shown to have exerted great influence in shaping thought of modern England. Refers to W. G. Tarrant's *Milton and Religious Freedom* (London, 1903) and W. Willis' *Milton as a Political Thinker and Statesman* (London, 1909).

2414 W. T. Myers. The Relations of Latin and English as Living Languages in England during the Age of Milton. Dissertation at University of Virginia. Dayton, Virginia: Ruebush-Elkins Co., 1914. Pp. 163.

Sketches on the school, international, and living uses of Latin. Slight bibliography. Rev. by R. T. Kerlin in *MLN*, XXIX, 187.

2415 E. S. Roscoe. Penn's Country: Being Literary and Historical Studies of the Country of Penn, Milton, Gray, Burke, and the Disraelis. London: Longmans, 1914. Pp. x+212.

2416 Elbert N. S. Thompson. Essays on Milton. New Haven: Yale University Press, 1914. Pp. 217.

An interesting collection of studies with original contributions. Contains: "Milton, The Last of the Elizabethans"; "Milton's Temperament and Ideals"; "The True Bearing of Milton's Prose"; "Epic Structure of *Paradise Lost*"; "The Sources of *Paradise Lost*"; "The Theme of *Paradise Lost*"; "Milton's Art."

2417 John C. Bailey. Milton. London: Williams & Norgate. 1915.

An introduction to the scope of Milton's art that has merit. The major poems are dealt with in brief but definite analysis. Some bibliography.

Reviews in *British Review*, XI, 152; *Spectator*, CXIV, 407–8; *Athen.*, April 24, 1915, p. 379.

2418 C. C. B. Notes and Queries, Series XI, No. X (1915), pp. 212–13.

Explains Johnson's strictures on Milton's use of "ellops" and of "scorpion." See also a note on page 150 of the same volume.

2419 J. E. G. De Montmorency. "Milton on War and Peace." *Contemporary Review*, CVII (1915), 385–89.

Uses quotations from Milton to show that he believed in war for a just cause.

2420 T. R. Glover. Poets and Puritans. London: Methuen, 1915.

Milton, pp. 34–73. Second edition, 1916.

2421 Anna von der Heide. Das Naturgefühl in der englischen Dichtung im Zeitalter Miltons. Heidelberg, 1915. Pp. 131.

Milton, pp. 5–18 and *passim*.

Author asserts that Milton's objectivity and blindness both prevented normal nature sense. Refers to Schlesinger, 1892, and to Scheifers, 1901.

Reviews in *Beiblatt* (by Bernhard Fehr), XXIX (1918), 289–92; *ES* (by Mutschmann), LIII (1919), 441–44.

2422 E. E. Kellett. "Milton as a Mediaevalist." *British Review*, XII (1915), 430.

2423 Macaulay's Essay on Milton: Edited and Annotated by C. W. French. New York: Macmillan, 1915. Pp. xlviii+128.

Bibliography, pp. xliii–xlvi.

2424 A. Mordell. Dante and Other Waning Classics. Philadelphia, 1915. Pp. 127.

Essays on Milton and on *Paradise Lost.*

2425 H. Mukhopadhaya. Nature in the Poetry of Milton. Calcutta: privately printed, 1915. Pp. 69.

Elementary. Written to interest young Indian students of English verse.

2426 John Cowper Powys. Visions and Revisions. A Book of Literary Devotions. London, 1915. Pp. 258.

Milton, pp. 87–101. Asserts that he had final faith in will and that he was less a Christian than any other great writer of Europe.

2427 E. de Sélincourt. English Poets and the National Ideal: Four Lectures. London: Oxford Press, 1915. Pp. 119.

Milton, pp. 34–60. Of popular interest.

2428 J. B. Williams. "Dr. Johnson's Accusations against Milton." *British Review*, IX (1915), 431.

2429 Ralph G. Lommen. The Religious Milton. Manuscript dissertation at the University of Chicago. Chicago, 1916.

A preliminary study.

2430 Pridwin. "Milton on Free Speech." *SR*, CXXI (1916), 465–66.

Application of Milton's statements for freedom of speech to conditions imposed by the war.

2431 Elbert N. S. Thompson. "Toleration in Puritan England." *Mid-West Quarterly* (University of Nebraska), IV (1916–17), 204–22.

Relates Milton to contemporary agitation for freedom.

2432 Gilbert K. Chesterton. "Milton: Man and Poet." *Catholic World*, CIV (1917), 463–70.

Contrasts the pleasing poetry and unpleasant personality of Milton with certain parallels between the pride of Milton and of his Satan.

2433 Walter Graham. "Sensuousness in the Poetry of Milton and Keats." *South Atlantic Quarterly*, XVI (1917), 346–56.

Milton held to be superior in descriptions of sound; Keats, in descriptions of taste and odor.

2434 Edwin Greenlaw. "A Better Teacher than Aquinas." *SP*, XIV (1917), 196–217.

On Milton's indebtedness to Spenser. Lives of these two poets compared in an able manner.

2435 Paul Emmons Whitmer. The Christology in Milton's English Poems. Manuscript dissertation at the University of Chicago, 1917.

2436 James Holly Hanford. "The Temptation Motive in Milton." *SP*, XV (1918), 176–94.

A careful study of the development of Milton's moral principles. The keen sense of enjoyment evident in his early poems gave way to the Puritan concept that life is a moral conflict.

2437 S. B. Liljegren. Studies in Milton. Land: Gleerup, 1919. Pp. xlii+160.

Calls Milton a Renaissance type—egotistic, unscrupulous, Stoic (like Raleigh and Marlowe). Attempts to demonstrate that Milton could not have visited Galileo; that he and the printer Dugard interpolated the Pamela prayer from *Arcadia* in *Eikonbasilike*. Obviously wrong in saying English criticism has been governed by Puritan tradition in judging Milton.

Decisively criticized in *ES* (by Walter Fischer, LII (1918), 390–96 (reply, *ibid.*, LIV, 358–66); *Deutsche Literaturzeitung* (by G. Hübener), XL, 150–51; *Archiv* (by A. Brandl), CXXXVIII, 246–47; *Beiblatt* (by H. Mutschmann), XXIX, 228–35; *Literaturblatt für . . . . Philo* (by Stern), XLI, 242–46; *Neophilologus* (by Fr. A. Pompen), V (1920), 88–96 (reply, pp. 354–55).

2438 Robert L. Ramsay. "Morality Themes in Milton's Poetry." *SP*, XV (1918), 123–59.

Milton was the gateway through which the medieval morality technique passed into later literature. Milton borrowed widely from the four main themes of medieval morality. Contrasts the medieval "personification" type of allegory with the "metaphorical" type of the Renaissance.

2439 W. F. P. Stockley. "Prose and Poetry: Newman and Milton." *N & Q*, Ser. XII, No. IV (1918), pp. 181–82.

Compares passages from the two poets on Athens.

2440 W. A. Webb. "Milton's Views on Education: Their Present Significance and Value." *Educational Review* (New York), LV (1918), 137–48.

2441 Allan H. Gilbert. A Geographical Dictionary of Milton, "Cornell Studies in English," Vol. IV. New Haven, Connecticut: Yale University Press, 1919. Pp. viii+322.

2442 [By the King. A Proclamation for Calling In, and Suppressing of Two Books Written by John Milton. . . . . 13 August 1660. [Boston: Massachusetts Historical Society, 1919.] Pp. 2.

A broadside in facsimile.

2443 Allan H. Gilbert. "Pierre Davity: His 'Geography' and Its Use by Milton." *Geographical Review*, VII (1919), 322.

Milton said to have used Davity for geographical ideas, in part also as a French text for his nephews. The concise statement of classical notions made the book adaptable to the requirements of pedagogy and thereby familiarized Milton with its terms.

2444 James Holly Hanford. "Milton and the Return to Humanism." *SP*, XVI (1919), 126–47.

Milton a humanist who likewise wrote in accord with the best traditions of his time. Important discussion of Milton's relation to the Renaissance.

2445 R. Lawson. Milton. Melbourne: Whitcombe & Tombs, [1919]. Pp. 128.

In "Australasian Literature Primers." "A useful introduction" (*Athen*).

2446 Thomas Lyster. "Milton's Predecessors." *TLS*, XVIII (1919), 251.

Note of manuscript copy of Martin MacDermott's study of Irish sources in English poetry.

2447 Henry Newbolt. A New Study of English Poetry. New York: E. P. Dutton & Co., 1919.

Milton, pp. 224–50.

2448 A. H. Moncur Sime. "Milton and Music." *Contemporary Review*, CXV (1919), 337–40.

Influence of Milton's knowledge of music on his poetic art. A well-phrased general estimate, with selections.

2449 Elbert N. S. Thompson. "Milton's Knowledge of Geography." *SP*, XVI (1919), 148–71.

His knowledge of geography shown to be extensive and exact. In his *History of Moscovia* he followed Hakluyt and Purchas. This is Milton's most careful treatment of a geographical subject. Asserted also that Milton probably drew from Knolle and Sandys, and likewise made extensive use of maps. His aim in geographic studies was the collection of all the knowledge about the earth known by the Elizabethans.

2450 Edward Chauncey Baldwin. "Milton and Plato's *Timaeus*." *PMLA*, XXXV (1920), 210–17.

Points out important parallels in the thought of Milton and Plato: i.e., their ideas that departed spirits inhabit the stars, that the world was formed out of chaos, and that the origin of evil may be explained by dualism.

2451 "The Caedmonian Genesis." *Essays and Studies by Members of the English Association*, VI (1920).

Henry C. Bradley, on Milton's theology, pp. 24–29.

2452 Allan H. Gilbert. "Milton on the Position of Women." *MLR*, XV (1920), 240–64.

Discrimination of traits in leading feminine characters, with due regard for the superior development of contrasting moods in Eve.

2453 C. Hedde. Klinische Monatsblätter der Augenheilkunde, LXV (1920), 71–72.

Two medical authorities on Mutschmann's theory of Milton's albinism.

2454 Gustav Hübener. "Milton—der Albino." *ES*, LIV (1920), 473–77.

Acquits Milton of the charge brought by Mutschmann in *Beiblatt* of November, 1919.

2455 Richard Jones. The Background of the Battle of the Books. "Washington University Studies, Humanistic Series," Vol. VII, No. 2 (1920).

2456 S. B. Liljegren. "Bemerkungen zur Biographie Miltons." *ES*, LIV (1920), 358–66.

Comments on Fischer's review of his *Studies in Milton*. Asserts that Milton was nearer Roman Stoicism than English Puritanism.

2457 ———. "A Note on the *Neophilologus*, 1919, pp. 88–96." *Neophilologus*, V (1920), 354–56.

Replies to Pompen's review of *Studies in Milton*. Discusses Milton's part in the *Eikon* controversy.

2458 U. Lindelöf. Milton. Helsingfors: Helger Schildts, 1920. Pp. 110.

Illustrated. The standard brief biography of Milton in Swedish.

2459 Heinrich Mutschmann. Der andere Milton. Bonn: K. Schroeder, 1920. Pp. xii+112.

Calls Milton a non-moral egoist; says that he glorified and served virtue only as a means to fame. Expands his albino theory, but is quite unconvincing.

Reviews in *Literaturblatt* (by Walter Fischer), XLII, 174–83; *ES* (by Rudolf Metz), LIV (1920), 437–39; *ibid.*, LV, 313–18 (see reply, *ibid.*, pp. 479–80); *Beiblatt* (by Liljegren), XXXII (1921), 479–80; *Neueren Sprachen* (by M. J. Wolf), XXVIII, 190.

2460 ———. "Milton und das Licht. Die Geschichte einer Seelenerkrankung." *Sonderdruck aus Anglia Beibl.*, XXX (1919), 320–36, 339–59.

An unconvincing attempt to interpret Milton on the assumption that he was an albino. Discusses the effect of blindness on his work and also covers some source materials of *Paradise Lost*.

Reviews in *Archiv* (by Liljegren), CXLII, 147–48; *Literaturblatt* (by Fischer), XLII, 174–83 (see also *ibid.*, 429–32); *MLR* (by Grierson), XVI, 343–50.

2461 ———. "Der Albino als Dichter." *Kölnische Zeitung*, December 19, 1920, Literaturblatt.

Defends his theory of Milton's albinism; appeals to medical authority. *See* Item 2453 for reply.

2462 Denis Saurat. La pensée de Milton. Paris: Alcan, 1920. Pp. 770.

An important book among the Continental studies of Milton since 1900, being partly historical in interpretation but more psychological in its grounds of evidence. The attempt to prove Milton a subtle thinker leads the author to work for his own premises and to ignore the changing circumstances of Milton's surroundings, his intellectual limitations, and his idealism.

Reviews in *SP* (by Hanford), XVIII (1921), 375; *MLR* (by Grierson), XVI, 343–50; *ES* (by Liljegren), LVII (1923), 302–6; *Revue germanique* (by Cazamian), XII (1921), 188–92; *Athen.*, June 25, 1920, p. 843.

2463 Alfred Stern. [On the albino theory, etc.] *Frankfurter Zeitung*, May 23, 1920, Literaturblatt.

Treats Mutschmann's theories ironically.

2464 Edward Chauncey Baldwin. "The Authorized Version's Influence on Milton's Diction." *MLN*, XXXVI (1921), 376–77.

Influence noted in *Paradise Lost*, Book VII, ll. 224–31, and in the sonnet "On the Late Massacre in Piedmont."

2465 Edward Bensly, Gerald Loder, *et al.* "Milton and Elzevier." *N & Q*, Ser. XII, No. IX (1921), p. 116.

Explains Elzevier's letter on Milton. See also notes by W. del Court, *N & Q*, pp. 28 and 158.

2466 R. Burkitt. "Authors' Favourite Words." *Spectator*, CXXVII (1921), 891.

Comments on Milton's frequent use of the word "orient."

2467 Jefferson B. Fletcher. "The Comedy of Dante." *SP*, XVIII (1921), 400.

Milton and Dante compared in the matter of their treatment of "the state of blessed souls after death."

2468 Allan H. Gilbert. "A Note on Shelley, Blake, and Milton." *MLN*, XXXVI (1921), 505–6.

Phrases cited by Beljame used to prove that Blake's influence on Shelley may be due to Milton's influence.

2469 James Holly Hanford. "The Chronology of Milton's Private Studies." *PMLA*, XXXVI (1921), 251–314.

An important study based on Milton's *Commonplace Book*. Corrects Horwood's datings of some of Milton's studies and shows that Milton followed a systematic plan of historical reading.

2470 ———. "Milton and the Art of War." *SP*, XVIII (1921), 232–66.

2471 Gustav Hübener. "Erwiderung." *ES*, LV (1921), 318–19.

Further discussion of Mutschmann's theory of Milton's albinism.

2472 Rudolf Metz. "Nochmal der andere Milton." *Ibid.*, LV (1921), 313–18.

Discusses Mutschmann's theory.

2473 Heinrich Mutschmann. "Zur Milton-Frage." *Ibid.*, pp. 140–46; 479–80.

Defends his work *Der andere Milton* against the criticism of Metz and Hübener. Not convincing.

2474 G. R. Potter. "Milton and Roger Williams." *Rhode Island Historical Society*, XIII (October, 1920), 113.

2475 G. Roth. Sur un exemplaire de Milton ayant appartenu à J.-G. Herder." *RLC*, I (1921), 155.

On the two volumes in the Strasburg library; a French edition of 1760 attested by Herder's daughter.

2476 Denis Saurat. "La Cabale et la philosophie de Milton." *Revue des études juives*, LXXIII (1921), 1–13.

2477 ———. "Les sources anglaises de la pensée de Milton." *Revue germanique*, XII (1921), 353–70.

Study of Milton's connections with the Mortalists, 1643, and his influence on the revised edition of the pamphlet *Man's Mortality* (1655). An important study of Milton's place in the thought of the seventeenth century.

2478 R. Scott Stevenson. "Milton and the Puritans." *North American Review*, CCXIV (1921), 825–32.

Appreciative presentation of Milton's defense of liberty and peace.

2479 Elbert N. S. Thompson. "Milton's Part in Theatrum Poetarum." *MLN*, XXXVI (1921), 18–21.

Regards as probable some contributions by Milton to the work of Phillips. Rejects Warton's statement to the contrary.

2480 ———. "Mysticism in Seventeenth-Century English Literature." *SP*, XVIII (1921), 170–231.

Brief comment on Milton's contempt for pure love verse. Milton cannot be classified simply as mystic; he failed to harmonize diverse moral and ethical elements. Comment on his view of life in the other world.

2481 Henry Van Dyke. Studies in Tennyson. New York: Scribner, 1921.

"Milton and Tennyson," pp. 151–207. Asserts that the two are alike in love of the beautiful, of classical learning, in exact observation of nature (especially in their "landscape-poetry"), in purity of tone, spiritual activity, use of marriage theme, etc. Milton's method is rational; Tennyson's, emotional.

2482 Gilbert K. Chesterton. "Milton and Merry England." *LM*, V (1921–22), 134–43.

A somewhat quixotic essay asserting that Milton's greatness is due not to moral earnestness but to art. Many Cavaliers more noteworthy for standards of conduct than were Puritans.

2483 Paull Franklin Baum. "The New Milton." *Freeman*, V (1922), 225–28.

Milton not a cold Puritan but a man of passionate nature, possessing Renaissance characteristics of pride, ambition, egoism. At times he shows the mood of Puritan moroseness, but not uniformly.

2484 Hugh C. H. Candy. "The Milton-Ovid Script." *N & Q*, Ser. XII, No. XI (1922), pp. 201–6, 221–23, 242–45, 265–69, 281–84, 305–7, 324–26, 344–46, 363–65, 387–89, 406–8, 427–29, 446–48, 463–65, 487–88, 508–10, 525–27; XII, 8, 28, 49, 65, 86, 105, 126, 158, 426.

Opening notes forming the outline of Candy's book. Concludes that script is juvenile work of Milton. Compares with facsimiles of accepted manuscripts.

See also Edward Bensly, *N & Q*, Ser. XII, No. XII, pp. 76, 112, 139.

2485 Walther Fischer. "Der alte und der neue Milton." *GRM*, X (1922), 292–305.

Also appears (condensed) in 18. Allg. Deutschen Neuphilologentage zu Nürnberg, June 9, 1922. Reviews the conceptions of Milton held by scholars from Johnson's time to the present. Emphasizes results of Saurat's work and the new psychologically established unity between Milton's life and his works.

2486 Allan H. Gilbert. "Milton and Galileo," *SP*, XIX (1922), 152–85.

No evidence that Milton knew his writings. A good summary of the Copernican and Ptolemaic elements in *Paradise Lost*, and a good hypothetical case for Milton's selection of Galileo as the sole contemporary to be named in *Paradise Lost*.

2487 Anne M. B. Guthrie. Wordsworth and Tolstoi, and Other Papers. With Preface by H. J. C. Grierson. Edinburgh University Press, 1922. Pp. xviii+124.

"Milton and Shakespeare as Lovers," pp. 37–73.

Grierson's Preface excellent; on Milton. The essays have the unusual quality of emotional power without exaggeration of the known facts concerning the vexed question of Milton's married life.

2488 James Holly Hanford. "The Evening Star in Milton." *MLN*, XXXVII (1922), 444–45.

Comment on the allusions to the evening star in *Comus*, ll. 93–94, and "Lycidas," ll. 30–31, replying to Emerson, *MLN*, XXXVII, 118, and *Anglia*, XXXIV, 495.

2489 Raymond D. Havens. The Influence of Milton on English Poetry. Cambridge, Massachusetts: Harvard University Press, 1922. Pp. xii+722.

A full and finely documented record of the continuous influence of Milton's meter, diction, and ideas up to the year of the Romantic revival.

2490 Newell Dwight Hillis. Great Men as Prophets of a New Era. New York: Revell, [1922]. Pp. 221.

"The Scholar in Politics," pp. 115–42, is an idealized treatment of Milton.

2491 S. B. Liljegren. "Ethisches und Literaturanalytisches zur Milton-Frage." *ES*, LVI (1922), 59–68.

Hübener, in a recent article in *Englische Studien*, had brought up the resentment-motif in *Paradise Lost*, stressing the biblical tradition.

Liljegren stresses the non-scriptural elements, in which he sees an expression of Milton's own passionate and revolutionary character.

2492 Albert Ludwig. "Französische Miltonforschung." *Archiv*, CXLIII (1922), 204–8.

Based on Saurat's *La pensée de Milton*, and his Blake and Milton.

2493 Jesse F. Mack. "The Evolution of Milton's Political Thinking." *Sewanee Review*, XXX (1922), 195–205.

Traces the changes in Milton's political alignments, 1639–73.

2494 Heinrich Mutschmann. "Macaulay and Milton." *Beiblatt*, XXXIII (1922), 170–73.

Comments on the attitude toward Milton's political activities held by Hayley, Macaulay, and others. Shows how Cresswell, in his edition (1912) of Macaulay's essay, opposes the traditional view of Milton.

2495 Fr. R. Pompen. "Recent Theories about Milton's Personality." *Neophilologus*, VII (1922), 272–79.

Reviews Liljegren's and Mutschmann's theories; shows their weaknesses.

2496 Sir Arthur Quiller-Couch. Studies in Literature. Second Series. New York: Putnam; Cambridge: University Press, 1922.

"Talks" on Milton, pp. 88–168.

Reviews in *N & Q*, August 26, 1922; *TLS*, June 8, 1922; *Nation-Athenaeum*, July 8, 1922; *New Statesman*, XIX, 361–62; *Spectator*, September 9, 1922; *Nation* (by John Macy), CXV, 621.

2497 E. K. Rand. "Milton in Rustication." *SP*, XIX (1922), 109–35.

On Milton's presumed study of Latin during rustication, and his imitations of Vergil and Ovid. A summary of the influence of ancient poets on Milton's thought and style.

Review in *Beiblatt*, XXXIV (1923), 173–77.

2498 Denis Saurat. "Milton and the Zohar." *Ibid.*, pp. 136–51.

Originally in *Revue germanique*, XIII (1922), 1–19.

Attempts to show that Milton derived practically all of his philosophical ideas from the *Zohar* and other Kabbalistic documents. Presumes was directed to the *Zohar* by influence of Robert Fludd and Henry More. The extent of Milton's knowledge of this material and his direct reliance on it are not proved.

Reviewed by S. B. Liljegren in *Beiblatt*, XXXIV, 173–77.

2499 M. E. Seaton. "Milton and the Myth of Isis." *MLR*, XVII (1922), 168–70.

Milton a close observer of Italian art, as indicated in the comparison of his search for truth to the picture in the Vatican of Isis searching for body of Osiris.

2500 G. C. Moore Smith. "Milton and Randolph." *TLS*, January 19, 1922, p. 44.

2501 C. T. Winchester. An Old Castle, and Other Essays. New York: Macmillan, 1922. Pp. 395.

On *Comus*, pp. 32–35.

2502 Wollenteit. Milton als Romantiker. Manuscript dissertation, Marburg, 1922.

2503 "Blake and Milton." *TLS*, XXII (1923), 1927.

In part a review of the Keynes edition of the "Ode on the Nativity."

2504 John Buchan (ed.). A History of English Literature, with an Introduction by Sir Henry Newbolt. London: Nelson & Sons, 1923. Pp. xvi+675.

Milton, pp. 202–12.

2505 Ronald S. Crane. "Milton's Lighter Moments." *Freeman*, VII, No. 163 (1923), 159–60.

Indicates that *Paradise Lost* is not essentially a Puritan epic; that concepts of sex therein are outgrowths of such indications as Hebel noted in earlier issue. Hebel, however, restated much of Moody's comment.

2506 Oliver Elton. Sheaf of Papers. University of Liverpool Press, 1923; Boston: Small, Maynard, 1924.

An essay on Milton included.

2507 W. Melville Harris. John Milton; Puritan, Patriot, Poet. A Biography for Young People. London: Congregational Union of England and Wales, [1923]. Pp. 63.

2508 J. William Hebel. "Milton's Lighter Moments." *Freeman*, VII, No. 159 (1923), 58–60.

Assumes that in Latin Milton wrote with a veracity and freedom not permitted in his work made available in English for unlettered readers of that day.

2509 E. E. Kellett. Suggestions. Literary Essays. Cambridge: Cambridge University Press, 1923.

Last essay, "The Literary Essay," concerned largely with Milton.

2510 McEwan Lawson. Master John Milton of the Citie of London. London: Congregational Union of England and Wales, [1923]. Pp. 47.

Brief chapters on seventeenth-century London and Milton's youth, with questions for children.

2511 S. B. Liljegren. "La pensée de Milton et Giordano Bruno." *RLC*, III (1923), 516–40.

Study of the pervasive quality of Bruno's thought in English letters and of his transmitting function for Plato and Plotinus. Not a source study for Milton, but a paralleling of the concepts of Bruno and Milton.

Review in *Beiblatt*, XXXV (1924), 76–78.

2512 ———. "Miltonic Philosophy in the Light of Recent Research." *Scandinavian Scientific Review*, II (1923), 114–23.

Résumé of recent work on Milton's thought by Saurat and others.

2513 Walter MacKellar. "Milton, James I and Purgatory." *MLR*, XVIII (1923), 472.

Gives quotation from *Apologie for the Oath of Allegiance of James I*, in which the king derides the Roman Catholic belief in purgatory—a piece of documentary evidence for the line in Milton's third Latin epigram in the group *In Proditionem Bombardicam:* "Purgatorem animae derisit Jacobus ignem."

2514 John Morley. Critical Miscellanies. London: Macmillan, 1923. Pp. xiv+424.

On Pattison's *Milton*, pp. 308, 333.

Also in Volume III (1886).

2515 [Mark Pattison on Milton.]

Criticisms in *TLS* by C. W. B., March 29, 1923, p. 217; by J. B. W. and H. Mackay, April 19, 1923, p. 269; by C. Allbutt, May 17, 1923, p. 340; and by J. E. Hogg, July 26, 1923, p. 504.

2516 Denis Saurat. "La conception nouvelle de Milton." *Revue germanique*, XIV (1923), 113–41.

Reviews articles on Milton by Hanford, Greenlaw, Liljegren, and others; shows change in the attitude of critics since 1916.

Critical bibliography of Milton scholarship, 1917–21, supplementing Thompson's bibliography of 1916. Duly expanded in the Appendix of *Milton: Man and Thinker* (1925).

2517 ———. "Les éléments religieux non chrétiens dans la poésie moderne." *RLC*, III (1923), 337–68.

Deals with Milton's non-Christian thought as well as that of other English and German poets.

2518 Denis Saurat and C. Cabannes. "Milton devant le médicine." *RAA*, I (1923), 120–34.

Refutes Mutschmann's theory of Milton's albinism and illegitimacy, showing that Mutschmann ignored some evidence and misconstrued various passages from Milton's poetry. A discussion of Milton's health, tending to show that it was bad for a considerable part of his life and was made worse by overwork. Sets up the dubious assertion that his weakness of sight and later blindness were due to hereditary syphilis, a theory restated in his *Milton: Man and Thinker* (1925).

2519 E. A. Sonnenschein. "Stoicism in English Literature." *Contemporary Review*, CXXIV (1923), 355–65.

Chiefly on Shakespeare, but notes Milton as imbued with Stoicism while inveighing against it in *Paradise Regained*, Book IV, ll. 300 ff.

2520 C. A. Tucker. "John Milton and Religious Liberty." *Methodist Quarterly Review*, LXXII (1923), 454–59.

Summary of Milton's views on the subject of religious liberty.

2521 E. H. Visiak. Milton Agonistes: a Metaphysical Criticism. London: Philpot, 1923.

A psychological study, not literary in purpose and not fully tempered by a knowledge of Milton's mind; attempts to show his interest in Satan due to war with self.

Review in *QR*, July, 1923, p. 125; *TLS*, May 3, 1923; *New Statesman* (by Owen Barfield), XXI, 524–25; *Bookman* (London), LXV, 50; *ER* (by G. Sampson), CCXLII, 165–78.

2522 Mary Bradford Whiting. "Dante's Beatrice and Milton's Eve." *Fortnightly Review*, CXIX (1923), 475–83.

Contrast of Dante's idea of woman as the "uplifter" and Milton's as the "temptress."

Milton's attitude due to an unhappy love affair in Italy is the undemonstrated conclusion.

2523 Quarterly Review, CCXLI (1924), 281–82.

Allusions in *Paradise Lost*, *Samson Agonistes* and "Il Penseroso," reveal the extent of Milton's knowledge of bee culture. Quotations.

2524 "New Conception of Milton." *N & Q*, CXLVII (1924), 329.

Saurat, lecturing at Edinburgh, stated the recognized fact that Milton was a man of the Renaissance, not a Puritan.

2525 Lascelles Abercrombie. The Theory of Poetry. London: M. Secker, 1924. Pp. 222.

Milton, *passim*.

2526 Louis I. Bredvold. "Milton and Bodin's *Heptaplomeres*." *SP*, XXI (1924), 399–402.

Milton possessed a copy of the rare and dangerous *Heptaplomeres*.

Shows Milton's interest in radical or "libertine" thought.

2527 Longworth Chambrun. "Encore un mot sur Milton." *RAA*, I (1924), 431–32.

A trivial note pointing out that Mutschmann got no data for the albino theory from Aubrey.

2528 Paul Chauvet. "Milton et la critique française." *Les langues modernes*, XXII (June, 1924), 322–26.

Criticism of Saurat and Douady.

2529 W. M. Conacker. "The Puritanism of Milton." *Queen's Quarterly*, XXXII (1924), 69.

2530 H. N. Fairchild. "The Classic Poets of English Literature: John Milton." *Literary Digest International Book Review*, II (1924), 603, 623.

2531 Walther Fischer. "Defoe und Milton." *ES*, LVIII (1924), 213–27.

A composite picture of influences on Defoe's *Political History of the Devil*. Defoe the first critic to assail Milton's orthodoxy.

2532 J. H. Harder. "Milton, Puritan or Calvinist." *Neophilologus*, IX (1924), 199–203.

Reviews opinions on Milton's Puritanism, and asserts that Milton was not a Calvinist, as Liljegren attempted to show.

2533 C. H. Herford. Dante and Milton. Manchester: University Press, 1924. Pp. 47.

Reprinted from the *Bulletin of the John Rylands Library*, Vol. VIII (January, 1924).

Both prophetic, but "Dante had also, and in a yet more surpassing measure, the sympathetic and synthetic imagination which enables a poet of the Sophoclean or Shakesperian type, ... to bring all the elements of a vast culture harmoniously together."

2534 Elizabeth Holmes. "Some Notes on Milton's Use of Words." *Essays and Studies by Members of the English Association*, X (1924), 97–121.

Attempts "to bring out the interplay of distinct but related shades of meaning in some of Milton's characteristic words." Useful criticism of Milton's use of strange words.

2535 Lyla G. Hugill. A Record of the Friends of John Milton. Manuscript dissertation, University of Chicago. Chicago, 1924. Pp. 241.

A detailed record of the names of persons in any way connected with Milton. Valuable for reference work on sources and personalities.

2536 Ida Langdon. Milton's Theory of Poetry and Fine Art. An Essay with a Collection of Illustrative Passages from His Works. New Haven: Yale University Press, 1924. Pp. x+342.

A well-arranged gathering of passages to illustrate the author's conclusions regarding the varied interests of Milton in the records of critical theory as well as in current experiences of his day.

2537 S. B. Liljegren. [Review of Herbert Schöfflers' *Protestantismus und Literatur.*] *Neophilologus*, IX (1924), 304–8.

Refutes Schöffler's argument that Milton refrained from entering church in order to give himself to writing profane poetry, the two careers being incompatible.

2538 ———. "Miltons Wahl des Berufs." *Beiblatt*, XXXV (1924), 158–60.

Criticism of Schoffler's comments on Milton's religious opinions in *Protestantismus und Literatur*, pp. 39 ff.

2539 ———. "Milton's Personality." *Neophilologus*, IX (1924), 119–21.

Insists on Calvinism as one of the influences on Milton, but maintains that religion was to him of secondary importance.

2540 Heinrich Mutschmann. Milton's Eyesight and the Chronology of His Works. Dorpat, 1924. Pp. 50.

Interesting only as a curiosity of research procedure.

Reviews in *ES*, LX, 354–60; *RC*, XCII (1925), 195–96; *Archiv*, CXLVII (1924), 303.

2541 ———. Milton in Russland. Dorpat: privately printed, 1924. Pp. 10.

To discover an account of a Russian invasion in the lines of *Paradise Lost* is the unfulfilled hope of this pamphlet, based on uses of words that Milton had varied means of securing other than in the presumed source.

2542 M. Raisin. John Milton: the Man, the Poet, the Prophet. Berlin; London: Remon, 1924.

In Hebrew.

2543 Denis Saurat. "Les sources anglaises de la pensée de Milton: Robert Fludd." *RAA*, II (1924–25), 515–23.

Similarities between Milton and Fludd are in their pantheism and materialism, and in their conception of light as primitive matter. No direct influence of Fludd on Milton found. Similarities more in use of images than in philosophy. The essay relates Milton to the current of contemporary thought.

2544 J. Veldkamp. "Calvinism and Pride." *Neophilologus*, IX (1924), 281–83.

Shows Liljegren wrong in assuming Milton's pride to be a result of Calvinistic tendencies.

2545 "Milton." *TLS*, May 21, 1925, pp. 241–42.

Leading article. Summary of recent Milton scholarship.

2546 "Milton Memorial." *N & Q*, CXLIX (1925), 163.

Notice of Milton memorial at Vallombrosa.

2547 Edward Chauncey Baldwin. "*Paradise Lost* and the *Apocalypse of Moses*." *JEGP*, XXIV (1925), 383–86.

2548 Philo M. Buck. "Milton on Liberty." *University Studies* (Lincoln: University of Nebraska), XXV, No. 1 (1925), 1–40.

A clear and stimulating summary of Milton's utterances on true liberty.

2549 John H. Collins. "Milton and the Incomprehensible." *South Atlantic Quarterly*, XXIV (1925), 373–84.

Milton failed to create living characters because he reduced life to terms of inflexible formulas. He failed to see life as a whole.

2550 S. F. Damon. A Note on a Discovery of a New Page of Poetry in William Blake's *Milton*. Illustrated by Facsimile Reproductions from the Original. Boston: Merrymount Press, 1925. Pp. 14.

2551 J. W. Draper. "Milton's Ormus." *MLR*, XX (1925), 323–27.

History of the island to which Milton refers.

2552 John Drinkwater. The Muse in Council. London: Sedgwick & Jackson, 1925.

Milton, pp. 77–94.

2553 G. Ferrando. "Milton in Toscana." *Illustrazione Italiana*, October, 1925.

See also an anonymous article on "Milton a Firenze" in *Marzocco* (November 9, 1925), which parallels closely this article.

2554 Darrell Figgis. "Milton's Spelling." *TLS*, June 25, 1925, p. 432.

Credits Milton's texts with absolute representation of the poet's intent in irregular spellings, leaving no discretion to the editor. Letters follow from Grierson and the Nonesuch Press, July 9, 1925, p. 464.

2555 H. J. C. Grierson. "The Text of Milton." *Ibid.*, January 15, 1925, p. 40.

Would read "in glorious themes," with meaning of "musical strains" in the sonnet "On the Religious Memory of Mrs. Catherine Thomason."

2556 James Holly Hanford. [In] *Studies in Shakespeare, Milton, and Donne.* New York: Macmillan, 1925. Pp. 232.

"The Youth of Milton. An Interpretation of His Early Development," pp. 89–163. The parts played by reading, imitation, and experience of active life are integrated into a pattern depicting Milton's youthful development. An excellent introductory document for a balanced judgment of the *Minor Poems.*

Review in *JEGP*, XXV (1926), 425–26.

2557 Merritt Y. Hughes. "Lydian Airs." *MLN*, XL (1925), 129–37.

On Milton's attitude toward the Platonic tradition of the effect of music upon character. Milton believed music, like poetry, might be sensuous and passionate in creative strains.

2558 G. Humphrey. The Story of the Johns. Philadelphia: Penn Publishing Co., 1925. Pp. 214.

Milton, pp. 39–58. Appreciative.

2559 S. B. Liljegren. Några nya synpunkter på Miltons personlighet ["A new view of Milton's personality"]. *Sällskapet den nya årsbok, Stockholm*, 1925, pp. 128–44.

2560 Heinrich Mutschmann. The Secret of John Milton. Dorpat, 1925. Pp. 104.

Noted in *TLS*, October 8, 1925.

2561 Marjorie H. Nicolson. "The Spirit World of Milton and More." *SP*, XXII (1925), 433–52.

Milton's spirit world identical in many points with that of Henry More. Both received their ideas at Cambridge.

2562 U. Ojetti. "Commemorazione di G. Milton a Vallombrosa." *La parola*, October, 1925.

2563 E. K. Rand. Ovid and His Influence. Boston: Jones, 1925. Pp. xii+184.

Milton is accepted as the author of the 171 stanzas accompanying the illustrations in an edition of the *Metamorphoses* (*see* Item 2673). No discussion of the evidence, which is not generally accepted as conclusive.

2564 G. Sampson. "Macaulay and Milton." *Edinburgh Review*, CCXLII (1925), 165–78.

Composite review of Smart, Visiak, and Saurat. Defends Macaulay's essay on Milton as having breadth and effective knowledge.

2565 Denis Saurat. Milton: Man and Thinker. London: Jonathan Cape; New York: Dial Press, 1925. Pp. xvii+363.

Least convincing in its assertions regarding Milton's physical inheritance. Important as a fresh casting of Milton's ideas under modern ways of analysis. Only partially accurate in interpretations of relationships with Christian materials, it opens new channels of research into Jewish interpretations of biblical themes; yet neither the biblical nor the Hebraic evidence is handled with care. Based in good part on his 1920 book, the volume offers a study of Milton's personality through quotations; a discursive survey of his philosophy, psychology, ethics, and religion; a source study of *Paradise Lost;* essays on Fludd and the Mortalists; a translation of an earlier essay on Milton's blindness. Brief critical bibliography by R. S. Crane, in summary of the two current trends in Milton studies, shows the activity in new fields of Milton study between 1917 and 1925.

Reviews in *New Republic* (by Lovett), XL, 346–47; *Nation-Athenaeum* (by Saintsbury), XXXVII, 178; *New York Tribune* (by Hanford), May 17, 1925; *Beiblatt* (by Liljegren), XXXVI, 274–76; *MLR* (by Grierson), XXI (1926), 440–42; *RAA* (by Legouis), III (1926), 254–55; *ER* (by Sampson), CCXLII, 165–78; *MLN*, XLI, 55–59; *TLS*, May 21, 1925; *Saturday Review of Literature* (by Havens), II (1925), 276; *LM* (by Mirsky), XII, 547–49; *JEGP* (by Greenlaw), XXV, 437–43.

2566 Alwin Thaler. "The Shakesperian Element in Milton." *PMLA*, XL (1925), 645–91.

Shows by parallel passages that Milton did not forget Shakespeare in his later years. Shakespeare's influence on Milton is great, both by way of verbal and figurative recollection and in matters of dramatic technique.

2567 Stanley T. Williams. "Landor's Criticisms in Poetry." *MLN*, XL (1925), 413–18.

On Landor's admiration of Milton as evidenced in critical essays and in verse.

2568 "In Memory of Lionel Harvard." *Harvard Library Notes*, No. 17, April, 1926.

Items purchased as memorials from subscribed funds: French version of "L'Allegro" and "Il Penseroso," 1766; Thomas Farnaby, *Systema Grammaticum*, London, 1641 (*N & Q*, July, 1858, notes Milton's autograph on title-page); folio edition of Pindar. Milton's autograph notes of 1630—; Geneva autograph album of Camillo Cerdoque, with Milton's *Comus* couplet, July 10, 1639.

2569 [The "Milton Ovid Script." Manuscript of Hugh C. H. Candy. In] Sotheby & Co. Catalogue of Valuable Printed Books. Illuminated & Other Manuscripts. London, 1926. Pp. 82. Illustrated.

Lot 461, pp. 78–82, is an illustrated copy of *Johan Posthü Germershemü Tetrasticha in Ovidü Metamorphoses*, Lib. XV (Frankfurt-am-Main, 1563); it contains 166 eight-line stanzas, in heroic couplets, that on handwriting evidence Mr. Candy attempted to prove Milton's amateur compositions to describe the pictures. The item was withdrawn and has not been sold by its owner, who discovered the book in a second-hand bookshop in 1921.

2570 Beverly Chew. Essays and Verses about Books. New York: privately printed, 1926.

Includes paper on portraits of Milton.

2571 Harris F. Fletcher. Milton's Semitic Studies and Some Manifestations of Them in His Poetry. Dissertation at the University of Michigan. Chicago: University of Chicago Press, 1926. Pp. x+155.

Reaches firmly into new evidence that Saurat had touched, while obviously giving only an opening into the most fruitful present field of Milton research outside of English records. The author affirms that Milton's concept of the Holy Spirit is in the Jewish Shekinah and other rabbinical matter; that his ideas can be demonstrated as derived from Semitic origins.

Reviews in *TLS*, February 3, 1927, p. 78; *N & Q*, CLII, 234; *JEGP*, XXVI, 582–85; *MP*, XXIV, 497–98; *RES*, III, 356–58; *Beiblatt*, XXXIX (1928), 364–67.

2572 James Holly Hanford. A Milton Handbook. New York: Crofts, 1926. Pp. x+304.

Bibliography, [287]–96.

Useful for students needing rapid surveys of Milton texts and of recent scholarship. The bibliography gives the final reason for considering this the best current handbook on Milton.

Reviews in *LM*, XVI (1927), 216; *RES*, III (1927), 355; *Beiblatt*, XXXIX (1928), 21–23.

2573 Marjorie H. Nicolson. "Milton and Hobbes." *SP*, XXIII (1926), 405–33.

It is asserted that Milton's central point in justifying the ways of God was in refutation of the ethics of Hobbes. Milton had contrasting views on human nature, reason, the nature of God, and of arbitrary morality. The treatment of these themes in *Paradise Lost* may have had origin in *De Cive* (1642). Obviously Milton was exposed to the pervasive influence of Hobbes, so that the study is valuable apart from the idea that Milton wrote in direct refutation. Other values arise from the contrasted definitions and from tracings of thought in similar veins in the *Doctrine and Discipline*.

2574 George Sampson. "Macaulay and Milton." *Edinburgh Review*, CCXLII (1926), 165–78.

Review of Smart, Visiak, and Saurat. A defense of Macaulay's essay.

2575 Thomas Vernor Smith. "Two Philosophic Observations upon Denis Saurat's *Milton: Man and Thinker*." *SP*, XXIII (1926), 184–88.

As a corrective to the assertions of Saurat, the article states Milton's theology to be related to nineteenth-century idealism by historical continuity, logical similarity, motivation, and method. Milton's concept of the universe as not in harmony with modern scientific views discussed.

2576 George Coffin Taylor. "Shakspere and Milton Again." *Ibid.*, pp. 189–99.

Milton drew from Shakespeare certain dramatic situations and devices to give variety to his epic form. The greatest influence of Shakespeare is found in *Samson Agonistes*, which is an expanded fifth act of a Shakespearian tragedy. Evidence presented is not finally convincing, being based on similarities found in various works.

2577 F. M. C. Turner. The Element of Irony in English Literature. Cambridge, 1926.

Chap. ii: "Milton and the Dawn of the Age of Irony."

2578 J. P. R. Wallis. "Blake's Milton." *TLS*, March 11, 1926, p. 182.

2579 C. A. Moore. "Miltoniana (1679–1741)." *MP*, XXIV (1926–27), 321–39.

Deals with influences and schools of verse.

2580 D. Angeli. Giovanni Milton. Rome: Formiggini, 1927. Pp. 91.

2581 Ernest Boyd. Literary Blasphemies. New York: Harper, 1927. Pp. 265.

Unsympathetic toward Milton, the author thereupon dubs him "academic."
Review by R. M. Lovett, *New Republic*, January 11, 1928, pp. 224–25.

2582 Edward Bensly. "William Hog." *N & Q*, CLIII (1927), 264–65.

Biographical note on the man who published the Latin paraphrase of *Paradise Lost* in 1690.

2583 E. M. Clark. "Milton's Earlier Samson." *University of Texas Studies in English*, VII (1927), 144–54.

On the telling of the story in *The Reason of Church Government.*

2584 Keith Feiling. England under the Tudors and Stuarts. London: Williams & Norgate, 1927.

Review in *TLS*, April 7, 1927.
Condensed but suggestive treatment of literary and intellectual tendencies of the period.

2585 Harris F. Fletcher. "Milton's Use of Biblical Quotations." *JEGP*, XXVI (1927), 145–65.

Deals with Milton's peculiarities of citation and quotation. He used a folio edition of Junius and Tremellius Bible, which contained Beza's Latin translation of the Greek New Testament. He tended to push back to ultimate authority, to Hebrew in the Old Testament, and to the Greek in the New Testament. Virtually all of the scholarly apparatus of the biblical student of his day was at his command.

2586 ———. "Milton and Walton's Biblia sacra polyglotta." *MLN*, XLII (1927), 84–87.

Provides further proof of Milton's use of the Polyglot Bible, edited by Brian Walton, 1657.

2587 Alfred Gertsch. Der steigende Ruhm Miltons: die Geschichte einer Heteronomie der literarischen Urteilsbildung. Leipzig: Tauchnitz, [1927]. Pp. 76.

Bibliography, pp. 73–76.
See *ES*, LXII (1927), 234–37.

2588 G. P. Gooch. English Democratic Ideas in the Seventeenth Century. Second Edition. Cambridge: University Press, 1927.

2589 James Holly Hanford. "Creative Personality: the Case of John Milton." *Johns Hopkins Alumni Magazine*, XV (June, 1927), 328–52.

A lecture delivered on March 11, 1927, resisting the extravagances of psychoanalytic critics.

2590 Charles H. Herford. The Post-War Mind of Germany and Other European Studies. Oxford: Clarendon Press, 1927. Pp. 248.

Essay on "Dante and Milton," pp. 58–114.

2591 Martin A. Larson. The Modernity of Milton. Dissertation at the University of Michigan. Chicago: University of Chicago Press, 1927. Pp. 277.

Too enthusiastic in its interpretations of Milton's ideas as modern; interesting for its collection of related passages from his works.
Review by E. C. Hassold, *MP*, XXV, 245.

2592 ———. "Milton's Essential Relationship to Puritanism and Stoicism." *PQ*, VI (1927), 201–20.

Undue stress put upon Stoic qualities as though incompatible with Puritan traits, with little care for the shifts of taste or the pervasive nature of many of the opinions noted.

2593 Ernest Law. "Milton and Mabuse." *TLS*, February 24, 1927, p. 126.

Probable that Milton saw and studied pictures (at Whitehall and Hampton Court) inventoried and sold by Commonwealth Commissioners.
This item discredited by C. W. B. in *TLS*, March 3, 1927.

2594 Thomas O. Mabbott. "Milton's Books." *Ibid.*, December 1, 1927, p. 910.

Inquiry after present location of Milton's copy of Euripides and other works from his library.

2595 F. P. Magoun. "The Chaucer of Spenser and Milton." *MP*, XXV (1927), 129–36.

Demonstrates that Milton used Speght's 1602 (second) edition.
Review in *MP*, XXV (1927), 129–36.

596 Heinrich Mutschmann. "Methodische Bemerkungen zur Milton-Frage." *ES*, LXI (1927), 316–17.

Further defending the conclusions of his "Milton's Eyesight and the Chronology of His Works" (*ES*, LX, 354 ff.).

2597 Marjorie H. Nicolson. "Milton and the Conjectura Cabbalistica." *PQ*, VI (1927), 1–18.

Reason for interest in cabbalism during seventeenth century. Henry More's English version of the Cabbala, 1654, and More's relation to cabbalism. Comparison of Milton's relation to cabbalism and More's, without an extension of the search into the original sources in any vital reference to Milton's own works.

2598 S. A. Nock. "Denis Saurat on Milton's Color Vision." *MLN*, XLII (1927), 146–50.

Criticizes Saurat for misusing V. P. Squires' article (*MLN*, December, 1894), and arguing from his own notions of color names rather than from Milton's use of them.

99 Frederick E. Pierce. "The Genesis and General Meaning of Blake's *Milton*." *MP*, XXV (1927–28), 165–78.

Blake's interest in Milton due to some extent to associations with William Hayley, from whose *Life of Milton* (1796) he derived the central theme of his poem. By parallel passages, critic tries to show that Blake had read Milton's prose works. Asserts that it was Blake's purpose to save Milton from "stupid misinterpretation and malignant libel."

2600 S. H. Steadman. "Milton and a School Prayer." *TLS*, August 11, 1927, p. 548.

Paradise Lost, Book IV, ll. 213–20, having "disputant," "teaching not taught," apparently draws on Latin prayers of St. Paul's School rather than on any biblical materials.

2601 Elbert N. S. Thompson. "Milton's Puritanism; or, the Issue Clouded." *PQ*, VI (1927), 291–94.

Sound judgment of the qualities in Milton that cannot be classified by inclusive nomenclature; largely induced by Larson's article in the preceding issue.

2602 Austin Warren. "The New Milton." *EJ*, XVI (1927), 811–13.

Milton attractive to modern readers as a figure of the Renaissance, not as a Puritan. Favorable comments on Saurat and Hanford.

2603 Oliver M. Ainsworth. Milton on Education. The Tractate *Of Education* with Supplementary Extracts from Other Writings of Milton. New Haven: Yale University Press, 1928.

The introduction on educational theories of the seventeenth century and the Milton extracts give unusual critical value to the volume.

2604 H. J. C. Grierson. Criterion, VIII (1928), 7–26.

A study based upon autobiographical evidence in the works of Milton to indicate how his fixed resolves of youth, induced by parental guidance, made him unfit for development through experience. Ruskin compared as hampered by the same early fixation.

2605 Rhoda Crane Haussamen. The Use of Color and Light in Milton's *Paradise Lost.* Manuscript dissertation at University of Chicago, 1928. Pp. 83.

2606 Evangeline Lawson. Milton's Theology. *Open Court,* XLII (1928), 407–13.

2607 Thomas O. Mabbott. "Milton's Letters." *TLS,* February 16, 1928, p. 112.

Announces the finding of seven new Milton letters in the Oldenburg state archives, the texts of the letters to be issued later. Apparently not of literary significance.

2608 S. A. Nock. "Notes on Milton's Appearance." *MLN,* XLIII, (June, 1928), 391–93.

A surmise inspired by Mutschmann.

2609 Denis Saurat. Milton et le matérialisme chrétien en Angleterre. Paris: Rieder, 1928. Pp. 243.

"De Fludd à Milton"; "Le système de Milton."

Further search in cabbalist source materials by Saurat has brought up certain parallels to Milton's concept of "absolutism," or rather the later understanding given that term. He makes Milton a transmitter in his theology, particularly in *Paradise Lost,* of the formula of evil and good incarnate, the cabbalist base being used for his theory of free will as bearing on the fall. Introduces further detailed relationships to the seventeenth-century mortalist, Richard Overbury, as well as to the ideas of Robert Fludd, but does not enlarge significantly the known relationships of Milton's works to materials outside the Christian tradition.

2610 Walter F. Schirmer. Antike Renaissance und Puritanismus. Munich: Max Huebner, 1928.

The literary relationships of Puritanism and the Renaissance, illustrated throughout by points from Milton. The definitions of Continental and English standards in the sixteenth and seventeenth centuries are drawn critically from historical facts.

Review in *TLS,* December 27, 1928.

XV. TRIBUTES AND ASCRIBED WORKS

TRIBUTES TO MILTON

2611 Milton's "Bright Morning Star," as a Duet for Soprano Voices, with an Accompaniment for the Piano Forte. By William Carnaby. Goulding & D'Almaine, [1800].

Folio, music and words.

2612 Science Revived, or the Vision of Alfred. A Poem, in Eight Books. London: Gameau, 1802.

A tribute to Milton, in heroic couplets.

Review in *Monthly Rev.*, XL (1803), 27–30.

2613 J. C. Hubbard. The Triumph of Poesy. London, 1803.

An appreciative tribute in verse. Quoted and criticized in the *Monthly Review*, XLI (1803), 439–40.

2614 Gentleman's Magazine, LXXXVI (June, 1816), 526.

Poem on Milton, in a review of Smedley's *Prescience: or the Secrets of Divination.* Refers to the slow growth of his reputation.

2615 Johnson Grant. "Arabia" . . . . to Which Are Added Several Smaller Pieces. London: Hatchard, 1815.

A sonnet to Milton based on the story of Ellwood's proposal that he write a *Paradise Regained.*

Review in *Monthly Review*, LXXIX (1816), 436.

2616 Leigh Hunt. Sonnets to the Donor of a Lock of Milton's Hair. *Foliage* (1818), pp. 131–33.

One is quoted in Ashton's *Eighteenth Century Waifs*, p. 56.

2617 "Lines for the Bust of Milton." *New Monthly Magazine*, I (1821), 250.

Copy of verses inscribed on bust of Milton in a small Grecian temple at Mount Edgecumbe. Three stanzas (Spenserian).

2618 John Greenleaf Whittier. "Apostrophe to Milton." *Independent*, LXIX (1910), 1357.

Early poem of Whittier; appeared first in the *Haverhill Gazette*, 1824.

2619 Wiffen. Lines to a Lady, with a Leaf of the Mulbery-tree Planted by Milton in the Garden of Christ's College, Cambridge.

Quoted in a review of *The Literary Souvenir*, in *Monthly Review*, CV (1824), 443.

2620 Monthly Review, N.S., I (1826), 309.

Quotations from a novel of 1826, *Bramletye House*, giving descriptions of scenes in which Milton had a part.

2621 Lord Edward Bulwer-Lytton. "Milton," a Poem. London, 1831.

At the end of *The Siamese Twins.*

Edinburgh Review, LIII (1831), 146–50, has a quotation and commendatory commentary.

2622 Edinburgh Review, LIV (1831), pp. 165–66.

Comment on Fuseli's paintings on Miltonic themes.

2623 J. de Duçat. Milton, ou la gloire du repentir; drame en trois actes et en prose. Paris, 1843.

2624 "Paradise Restored"; a Poem. Cincinnati: R. P. Donogh, 1844. Pp. 40.

2625 T. Ouseley. "'Milton': a Sonnet." *New Monthly Magazine,* LXXVIII (1846), 364.

2626 [Anne Manning.] The Maiden and Married Life of Mary Powell, Afterwards Mistress Milton. [From *Living Age,* Vol. XXII (1849–50).] Pp. 38.

Originally in *Sharpe's Magazine.* A clever fictitious diary built upon the statements of Phillips.

2627 Major Vetch. Milton at Rome: a Dramatic Piece. Edinburgh: Hogg, 1851. Pp. 24.

2628 A. A. Lipscomb. "Milton." *Harper's Magazine,* XX (1860), 771–78.

An ode to Milton.

2629 "Milton, Morley, and the British Museum." *Censor,* August 1, 1868.

"Some Dons at the British Museum
Say the Epitaph's by one P. M.
On H. M. they press hard,
But J. M. is the bard,
Despite all the swells at the B. M."

An echo of the "Morley controversy" over a supposed find. A full record of the newspaper articles is in the British Museum.

2630 Gatinelli's Play on Milton. *Nation,* VII (1868), 328–29.

Based on Milton's life, but extremely fanciful. Represents Mary Powell as intriguing with Cavaliers, Charles II visiting Milton to compliment him on *Paradise Lost,* etc.

2631 Maurus Jókai. Milton: dráma négy felvonásban [and in verse]. Budapest, 1877. Pp. 99.

Tragedy: Milton as hero.

2632 H. Giner de los Rios. Milton: cuadro dramatico en un acto y en verso, original. Madrid: Alaria, 1879. Pp. 38.

2633 Villiers de L'Isle. "Milton's Daughters; a Story." *Poet-Lore*, VII (1895), 601 ff.

Imaginary conversations of Milton and his daughters.

2634 [Anne Manning.] The Maiden and Married life of Mary Powell, and the Sequel Thereto [Deborah's Diary]. Introduction by W. H. Hutton. London, 1898. Pp. 358.

2635 Programme of Music. . . . . To Be Performed by the Students of the Guildhall School of Music, under Direction of W. H. Cummings, at Mansion House [London], Dec. 9, 1908. London, [1908]. Pp. 17.

A tercentenary-celebration item. Contains the musical program and reproductions of some of the portraits.

2636 Lawrence Binyon. "Milton." *Living Age*, CCLIX (1908), 760–62.

Ode read at a memorial service on Milton's birthday.

2637 Austin Dobson. "A Miltonic Exercise." *Christ's College Magazine*, XXIII (1908), 35–36.

Five stanzas written for the Christ's College tercentenary celebration.

2638 George Meredith. "The Tercentenary of Milton's Birth. Lines Written in Honour of the Occasion." *Proceedings of the British Academy*, III (1907–8), 353–55.

A short poem in blank verse.

2639 George N. Northrop. "In Christ's College, Cambridge. In Memoriam, J. M." *Christ's College Magazine*, XXIII (1908), 7.

A sonnet on the occasion of the celebration.

2640 Henry Van Dyke. "Milton." *Scribner's Magazine*, XLV (1908), 160.

2641 Horace Spencer Fiske. "To Milton's Mulberry Tree." *University of Chicago Magazine*, I (1909), 96.

A sonnet.

2642 Richard Watson Gilder. "Milton." *Putnam's Magazine*, V (1909), 546.

Sonnet read at Columbia University on December 9, 1908.

2643 Ernest Myers. "Milton." *Chautauquan*, LX (1910), 429.

A sonnet on Milton.

2644 Peter E. Wright. "Milton." *ER*, XXXII (1921), 481–82.

A poetic tribute to Milton.

2645 E. Lloyd. Milton's Prayer of Patience.

A verse tribute in *Whittier's Unknown Romance* (Boston, 1922), pp. 71–72.

2646 E. J. Price and Harriet Byles. Scenes from the Life of John Milton. London: Congregational Union of England and Wales, 1923. Pp. 48.

A play for 19 characters; first staged in November, 1921.

2647 Paul Selver. Galileo with Milton at Torre del Gallo. (Translated from J. S. Machar's *The Apostles.*) *Sewanee Review*, XXXII (1924), 30–31.

Represents Galileo discussing with Milton the mysteries of the universe.

2648 V. Beonio Brocchieri. "Giovanni Milton: dramma individuale e problemi universali." *Nuova Antologia*, CCXLVIII (1926), 388–400.

2649 William Blake. The Prophetic Books of William Blake. Edited by E. R. D. Maclagan and A. G. B. Russell. London: Bullen, 1927. Pp. xvi+57.

Originally published in 1804. Has the illustrations for *Paradise Lost.*

WORKS ASCRIBED TO MILTON

2650 J. M. News from Hell, Rome and the Inns of Court. . . . . Published for the Future Peace . . . . of the Inhabitants of Great-Britain by J. M. *Harleian Miscellany*, Vol. VII (1811).

Pp. 212–22. A note, never justified by evidence, represented the tract as Milton's.

2651 "Original Lines, by Milton." *Monthly Magazine*, XLV (1818), 44.

Copy of lines written on a glass at Chalfont, believed to have been written by Milton at the time of the Plague. From Bibl. Birch, 4253, in the British Museum.

2652 An Account of an Original Autograph Sonnet by John Milton, Contained in a Copy of Mel Helonicum Written by Alexander Rosse, 1642, in the Possession of William Tite. . . . . With Facsimiles and Literary Illustrations. [By Sir William Tite.] London: privately printed, 1859. Pp. 38.

An ascription based on initials; not in Milton's hand.

2653 Nation, I (1865), 245.

Copy of the inscription in verse on a window in Chalfont St. Giles. Reference to Pope's notice of 1737.

2654 Henry Morley. "The Poem Attributed to Milton."

The epitaph discussed at such length in the *London Times* was reprinted in the *New York Tribune* (August, 1868) and in Morley's Introduction to *The King and Commons* (Cavalier and Puritan Song), 1868. Morley still held to his unfounded ascription to Milton.

See *Nation*, VII (August 6, 1868), 112, 150–51; also Item 2629.

2655 Sir Charles H. Firth. "A Tract Attributed to Milton." *Athen.*, February 6, 1897, pp. 183–84.

Attributes to John Hall a tract which Masson (IV, 520–23) assigned to Milton. Conclusive.

2656 "Milton's Unpublished Poem. . . . . Epitaph on a Rose Tree, Confined in a Garden Tub." *N & Q*, Ser. IX, No. VI (1900), pp. 182–83; No. VII (1901), pp. 90 and 235; No. XII (1903), p. 67.

One of the false trails of searchers after lost poems by Milton. See also *N & Q*, Ser. IV, No. II (1868), pp. 75–76.

2657 Nova Solyma, the Ideal City; or Jerusalem Regained . . . . Attributed to the Illustrious John Milton. Edited by W. Begley. 2 vols. London, 1902.

2658 Book-buyer, XXV (1902), 223–28.

A review of Begley's edition of *Nova Solyma*, accepting his ascription.

2659 Athenaeum, January 24, 1903, p. 104.

Begley's work not accepted. The authorship of *Nova Solyma* discussed on the grounds of learning and urbanity.

2660 Fanny Byse. "Authorship of *Nova Solyma*." *Book-buyer*, XXV (1903), 223–28.

2661 ———. "Nova Solyma." *N & Q*, Ser. IX, No. XII (1903), pp. 168, 232.

2662 F. G. "An Utopia Attributed to Milton." *Atlantic Monthly*, XCI (1903), 695–98.

Nova Solyma probably Milton's but external evidence must be forthcoming to establish authorship.

2663 Frederic Ives Carpenter. "A Romance Ascribed to Milton." *Dial*, XXXIV (1903), 238–39.

Criticizes Begley's assertions and refutes the claims for Milton as author.

2664 J. W. Mackail. "A Miltonian Romance." *QR*, CXCVII (1903), 484–502.

Review of Begley's translation of *Nova Solyma*. Rejects attribution to Milton, but commends Begley's study of cultural life of the period.

2665 Paul Elmer More. "A Romance Attributed to John Milton." *Independent*, LIV (1903), 434–37.

Accepts Begley's theory of Milton's authorship of *Nova Solyma*.

2666 "Nova Solyma." *Nation*, LXXVI (1903), 251–53.

No external evidence to prove Milton's authorship. Begley's translation well done.

2667 J. Churton Collins. "Miltonic Myths and Their Authors." *National Review*, Vol. XLIII (1904).

Significant criticism. Reprinted in *Studies in Poetry and Criticism* (London, 1905), pp. 167–203.

2668 Richard Garnett. "Milton as a Romancer: *Nova Solyma*." *International Quarterly*, IX (1904), 140–53.

Praises Begley's edition; evidence for Milton's authorship inconclusive.

2669 William Allan Neilson. "*Nova Solyma:* a Romance Attributed to Milton." *MP*, I (1903–4), 525–46.

Begley probably wrong, but his discovery and study of the book is valuable. A good conclusion to the speculations in earlier discussions.

2670 A. L. Clarke. "Allibone's *Critical Dictionary of English Literature*." *Library*, V (1904), 427.

A review that discusses spurious letters "in which Milton refers to Roger Williams" in a novel of 1852. See the *Library Journal*, II (1877–78), 80.

2671 S. K. Jones. "The Authorship of *Nova Solyma*." *Ibid.*, 3d Ser., I (1910), 225–38.

The evidence for Samuel Gott as author is convincing.

2672 "An Attribution to Milton." *TLS*, August 14, 1924.

Reviews Candy's *Some Newly Discovered Stanzas*. . . . . Suggests that author of stanzas used translation of Ovid by Golding (1567) and by Sandys (1626). Probable that he used prose commentary which first appeared in Sandys' second edition (1632). If so, stanzas must be dated nine years later than date assigned by Candy. The review presents no settled opinion.

2673 Hugh C. H. Candy. Some Newly-discovered Stanzas Written by John Milton on Engraved Scenes Illustrating Ovid's Metamorphoses. London, 1924. Pp. viii+192.

First form appeared in *TLS*, January 26, 1922, and in *N & Q*, September 9, 1922—February 17, 1923, and June 2, 1923.

An elaborate handwriting test of Milton's early manuscript materials and of the autograph verses in a 1563 edition of Ovid published at Frankfort, with further details on diction, phrasing, and spelling, the effort being to prove that Milton did these verse experiments to describe the illustrations of Ovidian passages. Not conclusive, though accepted by a few critics with surprising alacrity.

Reviews in *Sheffield Independent*, August 18, 1924; *Liverpool Courier* August 30, 1924; *Liverpool Post*, August 20, 1924; *Birmingham Post*, July 25, 1924; *Newcastle Chronicle*, July 17, 1924; *T. P. and Cassell's Weekly*, October 11, 1924; *New Statesman*, August 16 and 30, 1924; *Manchester City News*, July 12, 1924; *London Times*, July 13, 1924; *Observer*, July 6, 1924; *Yorkshire Observer*, October 28, 1924. Most of these are uncritical reviews.

2674 ———. "Ovid, Sandys, and Milton." *N & Q*, CXLVII (1924), 122.

Replies to Brodbie's assertion (*N & Q*, CXLVII, 77) that poems supposed to be Milton's are by Sandys.

XVI. EDITORS OF MILTON

2675 The Poetical Works of John Milton. With the Principal Notes of Various Commentators. To Which Are Added Illustrations with Some Account of the Life of Milton. By H. J. Todd. London: J. Johnson, etc., 1801. 6 vols.

The four editions of Todd have countless remarks on other editors of Milton's poetry from the earliest date to 1842.

2676 "Burnett's Edition of Milton's *Prose Works* (1809)." *Monthly Review*, LXV (1811), 247–48.

Burnett's qualifications as an editor noted. One praiseworthy feature of his edition is that it tells the reader where to skip, for "the prose of Milton, however beautiful and majestic, is somewhat scholastic and heavy."

2677 Gentleman's Magazine, LXXXI (1811), 42.

Discussion of a proposed edition of Milton. Critic notes that Todd used Stillingfleet's manuscript.

2678 "Newton's Milton" *Monthly Magazine*, XXXIV (1812), 234.

Suggestion as to the best method of preparing an edition of Milton, with comment on difficulty of making his work intelligible to lay readers.

2679 Gentleman's Magazine, LXXXIII (1813), 25–26, 326.

Criticism of Symmons' edition.

2680 Monthly Review, LXXXIX (1819), 83–84.

Survey of Milton's literary reputation. Account of the publication of his *Character of the Long Parliament.*

2681 *Ibid.*, CIII (1824), 378–81.

William Hayley as editor discussed. Much interesting data included.

2682 D. Laing. "Report on the Unpublished Manuscripts of Callander's Notes on Milton." *Arch. Scotica*, Vol. III (1826).

2683 Quarterly Review, XLVI (1832), 159–62.

Bentley's Milton discussed in connection with a review of Monk's *Life of Bentley.*

2684 "Milton and His Biographers." *Museum*, XXII (1833), 173–83.

Estimate of Johnson, Hayley, Cowper, Todd, Symmons, and Mitford as editors and biographers.

2685 Eugenio Camerini. Profili letterari. Firenze: Barbera, 1870. Pp. x+525.

"Milton e l'Italia" presents a brief list of the Italian translators of Milton.

2686 "Plagiarism in Milton Scholarship." *Nation*, XXV (December 13, 1877), 365.

Attacks Nadal (*Harper's Magazine*, LVI, 137–40) for plagiarizing Masson's work. See Nadal's reply, *Nation*, XXVI, 43.

2687 Alois Brandl. "Zur ersten Verdeutschung von Miltons *Verlorenem Paradies*." *Anglia*, I (1878), 460–63.

Evidence of translation of *Paradise Lost* by Th. Haake (1605–90) discovered in letter of J. U. König to J. J. Bodmer, printed in *Literärischen Pamphleten*, 1781.

2688 J. F. Payne. "Milton's *Prose Works:* the Folio of 1697." *Athen.*, June 18, 1898, pp. 791–92.

Description of a volume published in 1697, entirely different from Toland's edition of 1698. Published perhaps by Tonson; Hodgkin probably the printer.

2689 Edmund Gosse. "Milton Manuscripts at Trinity." *Atlantic Monthly*, LXXXV (1900), 586–93.

Same article, in *Current Literature*, XXIX (1900), 38. Comments on Aldis Wright's facsimile edition and on the history of the manuscript at Cambridge. Mentions corrections made in poems, but has little original comment to present.

2690 J. Schmitter. J. J. Bodmers Übersetzungen von J. Miltons *Verlorenem Paradies*, 1732, 1742, 1754, 1759, 1769, sprachlich verglichen. Inaugural dissertation, Zurich. Zurich: Von Marbach, 1913. Pp. 283.

A studious anatomizing of forms in the successive editions.

2691 John W. Mackail. "Bentley's Milton." *Proceedings of the British Academy*, XI (1924), 21.

The Warton lecture on English poetry.
Review in *Archiv*, CXLVIII (1925), 158–59.

2692 Johannes C. Andersen. "Bentley and Milton." *TLS*, August 27, 1925, p. 557.

An unpublished letter from Bentley's nephew.

2693 Frank L. Clark. A Study of the *Iliad* in Translation. Chicago: University of Chicago Press, 1927. Pp. x+354.

Many points regarding Milton's use of the *Iliad* are illustrated by parallel passages.

XVII. EPIC

2694 William Barron. Lectures on Belles Lettres and Logic. London, 1806. 2 vols.

Milton discussed, II, 281–300. The critic defends *Paradise Lost* as epic, even though Milton uses only supernatural power, because "the great end of epic composition is to enlarge and exalt the mind by the contemplation of magnificent objects."

2695 George Walker. "On the Machinery of the Ancient Epic Poem." *Memoirs of the Literary and Philosophical Society of Manchester*, 2d Ser., Vol I (1806).

Milton and Homer compared. "As Homer's has been observed to be the history of the gods, Milton's may be said to be that of the devils." Milton held superior in epic style to Homer.

Review in *Monthly Review*, L (1806), 362-64.

2696 Monthly Review, LXXIII (1814), 473–85.

Critic of M. Breton's *New Elements of Literature* discusses Milton as an epic poet.

2697 Quarterly Review, X (1814), 380–81.

Comparison of Milton and Klopstock.

2698 "Macpherson and Milton." *Monthly Magazine*, XLII (1816), 232.

M. Breton, a French critic, in *Elements of Literature*, awards preference to Ossian over Milton. Ossian also preferred to Milton in Italy. Both poets have been translated with equal felicity—Milton by Rossi, and Macpherson by Cesarotti.

2699 J. C. Gray. "Milton and Dante." *North American Review*, VIII (1819), 342–47.

Comparison shows Dante superior in conception of subject, but Milton succeeded in giving more vivid pictures of the scenery and inhabitants of Eden.

2700 "Milton and Homer Contrasted" *Analectic Magazine*, XIV (1819), 224.

2701 E. P. "Remarks on the Subjects of Epic Poems." *GM*, LXXXIX (July, 1819), 36.

Milton's creative power greater than Homer's. Framed subjects from his own imagination. Greatness lies in range and sublimity of ideas, although sometimes he was capable of "languor and insipidity."

2702 Monthly Review, N.S., I (1826), 470–79.

Comparison of Camoëns and Milton, particularly of the circumstances of their writing.

2703 *Ibid.*, CXXIV (1831), 295–305.

Dante and Milton compared, in a review of Stebbing's *Lives of the Italian Poets.*

2704 "Poetry and Romance of the Italians." *North American Review*, XXXIII (1831), 32–33.

Milton held an ideal poet who delighted in generalization; Dante, most literal of artists, who painted in great detail.

2705 Edinburgh Review, LVII (1833), 412–34.

Milton compared to Dante in subject matter, genius, and spirit.

2706 "John Milton and Robert Montgomery." *Knickerbocker Magazine*, III (1834), 120–34.

A severe criticism of Montgomery's *Messiah*, comparing its plan and execution with the structure of *Paradise Lost* and *Paradise Regained.*

2707 Edinburgh Review, LXVI (1838), 261–94.

Summary of ideas of epic in Milton's day; notes on William Herbert's imitation of Milton in his *Attila.*

2708 Quarterly Review, LXI (1838), 430–31.

Milton held to have been held to self-restraint by classical models. Alludes to himself only twice in *Paradise Lost.* His self-exclusion remarkable, for "no writer seems so completely concentered in his own individual being."

2709 Raymond de Vericour. Milton et la poésie épique; cours professé à L'Athenée Royale de Paris. Paris; London: Baillière, 1838. Pp. viii+422.

Highly appreciative of *Paradise Lost.* Indicative of changed French attitude toward Milton; ranked above Dante and Klopstock.

Reviews in *Monthly Review*, CXLVI (1838), 342–51; *Athen.*, September 3, 1842, pp. 783–84.

2710 Carolus Hillebrand. De sacro apud Christianos carmine epico dissertationem, seu Dantis, Miltonis, Klopstockii poetarum collationem. Paris: Durand, 1861. Pp. 82.

2711 "Milton and Dante." *St. James Magazine*, 1866, pp. 243–50.

2712 A. Chassang and F. L. Marcou. Les chefs-d'œuvre épiques de tous les peuples. Paris, 1879. Pp. xxxviii+339.

Milton, pp. 279–97.

2713 W. T. Dobson. The Classic Poets; Their Lives and Their Times, with the Epics Epitomized. London: Smith, Elder & Co., 1879. Pp. ix+452.

2714 E. Bailly. Étude sur la vie et les œuvres de Frédéric Gottlieb Klopstock. Paris: Hachette, 1888. Pp. 450.

"Comparaison des très épopées, *La divine Comédie, Le Paradis perdu, La Messiade*," pp. 136–62.

2715 W. E. Buckley. "Milton's Translations from Dante and Ariosto." *N & Q*, Ser. VII, No. V (1888), p. 445.

A list of translated passages.

2716 Pardo Bazán. "Los poetas epicos cristianos: Milton." *La España moderna*, VI (November, 1894), 108–22; VI (December, 1894), 116–48.

2717 Pardo Bazán. Los poetas épicos cristianos. Madrid: A. Avrial, 1895. Pp. 350.

In his *Obras completas*, Vol. XII. Dante, Tasso, Milton.

2718 S. H. Gurteen. The Epic of the Fall of Man. A Comparative Study of Caedmon, Dante, and Milton. New York: Putnams, 1896. Pp. xi+449.

Plates. Discusses Christian epic forms, not defining his idea of Milton's possible use of Caedmon.

Review by W. H. Browne, *MLN*, XII (1897), 91.

2719 R. E. Neil Dodge. "Spenser's Imitations from Ariosto." *PMLA*, XII (1897), 165–66.

Probable attitude of Milton toward *Crlando Furioso* discussed.

2720 I. T. Myers. A Study in Epic Development. "Yale Studies in English," Vol. XI. New York: Holt, 1901. Pp. 160.

Bibliography, pp. 149–56. Milton, pp. 24–28.

2721 W. Thomas. De epico apud Joannem Miltonium versu. Dissertation at the University of Paris. Paris: Hachette, 1901. Pp. xii+[89].

"Epica Miltonii poemata perscrutati ejus in re metrica immotum aliquid invenimus."

2722 A. Scrocca. Studio critico sul *Paradiso Perduto* del Milton. Naples, [1902]. Pp. 39.

On French and Italian relationships with Milton, particularly in epic forms.

2723 Friedrich Buff. Miltons *Paradise Lost* in seinem Verhältnisse zur *Aeneide, Ilias*, und *Odyssée*. Inaugural dissertation at München, 1904. Pp. 77.

Good on epic devices.

2724 Henry Cloriston. Later Work of Torquato Tasso Rendered into English Verse. London: Postal Literary Alliance, 1907. Pp. 47.

"Affinities Tassian and Miltonic," [pp. 30–47].
Reviewed by Helene Richter, *ES*, XLI, 146.

2725 Marianna Woodhull. The Epic of *Paradise Lost*. New York: Putnam's Sons, 1907. Pp. xi+375.

Bibliography, pp. 351–68.

2726 W. M. Dixon. English Epic and Heroic Poetry. London: Dent, 1912. Pp. 339.

Classical epic, Milton, pp. 189–223.

2727 Allan H. Gilbert. "Milton's Translation from Ariosto." *MLN*, XXVII (1912), 229.

Comment on Milton's use of eight lines translated from *Orlando Furioso*, Canto 34. Milton revised Harrington's translation of the last four of these lines.

2728 K. Assman. Miltons epische Technik nach *Paradise Lost*. Berlin, 1913. Pp. viii+90.

Brief bibliography and chapters on Milton's adaptations of classical formulas.

2729 H. A. Guerber. The Book of the Epic: the World's Great Epics Told in Story. Philadelphia, 1913.

Paradise Lost and *Paradise Regained* in prose paraphrase, pp. 353–94. Published also in London: Harrap, 1916. Pp. 631.

2730 Lascelles Abercrombie. The Epic. London: Secker, 1914. Pp. 95.

Bailey: "full of fine and suggestive criticism of Milton."
Critic discerns in Milton unlimited reality beyond self. He had to "dissolve his human action completely in a supernatural action . . . . a development, a recreation of epic art."

2731 L. Falchi. Studi di poesia cristiana. Rome, 1914. Pp. 176.

Author asserts (pp. 154–57) that while in Naples, in 1638, Milton received Tasso's epic from Manso. No evidence.

2732 Elbert N. S. Thompson. "The Epic Structure of *Paradise Lost*." *Essays on Milton*. New Haven: Yale University Press, 1914.

2733 Marjorie Barstow. "Milton's Use of the Forms of Epic Address." *MLN*, XXXI (1916), 120–21.

On the use by Adam and Eve of epic address in Eden. After the fall, they call each other by name.

2734 C. W. Crane. Some Points of Comparison in Dante and Milton. Manuscript dissertation at Cornell University. Pp. 60.

2735 Allan H. Gilbert. "The Cambridge Manuscript and Milton's Plans for an Epic." *SP*, XVI (1919), 172–76.

The manuscript is fragmentary. His plan of writing a heroic poem was conceived before the Italian journey. Milton had in mind both epic and tragedy, and suitable subjects for them; he did not reject epic in favor of tragedy.

2736 Elizabeth Nitchie. Vergil and the English Poets. New York: Columbia University Press, 1919.

Chapter vi, "Milton and the Classical Epic," "affirms that Milton's classicism is Greek rather than Latin, but that *Paradise Lost* uses the *Aeneid* chiefly as the model for epic structure."

Review by Paul Shorey in *Classical Philology*, XVI (1921), 401.

2737 Proctor Fenn Sherwin. "Detached Similes in Milton's Epics." *MLN*, XXXVI (1921), 341–48.

A good sketch of Renaissance, classical, and romantic elements in Milton's art.

2738 P. F. Jones. "Milton and the Epic Subject from British History." *PMLA*, XLII (1927), 901–9.

A plausible explanation of the turn from Arthurian materials to biblical.

XVIII. METRICS

2739 Edinburgh Review, VII (1806), 259–328.

On the versification of *Paradise Lost*, with special regard for R. P. Knight's strictures.

2740 William C. Hazlitt. "On Milton's Versification." *The Round Table.* London, 1817.

2741 Quarterly Review, LI (1834), 24–25.

On Milton's mastery of lyrical measures and his knowledge of Greek drama.

2742 *Ibid.*, LII (1834), 7, 13, 35.

Versification of *Comus* compared with that of *Paradise Lost.* Held to be subjective in his artistry.

2743 John Addington Symonds. "The Blank Verse of Milton." *Fortnightly Review,* XXII (1874), 767–81.

Summary of criticism of Milton's blank verse.

2744 Edwin Guest. A History of English Rhythms. New edition, by W. W. Skeat. London: Bell, 1882. Pp. xii+730.

First edition, Vol. I, 1838; Vol. II, 1840.
Milton, pp. 530 ff. On Milton's apt numbers, fit quantities of syllables, etc.

2745 Modern Language Notes, I (1886), 22–23.

Review of Gosse's *From Shakespeare to Pope*, by T. W. Bancroft. Discussion of Milton's subservience of expression to thought and the classical distich.

2746 "Milton's False Quantity." *N & Q*, Ser. VII, No. V (1888), 147, 216.

Query and replies on Milton's compositions in Greek.

2747 On the Prosody of *Paradise Regained* and *Samson Agonistes.* Being a Supplement to the Paper "On the Elements of Milton's Blank Verse in *Paradise Lost*," Which is Printed in the Rev. H. C. Beeching's Edition of *Paradise Lost*, Bk. I. Oxford: Blackwell, 1889. Pp. 12.

Anonymous; by Bridges.

2748 William Hand Browne. "Certain Considerations Touching the Structure of English Verse." *MLN*, IV (1889), 97–101.

Deals with Milton's blank verse.

2749 Oliver Farrar Emerson. "The Development of Blank Verse." *Ibid.*, pp. 233–36.

Blank verse of Milton and Shakespeare contrasted with that of Surrey.

2750 Jonathan Boucher "Milton's Poetic Theory." *N & Q*, Ser. VII, No. IX (1890), p. 269.

Query as to the statement of Milton's poetic theory.

See replies by Henry Gerald Hope and W. E. Buckley, *N & Q*, Ser. VII, No. X, pp. 17–18.

2751 W. Watkiss Lloyd. "Miltoniana." *Ibid.*, Ser. VII, No. XII (1891), p. 5.

Milton's use of Greek scansion of proper names.

2752 J. Schipper. "English Metres." *MLN*, VI (1891), 121–23.

Comments on meter of "L'Allegro" and "Il Penseroso."

2753 Robert Bridges. Milton's Prosody. Oxford: Oxford University Press, 1893.

Limited edition, Oxford, 1893. Pp. 80. Revised, final edition, 1921 (*q.v.*).

Reviews in *Nation*, LX (1895), 166; *School Review*, IV (1896), 553–54; *Athen.*, March 24, 1894, p. 372.

2754 Modern Language Notes, VIII (1893), 245–47.

On Milton's meters, in a review, by A. H. Tolman, of Corson's *Primer of English Verse.*

2755 Richard Hemming. "Milton's Pronunciation of Latin." *N & Q.*, Ser. VIII, No. VII (1895), p. 436.

On the two modes of pronouncing Latin vowels, a topic discussed previously (in No. VI, pp. 146, 253, 489).

2756 Robert Bridges. Milton's Prosody. With William Johnson Stone's Classical Metres in English Verse. Oxford, 1901. Pp. vi+174.

Reviews in *Nation*, LXXIV (1902), 370–71, 406; *ES* (by B. A. P. Van Dam), XXXII (1903), 98–109.

2757 George Dobbin Brown. Syllabification and Accent in the *Paradise Lost*. Johns Hopkins dissertation. Baltimore: John Murphy Co., 1901. Pp. v+73.

Summary of studies of Milton's meters. Study of syllable division, number and position of accents, etc.

2758 B. A. Dam and C. Stoffel. Chapters on English Printing, Prosody, and Pronunciation (1550–1700). Heidelberg, 1902. Pp. 206.

2759 Robert Bridges. "Miltonic Elision." *Athen.*, I (1904), pp. 83–84, 113, 147–48.

Milton intended to enrich rhythm of blank verse by trisyllabic effects; his system of elision designed for this purpose. Therefore, "elided" syllables not intended to be cut out in the reading.

2760 Walter Thomas. "Milton's Heroic Line Viewed from an Historical Viewpoint." *MLR*, II (1907), 289–315; III (1908), 16–39, 232–56.

Argues for a 10-syllable basis of Milton's lines as the fundamental element and for the pronunciation of the century as the means of forming a regular structure.

2761 T. S. Omond. "Milton and Syllabism." *Ibid.*, IV (1909), 93–101.

Comment on Milton's versification, and especially on the ideas in Walter Thomas' articles in *MLN*, 1907.

2762 Edward Payson Morton. The Technique of English Non-dramatic Blank Verse. Chicago: Donnelley, 1910. Pp. viii+129.

Able discussion of the changes due to Milton's practices.

2763 John M. Robertson. "Form in Poetry." *ER*, VIII (1911), 377–97.

Comments on form of some of the *Minor Poems* and offers his opinion that *Paradise Lost* would have been more popular in rhyme.

2764 English Review, XIX (1915), 389–404; XX, 13–24.

Frederic Harrison on the blank verse of Milton and Shakespeare, the only medium to dignify English epic.

2765 Ada L. F. Snell. "An Objective Study of the Syllabic Quantity in English Verse." *PMLA*, XXXIII (1918), 396–408.

Shows 90 per cent of stressed syllables are longer than those unstressed in *Paradise Lost*, Book II, ll. 604–28.

2766 M. A. Bayfield. The Measures of the Poets: a New System of English Prosody. Cambridge: Cambridge University Press, 1919. Pp. 112.

Review by Hulbert in *MP*, XVII, 727–29.

2767 Robert Bridges. Milton's Prosody: with a Chapter on Accentual Verse, and Notes. Revised Edition. Oxford: Oxford University Press, 1921. Pp. v+119.

The final statement of the author on Milton's prosody as syllabic in construction. His insistence on fixed line-type tests is not justified by the facts regarding accentual verse that are presented in the work for contrast purposes, but the book has a good stock of examples illustrating Milton's metrical variety.

Reviews in *TLS*, April 14, 1921, p. 240; *MLR* (by Omond), XVII (1922), 90–96, *MLN* (by Bright), XXXVII, 316, *Literary Review* (by Mason), June 25, 1921.

2768 T. S. Omond. English Metrists: Being a Sketch of English Prosodical Criticism from Elizabethan Times to the Present Day, 1907. New Edition, Condensed and Revised. Oxford: Clarendon Press, 1921. Pp. viii+336.

Review in *TLS*, September 1, 1921.

2769 T. H. Banks, Jr. "Miltonic Rhythm; a Study of the Relation of the Full Stops to the Rhythm of *Paradise Lost*." *PMLA*, XLII (1927), 140–45.

Nearly half the sentences end in the middle of lines. Milton makes free use of inversion of accent.

XIX. MILTON'S INFLUENCE

2770 Octavius. "Milton and Warton." *Monthly Mirror*, XI (1801), 153–58.

Warton has pointed the way for commentators on Milton. Warton's debt to him is indicated by parallel passages from *Pleasures of Melancholy* and *Comus*, and by "sombrous colouring" which "throws a gloom over his versification, happily corresponding with the nature of his subject."

2771 Chateaubriand. Génie du christianisme, ou beautés de la religion chrétienne. Paris, 1802. 5 vols.

"Gave the emigrant literature of France its Miltonic stamp and coloring."
Issued in many editions.

2772 Edinburgh Review, II (1803), 64–86.

In review of Hayley's *Life of William Cowper*. Critic quotes (p. 73) letter showing Cowper's estimate of Milton.

2773 Manuel José de Quintana. Variedades de ciencias, literatura y artes. 1804.

For estimate of Milton from standpoint of French classicism see, III, 164 ff., 241 ff., 361 ff.

Attacked by Blanco White in *Correo literario y económico de Sevilla*, IV, 177 ff., 201 ff., 209 ff., 217 ff.

2774 "Milton's Fame." *GM*, LXXVI (July, 1806), 595–96.

Anonymous letter reviewing Symmons' *Life*.

2775 Monthly Review, LII (1807), 67–79.

A review of Symmons' *Life* that praises it as a corrective of misconceptions regarding Milton chargeable to Hume, Warton, and Johnson.

2776 *Ibid.*, LVIII (1809), 285–302.

Review of Cowper's translations containing valuable commentary on the contemporary reputation of Milton. Discussion of Cowper's meter included.

2777 Edinburgh Review, XXII (1813), 198–238.

Milton's influence on Klopstock discussed.

2778 G. H. T. "Poesy—an Ode. In Imitation of Milton." *GM*, LXXXVI (1816), 614–15.

2779 "Strutt's Translation of Milton's Latin and Italian Poems." *Monthly Review*, LXXX (1816), 91–95.

Strutt inaccurate in his rendering of Milton's meaning and in his knowledge of the Milton biographical literature.

2780 Monthly Review, LXXXVII (1818), 339–40.

Criticism of Milton's style. Milton considered unique in his "unison of Latinized frame, or classical taste, with the peculiar strength and brevity of his construction." Influence on Milman presented.

2781 Quarterly Review, XXIII (1820), 209–10.

Imitation of passages from the "Ode on the Nativity" by Milman in his song of Miriam in the *Messiah* presented in a review of his work.

2782 Monthly Review, XCIV (1821), 386–95.

Milton's pastoralism considered in a review of *Amarynthus*, a pastoral drama.

2783 New Monthly Magazine, XLI (1834), 98.

A comment on an imitation of Milton's style in a translation of a poem by Sorelli

2784 "A Parody on Milton." *Western Monthly Magazine*, V (November, 1836), 666–67.

Parody of *Paradise Lost*, Book VI, ll. 207–56.

2785 "William Herbert's Imitation of Milton." *Monthly Review*, CXLV (1838), 392–93.

Although in *Attila* Herbert obviously imitates Milton, he utterly fails to achieve sublimity of style.

2786 W. H. Gardiner. "Milton and Prescott Compared." *North American Review*, XLVI (1838), 216–17.

Prescott encouraged to pursue his labors by reading Johnson's account of the difficulties Milton encountered in writing his *History*.

2787 A. R. Vinet. Études sur la littérature française au XIXe siècle. Paris, 1849–51. 3 vols.

See I, 500–74. On primitivistic use made of Milton, 1800 ff., in France. Milton's true spirit praised as against change of his spirit made through French imitation. "On n'a jamais mis en doute que le dessein de l'auteur du *Paradis perdu* n'ait été profondément serieux. Il a songé moins à orner son sujet de poésie, qu'à honorer la poésie en l'appliquant à son sujet."

2788 J. B. Angell. "Influence of English Literature on the German." *North American Review*, LXXXIV (1857), 311–33.

Milton, pp. 314–17, 318–19. Chiefly on Bodmer and Klopstock.

2789 "Milton a Lexicographer." *GM*, N.S., III (March, 1867), 338.

Littleton, in fourth edition (1703) of his Latin dictionary, acknowledges his debt to Milton.

2790 R. Rosières. "La littérature anglaise en France, de 1750 à 1800." *Revue bleue*, August 19, 1882.

2791 Alfred Schaffner. Lord Byrons *Cain* und seine Quellen. Strassburg, 1880.

Milton as a source for Byron.

2792 Religion et libre pensée (contient une imitation du *Paradis reconquis* et une traduction du XIXe sonnet). Genève, 1886.

2793 F. Servaes. Die Poetik Gottsheds und der Schweizer. Strassburg, 1887.

On the Bodmer-Breitinger controversy.

2794 Franz Muncker. Friedrich Gottlieb Klopstock. Stuttgart, 1888. Pp. xii+566.

Data of Milton's influence, *passim;* also pp. 32–35, 82–87, and 164 ff.

2795 G. von Wenzel. "Miltons und Byrons Satan." *Archiv*, LXXXIII (1889), 67–90.

2796 Gustav Jenny. Miltons *Verlorenes Paradies* in der deutschen Literatur des 18. Jahrhunderts. St. Gallen, 1890. Pp. 97.

Does not cover the field, but discusses editors and translators carefully and treats the use of Milton by Klopstock and others as a help toward a new German literature.

2797 M. Menendez y Pelayo. Historia de las ideas esteticas en España. Madrid, 1890–1908.

See Vols. III, IV, and VIII. Milton's forms and influence discussed, *passim.*

2798 Friedrich Blumenthal. Lord Byron's Mystery *Cain* and Its Relation to Milton's *Paradise Lost* and Gessner's *Death of Abel.* Oldenburg: G. Stalling, 1891. Pp. 12.

Review by E. Kölbing, *ES*, XVI (1892), 310.

2799 H. S. Pancoast. "Some Paraphrasers of Milton." *Andover Review* (Boston), XVII (1891), 35–54.

Mentions Dryden's play, 1674; Hopkins' paraphrase, 1699; Bentley's 1732; Howard's, 1738; and Jackson's, 1740. Reasons for many versions of *Paradise Lost* presented.

2800 L. A. de Cueto-Valmar. Historia crítica de la poesía castellana en el siglo XVIII. Madrid, 1893.

See I, 407, for comment on Milton's influence on Spanish epic.

2801 Auguste Angellier. De Joh. Keatsii vita et carminibus. Paris: Hachette, 1893.

Part II, chap. vi, compares Keats with Milton and Spenser.

2802 Hans Bodmer. "Die Anfänge des Zürcherischen Milton." *Studien . . . . Michael Bernays gewidmet.* Hamburg und Leipzig, 1893. Pp. 330.

On influence of Bodmer on German literature, see pp. 179–99.

2803 R. Sprenger. "Anklänge an Milton in Goethes *Faust.*" *ES*, XVIII (1893), 304–6.

Goethe's indebtedness to Milton shown in parallel passages of *Paradise Lost* and *Faust.*

2804 J. Demogeot. L'histoire des littératures étrangères considérées dans leurs rapports avec le développement de la littérature française. Paris: Hachette, 1895. 2 vols.

Good general comment. First edition, 1884.

2805 A. F. Agard. "Poetic Personifications of Evil." *Poet-Lore*, IX (1897), 206–16.

2806 G. Waniek. Gottshed und die Literatur seiner Zeit. Leipzig, 1897.

On Milton's influence in Germany, *passim.*

2807 Vernon Purinton Squires. "John Milton: Influence on Wordsworth." *Poet-Lore*, IX (1897), 540–51.

Comparison of life and works of Milton and of Wordsworth.

2808 Mary Steward Leather. "Pope as a Student of Milton." *ES*, XXV (1898), 398–410.

Pope early read and genuinely admired Milton. Many echoes of his style in Pope's translations; some imitations in the *Dunciad*, but no intention of disparagement is evident.

2809 F. Muncker. F. G. Klopstock, Geschichte seines Lebens und seiner Schriften. Berlin, 1900.

See pages 117 ff. on Milton and Klopstock.

2810 Quarterly Review, CXCVI (1902), 190–92.

Influence of "Lycidas" and "Il Penseroso" on Darley's "Nepenthe" discussed.

2811 Frank Edgar Farley. Scandinavian Influences in the English Romantic Movement. Harvard dissertation. Boston: Ginn & Co., 1903. Pp. viii+250.

On Milton's influence upon early nineteenth-century writers through his *History of Britain.*

2812 A. Waites. A Brief Account of John Milton and His Declaration of Independence. Worcester, Massachusetts: Davis, 1903. Pp. 32.

A study of Jefferson's text as possibly influenced by Milton's prose.

2813 John Martin Telleen. Milton dans la littérature française. Thesis at Paris. Paris: Hachette, 1904. Pp. ii+151.

On French interest in Milton in the eighteenth and early nineteenth century. Excellent bibliography, and important summary.

Reviews in *TLS*, III (September 2, 1904), 268; *ES* (by J. Delcourt), XXXVII (1907), 244–47. First review listed here gives references to Milton antedating Telleen's.

2814 N. G. Chase. Miltonic Influence in the Poetry of Coleridge. Manuscript thesis at Cornell University. Pp. ii+108.

2815 Quarterly Review, CCVI (1907), 79.

Milton noted as the "well-head of the English romantic movement." His influence on the melancholy cult of the eighteenth century is also considered significant.

2816 "A Note on Milton and Keats." *Century Magazine*, LXXVII (1908), 308–12.

Influence of Milton on Keats as shown through Keats' annotations in his copy of *Paradise Lost*.

2817 Charles F. Adams. "Knowledge of Milton in Early New England." *Nation*, LXXXVII (1908), 599–600.

Milton's poems unknown in New England until 1750. No edition of *Paradise Lost* in America until after 1775. First Massachusetts edition, 1794.

2818 Jessie Crosland. "J. Fr. W. Zachariä and His English Models." *Archiv*, LXII (1908), 291–95.

On the influence of Milton, Thomson, and Young. A particularly useful comment upon Milton in translation. Berge's (1682) German translation of *Paradise Lost* the only one to anticipate Zachariä's.

2819 Edward Dowden. "Milton in the Eighteenth Century." *Proceedings of the British Academy*, III (1907–8), pp. 275–94.

Read December 10, 1908. Discusses Milton's influence on poetic style before 1750; on the sentiment of the early romantic writers; and on ideas.

2820 Albert Matthews. "Knowledge of Milton in Early New England." *Nation*, LXXXVII (1908), 624–25.

2821 Agnes Blanche Powell. The History of Milton's Literary Reputation until the Time of Wordsworth. Manuscript dissertation at the University of Chicago, 1908.

Made of slight value through Havens' extensive studies.

2822 "Milton's Impress on the Provincial Literature of New England." *Report of the Massachusetts Historical Association, February, 1909.*

2823 Richard Ackermann. "Neuere Forschungen über Byron." *GRM*, I (1909), 376.

Shows relation of Byron's Satan to Milton's conception.

2824 Alice M. Dunbar. "Wordsworth's Use of Milton's Description of the Building of Pandemonium." *MLN*, XXIV (1909), 124–25.

2825 A. Vambéry. "Milton in Hungary." *Milton Memorial Lectures*. Oxford, 1909.

Pages 221–22.

2826 Ernst Dick. "Chateaubriands Verhältnis zu Milton." *Festschrift zum 14. Neuphilologentage in Zürich*. Zürich: Rascher & Co., 1910. Pp. 396.

Critic tries to show that Milton was the father of French romanticism. See pp. 1–50.

2827 W. Wright Roberts. "Chateaubriand and Milton." *MLR*, V (1910), 409–29.

Detailed survey of Milton's influence on style and subject matter of Chateaubriand's works, especially of *Les Martyrs* and *Les Natchez*. Shows Milton's influence in development of epic tendencies.

2828 Ernst Dick. "Plagiat, Nachahmung und Originalität bei Chateaubriand." *GRM*, III (1911), 394–410.

On Milton's influence upon Chateaubriand.

2829 Arturo Graf. L'Anglomania el l'influsso inglese in Italia, nel secolo XVIII. Turin: Loescher, 1911. Pp. xxxiv+341.

Milton, pp. 251–57.
Quotes interesting letters on Milton.

2830 W. A. Bradley. The Early Poems of Walter Savage Landor: a Study of His Development and Debt to Milton. Münster, 1913.

Bibliography, vii–viii. Published again in 1914 by Bradbury, London. Pp. viii+121.

2831 Enrico Pizzo. Miltons *Verlorenes Paradies* im deutschen Urteile des 18. Jahrhunderts. Berlin: Felber, 1914. Pp. 144.

Has definite references in abundance, and some bibliography in footnotes.

2832 John Walter Good. Studies in the Milton Tradition. "University of Illinois Studies in Language and Literature" (Urbana, Illinois), I, Nos. 3 and 4 (1915), 1–310.

A detailed survey giving some points not treated so exactly by Havens.
Reviews in *Literaturblatt* (by Walter Fischer), XLIII (1922), 371–76; *MP*, XV, 60–63; *Archiv*, CXLVII (1924), 155.

2833 Cora Aldis Hutchens. The Influence of Milton on Wordsworth. Manuscript dissertation at the University of Chicago, 1916.

2834 Alwin Thaler. "Milton and Thomson." *MLN*, XXXI (1916), 439.

Much of Thomson's romantic quality is traced to his imitations of Milton.

2835 C. A. Moore. "The Return to Nature in English Poetry of the Eighteenth Century." *SP*, XIV (1917), 243.

Milton's influence in the eighteenth century discussed with special regard for some long-standing theories.

2836 Ronald S. Crane. "Imitation of Spenser and Milton in the Early Eighteenth Century; a New Document." *Ibid.*, XV (1918), 195–206.

That imitations sprang largely from classical doctrines, rather than from use of earlier English models is the central theme.

Discussion of Henry Felton's *Dissertation on Reading the Classics and Forming a Just Style* (1709).

2837 A. T. Baker. Milton and Chateaubriand. Manchester, 1919.

Review in *French Quarterly*, I, 87–104.

Shows Milton's place in the French romantic movement and his pervasive influence upon Chateaubriand.

2838 C. Kramer. "Les poèmes épiques d'André Chénier." *Neophilologus*, V (1920), 210–18.

Milton's influence shown to have been great in *Susanne.*

2839 Denis Saurat. Blake and Milton. Bordeaux: Cadoret, 1920. Pp. 74.

An outline of Milton's philosophy that is useful to Blake criticism and as an introduction to Saurat's larger work of the same year dealing with Milton alone.

Review by Liljegren, *Beiblatt*, XXXIII (1922), 39–48.

2840 William Morrison. "Affinities in Wordsworth to Milton." *Poetry Review*, May–June, 1921, pp. 130–41.

2841 John Edwin Wells. "The Story of Wordsworth's *Cintra*." *SP*, XVIII (1921), 15–16.

Comparison of Wordsworth and Milton.

2842 Raymond D. Havens. The Influence of Milton on English Poetry. Cambridge, Massachusetts: Harvard University Press, 1922. Pp. xii+722.

A great compilation of evidence showing the pervasive influence of Milton upon later poetry. Bibliography, 63 pages.

Reviews in *MLN*, XL, 105–8; *JEGP*, XXII, 457–61; *MP*, XXII, 107–8; *MLR*, XVIII, 345; *Beiblatt*, XXXVI, 1–7; *LM*, VII, 321–22; *TLS*, November 9, 1922, p. 730.

2843 C. H. Ibershoff. "Bodmer as a Literary Borrower." *PQ*, I (1922), 110–16.

Bodmer's indebtedness in his *Noah* to *Paradise Lost.*

2844 Martin A. Larson. "The Influence of Milton's Divorce Tracts on Farquhar's *Beaux' Strategem.*" *PMLA*, XXXIX (1924), 174–78.

Shows Farquhar's use of Milton's phraseology in the dialogue and of Milton's sentences on divorce by mutual consent.

2845 The Demos in Council: or 'Bijah in Pandemonium. Being a Sweep of the Lyre, in Close Imitation of Milton. Boston: James Cutler, 1799.

Reprinted by W. Abbott, Tarrytown, New York, 1925.
In *Magazine of History*, XXVII, [7]–18.

2846 W. E. Doubleday. "Milton and Keats." *TLS*, November 5, 1925.

The curator of Wentworth-place answers Bradley's query (October 22) with word that Keats had no note or marking in his *Paradise Lost* on the line under discussion.

2847 G. Ferrando. "Milton in Toscana." *Illustrazione Italiana*, October, 1925.

See also an anonymous article on "Milton a Firenze" in *Marzocco*, November 9, 1925, which closely follows Ferrando's article.

2848 E. Allison Peers. "Milton in Spain." *SP*, XXIII (1926), 169–83.

Traces use of Milton by Spanish writers from the eighteenth century to the end of the nineteenth, showing that *Paradise Lost* alone was widely known and that even that work had little influence on Spanish literature.

2849 Alfred E. Richards. "Milton's Popularity in the Eighteenth Century." *MLN*, XLI (1926), 322.

Recalls a statement on popularity of Milton by Carl Philip Moritz, *Reisen eines Deutschen in England im Jahr 1782.* Compare with Osgood's statement, *New York Evening Post*, June 16, 1923, p. 764: "Few read Milton now, unless under academic compulsion."

2850 C. H. Ibershoff. "Bodmer and Milton Once More." *PMLA*, XLIII (1928), 1055–61.

Parallel passages showing Bodmer's indebtedness to Milton in descriptions of spirits of evil.

See *JEGP*, XVII, 589–601.

INDEX

Reference figures are to item numbers.

PRINTED IN U·S·A·